STUDENTS OF THE WORLD

A THEORY IN FORMS BOOK
Series Editors Nancy Rose Hunt and Achille Mbembe

STUDENTS

GLOBAL 1968 AND

OF THE

DECOLONIZATION IN THE CONGO

WORLD

PEDRO MONAVILLE

Duke University Press *Durham and London* 2022

© 2022 DUKE UNIVERSITY PRESS

Designed by A. Mattson Gallagher
Typeset in Sabon and ITC Avant Garde Gothic
by Westchester Publishing Services
Printed and bound by CPI Group (UK) Ltd, Croydon, CR0 4YY
Library of Congress Cataloging-in-Publication Data
Names: Monaville, Pedro, [date] author.
Title: Students of the world : global 1968 and decolonization
in the Congo / Pedro Monaville.
Other titles: Theory in forms.
Description: Durham : Duke University Press, 2022. | Series:
A Theory in forms book | Includes bibliographical references
and index.
Identifiers: LCCN 2021037921 (print)
LCCN 2021037922 (ebook)
ISBN 9781478015758 (hardcover)
ISBN 9781478018377 (paperback)
ISBN 9781478022985 (ebook)
Subjects: LCSH: Student movements—Congo (Democratic
Republic)—History—20th century. | College students—
Political activity—Congo (Democratic Republic) |
Decolonization—Congo (Democratic Republic) | Cold War—
Social aspects—Africa. | Congo (Democratic Republic)—
Politics and government—1960–1997. | Congo (Democratic
Republic)—History—1960–1997. | Congo (Democratic
Republic)—Social conditions—History—20th century. |
BISAC: HISTORY / Africa / Central | POLITICAL SCIENCE /
Colonialism & Post-Colonialism
Classification: LCC DT658.22 .M66 2022 (print) |
LCC DT658.22 (ebook) | DDC 967.5103—dc23/eng/20211027
LC record available at https://lccn.loc.gov/2021037921
LC ebook record available at https://lccn.loc.gov/2021037922

Cover art: (top) Black students demonstrate against Lumumba's execution (January 17, 1971) on February 2, 1961,
in Paris. Photograph by Keystone Press / Alamy Stock Photo.
(bottom) Student procession during the commemoration of
the second anniversary of the June 4 massacre, June 4, 1971.
Photographer unknown. Courtesy of Alexandre Luba.

For Adia Yvonne Tshiabu,
beloved and shrewd student of the world

CONTENTS

MEMORY WORK IN THE AGE OF THE CINQ CHANTIERS

And this world, which appears to us as a fable . . . and never ceases to deny our reason; this world which envelops us, penetrates us, agitates us, without us even seeing it in any other way than the mind's eye, touching it only by signs, this strange world is society, it is us!

Pierre-Joseph Proudhon, *System of Economic Contradictions, or the Philosophy of Misery* (1846)

When I arrived at his office in the National Union of Workers of the Congo (UNTC) in downtown Kinshasa, François Mayala was sitting in front of a small radio set, listening to a news broadcast on Radio France Internationale. Meanwhile, a colleague of his had his head buried in a well-worn book on neurosis. The room contained neither computers nor cabinet files, and seemingly, no urgent tasks required completing. Fading green walls recalled the time when all the country's administrative buildings were painted in the color of President Mobutu's one-party state. In those years, the UNTC had been a powerful labor organization, but trade union liberalization and the shrinking of the formal economy had made it a shadow of its former self.

Mayala welcomed the distraction of my impromptu visit. I came with questions about the Congolese left in the 1960s, a topic he always discussed with passion. Revisiting this bygone era was not merely a matter of chatter. Mayala's leftist memories connected him to the world existentially.

Reminiscences of past politics sustained his peripatetic mind, years after opportunities to travel abroad and attend international labor conferences came to an end. Mobility was key for my own research, as I followed archival trails and developed networks of informants across the Congo and abroad. Mayala was curious to know where I had been and whom I had met. And as I was to fly to Europe a few days later, he asked me to bring him a copy of Pierre-Joseph Proudhon's *The Philosophy of Misery* when I came to the Congo again. "Did you know that Marx wrote his *Poverty of Philosophy* in response to this book? Marxists do not like Proudhon, but I regret disregarding him for so many years," he explained.[1] Although Mayala deplored that Congolese, including himself, knew too little about anarchist thinkers like Proudhon, the tentacled city of more than ten million that was roaring outside of his office windows exuded its own kind of statelessness.[2] Cycles of war that started in the aftermath of the Rwandan genocide in 1994 continued to destabilize the country, while the social fabric had come to be pervaded with a new religiosity fixated on the figure of evil.[3] These and other developments unsettled long-standing certitudes. For Mayala and others from his generation of left activists, telling stories about the past was an act of resistance, an attempt at mending a fractured sense of time and reality.

Mayala's political imagination complicated widespread characterizations of postcolonial cities like Kinshasa as spaces of abjection and exclusion. A native of the lower Congo, Mayala had lived in Kinshasa since the 1950s. He had witnessed the proverbial transformation of "Kin-la-Belle" (Kin-the-Beautiful) into "Kin-la-Poubelle" (Kin-the-Garbage), a city now plagued with overpopulation, land erosion, a failing sewage system, and inadequate electricity supply. Yet, Mayala claimed full citizenship in the world, not in a distinct planet of slums.[4] Memories populated his lifeworld in Kinshasa, making distant times and places part of the everyday.

This book interrogates how a generation of university students redefined Congolese politics in the aftermath of independence, with a movement that made a call to decolonize higher education, build a strong and just nation-state, and cultivate solidarity across borders. Not having studied at university, Mayala did not directly participate in the student movement. But he did serve as a mentor to several student activists at the University of Lovanium in Kinshasa, including his younger brother, the late Moreno Kinkela. Sharing his personal collection of leftist publications with these students, Mayala enabled a turn toward Marxism that shifted the horizon of the student movement. Reading Karl Marx and Friedrich Engels's writings on colonialism had been Mayala's own "introduction to life" while working as a clerk in the Office des Transports Coloniaux (Colonial Transportation Office) in the 1950s.[5] Back then, Marxism, both intellectually and in the materiality of its circulation, had an aura of danger and mystery. And after Mayala began work as a union employee, he did not fail to bring back revolutionary books, which he tucked under his shirt or sewed into the lining of his suitcase, whenever he traveled abroad. The "red library" that Mayala built in this way provided the group formed around his brother with precious weapons. The histories of revolutionary struggles and the radical critiques of imperialism that they read in Mayala's library emboldened these young men to break with the expectations to conform that weighed heavily on university students. The left outlined a path of subversive deviation, but it also offered an avant-gardist rhetoric compatible with the elitist bent of colonial and early postcolonial education. Mayala's brother and his friends came to see themselves as a political vanguard and their campus as a microcosm of the wider world of decolonization. They created a clandestine student structure that aimed to overthrow Mobutu's dictatorship. The authorities quickly arrested them and crushed their movement, but their initiative left a deep imprint on the Congo's postcolonial history.

Although their struggle returns us to the singularity of the era of the African independences, it also presents itself as a chapter in an unfinished story. Decolonizing the university has indeed reemerged as a powerful rallying cry in Africa and beyond since the early 2010s. However, discussions of this question are framed around epistemological stakes that too rarely account for historical precedents.[6] By reestablishing how, more than half a century ago, young Congolese connected the transformation of higher education with the broader struggle against imperialism and neocolonialism, *Students of the World* outlines an alternative history of the present.

(Af)filiations

In the 1960s, with a vibrancy reflecting the sudden freedom from colonial domination, Congolese political imaginaries branched off toward distant horizons. For the people who shared their stories with me decades later, this era was not fully past. And when I brought back books from Europe for Mayala and others, I could not help think that the configuration of my work reactivated material and intellectual transactions from the youth of my interlocutors.

Various dynamics shaped my historical ethnography in the Congo. My mother is Congolese—she moved to Belgium in the mid-1970s, a few years

before I was born there—and interviewees keenly used a language of kinship with me, "our sister's son," as Mayala and others would call me.
This imagined familial connection mattered but maybe less so than my
affiliation with American academia or the fact that my work involved
multiple trips, long conversations about events and networks, and a general attention to questions of ideology and organization. All these things
invited informants to reminisce the transnational structures of activism
and knowledge production in the 1960s. At this time, foreigners were
particularly hungry for information about Congolese society and politics.
And many students, because they were themselves seeking to expand their
knowledge of the world, happily engaged with these interlocutors.

This kind of cross-fertilization seemed far away in the 2000s and
2010s, long after a self-declared apolitical humanitarianism had replaced
the radical horizons of the 1960s as the new dominant discursive thread
connecting the Congo to the world.[7] Yet, the habitus forged at earlier
points of internationalist convergences have endured into the neoliberal
era. Former activists' ways of speaking and looking at the world testified to this continuity. And the reverberations of past modes of political
engagement that appeared during meetings with them directly enter into
the framing of this book.

During my research, the 1960s came to life in multiple ways. Memories
of this decade have held a specific value ever since Laurent-Désiré Kabila
came to power in 1997. A leader in the Simba armed insurrection of the
mid-1960s, Kabila reemerged three decades later as the spokesman of a
new rebel group, the Alliance des Forces Démocratiques de Libération
(AFDL). Together with the active support of Rwanda, Uganda, and a few
other African countries where insurrectionary movements with roots in
the era of revolutionary tricontinentalism had also captured power in recent years, he routed Mobutu's army.[8] As president, Kabila initially sought
to erase the Mobutu era. One of his first measures was to change the country's name from Zaire (a name imposed by the late dictator in 1971) back
to Congo.[9] Longtime opposition to Mobutu became a source of legitimacy,
and several former figures on the student left served as ministers in the first
Kabila governments, including Mayala's brother Kinkela as the minister
of post and telecommunications. Kabila's mercurial personality and the
war that followed his rupture with his Ugandan and Rwandese allies in
1998 created turbulences at the center of power, but the old rebel leader
remained committed to the anti-imperialist rhetoric of his youth. After his
assassination by one of his bodyguards in 2001, these ideological references lost much of their purchase.[10] Kabila's son Joseph succeeded him as

president. At just thirty years of age, he was one of the world's youngest heads of state. Less constrained than his father by the postcolonial political history of the Congo, Joseph reconciled with former Mobutu supporters, further empowered members of his extended Katangese family, sought the guidance of the so-called international community, and did not hesitate to marginalize leftist figures who had worked with Laurent.[11] In 2006, the young Kabila began to articulate his vision for the Congo as that of a "revolution of modernity" and billboards around Kinshasa advertised the cinq chantiers, the so-called construction sites that symbolized the state's voluntarism in developing infrastructures, employment, education, water and electricity, and health.[12] Memory was absent from the spectral rhetoric of this campaign.[13] It still became a chantier in its own right for the former student activists who had opposed Mobutu and worked with the old Kabila before his assassination. Having lost access to the presidency, they were invested in restoring the polarization between the left and the right that had structured their approach to politics for years but that now seemed illegible. By deploying memories of their activist past in newspaper columns, televised debates, and interviews with a young historian, they strategically reasserted their relevance in the present.

These former activists claimed fidelity to the ideals of their youth. They continued to debate ideas, write manifestos, and fight over strategy and leadership, just as they had in their student years. However, not all former students related to the past in this way. Some were prone to criticizing the shortcomings of the student movement. They considered that their generation had failed. In the words of the late Richard Mugaruka, a charismatic Catholic priest and university professor, the educated elite trained in the 1960s had taken for granted the symbolic and financial rewards of university education: he labeled them "the generation of the three keys," students who had expected to receive keys to a car, a house, and an office directly upon graduation. Despite their nationalist and revolutionary rhetoric, they served themselves, not the people, Mugaruka claimed.[14]

Self-criticisms denouncing these selfish aspirations were not new. For instance, a book written by a student activist in 1964 already opened with a preface that depicted the Congolese educated elite as "an amorphous mass of would-be bourgeois without any ideal or courage."[15] Yet, during my conversations with former activists, nostalgia was often more prevalent than lament. Many people, like Mayala, remembered the post-independence years as a golden age, when towering heroes that compared to Marx dominated African politics. Since then, nobody had managed to fill the shoes of these Lumumbas and Nkrumahs. Beyond questions of leadership, a whole collective relationship to politics was lost. "Our children have become too focused on money," one of Mayala's colleagues commented during my visit at the UNTC—redirecting, toward the youth, a criticism first leveled at his own generation.[16]

Reverberations, Refractions, Resonances

Unlike Accra, Brazzaville, or Dar es Salaam, Kinshasa was not a state-sanctioned hub of revolutionary politics in the 1960s.[17] In the Congo, the left existed at the margins of the state, in semiclandestine reading groups, student clubs, and radical labor circles. One interviewee advised me to change my research focus and look at the history of the right, since the left had never been a real thing in the Congo.[18] This comment came with a certain dose of provocation. It also evoked the difficulty involved in determining the essence of the left. Initially associated with the Belgian polarization between Christian conservatives and anticlerical liberals, the left made its appearance in the Congo in the mid-1950s. By the time of independence, it came to index radical anti-imperialism and served as an important point of reference throughout the 1960s. Still, references to the left always remained overshadowed by the rhetoric of nationalism. Left politics did not manage to become institutionalized in practice, nor did they generate any authoritative memories. They nonetheless opened a space of possibilities and carried a strong sense of worldedness that continued to resonate among former activists of the 1960s. This generation had performed key mediations between the Congo and the world. Moving between rural boarding schools and urban spaces, universities in the Congo and abroad, classrooms and rebellion fronts, these students occupied interfaces of refraction that redirected political waves of great magnitude. Even after the Cold War bore its full weight on the Congo, student activists refused to accept the closing of the temporal horizon of radical emancipation that the struggle for independence had opened. This spatial and temporal imagination continued to reverberate as I was researching this book. Despite the tumultuous events of the past few decades, the wars of the 1990s and the 2000s, Congolese still related intensely to the first years of independence as an unfinished business. *Students of the World* engages with this memory work and situates the 1960s within a broader resonance chamber defined by struggles for emancipation and belonging of a longer duration. Bringing together archival materials and life stories, the political and the intellectual, events and the everyday, modes of being and modes of thinking, self-representations and outside constructions, I strive to embrace historical complexities and move away from simplistic accounts that fail to problematize Congolese experiences of violence and oppression. While the students who are at the center of the book have often been overlooked in these accounts, their engagement with the question of the world in the age of decolonization offers a precious vantage from which to view our global present and its subaltern, insurgent cosmopolitanisms.[19]

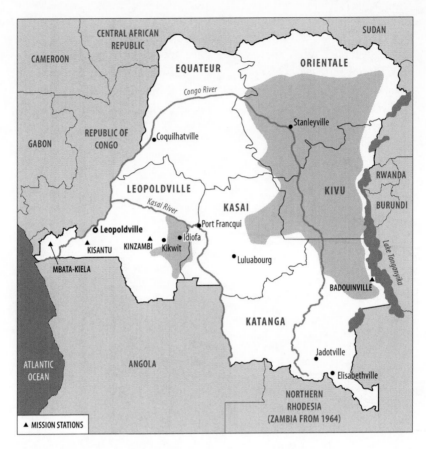

Map of the Congo, ca. 1964. The gray areas represent the territories directly affected by the Mulele and Simba rebellions.

In 1966, the Mobutu regime decided to rename most urban centers in the Congo, abolishing old colonial-sounding toponyms and replacing them with more authentic names. The book uses the old colonial names when referring to the pre-1966 period and the current names when referring to the period after the change.

The relevant city names are as follows:

Leopoldville	Kinshasa
Elisabethville	Lubumbashi
Stanleyville	Kisangani
Coquilhatville	Mbandaka
Jadotville	Likasi
Costermansville	Bukavu
Port Franqui	Ilebo
Luluabourg	Kananga
Bakwanga	Mbuji-Mayi

My first debts of gratitude are to the many people who shared their stories about the Congolese student movement of the 1960s with me. I thank all of them for their time, hospitality, and generosity. Many of their names appear in the pages of this book. Some I must also acknowledge here individually, as their trust and clairvoyance had an unparalleled impact on my work. In Liège, years before I embarked on this project, Ambroise Kalabela Misombo planted the first seeds that would lead me to research this history. Ambroise's unflinching loyalty to the ideals of his youth made clear to me the unquestionable importance to document the trajectory of his generation of Congolese left cosmopolitans. My uncle, Grégoire Muke-ngeshayi, belonged to this generation as well. Hearing him speak about the many paths he traveled in the 1960s, from Tshikapa to Berlin via Poznan, was another early source of inspiration. In Kinshasa, Yoka Lye Mudaba and Isidore Kabongo were two absolute founts of knowledge, always welcoming, always witty. Jean-Baptiste Sondji, Guy Yangu, and the late Célestin Kabuya never tired of my requests to guide me through the history of their student cell at Lovanium University, including during a memorable trip to the infamous Luzumu prison where they had been detained for two years in the early 1970s. Ernest Wamba dia Wamba again and again challenged me to ask better questions. I am humbled that he believed so much in my work and saddened that he will not be able to see this book in print. Jean-Baptiste Mulemba, Elisabeth Mweya, Antoinette Da Silva, Paul Inongo,

Aubert Mukendi, Valérien Milingo, and Mukendi Wa Nsanga were story-tellers extraordinaire whose voices will long resonate with me.

Colleagues at the University of Kinshasa, the University of Lubum-bashi, and the University of Kisangani—including several who had been part of the student movement themselves—made fieldwork possible, while offering precious guidance and feedback. I want to thank in particular Marie-Madeline Mwifi, Kiangu Sindani, the late Jacob Sabakinu, Noël Obotela, Jean-Marie Mutamba, Elikia M'Bokolo, Isidore Ndwayel, Do-natien Dibwe, and Léon Tsambu. Many foreign faculty and researchers who had worked in Congolese academia in the early postcolonial era also answered my questions and critiqued early findings. I am especially grateful to Johannes Fabian, Bogumil Jewsiewicki, Martin Klein, Herbert Weiss, Crawford Young, Jan Vansina, and Tamar Golan for their generous engagement with my work.

The idea for this project first emerged in 2004, during a semester I spent as an exchange student in New York. Fred Cooper and Ann Stoler provided the best introduction to North American graduate education; both also con-nected me with Nancy Hunt. Reading A Colonial Lexicon had changed my perception of the possibilities of historical writing, and when Nancy invited me to study with her as a doctoral student at the University of Michigan, I was ecstatic. An exceptional mentor and constant source of inspiration, Nancy made this work and many other adventures possible. At Michigan, I am also grateful for the insightful mentorship of the members of my disserta-tion committee: Kelly Askew, Butch Ware, and Geoff Eley. Mbala Nkanga connected me to key interlocutors early on. And even though they are too many to list here, I am very thankful to all the faculty and fellow graduate students who shared ideas, feedback, and constructive criticisms of my work. Absolutely essential in Ann Arbor was the friendship of Maxime Foerster, Bertrand Metton, Tasha Rijke-Epstein, Isabelle de Rezende, Kai Mishuris, Candice Hamelin, Monique Johnson, Frieda Ekotto, and Monica Patterson. Fernando Arenas was another dear friend. His optimism and kindness mat-tered so much. How I wish he could read these few words of gratitude.

The journey from doctoral dissertation to book manuscript began while I was teaching as a visiting faculty at Williams College. Aparna Kapadia, Lesley Brown, Eiko Siniawer, Shanti Singham, and (in absentia but no less critically) Kenda Mutongi were all particularly precious supporters in Williamstown. At NYU Abu Dhabi, my institutional home since 2015, the support of Robert Young, Taneli Kukkonen, Awam Amkpa, Tina Gala-nopoulos, Nisrin Abdulkhadir, Jesusita Santillan, and Caitlin Newsom has been instrumental. I am greatly indebted to Martin Klimke for inviting me to coteach a course on the global sixties, as well as for his guidance as my faculty mentor over the past few years. Erin Pettigrew deserves a loud shout-out for her dedication to creating a community around African studies on our campus. Erin, together with Masha Kirasirova, Giuliano Garavini, Arvind Rajagopal, Bob Stam, Martin Bowen, Tuomo Tiisala, the late Michael Dash, and Mahnaz Yousefzadeh have offered generous encouragement, asked important questions, and made precious suggestions. I also feel very privileged for the impeccable collegiality of Mark Swislocki, Fiona Kidd, Nelida Fuccaro, Andy Eisenberg, Andrew Bush, Maurice Pomerantz, Sam Anderson, Camilla Boisen, Justin Stearns, Toral Gajarawala, Maya Kesrouani, and many other colleagues in the division of Arts and Humanities.

The year I spent in 2017 and 2018 at the New York campus of NYU was pivotal for the completion of this project. Robyn d'Avignon, Fred Cooper, Michael Gomez, Barbara Weinstein, and David Ludden made me feel welcome on the square. Julie Livingston helped me figure out what this book was about. I learned much from Marek Eby and Arash Azizi. And lunches with Sandrine Colard were one the best perks of my time in the city. A fellow Belgian Congolese expatriate who is charting new territories in Congolese history with her research on photography, Sandrine became one of my favorite coconspirators. Our overlap at NYU was a great motivation to organize a workshop around emerging works in Congolese history at the NYU Abu Dhabi House in New York. Didier Gondola, Sarah Van Beurden, Christina Mobley, Fiston Mwanza, Yayra Sumah, Jason Stearns, Kambale Musavuli, and Tatiana Carayannis also participated, and I thank them for their feedback on a draft of a chapter I presented at the workshop.

A large part of the research for this book dates from my time at Michigan. Generous funding from several entities within the university—the Eisenberg Institute for Historical Studies, the Institute for Research on Women and Gender, the Rackham School of Graduate Studies, the Institute for the Humanities, and the African Studies Center—as well as from the Social Science Research Council, the Spencer Foundation, the Council on Library and Information Resources, Vocatio, and the National History Center allowed me to conduct archival and oral history research in multiple locations in Europe, Africa, and the United States. Further support from NYU Abu Dhabi, as well as a grant from the Friends of the University of Wisconsin Libraries, made possible key follow-up research stays in more recent years.

Kinshasa was the most central location in my research. My debts of gratitude there are numerous. Out of the many friends and family members who cared for me in the city, I would be remiss if I did not acknowledge

Doodoo Lanza, Kaniki Kasongo, Sapin Makengele, Triphe Kialungila, Tcheques Bukasa, Théophile Kanyinda, Hervé Ngandu, Thomas Lumbi, Dorothée Clette, Didier de Lannoy, Agnès Bandimbi and her children, and my dear cousin John Tshitoko Malele. In Lubumbashi, I thank Emilie Zola, the late Georgette Borremans, as well as Maman Suzanne and her children. Of the various destinations where this work took me, I also have to mention Berlin. I am extremely thankful for Daniel Tödt's and Andandita Bajpai's invitations to visit the city as a guest researcher, respectively at Humboldt in 2011 and the Zentrum Modern Orient in 2017. Anandita and Daniel, together with Peter Lambrechts, Candice Hamelin, Koen Claerhout, Farah Barakat, Abdoulaye Sounaye, and the Mukengeshay and Kabasela families helped me move this project along in critical ways, both in Berlin and beyond.

Over the years, many colleagues who are also working on the Democratic Republic of the Congo facilitated my research. I am very thankful for the essential advice and encouragement of Filip De Boeck, Katrien Pype, and Kristien Geenen. I learned a tremendous amount from conversations with Johan Lagae, Luce Beeckmans, Isabelle de Rezende, Jo Trapido, Emery Kalema, Nikki Eggers, Amandine Lauro, Nephtali Fofolo, Benoit Henriet, Gillian Mathys, Leslie Sabakinu, Chérie Ndaliko, Silvia Riva, Rosario Giordano, Nyunda Ya Rubongo, Guillaume Lachenal, Pierre Halen, Karen Bower, Bob White, Anne Mélice, Catherina Wilson, Gauthier de Villers, Yolanda Convington-Ward, Miles Larmer, Sarah Van Beurden, Danielle Sanchez, Jeremy Rich, and Joshua Walker. At different moments of my research, I had the chance to work closely with artists whose work inspired me to think more creatively about memory and narratives. Sapin Makengele was there all along. He helped me orient myself in Kinshasa, assisted me during several interviews, and produced several paintings that reflected on my work. Together with Sapin, I also collaborated with our friend Cécile Michel on a documentary film about Mobutu's repression of the student movement in 1969 and 1971. I am forever grateful to Cécile for initiating this project. Her film, *Les fantômes de Lovanium*, is a wonderful visual complement to this book. Being in conversation with Vincent Meessen while he prepared his curatorial intervention for the 2015 Venice Biennale was an absolute delight. Vincent's meticulous approach to research and his rhizomatic imagination generated crucial insights about the Situationist International. I also learned much from my exchanges with Sammy Baloji on young Congolese communists in the early 1960s. I am particularly thankful to Sammy for his invitation to give a talk at the Garage Museum of Contemporary Art in Moscow and to the Garage's field research team for organizing a visit of the former Lumumba University's archive for me during my stay in the city.

Being part of a writing group helped immensely in drafting this book. Andy Cavin, Bertrand Metton, and Shane Dillingham were invaluable readers, kind and unsparingly constructive. I learned much from their own work on France, Germany, and Mexico. Barbara Weinstein, Nelida Fuccaro, Fred Cooper, Andy Ivaska, Kelley Askew, Nancy Hunt, Ernest Wamba dia Wamba, Heith Sledge, Bogumil Jewsiewicki, Kiangu Sindani, Florence Bernault, Herbert Weiss, Crawford Young, Daniel Tödt, and Tasha Rijke-Epstein offered comments on various chapters, while Cian Dinan and Steve Corcoran read the full manuscript. The book is better as a result. I also benefited from questions and suggestions from numerous colleagues who engaged with my work during seminars and conference in Abu Dhabi, Ann Arbor, Antwerp, Brussels, Cape Town, Chicago, Paris, Nashville, New Haven, New York, Sheffield, Oxford, and Washington, DC. These include Isabel Hofmeyr, Jean Allman, Miles Larmer, Jocelyn Alexander, Moses Ochunu, Daniel Magaziner, Shobana Shankar, Greg Mann, Moira Fradinger, Michael Denning, Samantha Christiansen, Zachary Scarlett, Françoise Blum, Luke Melchiorre, Daniel Hodgkinson, Matthias De Groof, George Nzongola, Andreas Eckart, Jean-Luc Vellut, Mary Nolan, Guy Ortolano, Matt Swagler, Reuben Loffman, Ophélie Rillon, David Cohen, Penny Von Eschen, Kathleen Canning, Adam Ashforth, Derek Peterson, Gabrielle Hecht, Patricia Hayes, Ciraj Rassool, Premesh Lalu, Philippa Levine, Jason Parker, Dane Kennedy, and Wm. Roger Louis.

Several people helped me with archival research and transcriptions of interviews at various stages of the project. I thank for their skillful assistance Amélie Roucloux, Vénétia Apondja, Aurélie Bouvart, Sungoh Yoon, Jenny Fichmann, Léo Frankhauser, Crystal Lee, Anne Schult, Faustine Karasira, St. Jose Camille Inaka, Emery Kalema, as well as my friends François Colard, Francis De Bruyn, and Tijl Vanneste. Gloria Bilbili offered precious guidance in Tirana and translated documents from Albanian into English. I am also grateful for the professionalism of many archivists and librarians, most notably at the Carcob in Brussels, the University of Leuven, the University of Kinshasa, the International Institute of Social History in Amsterdam, ARNACO and the Centre Inter-Diocésain in Kinshasa, and NARA in College Park. While I was finishing drafting my manuscript, Iva Pesa and Julien Bobineau kindly shared with me two key documents that I could not access. I am deeply thankful for all the support received at Duke University Press, and particularly for Elizabeth Ault's careful guidance and precious encouragements.

Two chapters of the book expand on already published works: a shorter version of chapter 4 appeared as "The Political Life of the Dead Lumumba: Cold War Histories and the Congolese Student Left," *Africa* 89, no. S1 (2019): 15–39, and the second part of chapter 7 is a revised version of "Making a 'Second Vietnam': The Congolese Revolution and Its Global Connections in the 1960s," in *Routledge Handbook of the Global Sixties*, ed. Chen Jian, Martin Klimke, Masha Kirasirova, Mary Nolan, Marilyn Young, and Joanna Waley-Cohen (New York: Routledge, 2018), 106–18.

My mother belongs to the generation of the students I write about in this book. Very few Congolese women of this generation were allowed to access university education, and she was not one of them. However, as I finally reach the end of this long research project, I realize how much her struggle for survival has inspired much of what I have done. I am so thankful to her, to my father, and to my siblings, François, Luc, and Amalia, for their support, trust, and understanding. I also warmly thank Alice, Elise, Yvan, and Ghislaine Mouton for welcoming me in their family. I stayed with Yvan and Ghislaine many times during the writing of this book, and I so much appreciate how they always went out of their way to allow me to do my work. Many close friends similarly cared and helped: thank you, Philippe, Roland, Julien, Laurent, Nadia, Didier, Nicolas, François S., and François C. Without Amélie, there would be no book. An exigent writer, she has been a major source of inspiration. She read through many drafts cheered me up through difficult times and kept me going. Her love makes it all more beautiful.

THE SCHOOL OF THE WORLD

The radical contemporaneity of mankind is a project.

Fabian, Time and the Other, xi

Hubert and Muriel Humphrey spent the first night of 1968 waltzing on a dance floor in Liberia. The US vice president and his wife were attending a ball in Monrovia for the inauguration of President William Tubman's sixth term in office. Liberia was the first stop on a trip that took the Humphreys to eight other countries across Africa. The tour was meant to strengthen US positions in the disputed Cold War battleground. At the beginning of an electoral year, the Johnson administration was also willing to impress voters at home that it supported independent nations in Africa.[1] Humphrey, well versed in this kind of political salesmanship, had been on so many missions to defend the Great Society that one journalist described him as "the most travelled presidential backstop in history."[2] Jet lag may have been an inconvenience on these trips but more so the placard-bearing opponents to the Vietnam War whom Humphrey encountered wherever he set foot, from France to New Zealand.[3] In Africa, too, activists portrayed this "Happy Warrior" of American liberalism as the war criminal "Himmler Humphrey."[4] Although the vice president asserted that "Vietnam did not absorb more than 30 minutes" of his two-week tour, members of his delegation acknowledged that the war "came up everywhere."[5]

Vietnam was certainly on people's mind in Kinshasa, the fourth stop on the tour. Barely an hour after Air Force Two landed in the Congolese capital, two hundred students from the University of Lovanium blocked Humphrey's motorcade as it went from the airport to General Joseph Mobutu's presidential compound. The protesters used familiar elements from the grammar of international solidarity with Vietnam: they burned an American flag, pelted eggs at the delegation, chanted pro-Vietminh slogans.[6] But the protest's location added a further layer of meaning. The students gathered in front of a monument that commemorated Patrice Lumumba, the hero of Congolese independence, after hearing a rumor that Humphrey would stop there briefly. To them, this visit was simply unfathomable: had not the United States ruthlessly undermined Lumumba when he served as prime minister? Had not the Central Intelligence Agency (CIA) played a prominent role in the events that led to his assassination on January 17, 1961? How could Humphrey salute Lumumba's memory in these circumstances?[7] The students felt compelled to stand up to this "shameless hypocrisy" and "show [their] hatred of American foreign policy to the world."[8] That so many "democratic and progressive movements around the world unabashedly opposed American imperialism's criminal actions in Vietnam" made their action against Humphrey an "internationalist duty."[9] By bringing Lumumba and Ho Chi Minh together, the students placed Kinshasa and Saigon as two interconnected dots on a map of anti-imperialist resistance. Imagining themselves as a part of a transnational political community, they found the resolve to brave police repression when nobody else in Kinshasa was daring to challenge the Mobutu regime.

The protest at the Lumumba monument lasted only a few minutes. Soldiers quickly freed the US delegation, using their rifle butts to hit students in the face before hauling them off to jail.[10] Meanwhile, Humphrey reached the presidential compound for his meeting with Mobutu. The general intended to use the visit to plead for an increase in the US support to his military.[11] He may have believed that his guest's unpleasant encounter with the rebellious mindset of Congolese students contained a silver lining, as his main argument in support of his request for US money and equipment was that communist subversion was growing in the Congo. Yet, Mobutu was anxious to have Humphrey leave with a good impression of Kinshasa. At a dinner later that day, he offered Muriel Humphrey an eight-carat, uncut diamond, reportedly to make up for the tomatoes that students had thrown at her husband.[12] His gift to Hubert was a leopard-skin hat, headwear associated with Lumumba and his radical supporters, which Mobutu had appropriated to claim the revolutionary bona fides of his regime.[13]

Figure I.1 "At the stopover in Kinshasa for refueling. With the vice president [Hubert Humphrey] is the minister of the interior Etienne Tshisekedi." Photographer unknown, January 9, 1968 (source: Minnesota Historical Society, Hubert Humphrey Papers).

Cosmopolitan Horizons

This book traces the history of the Congolese student movement from its roots in the Belgian colonial era to its confrontation with the state in Mobutu's post-colony. Students formed only a small minority during this period, but they occupied a central position, one situated at the crossroads of development and nation building. More than any other group, they lived the future-oriented sensibility of the time. Working in the margins of formal politics, they outlined problems, reformulated issues, and gave criticisms. After the coup that brought Mobutu to power in 1965, the new regime initially attempted to co-opt the students' ideas and energies. Failing to win their complete loyalty, Mobutu resorted to violence. In 1969, soldiers killed dozens of students during a street rally in Kinshasa. Then, two years later, scores of their peers were compulsorily drafted into the military as a collective punishment.

This repression did not totally eradicate the student protests. However, it did give way to a "catastrophic loss of political ideals."[14] What was lost in the Congolese case was not futurity and the idea that time might bring radical change. Indeed, after Mobutu's attack on the students, revolutionary movements became more numerous, if increasingly fractioned. What was lost was the cosmopolitan edge that authorized students to act as mediators between the Congo and the world.

Humphrey was a minor figure in the trajectory of antagonism between the students and the state. Yet, his visit emblematized the importance of spatial considerations in the political psyche of the 1960s. Students mattered in the politics of independence in postcolonial Congo thanks to the mediations they performed and not due to their numbers.[15] Their geographical imagination challenged colonial assignations. Defending Lumumba's memory and expressing solidarity with Vietnam, students projected themselves beyond the political architecture bequeathed to the Congolese at the time of independence: they acted neither as ethnic subjects nor as moderate Congolese patriots but as African nationalists and third world internationalists who saw the Congo as open to many revolutionary winds.

Decolonization had increased the valence of youth as a political category throughout the world.[16] Governments in "young countries" promoted visions of their young citizens as preeminent makers of the nation.[17] State schemes to mobilize the youth also created conditions for dissent. In the Congo as in several other African countries, university students held far higher academic qualifications than those of most people in power, credentials they used to defend their own views and oppose the political establishment.[18]

Their mobility, more than anything else, set young educated Congolese apart in their society. Students were socialized in institutions that claimed the borderlessness of knowledge and science. Scholarships to travel and study abroad were easily attainable. Many young Congolese were also prolific letter writers, able to expand the space of their activism through international postal exchanges. The capacity to circulate across different intellectual, political, and social worlds, as well as the books they read, the clothes they wore, the music they listened to, and the worldviews they professed—all this brought distant horizons closer. These diverse cosmopolitan dispositions allowed students to shape, contest, and redefine the meaning of decolonization.[19]

The cosmopolitanism of Congolese students hinged on feelings of generational distinction.[20] This cosmopolitanism was also thoroughly gendered in accordance with a normative masculinity that constrained how the few women able to access university education could participate in campus politics. The colonial system had showed little interest in female education, and high schools only began graduating young women with qualifications for university entrance well after independence. This imbalance reflected the type of subjects that Belgians had sought to engender when they established the first Congolese universities at the end of the colonial period: mobile, rational, and efficient collaborators and technicians who would modernize the Congo and foster a society marked by middle-class values. In Belgian colonial eyes, only males could be candidates for such positions.[21] Many Congolese internalized this view, and male students used colonial gender norms to their own advantage. They were attached to an image of themselves that supported their pretensions to serve as a political and social avant-garde.[22] Their perception of a certain masculine ethos as consubstantial with respectability and expertise created frictions after women gained more prominence on campuses at the end of the 1960s, but it was deeply ingrained.[23]

In the eyes of many, being a student meant being a man of the world. This logic of distinction was self-limiting at times, but claims to worldliness helped students build a counterhegemonic movement against the power of the state. Mobutu sought to legitimize his rule by imposing a specific understanding of national identity and cultural authenticity. He could only resent the authority and autonomy that students gained by evading his state-sanctioned epistemologies and aesthetics.[24]

The Congo Crisis, Sartre, Senghor, and the Politics of Distance

When they protested against Humphrey's visit, Congolese students expressed their strong sensitivity to external political determinations. As Kwame Nkrumah argued when he exposed the predicament of neocolonialism in Africa, the Congo offered the clearest example of how economic, military, and political interference from foreign corporations and governments could weaken state sovereignty in recently decolonized countries.[25] These sorts of interference immediately followed the Congo's celebration of its independence on June 30, 1960. Within a few days, the country turned into a hotspot in the Cold War. Soon the whole world found itself there. The trigger was a mutiny in the army at the beginning of July. Belgium responded by unilaterally dispatching paratroopers to contain the mutiny, and Lumumba then broke diplomatic ties with the former colonial power. After the province of Katanga seceded from the central state with financial backing from Belgian mining interests, the Soviet Union offered Lumumba its support. Around the same time, the United Nations voted to send a major civilian and military mission, with contingents from countries including India, Ghana, Malaya, and Sweden. Meanwhile, envoys from anti-colonial movements in Algeria and Cameroon, diplomats from China and the United Arab Republic, and spies from Czechoslovakia, France, the United Kingdom, and the United States all bustled about behind the scenes with competing agendas.[26]

The Congo crisis "became the ultimate litmus test for where one stood in the polarized global order of the early 1960s"; it crystallized existing tensions between the Afro-Asian bloc at the United Nations and the Western countries that dominated the liberal internationalist postwar order.[27] Events in Leopoldville or Elisabethville reverberated far and wide. A whole generation of activists, ranging from Malcolm X to Rudi Dutschke, turned toward the Congo to understand the stakes of "a world suspended in time," one in which "race, immigration, decolonization, [and] international politics . . . were all in a state of flux."[28]

Although the international echoes of the Congo crisis are well known, historians of the Cold War have paid little attention to what people in the Congo themselves thought, said, or made of this moment of intense suffering and turbulence. Not much has been written about how the Congolese, and students in particular, engaged reflexively with the internationalization brought by the tumultuous transition to self-rule. Decolonization was a political drama of worldwide magnitude, and Congolese students were deeply aware of the vital need to situate themselves in relation to a multitude of distant interlocutors.

This engagement with the world took shifting forms, but it encouraged a trajectory of radicalization, as students progressively moved from a position of reformism to revolutionary nationalism and militant Marxism. However, different worldviews always coexisted at any given time. In the last years of the colonial regime, when most young educated Congolese were still tuning into the African programs on the Brussels-based *La Voix de l'Amitié*, more than a few were already listening to Radio Cairo and dreaming of Afro-Asian liberation.[29] Conversely, after the left and a rhetoric of revolution became hegemonic in the mid-1960s, some students remained immune to the attraction of Che Guevara or Mao Zedong. This was the case of Dieudonné Kadima Nzuji. Although he joined Lovanium around the time of Humphrey's visit to Kinshasa, Nzuji did not take part in the protest at the Lumumba monument. He considered himself apolitical, distrusted collective action, and had little patience for doctrinaire statements. Yet, he felt attuned to the philosophical and intellectual debates of the time. As a writer of poetry, he was particularly receptive to Negritude, the Pan-African literary movement that was begun by African and Caribbean students in 1930s Paris. When the president of Senegal and Negritude veteran Léopold Sédar Senghor visited Lovanium on January 17, 1969 (a date that incidentally coincided with the eighth anniversary of Lumumba's assassination), Nzuji was absolutely thrilled.[30] He did not care that campus activists had called to boycott Senghor because of his brutal repression of the student movement of May 1968 in Dakar.[31] Had these activists caught Nzuji, they may well have roughed him up. But he nonetheless decided to attend the speech that Senghor gave at Lovanium.[32] The Senegalese president's allocution presented poetry as a politically engaged art, and Negritude as "the encounter of giving and taking," a movement that fully belonged to the twentieth-century and the "age of the universal." True culture, Senghor noted, was always about "rooting and uprooting" and Negritude poetry productively confronted African aesthetics with European forms.[33]

Senghor's mantra was the liberation of humankind from all forms of alienation.[34] He spoke to an important aspect of the student psyche—an existentialist stream that claimed a perfect correspondence between Africanity and universality. If solidarity with Vietnam brought Congolese students together in chorus with a global movement of refusal, Senghor provided another way of opposing imperial frameworks poetically and politically.[35] From the Bandung Conference to the Tricontinental, a shared desire to escape and transcend geopolitical determinisms nurtured new imaginary futures and encouraged dissident cartographies.[36] On Congolese university campuses, this consciousness of refusal animated poets and activists alike. Although a literary tradition like Negritude did not translate into a direct critique of power, it fostered critical reflections about cultural identity and the politics of knowledge. University students occupied the upper level of a hierarchical system that had been designed by the colonizers. They struggled with the contradictions of this alien educational system, while remaining intimately committed to the ideal of universalism.[37] Negritude, but also African theology, Afro-centrist Egyptology, and French existentialism, allowed them to reconcile the colonial essence of higher education with their ambition to decolonize Congolese culture, revive communal forms and patterns, and stand against the racism and condescension of white professors.[38]

These students experienced politics not as disjunctive but rather as cumulative. Take Anastase Nzeza. In 1968, he headed Lovanium's student government together with his friend Hubert Tshimpumpu. Both men belonged to the Catholic student association Pax Romana, sometimes presented as the rightist bastion on campus. Yet, Nzeza and Tshimpumpu were no less outraged than their Marxist peers when they heard about Humphrey's possible stopover at the Lumumba monument. In 2010, when I asked Nzeza what led to the spirit of revolt that expressed itself in the protest against the US vice president, he answered by recalling a journey he and Tshimpumpu had undertaken to attend the World Congress for the Lay Apostolate in Rome in 1968. This trip "sharpened our consciousness," Nzeza recalled. On their way back to Kinshasa, the two students stopped off in Brussels, where they collected a lot of information about Vietnam. During their visit to Belgium, they attended a talk about the war by Jean-Paul Sartre. This was a major event for them and it reinforced their belief that "the Americans were imperialists that regimented the world, making war in Vietnam and supporting Mobutu."[39]

Many paths—even trips to Catholic youth congresses—led to Sartre in the global 1960s.[40] Nzeza's anecdote also attests to a porosity between social Catholicism and anti-war activism at Lovanium. Regardless of the various political orientations of the students, a shared structure of feeling emerged when they drank from the words of a famous philosopher of engagement, crossed a picket line to listen to a Negritude poet, or put their bodies on the line to stop a visiting American dignitary's convoy. Nzeza, Nzuji, and the protesters at the Lumumba monument all sought to mediate the politics of distance. They all related to decolonization as an unfinished project. And they all cultivated an ability to transcend the isolation of history and geography—that is, a specific worldedness.[41]

Sixties Histories and the Question of the World

In his report to Lyndon B. Johnson about his stopover in Kinshasa, Humphrey only briefly mentions the protest at the Lumumba monument, calling it "a minor incident in which a small number of communist-organized students sought to embarrass the visit."[42] However, despite this reluctance to dignify students with too much attention, some of the people who traveled with Humphrey acknowledged that politicized young people were threatening the stability of the Mobutu regime. In the words of the Belgian-born diamond mogul Maurice Tempelsman, the member of Humphrey's delegation most informed about Congolese affairs, Mobutu's isolation from the "younger, more activist part of the population" was a problem to which the United States would need to carefully attend.[43] After further encounters with young protesters in other countries on the continent, Humphrey himself acknowledged the urgency of countering radical ideas among the youth in Africa.[44] This preoccupation reappeared a few months later in a report submitted by the CIA to Johnson and his cabinet. Titled *Restless Youth*, the report provided elaborate descriptions of student politics in nineteen countries around the world. Four of these countries were in Africa (the Congo, Senegal, Ghana, and Ethiopia), showing the CIA's awareness that the continent's educated youth were contributing to the worldwide radicalization of student politics.[45]

Ironically, until quite recently, the scholarship on the 1960s failed to emulate the CIA's encompassing approach by ignoring student politics outside of Europe and North America. More historians are now acknowledging the role that African students at home and abroad played in the global 1960s.[46] This new body of research does justice to the perceptions of young West African expatriates in Paris who, in May 1968, talked of a continuity between colonial violence in their home countries and the police repression against street protests in the Latin Quarter.[47] Historians have also unearthed just how prominent African students were in the imaginations of foreign powers on both sides of the Iron Curtain, as all Cold War powers sought to cultivate relations with young educated Africans.[48] *Students of the World* builds on these new comparative and connected histories of the 1960s, but it approaches the global as a field of struggle and not as "a neutral framework for the addition of singular histories."[49]

Scholars should problematize, and not simply emulate, the expansive geographical scope of documents like *Restless Youth*. The report's comparative methodology was not without problems of its own. Even though its section on the Congo was unsurprisingly well informed on local student organizations, the report's authors trivialized the Congolese students, describing them as self-entitled contrarians who suffered from a "leader complex" and espoused "some sort of socialism or vague Marxism."[50] In general, *Restless Youth* reproduced the mechanistic language of modernization theory, reducing youth protests to a by-product of affluence that became more acute as countries progressed through the stages of economic growth. This view may have escaped the trap of paranoid anticommunism, but it was ideological and essentializing nonetheless.

A desire to celebrate simultaneity and shared political affects sometimes drives scholarship on student politics in the 1960s. However, accepting the "global" as a neutral descriptive category effectively depoliticizes what were highly disputed questions at the center of a hegemonic struggle. As emic categories, the "global" and its historical cognates helped a multiplicity of insurgents to imagine new revolutionary futures. But the same terms also contributed to a "police conception of history" that aimed to contain the most radical potentialities of decolonization.[51] It is no accident that in parallel to operations that secretly channeled funds to anti-communist labor unions and student associations in the United States and around the world (including in the Congo), the CIA established a yearslong program of covert support to highbrow literary magazines in Africa, Europe, the Middle East, South Asia, and Latin America. These magazines, promoting the international circulation of literary works that were not seen as threatening American hegemony, created a fully engineered "experience of global simultaneity" that was meant to capture, transform, and neutralize the transnational imagination of Bandung and nonalignment.[52]

Congolese students initially responded rather positively to American attempts at projecting this tamed imagination of global connections. Later, many students related to radical projects that envisioned world politics as unabashedly revolutionary and antisystemic.[53] The main point, though, is that these students were world makers at a time when the question of the world was highly debated.[54] Cold War politics tangibly inscribed the Congo within maps of oppression and resistance. But the international affinities, lineages, and trajectories that defined student politics were never a given. They had to be made and imagined.[55] At the beginning of the 1960s, young Congolese denounced dictatorships in Latin America that were "supported by US dollars and US tanks, exactly as in our country."[56] Soon, they "worr[ied] about a possible Vietnamization of the Congo."[57] And when they stood in front of the Lumumba monument in January 1968, they challenged dominant geographical and historical perspectives. To Humphrey's US-centered one-worldedness, they opposed their own "global making politics."[58] Protesting brought them closer to insurgents from around the world, and this proximity, in turn, strengthened their determination to refuse the world as it was.

Students of the World analyzes how connections with distant peers— real and imagined—increased young Congolese's room for maneuver. Yet, it refuses to reify any local-global dyad, for this binary erases students' experience of the relative, discontinuous, and serendipitous nature of political space.[59] The activists and intellectuals discussed here did not simply import, adapt, and translate, nor did they just invent. They compared, juxtaposed, and also claimed their belonging in moving, overlapping, and unbounded geographies of struggle.

Politics as Pedagogy

The global transactions of Congolese students are not unique, but the timing of their movement is. Selected colonial subjects of the French and British Empires migrated to London and Paris as students and turned these cities into sites of anti-imperialist activism already before World War II.[60] By contrast, very few Congolese were allowed to travel internationally and virtually none studied at university level until the 1950s. This specific situation can be explained by an obsessive policy of ideological containment. The nervous state—Nancy Hunt's powerful metonym for Belgian colonialism's fixation on securitization—worried much about Marxist and Garveyist contaminations.[61] Colonial administrators scrutinized the movement of ideas and people, and they worked together with missionaries and private conglomerates to maintain the colonized within social and political enclosures.[62] The British scholar Thomas Hodgkin called this tropism the Platonism of Belgian colonialism: the belief that "the Congo can avoid corruption and revolution if it is insulated from the outside world."[63]

Not until 1952 did the colonial authorities first allow a young Congolese man to attend a university in Belgium. The man's name was Thomas Kanza and he joined the University of Louvain as a student in psychology.[64] By that time, Senghor, who had graduated from the Sorbonne two decades earlier, was serving his second term as member of the French National Assembly; Kwame Nkrumah, who had studied at the University of Pennsylvania and the London School of Economics in the 1940s, was overseeing the Gold Coast's transition toward self-government; and established African student organizations were active in both the French and British Empires.[65]

Two years after Kanza moved to the metropole to pursue his education, the Catholic Church and professors from the University of Louvain opened the first university in the Congo. Lovanium propelled the colony into a new time. Until then, the so-called évolués, the colonized elite, all occupied subaltern clerical jobs.[66] University education led students (sometimes the children of these évolués) to dream bigger. Curriculums in medicine, law, mathematics, economics, sciences, and the humanities prepared them for positions that did not yet exist. At the same time, higher education made the inner contradictions of late Belgian colonialism even more apparent. It promised forms of self-government that the colonial system was structurally unable to deliver. Students were not willing to wait for the realization of racial equality and their frustration led them toward anti-colonial politics.[67]

Independence was no longer a distant aspiration when students emerged as a distinct group in Congolese society. Instead, it was a tangible reality that produced state formations, bureaucracies, liberation struggles, new possibilities and urgent challenges.[68] Whereas colonial humanism, Bolshevism, or surrealism may have politicized earlier generations of students in West Africa, these Congolese students first and foremost belonged to the era of decolonization. This was a time when education took an unforeseen prominence throughout Africa. In the Congo, the Catholic Church continued to expand its network of schools and by the mid-1960s had formed the fourth largest Christian school system in the world.[69] The government, international organizations, and foreign foundations also invested actively in schooling, allocating many of their resources to secondary and higher education. University student numbers grew from a few hundred in the late 1950s to more than ten thousand a decade later. More young Congolese could imagine themselves as university students, and this transformed collective perceptions of the future.

From the very beginning, the students had seen well beyond colonial reformers' horizon of semi-emancipation, but they had few models to emulate in attempting to articulate their own vision. Stepping onto university campuses in the mid-1950s, these students entered virgin territories that significantly differed from other spaces of socialization for the colonized elites. No established traditions were directly available to help them figure out their place in the "world of tomorrow."[70] This does not mean that they felt stuck in "the space between the no longer and the not yet" that Simon Gikandi has identified as characteristic of Africa's age of decolonization.[71] Neither were they fully exposed to the vicissitudes of the world, as Jan Vansina writes that Equatorial Africans were in the mid-twentieth century.[72] Some students felt deeply connected to the past. They reappropriated Congolese cultural traditions through the lens of Africanism.[73] Many others experienced the present as a moment of germination. They sometimes groped and fumbled, but they were not lost. Education meant the development of individual and collective potentialities, and the students' ability to speak with authority about the future gave them fortitude. They found composure not only by mining the past but also by looking ahead and sideways.

Young Congolese learned about the world through official and hidden school curricula, as well as through various encounters outside of formal institutions. For many, politics appeared as an avenue for self-education. "We were in the school of the world," Kalixte Mukendi Wa Nsanga told me during an interview.[74] As a young man, Wa Nsanga found opportunities to learn as much at political rallies as in libraries. He studied first at Lovanium before moving to Germany, where he was part of a clandestine Maoist organization (see interlude III and chapter 7). At the time, he often deplored that many of his fellow students professed revolutionary ideas but actually dreamed of inclusion in the ruling class. When he met with Chinese or Albanian diplomats, he warned them about the fake radicals within the Congolese student diaspora.[75] He believed that some students had a narcissistic relation to radical politics and were more content to use theoretical references to impress others than to advance the struggle. This criticism pointed to a tension at the core of the students' political identity: on the one hand, many students aimed to serve the oppressed; on the other hand, their aspirations, the quality of the food they were served at university restaurants, the comfort of their campus bedrooms, their suits and ties, and the relative generosity of their state scholarships distanced them from the rest of the population. Yet, their influence—their capacity to speak for the people and be heard by the state—depended on these material conditions and on their cosmopolitan distinction as a mobile, educated, and politicized elite.

Postal Correspondences and Extraversion

Massive investment in higher education in the 1960s ushered in a new era in knowledge production around the world. Writing about South Asia, Kris Manjpara has talked of the decade as a time of "lettered decolonization," one that witnessed the emergence of postcolonial humanities.[76] In the Congo as well, decolonization produced a new literature and generated a critical discourse that challenged established scholarly disciplines. The following three examples are illustrative: Valentin Mudimbe's theorization of the colonial library, George Nzongola's attention to popular resistance, and Gérard Buakasa's sociology of the invisible. All these projects grew from the intellectual conversations enabled by the expansion of Congolese academia and by these scholars' direct participation in student politics (respectively at Lovanium, the University of Louvain, and Davidson College in North Carolina).[77] *Students of the World* documents the institutional, social, and political milieu that engendered Congolese postcolonial letters. The book also approaches the Congo's lettered decolonization literally, by looking at postal correspondences that enabled the Congolese to secure symbolic and material support in their pursuit of education and politics.[78] Young Congolese wrote to a multiplicity of individuals and to groups ranging from the Belgian Communist Party to the American Federation of Labor. They took part most enthusiastically in the transnational circulation of political affects that was facilitated by the context of decolonization, which they truly experienced in the way defined by Achille Mbembe as a process of "dis-enclosure of the world."[79] Correspondence, even more than formal education, produced students of the world.

A "way of manifesting oneself to oneself and to others," letter writing always combines introspection and exposure.[80] In this sense, letters constitute an ideal genre of historical sources for this book, which both builds on works that theorize Africa's position in the world and on studies that investigate the logics of African worlds.[81] Following Jean-François Bayart, some scholars have used the concept of extraversion to bring these two traditions together. In Bayart's words, political actors in Africa strategically "mobiliz[ed] resources derived from their (possibly unequal) relationship with the external environment," doing so to gain, reinforce, and challenge power within their own societies, thus showing that a "relationship with the rest of the world . . . is consubstantial with [the continent's] historical trajectory."[82] Bayart has argued that these strategies of extraversion have been constitutive of African societies for centuries, allowing Africans to make their own history despite the reality of an unequal inscription in the world economy that is age old. My approach departs from this longue durée optic. Although clear lines of continuity related to extraversion emerge in central Africa's history,[83] I unearth the specificity of a historical configuration and of a political generation. In this way, I am hoping for a far closer rendering of the historical experience of the students. When writing letters and otherwise engaging with distant interlocutors and imaginaries, they did not apply strategies from some existing playbook with the intent to reproduce the status quo. Rather, they experimented with a set of constraints and possibilities, their minds firmly fixated on the transformation of their immediate conditions and those of the world beyond.

Although Bayart's theorization of the "connection between the two spheres of the internal and the external" directly talks to a tension at the core of Congolese student politics in the 1960s, extraversion is an imperfect concept for use in the context of this study. Students themselves battled against the economic and intellectual extraversion of early postcolonial Africa. The Franco-Egyptian dependency theorist Samir Amin used the term in a 1967 book about capitalism in Ivory Coast that circulated widely among African students.[84] Later, the Beninese philosopher Paulin Hountondji (who taught in Congolese universities from 1970 to 1972) talked of extraversion as typical of the situation of a postcolonial generation who found itself captive to "an intellectual history centered elsewhere in the great industrial and scientific capitals."[85] Although students were aware that leveraging distant sources of support was a condition for political survival, many of them would also have identified with "the search for ourselves," the attempt to place Africa "at the center of its own history" that Hountondji posited as the opposite of extraversion.[86]

The Congolese international outgoing mail substantiates the participation of students and other young letter writers in an "anti-imperialist community of sentiment."[87] On a par with informal discussion circles and study groups, periodicals, dancing bars, and the radio, international correspondence also contributed to the construction of politicized publics in Congolese urban centers.[88] But even more importantly, these letters served as tools in the mediation of distance. As such, they testify to the contingent and nearly experimental ways in which the Congolese experienced the opening-up that originated with decolonization. Independence came with promises of equality, dignity, and better lives, while placing the Congo at the center of a world fractured by antagonistic forces and passions. This configuration explains how a whole generation of young educated Congolese came to relate intimately to the Sartrean notion of authenticity and the urgency to escape from the alienation of the colonial mindset.[89] They had to come to terms both with the fact that political sovereignty produced new relations of dependency and that the unfinished struggle for liberation demanded the careful appropriation of distant references and foreign vocabularies. In the act of correspondence, they negotiated the ambiguities and paradoxes inherent in the intense internationalization of the decolonization era.[90]

The Structure of the Book

Students of the World is not strictly speaking a social or intellectual history of student politics. By bringing together biographies, diverse archival fragments, and an attention to memory work, the book captures the history of a particular disposition, of a mode of knowing and being in and of the world that responded to new openings in an era of independence. As Adom Getachew recently reminded, anti-colonial nationalism carried global "revolutionary implications" as "a project of reordering the world" that frontally clashed with the "world-constituting force" of Western imperialism.[91] As thinkers and political actors, students paid attention to the reconfiguration of forms of sovereignty and statehood in the aftermath of empire, and they weighed in on debates about the institutional remaking of the international order. However, they did not intervene in these debates from the position of statesmen or scholars. Accordingly, in this book, I approach decolonization and world-making less as normative problems in political theory and more as intersubjective processes that transformed perceptions of selves and others.[92] The politics of the students was rooted in the specific juncture they occupied in Congolese society as the country's educated youth and in the generational and cognitive field of experience that this juncture created. Their intellectual skills allowed them to look at the international sphere as a space of connections in which they could insert themselves.[93] Doing so, they assembled a plurality of worlds together.[94] Their labor of imagination and mediation forms the core of this study.

Based on a broad and contrasting corpus of sources, the book's chapters focus alternatingly on institutional micropolitics, activism, and the many routes traveled by students. Conducting research in private and public archival repositories in the Congo, as well as in Albania, Belgium, Britain, Congo-Brazzaville, France, Germany, the Netherlands, and the United States, I browsed through the archives of various schools and universities, delved into papers by former activists and militant publications, as well as documents from political parties, labor organizations, foreign governments, and international institutions. Ethnographic research and conversations that lasted over many years with several dozen former students also provided me with the material to retrace individual trajectories and better understand the singularity of the global 1960s in the lives of this generation of educated Congolese. Many of these former students—whom I met in Kinshasa, Kisangani, Lubumbashi, Dar es Salaam, Nouakchott, Abu Dhabi, Berlin, Brussels, Paris, Bethesda, and Montreal—opened their libraries and shared their private papers with me. They also often told me about personal documents on the student movement that they had lost or had been forced to destroy. These stories in themselves revealed much about the turbulent half century of independence in the Congo. Similarly, the wide geographical dispersion of my informants and of the archives I researched reflected the many connections that entered into the making of the postcolonial era.[95] They also spoke of histories forgotten and of others that could have been—various threads that *Students of the World* develops through a textured narrative that moves across conceptual, spatial, and temporal scales.

The book is composed of four chronologically ordered parts, each with a distinct physiognomy: the first part investigates the material and spatial production of political imagination through Congolese postal routines; the second studies campus micropolitics and student subjectivity; the third provides a narrative of the Congo crisis centered on the educated youth; and the fourth turns toward the affects, passions, and dramas that marked the Congolese experience of the 1960s. Interludes present biographical refractions of Congolese world politics and introduce the sections.

Chapters 1 and 2 provide a historical background to the study by investigating the role of long-distance communications, and most notably postal exchanges, in shaping political imagination during the colonial period and at the very beginning of the independence era. As chapter 1 shows, the postal service enabled the literate Congolese to project themselves into the broader world in the first part of the twentieth century. The biography of Patrice Lumumba, who began his professional life as a postal employee, illustrates how postal communications enabled the colonized to circumvent the limitations of colonial education and learn about the world. Chapter 2 continues to investigate the postal articulation of politics but moves the chronological focus to the moment of decolonization in the late 1950s and early 1960s. International correspondence helped many letter writers navigate the chaos of the Congo crisis. Upon independence, more young Congolese were allowed to study abroad, which created communities of letter writers bearing new kinds of knowledge and new motivations for intervening in Congolese affairs.

The next part of the book explains how an education system meant to maintain the colonial status quo ended up producing the very activists that dismantled colonialism. Most Belgians feared that educated colonized would become too difficult to manage. Yet, in the 1930s and increasingly after World War II, Catholic seminaries and a few elite secondary schools introduced a highly select group of Congolese boys to the humanities and the sciences. As chapter 3 explains, the colonial state was continually pressured with demands for more schools. Indeed, many alumni from elite schools joined the ranks of the nascent anti-colonial movement. Chapter 4 explores this trajectory of politicization in one institution, Lovanium. Established in 1954 on a hill outside of Leopoldville, the university was set up to train a technical elite that would work hand in hand with the Belgians. Within the space of ten years, however, students had derailed this plan. By protesting against Lovanium's colonial character, they transposed global conversations about cultural alienation onto the scale of the campus.

The book's third cluster of chapters follows the evolution of student politics in the first half of the 1960s as the internationalization of the Congo crisis radicalized students. Lumumba's assassination in January 1961 was particularly instrumental. Although many students had been reserved about national politics before this pivotal event, the global outcry at Lumumba's

Figure I.2 "Black students demonstrate against Lumumba's slaying: Negro students with a sprinkling of white leftists demonstrated before the Belgian embassy in Paris this afternoon." Photo Keystone, February 1961 (source: author's collection).

death encouraged them to reflect on their place in the world (see figure I.2). Chapter 5 retraces the creation of the Congolese Student Union in 1961 and its emergence as a central force in Congolese nationalism in the months that followed. As chapters 6 and 7 explain, the subsequent Lumumbist armed rebellions further radicalized students. Some joined in the insurrections, often as its propagandists and advocates. And many among those who did not still responded to its revolutionary rhetoric and participated in moving student politics toward the left.

General Mobutu came to power in November 1965, when the Lumumbist insurrections were already starting to recede. The last two chapters in the book reveal how Mobutu used his relationship with the students to establish his regime and transform the Congo. Several student activists took up important positions within the new administration, bringing the radical rhetoric of the student movement to the center of power. As chapter 8 narrates, Mobutu's relationship with the students remained an asset for his regime until just before Humphrey's visit in January 1968. However, once the antagonisms became impossible to ignore, the general decided to suppress student discontent. Chapter 9 focuses on a cycle of repression that lasted from 1969 to 1971, when the state used violence to terrorize the students into submission and undercut the cosmopolitan dispositions that had supported their rise as a political force after independence.

Continuing reverberations from the unfulfilled promises of decolonization make it important to seize the singularity of Africa's global 1960s. Decolonization mobilized dreams of liberation that have found other figurations through history. But it did so at a moment marked by mutations in the structures of imperialism, new left ideas, and friction between liberal internationalism and third world solidarity. Attending to the hesitations, contradictions, and experiments of the students in their quest for knowledge is a way to account for the unpredictable and the contingent, a way to look at decolonization not as the deployment of an idea but as a struggle for and over meaning(s).[96] As Ali Mazrui noted a long time ago, colonial education produced a class of culturally captive Africans, yet it also endowed them with the tools needed to fight this cultural alienation.[97] The quest to process the contradictions of education was crucial in the transition to independence. Decolonization was not a context for Congolese students; it was the world in which they lived. It was their horizon—in the sense of "something that circumscribes all the particulars of a given landscape, its visual part, but transcends it," making present both what is immediately visible and what is possible.[98]

Curiosity killed the cat, missionary teachers in the Belgian Congo liked to remind their pupils. Zamenga Batukezanga failed to pay heed to this warning. As a young student at a prestigious Catholic boarding school in rural lower Congo, he was caught listening to Radio-Moscou on the school's receiver. The young man narrowly escaped expulsion, but the incident seems not to have diminished his inquiring mind. Following graduation, he moonlighted as a newspaper reporter while working as a schoolteacher by day. A few years later, when the opportunity of a fellowship to study in Belgium presented itself, Zamenga seized it as a chance to explore the wider world. The time was 1960, the year of the Congo's independence. Half a decade later, Zamenga returned to the Congo to take a position as administrator in student affairs at the University of Lovanium. And he also embarked on a parallel career as a fiction writer. It was now his turn to satisfy the curiosity of others. Within a few years, he became the most popular writer in the country.[1]

Zamenga's writings—locally printed novellas and bande-desinnées—often centered on the tensions between tradition and modernity. Zamenga shared wisdom drawn from multiple sources with his many readers, inviting them to reflect on the contradictions of the present. Together with rumba music and ubiquitous popular paintings, his unpretentious and humorous stories shaped national culture in the postcolonial era. A man who had tuned into highly subversive airwaves as a teenager, later worked as a newsman, traveled to Belgium at a time when few Congolese could do so, and set his mind on educating his people through stories that ignored European literary fashion trends, Zamenga himself embodied the search for cultural sovereignty that animated so many Congolese in the second part of the twentieth century. His work as well as his biography bring to mind the key role played by tools of communication—broadcasting, the printed press, cheaply produced pamphlets, and novellas—had in the collective redefinition of Congolese identities that occurred in the aftermath of Belgian colonialism.

In the following two chapters, I focus on yet another type of mediation to have shaped the process of decolonization: postal correspondences. Letters sent via the post operated at an unmatched level of horizontality and equivalence, the possibility of a response being inherent to the medium itself.[2] Although the post as an institution is often associated with the imagination of the nation, I emphasize international correspondence. The international mail is fascinating in that it precisely enabled circulations, networks, and relationships that crisscrossed the boundaries imposed by colonial and postcolonial states.

Zamenga had personally experienced the new mobilities and spatial expansion that resulted from and informed the course of Congolese decolonization. He captured the importance of international postal communications for that moment in *La carte postale*, one of his most well-known novellas.[3] The book tells the story of a young man sent by a political party to study in Belgium in the aftermath of independence, while his wife and children remained in the Congo. Zamenga shows how letters became a vital lifeline for maintaining contact between the student and his family. His point, however, is that postal communications were inherently prone to misunderstandings and could separate more than unite: at the center of the novel's plot is a postcard depicting a white woman, which the student's family misinterprets as an announcement that he has taken a second wife in Brussels.

The theme of politics is subdued in *La carte postale*. Zamenga mentions the necessity of abolishing "the exploitation of man by man," but he also defends a universalist gospel that explicitly shuns the ideological conversations in which many students reveled during the 1960s. The novella does not reveal much about what these students were most curious about at the time—radical nationalism, socialism, or Pan-Africanism. Yet, the book makes a trenchant observation in noting the centrality of postal communications, even when not fully functional, in bridging two fronts in the Congo's decolonization: the foreign front in the former metropole where the main protagonist pursues his education and learns to demystify Europe, and the domestic front where he is supposed to apply his knowledge and contribute to his family's welfare and his nation's development.

One seemingly minor character in *La carte postale* is the postman who delivers the letters sent by the student to his family in Leopoldville. Seeing that many of his politically connected friends have benefited materially from independence while his own standard of living has not improved in the least, this postman decides halfway through the novella to demand small bribes for every letter and parcel delivered. To his own surprise, nearly all of his customers, having become so dependent on the mail, readily agree to these extra fees.

The character of the postman in *La carte postale* reveals Zamenga's amusement with an infrastructure of affects that developed during the era of decolonization. In the following chapters, I revisit the history of the colonial and early postcolonial Congo by focusing on the role of long-distance communications in creating the world that Zamenga chronicled in his short stories. By preventing the Congolese from traveling abroad for many decades, Belgian colonialism actually created a situation in which postal correspondence came to embody a unique tool for the circulation of ideas. Literacy and the postal system allowed generations of Congolese to explore the outside world in a way that pushed against colonial enclosures. These experiments with the post laid the foundations for the cosmopolitan orientation of student politics that this book posits as a major force in post-independence Congo.

ONE
DISTANCE LEARNING AND THE PRODUCTION OF POLITICS

This post-office service spoke as by some mighty orchestra, where a thousand instruments, all disregarding each other, . . . yet all obedient as slaves to the supreme baton of some great leader, terminate in a perfection of harmony like that of heart, brain, and lungs in a healthy animal organization. But . . . that particular element in this whole combination . . . through which it is that to this hour Mr. Palmer's mail-coach system tyrannizes over my dreams by terror and terrific beauty, lay in the awful political mission which at time it fulfilled. The mail-coach it was that distributed over the face of the land, like the opening of apocalyptic vials, the heart-shaking news of Trafalgar, of Salamanca, of Vittoria, of Waterloo. These were the harvests that, in the grandeur of their reaping, redeemed the tears and blood in which they had been sown.

Thomas De Quincey, *The English Mail-Coach*, 1849

It is the invention of the post that has produced politics.

Montesquieu, *Mes pensées*, 1725

The white missionaries who curated libraries in the Belgian Congo would likely not have seen Thomas De Quincey's ruminations on the English mail-coach system or Montesquieu's maxims on politics, law, and history as appropriate readings for colonized évolués. They could not have discerned any pedagogical value in De Quincey's reflections on acceleration, dream, and sudden death.[1] And as Frantz Fanon famously intuited, Montesquieu's work acted as a racial marker in colonial situations.[2] Yet, both De Quincey's and Montesquieu's illuminations concerning the postal nature of politics resonate deeply with the experience of letter writers in colonial Congo.

Montesquieu thought that the post encapsulated the conundrum of modern European politics in the eighteenth century. The "refinement" of government depended on the circulation of the written word, which in turn multiplied the intermediaries between sovereign and subjects, while also encouraging excesses in secrecy.[3] Writing a century later, De Quincey expressed his fascination with the national horse-powered mail-coach network in England. When a convoy brought thrilling news of a distant victory during the Napoleonic wars, De Quincey saw the tragic and the sublime condensed in the contrasting emotions that the mail left in its wake: joy for patriotic peasants and despair for mothers and wives whose sons and husbands had been sacrificed to the victory.[4] Despite shifts in latitudes, times, and technologies, De Quincey's and Montesquieu's intuitions about the productivity of long-distance communication provide a useful road map with which to explore the pedagogy of the world in the Belgian Congo.

The post promised access for the Congolese who sought to transcend their colonial isolation. Correspondence, newspapers, and mail-order books that were otherwise unavailable in local libraries offered opportunities to learn about the world. Images, ideas, and modes of action traveled long distances and shaped cognitive horizons.[5] In the early 1960s, in the direct aftermath of independence, Ernest Wamba, a teenage student at a Protestant boarding school in rural lower Congo, was one of the many young Congolese who still looked at international postal communications as absolutely crucial lifelines. "This is amazing when you think about it," he remembered decades later. "I wrote to Jean-Paul Sartre . . . and he replied!"[6] Sharing the memory of this correspondence, Wamba struggled to describe the exact substance of these long-lost letters. What mattered to him was mutual recognition: he sent letters and received answers. For people like Wamba, the post was never only a state institution; it was also a mode of relation, a set of intellectual dispositions, a political rationality, a psychological principle, and a way to position oneself in the world.[7] Accordingly, multiple kinds of epistolary sources entered into the making of postal politics in colonial and postcolonial Congo—including letters that were never sent, or were lost, or remained in their writers' imaginations, never actually put to paper.

This chapter looks at the network of possibilities created by the post in the first part of the twentieth century, before the creation of political parties and before the opening of universities in Leopoldville and Elisabethville, a time when postal exchanges offered a first window to the world to young Congolese literates. These postal users belonged to the class of the évolués against which university students later built their identity. Yet, the same students emerged as political actors within a field of practice that the évolués had constituted in previous decades. Looking at the role of the post in the colonial period, this chapter uncovers patterns that endured into the 1960s, even if distorted and transformed. The chapter also introduces Patrice Lumumba, a key figure for the students, who before breaking away from the évolué mold had been a model colonial postal agent and committed distance learner.

In colonial contexts, postal communications made some people aware of their being part of "a network of imperial transactions" as if every stamped envelope delivered brought the centers of power to the margins.[8] For other colonial subjects, the post reinforced feelings of isolation.[9] Postal offices embodied this dialectic of distance and nearness, isolation and connection, serving as potent material symbols of "the desire to claim belonging to a range of elsewheres."[10] During the first decades of the colonial period, when postal distribution depended on the schedule of steamers, the Congolese shared in the excitement brought by the periodic arrival of mail from Europe.[11] Many became letter writers themselves and seized every opportunity to engage with distant others.

Letter writing offered the Congolese new modes of communication and made new demands on them. Correspondence lacked the fluidity and immediacy of oral communications.[12] Writers were forced to project themselves into the future and account for delays in reception when crafting letters, as envoys could take weeks before reaching their destination.[13] Letter writing required a form of introspection, a confrontation with pen and paper, and time away from everyday activities. Yet, the fixity of the written word and the reliability and vastness of the postal network were all highly productive and gave postal communications a precious edge over orality. The post transported ideas and images over great distances without the altering effects of vernacularization. As a technology of communication, letters were particularly well suited to help many Congolese making sense of the new mobilities (of people, objects, and ideas) that transformed their lifeworlds.[14] In a colonial context, the post created precious opportunities to learn about the world and assert one's authority over foreign bodies of knowledge. In this way, colonial postal exchanges prefigured the pedagogical and cosmopolitan promises that university education would further institutionalize after its beginnings in the mid-1950s.

Politically, postal communications remained ambivalent throughout the whole colonial period. The post was an instrument at the service of colonial domination, but it also connected the colonized to interlocutors that might be critical of the powers that be. In the first decade of the twentieth century, the campaign against the regime of atrocities associated with the exploitation of rubber under King Leopold's Congo Free State (CFS) exacerbated this duality—post as domination, post as liberation.[15] Then the authorities worried about the outgoing mail of British and American missionaries who corresponded with journalists and activists in the anti-Leopoldian movement. By contrast, during the decades that followed the so-called takeover (la reprise) of 1908, when the Congo officially became a colony of Belgium, it was the ideas that traveled into the Congo with communist and Pan-Africanist pamphlets sent from Europe and the Americas that appeared to threaten the colonial order. Congolese évolués who were at the receiving end of these communications, including those who worked for the postal service, became targets of the state's surveillance. Yet the post, however central, did not engender any important movement of resistance against colonialism during this period, in contrast with the 1950s and 1960s when students and political activists used long-distance communications as a tool in the struggle for power. In the first part of the twentieth century, the Congolese understood correspondence as an opportunity to learn, to advance themselves, to stretch boundaries, and to escape literal and metaphoric states of confinement.

"Some Mighty Great Orchestra"

In 1893, the *Scientific American* published an article on the convenience of modern postal communications. The piece marveled that a five-cent stamp could take "one of our mammoth Sunday newspapers from this country to the white stations on the far Upper Congo" and that "when white men among the cannibals and the dwarfs write to their friends at home, they have the neat postage stamps of the Congo Free State to affix to the envelopes."[16] The article expressed familiar colonial tropes: racist condescension, fascination with abolishing distance, and a hint of disenchanted regret at a world in which money orders, postage stamps, and Sunday newspapers reached even the most "remote" of places.[17] The CFS, because of its unique international nature, offered an apt setting for this vignette. When European powers recognized King Leopold's Congo as a neutral sovereign entity at the Berlin Conference of 1884–85, they evoked the same rhetoric of progress and the same aspirations of racial internationalism that had propelled the creation of the Universal Postal Union (UPU) in Bern ten years earlier.[18] Leopold's promises of an international state, a place of convergence and collaboration among all "civilized nations," echoed the premises of the postal union and its promotion of a universal set of rules and technical provisions to ensure the smooth worldwide circulation of the mail. And although the Berlin Act, which recognized Leopold's sovereignty over the Congo, is best known for its articles on the protection of Christian missionaries, the suppression of the trade in slaves, and the declaration of freedom of commerce and navigation, it also imposed the implementation of the UPU's convention in the Congo Basin.[19]

Scholarship on postal culture often weaves the thread of the post into the fabric of the nation-state. Postal bureaucracies, the iconography of postage stamps, the cheap circulation of correspondence and its egalitarian overtones all seem to posit the nation as postal communications' horizon of intelligibility.[20] However, this reading ignores the convergences between the rhetoric of postal universalism and imperial internationalism.[21] New technologies of communications enabled the domination of European networks of information in imperial peripheries, while "a monster of correspondence" made imperial governance possible.[22] In few places was the affinity between postal universalism and the new imperialism illustrated more clearly than in Leopold's Congo.[23]

The CFS was a unique institutional entity. It operated from offices adjacent to the royal palace in Brussels, but it was not Belgian. It depended on foreign capital and on the labor of soldiers, doctors, merchants, and typists who more often hailed from Venice, Warsaw, or Zanzibar than Antwerp or Liège. A colony without a metropole, the Leopoldian state inhabited a field of empires. In contrast with the imagined horizontality of nations, the CFS exemplified the verticality of empires and the transversality of imperialism.[24] The complex entanglements that enabled its inscription in the world clearly appeared in its postal service.[25]

International postal relations offer a powerful metaphor for visualizing the dynamics that inscribed the CFS at the heart of the new imperialism of the turn of the century. However, on the ground, the postal service remained rather rudimentary. Ten years after the Berlin Conference, the Congo reportedly had the lowest postal density in the world, with fewer than one post office per one hundred thousand square miles and only twenty-eight employees for the whole territory.[26] Around 1900, the post office in Leopoldville—not yet the colony's capital but already one of its most important centers—employed two Belgian agents and one Senegalese telegrapher, and the mail from Belgium arrived once every three weeks.[27] This modest infrastructure created breaks in the circulation of correspondence and gaps in the postal canvas.

Due to the small number of postal employees in the CFS, soldiers were often put in charge of transporting the mail.[28] That the same auxiliaries who terrorized whole regions into meeting impossible rubber or ivory collection quotas were in charge of mail delivery made the juxtaposition between power and the post difficult to ignore. Critics observed that the injunctions about tax collection volumes that engineered large-scale atrocities circulated through the mail sent from Boma and Brussels.[29] These critics denounced the impact of revenue projections crafted in the language of bureaucracy. Others also perceived the importance of letters that traveled with sentries, porters, and steamers, but they believed that the mail from Europe sought to restrain, even if without much success, the tyranny and the violence of colonial extraction. Anonymous rubber refugees, testifying to the violence they had endured in 1903, expressed the connection clearly: "We heard that letters came to the white men to say that the people were to be well treated. We heard that these letters had been sent by the big white men in 'Mputu' (Europe); but our white men tore up these letters."[30]

As far as the CFS authorities were concerned, postal communication was associated with the rhetoric of awe and subjugation, the terror and terrific beauty of the colonial sublime. Yet, the post also transported descriptions of the atrocities perpetrated by state agents and private companies.[31] Quite fittingly, one of the first indictments of Leopold's oppressive regime appeared in 1890 in the form of an open letter written by the African American writer George Washington Williams.[32] A bit less than fifteen years later, the British publicist Edmund Morel began a powerful campaign against Leopold's "Vampire State" and its systematic infringements of the principles of free labor and human rights. Part of the international movement that sought to reconcile humanitarian principles with imperialism,[33] Morel's Congo Reform Association used lantern slide shows that displayed shock photographs of mutilated bodies to raise awareness of CFS atrocities.[34] But postal networks were not less important in circulating narratives of Congolese suffering. A few missionaries put their epistolary skills, their ability to convey closeness over long distances, in the service of Morel's campaign against the "horrors of the rubber slavery."[35] In his *King Leopold's Soliloquy*, Mark Twain imagined an infuriated Leopold, alone in his palace, venting about missionaries and their writings: "They seem to be always around, always spying, always eye-witnessing the happenings; and everything they see they commit to paper."[36]

Morel himself labored as a kind of postmaster: he received testimonies from the Congo in the form of letters and mailed pamphlets and periodicals to correspondents around the world. The postal nature of his activism was apparent in the title of the weekly publication that he began editing in 1903 to accelerate the outward flow of information about the Congo: *The West African Mail*.[37] Collecting, selecting, and italicizing testimonies, Morel concentrated the trickling Congolese mail and infused it with the urgency and signposting conducive to producing mass indignation.[38] His crusade against the "evils of Congoland" influenced the timing of the transfer of sovereignty from Leopold to the Belgian state, which was finally achieved in 1908. Although, in Britain and elsewhere, public attention to Congolese affairs waned in subsequent years, Belgian colonial officials never forgot the dangerous power of international correspondence.

"A Perfection of Harmony"

In 1909, less than a year after Belgium's takeover of the Congo, Prince Albert, Leopold's nephew, toured the colony for several weeks. His major takeaway from the trip was that the Congo's future depended on "the multiplication of communication lines."[39] A few months after returning to Europe, Albert succeeded his uncle to the Belgian throne. One of his first projects as monarch was to develop the colony's wireless telegraphic network. He opened a telegraphic school in an outbuilding of his palace in Brussels and had half a dozen Congolese brought to Belgium as telegraphy students until the school closed abruptly with the German military invasion of August 1914.[40] The colonial authorities' opposition to the education of the Congolese in Europe was already well entrenched when the telegraphic school opened its doors.[41] Albert's failure to abide to this central tenet of Belgian colonial policy indicates his sense of the importance of long-distance communication.

The king's closest associate in Congolese telegraphy was the entrepreneur and inventor Robert Goldschmidt. "To govern is to telegraph," Goldschmidt believed. "Without the telegraph, the government of a colony is nearly impotent."[42] Goldschmidt was a fervent advocate of wireless telegraphy. As he argued, communication via telegraphic lines was slow, expensive, difficult to maintain, and dependent on British overseas cables: only wireless telegraphy could make the Congo fully Belgian and truly independent from the influence of other imperial powers. The new technology would establish "an immaterial and safe connection" between the colony and the metropole, and assure young Belgian men that if they chose an African career, they could "receive news from [their] mom[s] in less than twenty-four hours in any place on this terrible and mysterious continent."[43]

During the German occupation of Belgium, the telegraphic stations that Goldschmidt had established throughout the Congo continued to function. A Belgian magistrate stationed in North Katanga during that period remembered the excitement when the "mail boy" arrived every week, bringing "indigenous news" gleaned along the way, newspapers and letters from Europe, and war telegrams that transited through the wireless station in Lusambo: "We know, seven or eight days later, the principal events that happened on European fronts. . . . What a joy it will be when, one good morning, we will receive the so-long-hoped-for telegram that will announce the final victory!"[44]

Telegraphic relays were becoming major features on the mental maps of Belgian colonials, but they did not bring the immediacy that Goldschmidt dreamed of. In the 1920s, messages often took several days to cross the six thousand kilometers between Boma and Brussels; and the high costs of services limited what traveled via cables or through the airwaves.[45] Furthermore, the small size of the postal and telegraphic workforce impeded the speed of all communications. In 1922, around seventy European agents and thirty African telegraphers worked for the Congolese postal services. For budgetary reasons, the minister of colonies hoped to raise the proportion of local auxiliaries, but the postal administration argued that it would be difficult to find Congolese agents with the adequate qualifications. Postal officials reminded the minister of "the pitiful results" when Mauritians, "though educated and civilized," had been hired to oversee postal offices in Katanga before the war. They also compiled a series of infractions committed by Congolese employees in recent years: a telegraphist in Boma had forged a telegram to request a cash withdrawal from a bank; a postal agent in Tumba had stolen banknotes from a registered letter; a clerk in Banana had produced a fake acknowledgment to pocket the money sent by "a native to his wife"; and so on. As the inspector of the posts argued, the very development of the colony would be at stake if the postal services hired unqualified agents, since "a correspondence that is not well directed might suffer weeks, and even months of delays."[46]

"The Awful Political Mission"

Telegrams could not always fill the communication gaps that coincided with those between steamship arrivals. News, like the mail, traveled in fits and starts, which posed problems for journalistic accuracy. Around the same time that the Ministry of Colonies debated the cost and racial organization of the post office workforce, newspapers in Belgium reported completely unsubstantiated rumors about a group of Black Americans in Kinshasa who had allegedly started an armed rebellion upon reading a call for insurrection from Marcus Garvey.[47] Anti-colonial internationalism worried the colonial authorities. They suspected that Garveyism and Bolshevism encouraged the Congolese to challenge European rule. In Belgium, the colonial lobby harassed Panda Farnana, a leading voice in the tiny community of Congolese expatriates in the metropole and an interlocutor of Black luminaries like W. E. B. Du Bois and Blaise Diagne. To agitated Belgian minds, Panda's association with these Pan-Africanist figures evoked bitter memories of Morel's anti-Leopoldian international coalition.[48] The press warned of the dangers of Panda's letters to supporters in the Congo: one journalist argued that Panda almost certainly had accomplices in the post office in Boma and that African postal employees should be kept under surveillance.[49]

Even when not traveling via letters, the threat of subversion often followed postal routes. Hearsay and prophecies were brought by steamers sailing up and down the Congo River and its tributaries, carried by the followers of "subversive" religious movements who had been banished to faraway zones, and shared by workers traveling between their home villages and colonial mining towns.[50] Belgian anxieties stoked the spreading of rumors, turning stories of insurrection into self-fulfilling prophecies.[51] In contexts permeated by the specter of insurrection and "competing hierarchies of credibility,"[52] postal forensics became more than a mere surveillance tool; it anchored the colonizers' fears of conspiracy and subversion in the materiality of paper.[53] Censorship often appeared as a convenient remedy to these anxieties. In theory, while the authorities were entitled to control which newspapers entered the colony, the list of banned publications had to be communicated to the UPU in Bern, and the postal service was obliged by law to protect the secrecy of all correspondence.[54] In practice, however, colonial agents had few scruples about reading over the shoulders of African letter writers.[55]

Despite the colonizers' suspicions, letter writing increasingly entered Congolese lives. Missionaries promoted correspondence by publishing letters from their converts in religious periodicals. These letters, written in local languages, conveyed personal narratives of encounters with the colonial order and served "the brokering of knowledge and the formation of social identities in a colonial situation."[56] Literacy and letter writing contributed to the construction of religious publics and ethnic constituencies, while connecting growing segments of the population more closely to the state.[57]

One word emblematized the ineluctable growth of the Congolese mail: *mukanda*. Used in all the major Congolese lingua francas, mukanda became a central unit in the language of power. It could mean paperwork or voucher and, by extension, paper and metal money, note, folder, image, photograph, ink, book, certificate, labor contract, calendar, manuscript, decree, bulletin, and of course, letter.[58] Mukanda permeated the lives of the literate Congolese (the Bena Mukanda—literally, the children or tribe of mukanda—as they were called in the Kasai),[59] but it also cast its shadow over their illiterate countrymen.[60] Paperwork was a necessity of governance and thus valorized. At the same time, the Belgians worried that literacy and postal communications could destabilize their colonial dominance. Undesirable letters, newspapers, and pamphlets entered the Congo anonymously, and Belgian talk of dishonest telegraphers and postal clerks betrayed a manifest apprehension about the control over communications within the colony.

The Production of Politics

A few months before the end of World War II, the police arrested a dozen clerks in Elisabethville on charges of conspiracy and attempting to overthrow the colonial order. A letter to a US army officer based in Katanga featured at the center of the prosecution. Liévin Kalubi, a former Catholic seminarian and primary school teacher turned state employee, had written the letter. Explicitly referring to the Atlantic Charter, Kalubi demanded freedom for the Congolese "in the full meaning of the word, as the above-mentioned Charter defines it, but not under the term 'protectorate' [tutelle], which is nothing else but the veiled domination of some European capitalists who dictate the government to prejudice us in all sorts of ways." The letter listed several requests: freedom of speech and the press; "the granting of necessary education for the intellectual development of the native and civilizational progress, like in other African colonies"; and "free access to other parts of the world so that we can be better informed about the progress of our country."[61]

The Elisabethville clerks' letter prefigured the nationalist manifestos of the mid-1950s.[62] Yet, neither was it received by its addressee, nor did it secure the clerks a seat at the table where statesmen, scholars, and activists were rethinking sovereignty, rights, and universal values. Kalubi and his associates did not inaugurate a new type of correspondence. They were banished to rural outposts instead. Unlike the people in Ruanda-Urundi, where Belgians were bound to the rules of the trusteeship system, the Congolese lacked the international interlocutors to whom they could address their grievances and share their hopes for emancipation.[63] In the years subsequent to the war, what occasioned politics was the domestication of postal routines, not militant letters.

Fast-paced urbanization and the progress of literacy rates certainly increased interest in letter writing among the Congolese, but postal density remained low, and the volume of letters exchanged in the Belgian colony was a rather poor two letters per person per year by the end of the 1940s.[64] The administration's skepticism about the ability of the Congolese to manage the postal offices unsupervised was the main obstacle to the system's development.[65] In Belgian representations, post office jobs were made out to be the typical professional occupation for a Congolese évolué; notwithstanding, the specter of the perfidious Black postman did not disappear.[66]

In 1946, the colonial government opened a school in Leopoldville to address the supposed moral and technical deficiencies of native postal employees. Patrice Lumumba, a promising twenty-two-year-old man who taught himself French soon after arriving in Stanleyville from his native Sankuru in the last few months of the war, was among the postal school's first student cohorts. After nine months of courses in accountancy, postal ethics, and postal geography, Lumumba graduated in third place from a class of thirty-five. First assigned to Yangambi, he found his way back to Stanleyville as a third-class assistant in 1950. Five years later, he had reached the position of main assistant in the checking accounts service.[67] Lumumba served as the leader of an association of évolués, presided over the local chapters of the association of native state employees and of the alumni association of the Scheutist missionaries' school network, and regularly wrote for the Brussels-based periodical *L'Afrique et le Monde* as well as for several newspapers in Leopoldville.[68] Even more importantly maybe, he cofounded and led the Oriental Province Native Postmen Association (APIPO).

The post gave Lumumba a professional identity. It allowed him to build a public persona despite the impediments of rigid colonial assignations. Having exhausted the local library's collections, he ordered books and pamphlets from France. Estranged from local Catholic colonials, he corresponded with the minister of colonies, Auguste Buisseret, and other politicians in the Belgian Liberal Party. Unable to register as a student at the newly created Lovanium University in Leopoldville due to family obligations, he subscribed to long-distance teaching programs in Belgium. "You can become a true university man from your home if you learn with tenacity and method," Lumumba wrote to a friend in April 1954.[69] Lumumba was indeed a true student of the world. His words are proof that the late colonial figure of the student—and its cosmopolitan associations—reverberated beyond the small group of colonized subjects who accessed the new universities. For those who did not but were curious about the world and desirous of learning, postal communications presented a powerful alternative.

Distance Learning

Like Lumumba, many Congolese used the post to circumvent obstacles to education.[70] In the early 1950s, a group of évolués working at the Lever palm oil plantation of Brabanta complained of interferences in the correspondence courses on human culture, self-control, and personal efficiency that they took at the Institute for Human Culture in Brussels.[71] Paul Nyssens, the institute's director, had offered correspondence courses since 1916 and was well known among Congolese évolués. Yet, in February 1950, the Belgian agent in charge of money orders at the post office in Port Franqui decided to stop accepting requests for Nyssens's correspondence courses and began intercepting letters sent by Brabanta clerks. The agent advised Léon Kingansi (see figure 1.3), one of the clerks who followed Nyssens's courses, to "stop wasting your money and your time with a charlatan."[72] The message failed to convince Kingansi and the other clerks. André Liwatwa, another student of Nyssens, complained bitterly, telling Nyssens, "We might as well stop calling ourselves citizens of the Belgian Congo, instead it is as if we have become the citizens of a foreign colony."[73]

The Congolese were Belgian subjects, not Belgian citizens. Nonetheless, postal exchanges encouraged strong feelings of belonging and participation. Feeding a sheet of paper into a typewriter, disentangling type bars, replacing spent ribbons, typing letters in French, visiting the post office— all of these routinized gestures were part of the évolués' attempts to inhabit and enlarge the tight confines of colonial assignations.

Nyssens vehemently protested the interruption of his correspondence with his students in 1950 and 1951. He denounced the interception as unlawful and defended himself from accusations of charlatanism, noting that despite many solicitations, he had always refused to send "talismans, amulets, or lucky charms" to Congolese correspondents.[74] The authorities ordered an investigation. Ultimately, the general governor concluded that the Belgian agent at Port Franqui had acted "in blatant contradiction with the duties of his charge." Yet, since his intervention sought "to protect some évolués, who too often fall victims of their own credulity," no disciplinary measure was taken against the agent.[75] The administration did not only condone his paternalism, but it also shared his suspicions about the nature of Nyssens's exchanges with Congolese évolués. During their

Figure 1.1 Léon Kingansi. Photographer unknown, 1962
(source: http://www.mimi.jc.free.fr/www_photos/famille.php).

investigations, the authorities frowned at what they read in this correspondence. A report, for instance, extracted the following lines from a letter from Nyssens to Kingansi dated November 1950: "You are a really good student. You are beginning to see clearly. You are already seeing more clearly than the majority of the whites. Continue this way, persevere."[76] Not incidentally, when colonial authorities worried about a resurgence in the efforts at "communist penetration" in the Congo a few years later, they suspected it may take the form of distance learning courses.[77]

It is not known which correspondence course Lumumba took, but Nyssens's stress on self-confidence resonates with the upward trajectory of the Stanleyville postal employee. Of his many activities, Lumumba's leadership of APIPO was one of the most significant. By January 1955, the association counted eighteen European agents and ninety African clerks, "without taking into account the postmen and the sentries."[78] It is as its leader that Lumumba moved away from a rather unpolitical agenda that sought to morally reform évolués and began to focus on the Belgian-Congolese community, subtly challenging colonial racism while seeming to reinforce the relationship between metropole and colony.

The idea behind APIPO emerged after a gathering in a bar where Stanleyville's Black and white postal employees celebrated the retirement of their director. The good companionship and "harmony between the races" that marked this celebration, Lumumba thought, should be cultivated.[79] Lumumba emphasized the idea that the postal service was a large family. In his articles for the association's periodical, *L'Echo Postal*, he evoked visions of the future that praised equality and "true friendship" among Congolese of different ethnic backgrounds as the way forward for "the development of our country."[80] He also contributed a series of articles on race and biology, which paraphrased a UNESCO booklet on the topic.[81] Undermining ideas of racial superiority, these articles clashed with a key tenet of Belgian colonialism and laid the ground for Congolese national pride.[82]

L'Echo Postal contributed to Lumumba's vision of distance education by offering lessons about the postal service's history and philosophy to readers across the vast Oriental Province.[83] Belgian and Congolese contributors sought to elevate the postman's intellect and develop his self-awareness as an évolué. They insisted that as a system, the post supported the "civilizing mission" and the construction of a "more prosperous Congo." In an article that also mentioned the postal service's censorship of pornographic material and its preservation of secrecy and discretion, Stanleyville's receveur en chef, Roland Tavernier, argued that the post encouraged commerce and cultural progress: "By providing the means for correspondence, we instill in a good number of natives the need to learn to read and write. Furthermore, our services are involved in circulating books, periodicals and distance courses at prices that are not profitable for us."[84] Because the post was a central institution in the civilizing mission, "drunken lustful or adulterous men" did not possess "the necessary qualities of a good agent in the postal service," Lumumba wrote in another article. "Men like these will sooner or later break the public trust by stealing and by neglecting their work."[85] Lumumba noted how dereliction of duty could affect postal service users: "How sad must a customer feel when, running hastily to the post office to drop an important and extremely urgent letter, he receives this ready-made answer: 'the office is closed.'"[86]

Contributors to *L'Echo Postal* promoted professionalism among postal workers. They argued that postmen should be honorable family men and should strive to improve themselves by listening to educational radio talks and reading instructive books.[87] In his own articles, Lumumba often insisted on these Belgian middle-class values and on notions that evoked the respectable masculinity of the évolué. He also pointed up traits such as honesty, temperance, punctuality, politeness, and personal hygiene. As he wrote, the fingers that were to handle other people's stamps and bank notes "should not be put in one's nose, mouth, or ear."[88] Lumumba also stressed the importance of a respect for hierarchy, particularly between Black employees of varying ranks, and stressed that postal workers should show as much deference toward Black customers—even illiterate postal users, he added—as toward white customers.[89] In these articles, as in other activities with APIPO, Lumumba used colonial discourse against itself: he combined together colonial notions of ethics, hygiene, and morals, producing a dissonant ferment that actually undermined the colonial order. Unlike the Elisabethville clerks of 1944, Lumumba did not confront Belgian colonialism head-on, but his work at the post helped him to build a model for political action that would deeply transform relations of power in the Congo.

Prison Letters

In April and May 1956, Lumumba took part in a state-sponsored study trip to Belgium, with a program that included visits to the postal administration in Brussels.[90] Very few Congolese enjoyed the privilege of traveling to Europe. Lumumba's trip crowned the success of his activism in Stanleyville and put him in good stead to expand his network beyond the Oriental Province. However, Lumumba had made enemies in Stanleyville—notably missionaries and rival members of local associations who were determined to counter his upward trajectory. While Lumumba was studying postal routines in Belgium, accusations of fraudulent practice at the post office arrived on a judge's desk in Stanleyville. The police opened Lumumba's mail, checked his registers, and discovered irregularities. On returning to the Congo, the young évolué was arrested and he confessed to charges of embezzlement: he had transferred money from the accounts of large companies into his own and covered up these transfers with manipulative bookkeeping. From being a dignitary on tour in Europe, Lumumba became a detainee in a colonial prison.

As a postal employee, Lumumba had become fluent in the language of colonial morality. His articles for *L'Echo Postal* called on readers to respect hierarchies. However, his own social mobility demanded the acumen of a forger. The Belgians paid Congolese clerks like the lower section of the white proletariat while demanding that they lived up to the material standards of their middle class. Salaries were low for évolués, and the cost of life in urban centers could be overwhelming. Lumumba had seen no other solution to the financial dilemma obstructing his social and political ambitions, so he helped himself to post office funds. In his defense, he argued that he had long stopped this malpractice and had already partially reimbursed the embezzled sums. On March 4, 1957, he was found guilty and sentenced to two years of imprisonment.

Lumumba had once written that all Congolese post offices "looked alike" and displayed "the same atmosphere, the same rumor, the same noise."[91] Congolese prisons had a similar modular character. Emblematic of the mental enclosure of colonialism, the prison system was an element of the everyday.[92] Tens of thousands of Congolese passed through prison doors every year.[93] The state turned to confinement as a way to relocate unemployed young men who illegally resided in urban centers and punish poor peasants who refused to pay taxes. Through the 1950s, more and more people of better means, who had some formal education, rode Raleigh bikes, and owned phonographs, also wound up behind bars.[94] As more évolués served time in prison in the 1950s, the authorities began to experiment with cellular incarceration, deemed too harsh for "noncivilized natives" but appropriate for "Europeanized Blacks." In Belgian eyes, évolués made the most obvious public for the penitentiary system, since they could best understand its logic and be affected by it.[95]

During Lumumba's time in prison, *L'Afrique et le Monde* published an article denouncing the conditions in Congolese prisons. Boniface Lupaka, an accountant and friend of Lumumba, signed the article. The piece vehemently denounced the unhygienic conditions, the discomfort of dormitories, the food, which "a European would never serve to his dog," and the everyday use of physical punishment.[96] Daily floggings in Congolese prisons disciplined prisoners who tried to avoid work duties, were caught having sex, refused to eat, threw food in latrines or at a guard's face, laughed during morning calls, smoked, spread rumors about plans to poison detainees, or used native medicines. But punishment was also meted out to detainees who possessed steno handbooks or clandestinely sent letters.[97]

Lumumba was more fortunate. As an immatriculé (a category of évolués subjected to European civil law), he escaped corporeal punishment and was allowed to correspond freely. He sent many requests to have his sentence revised,[98] and completed a book on the future of the Congo. In a letter to the publisher to whom he submitted the manuscript, Lumumba claimed that he was "on personal convenience leave" from the postal service and that he planned "to embrace a liberal and independent profession" that would allow him "to focus my efforts on the evolution of my country and further collaborate with Belgians for the Congo's civilization and industrialization."[99] Lumumba's manuscript read like a long epistle to the Belgian public, with cautiously crafted criticisms of the colonial system hidden behind declarations of his love for the "Belgian-Congolese community"—terms that reflected his awareness of censorship and his strategic attempt to rebound after a personal catastrophe. Confinement had exacerbated his reliance on foreign protectors and allies. In writing and sending letters, he resisted the arbitrariness of the judicial system. He had previously used the post to raise himself socially and knew that letters could bring deliverance.[100]

Conclusion

A few months after the Belgians released Lumumba from prison, they allowed the creation of political parties in the Congo. Lumumba took the presidency of one of them, the Congolese National Movement (MNC). His rhetoric shifted quickly, casting him as one of the most vocal advocates for Congolese independence. When campaigning, he talked about the Belgian Congo as an open-air prison. This was a metaphor that spoke to the countless Congolese who felt captive to the world of colonialism. For many of these people, and certainly for Lumumba himself, postal correspondence opened up gates that had otherwise seemed firmly closed.

The post was not unique in this regard. Communications across distance in general led the colonized to imagine new geographies and alternative futures. Various media fashioned urban Congolese outlooks and created opportunities for learning and overcoming colonial limitations on education. Popular music, cinema, radio broadcasting, newspapers, and magazines all provided important vehicles for enlarging spaces of cultural sovereignty, even if Belgians remained in control of all instruments of mass communication until the very end of the 1950s.[101] Letters functioned in conjunction with these other tools of mediation. They, too, affected the "experience of space, time, movement, and speed."[102] Yet, the cadence of postal delivery was distinctive, and the act of correspondence required a unique form of introspection.[103] As both a technique of the self and a highly dialogical tool of communication, letter writing came to embody a superior promise of deliverance from colonial enclosure. Postal exchanges enabled the colonized to connect to ideas, to goods, and to people located in remote places. They offered ways of exploring and experiencing the broader world. And they permitted experimentations with self-presentation. When

Figure 1.2 "Lumumba Makes a Famous Speech." Painting by Tshibumba Kanda Matulu, 1973–74 (source: Tropenmuseum, Amsterdam). Representing Lumumba standing in front of a crowd on the day of the Congo's independence, with King Baudouin at his side, the painting includes key symbols of sovereignty: the Congolese national colors, the broken chain of slavery, and the globe in Lumumba's hand. The artist's depiction of a postal office in the background of the painting serves as another marker of the Lumumbist symbolism of power and emancipation.

the perspective of decolonization became concrete in the late 1950s, this inward and outward dynamics was key to helping a generation of Congolese to think and act as political subjects.

Jean-Paul Sartre's preface to *La pensée politique de Patrice Lumumba*, a posthumous volume of Lumumba's speeches and articles, reflects on the centrality of the post in the maturation of Lumumba's political imaginary: "The Post Office network extended into all the provinces and even into the bush; through it, the government's orders were relayed to the local gendarmeries and the Force Publique. If one day the Congolese Nation were to exist, it would owe its unity to a similar centralism. Patrice dreamed of a general uniting power which would apply everywhere, impose harmony and a community of action everywhere, would receive information from remote villages, concentrate it, base the direction of its policies on it and send back information and orders by the same route to its representatives in every little hamlet."[104]

Lumumba's articles in *L'Echo Postal* confirms Sartre's intuition that the postal network informed his understanding of the Congolese nation (an intuition shared by many in the Congo, including the popular painter Tshibumba Kanda Matulu; see figure 1.2). But this was only one part of the story. For Lumumba, writing letters, using the postal service was also about skirting local constraints and connecting to "imagined communities" beyond the nation: the short-lived and elusive Belgian-Congolese community during his months in prison and the mighty anti-colonial international once he became the president of the MNC.

TWO
FRIENDLY CORRESPONDENCE
WITH THE WHOLE WORLD

Reading your letter, looking at your handwriting again, I was nearly able to picture you in front of me....You see how irresistible human love is! ...My dear Luis, my thoughts are flying towards you through the walls of my jail and, by the same love that has always united us, I embrace you fraternally.

Patrice Lumumba, letter to Luis Lopez Alvarez, November 1959, quoted in Lopez, *Lumumba ou l'Afrique*, 55–56

MOUYEKE DOMINIQUE, Ecole Nationale de Formation Para-Médicale et Médico-Sociale J. J. Loukabou, B. P. 1215, Pointe-Noire, RÉPUBLIQUE CONGO-BRAZAVILLE. Interested in friendly correspondence with the whole world.

"Pen Friends," *World Student News* 24, no. 3–4 (1970): 32

In December 1969, *Ebony* published an article on the "boom in stamps by and of blacks."[1] The American magazine illustrated the piece with a map of Africa on which were twenty-nine stamps, each representing a recently decolonized country. The stamps displayed the colors of national flags, precolonial emblems, fathers of the nation, and images of African wildlife. This iconography, *Ebony* suggested, symbolized Black sovereignty and the victory over imperialism. Yet, the magazine overlooked a contradiction between the stamps' semiotic function and their conditions of production: most of the stamps had indeed been designed and produced outside of Africa, by English, French, and Swiss printing companies. Had *Ebony*'s journalists focused more specifically on Congolese philately, they may have been more sensitive to the shadows that neocolonialism had cast on the colorful stamps of the immediate post-independence era.

Nowhere else in Africa had neocolonial violence and the Cold War made such a brutal entrance as they did in the Congo in July 1960. Days after the country's independence, thousands of disgruntled soldiers mutinied across the country. Belgium responded with a unilateral military operation that alienated the government of President Joseph Kasa-Vubu and Prime Minister Patrice Lumumba. Meanwhile, the provinces of Katanga and Southern Kasai, both backed by Belgian mining corporations, seceded from the central state. In response, the United Nations (UN) deployed a massive peacekeeping operation but failed to prevent the intensification of factionalism on the ground. Cold warriors blew on the embers of discord, with the Soviet Union leaving the door open to an intervention in support of Lumumba, while the United States threw its weight against him. In September, President Kasa-Vubu dismissed Lumumba from office. Soon after that, the prime minister's loyalists created a dissident government in Stanleyville. Conflicts continued unabated well into 1961—a year that began with Lumumba's murder. The Congo crisis rendered Nikita Khrushchev's opening toward the third world more pressing; it put decolonization at the forefront of American minds during a transformative presidential transition; and it changed how a multiplicity of actors across Africa—from the Algerian National Liberation Front to white settlers in Rhodesia—understood the web of constraints and possibilities in which they found themselves entangled.[2] In the midst of this crisis, the Congo witnessed a true explosion in stamps. Yet, the celebratory narrative about African sovereignty that *Ebony* related to its readers in its article on the iconography of postage does not align with the Congolese overflow of new postal values. The Congo crisis produced heterogenous stamps that were often in blatant infringement of international postal principles. These stamps evoked the confusion of a harsh struggle for outside legitimation and power. They responded to an intense competition over symbols of statehood among President Kasa-Vubu's Republic of Congo in Leopoldville, Moïse Tshombe's Katanga State in Elisabethville, Albert Kalonji's Autonomous State of South Kasai in Bakwanga, and Antoine Gizenga's pro-Lumumba People's Republic of Congo in Stanleyville. All these competing governments commissioned new series of stamps to entrench their mutually exclusive claims to sovereignty; they printed the chosen names for their polities over crossed-out mentions of the "Belgian Congo" on old colonial stamps; and they each issued overprints of each other's original productions.[3]

There was a biting irony in the stamp race of 1960: although a plethora of new postal values appeared on the market, there was no guarantee that any of these stamps could actually make letters move. Books of stamps were stolen, bags of letters lost, and accounting documents destroyed when Belgian postmasters joined their fellow countrymen in panicked exodus following the army's mutiny in July. Some postmasters helped themselves to cash from the postal coffers before leaving.[4] According to the Central Intelligence Agency (CIA) chief of station in Leopoldville, sending a letter through the post then amounted to throwing a bottle in the ocean.[5]

This American spy's jab at the Congolese post was rather hyperbolic. Even at the peak of the crisis, the disorganization of the service did not stem the flow of the Congolese mail. Independence internationalized Congolese politics, and mastering the art of correspondence had become a necessity for people wanting to understand and shape a new world. Stamps in the Congo may not have directly evoked the kind of satisfaction for African sovereignty that *Ebony* suggested (and after Joseph Mobutu imposed his image on a great portion of the Congolese philatelic production, many in the country may have associated the iconography of postage with neocolonialism). Yet, once put to use and attached to letters on the verge of being sent across the world, these stamps came to emblematize a promise of liberation and futurity. Not since Leopold's Free State had the Congo been the focus of so much attention. The rhetoric of internationalism, human rights, and socialism began to infuse the imagination of a growing number of Congolese. During the colonial period, letter writing had been a formidable tool for self-learning and personal advancement, and now with independence, it gave the impression of having limitless potential. The postal archive of the Congo crisis reveals how literate Congolese—students as well as others who shared the same interest for learning about the world—conceived of political participation as an exercise unbounded by national frontiers. Looking at the emotive language and affective rhetoric used across a wide variety of correspondence, this chapter claims that "the postal" acted as a potent interface in the emergence of new subjectivities in the 1960s. It also interrogates the gendered constructions to be found in these letters, as most exchanges happened among men.

Moments of Acceleration

If the colonial state authorized political parties in 1958, it was to contain a growing frustration among Congolese évolués. Yet, the measure had the effect of opening wide the floodgates of political passion. The number of parties multiplied, setting in motion a dynamic of radicalization. The anti-colonial struggle created incentives to co-opt the urban and rural masses. It also encouraged political entrepreneurs to search for external support beyond the Congo, something that Lumumba prioritized as the head of the Congolese National Movement (MNC). At the end of 1958, the former postal employee attended the All-African People's Conference in Accra, where he was alongside Frantz Fanon, Kwame Nkrumah, Sékou Touré, and others. His presence in the Gold Coast cemented his national and international stature as a leader. Returning from the conference, he was fully convinced of the rightness of his Pan-Africanist intuitions. Not to be outdone by Lumumba's successes, the ABAKO, the party of his main rival, Kasa-Vubu, called for a large popular meeting in Leopoldville on January 4, 1959. A last-minute decision to ban this rally led to street fights between ABAKO supporters, onlookers, and the Force Publique (as the colonial army was called). Riots paralyzed the city for several days and ended only after a brutal repression that cost hundreds their lives. In the following months, tensions simmered through the country. Several political leaders, including Lumumba, were arrested, while increasingly many Congolese were demanding independence forthwith.[6] At the end of January 1960, delegates from the main political parties ended up meeting with the Belgian authorities for a decisive round of negotiations in Brussels. To their great surprise, the Congolese delegates discovered that the Belgians had underwent a breathtaking change of mind. The colonizers now accepted the idea of a quick retreat and they agreed to grant independence to the Congo within six months.

Congolese politics evolved at a dizzying pace in 1959 and 1960. Things that had been unthinkable suddenly seemed achievable. This acceleration encouraged an "avidity for knowledge among the Congolese youth."[7] But it also produced confusion. After July, the crisis further exacerbated the existing climate of intrigue, fear, and pretense. Many Congolese turned to letter writing in hopes of making the moment more intelligible, but they did not all do it in the same way. Some grasped the act of writing as an opportunity to pause, analyze, and project order onto a chaotic present. Others embraced the tumult, penning urgent letters in nervous handwriting, striking through multiple passages, capitalizing and underlining words, and leaving unfinished sentences and abrupt transitions.

Pierre Wangata, a Congolese youth who briefly studied journalism in Belgium in 1961, belonged to the latter group. During his stay in Europe, he sent a series of exultant letters to Louis Mandala, a friend in Leopoldville. In his letters, Wangata marveled at the men's clothes that were being sold at a fraction of their asking price in Leopoldville, at Belgian night-clubs' policy of refusing entrance to unaccompanied males, and at other astonishing details about life in the former metropole. Wangata also de-scribed himself as a player in a game of masking and unmasking. He wrote about how he would hide his sympathy for Congolese nationalist political parties and present himself as a supporter of the Katangese secession, with the aim of exposing Belgian duplicity toward the Congo. His agitated, stream-of-consciousness messages to Mandala suggested the difficulty in-volved in making sense of the messiness that lay on the other side of the looking-glass of colonial illusions. In one letter, he mentioned that he had written to Cyrille Adoula, the then–Congolese prime minister, to warn him of new plans to "balkanize" the Congo. He also advised Mandala to mis-trust all Belgians in Leopoldville as potential spies and assassins. Belgium was a land of oppression, he wrote, and Belgian women all hated the Black race. Even so, when the Senegalese scholar Cheikh Anta Diop declined a job offer at the Institut Politique Congolais, a recently created research and educational center where Mandala worked, Wangata recommended a Belgian candidate to fill the position.[8] Wangata justified his recommen-dation with the assertion that young leftists in Belgium sometimes "know Congolese nationalism better than we do" and "can teach us the principles of the science of patriotism."[9]

Codes of Professional Correspondence

The drama of the Congo's decolonization played out on airmail writing paper, across diplomatic cables, and via the teleprinters that connected embassies and ministries in Elisabethville and Leopoldville to Brazzaville, Accra, Brussels, London, Paris, Moscow, Washington, and New York.[10] Lumumba, although often remembered as a charismatic orator, conducted most of his short political life from behind a typewriter and operated as a man of letters in the most literal sense. He did not like to delegate, as one of his Belgian friends noted after visiting his office on the eve of indepen-dence: "His mail sits here in front of me, solid piles of express-mails mixed with telegrams and ordinary letters. You can feel that at the decision level, he is the only one to see everything."[11] Six months later, while under deten-tion, Lumumba ended a letter to Rajeshwar Dayal, the UN representative in Leopoldville, by apologizing for the bad quality of the paper on which he was writing.[12] He had endured weeks of privations, had been forbidden to change clothes and kept shoeless, but still perceived postal etiquette as a source of dignity. His mail certainly mattered a great deal. Agents working for Joseph Mobutu had even broken into his office in September to steal piles of his letters. Conservative newspapers subsequently published facsimiles of some of these letters, together with others that were most certainly forged and were meant to expose Lumumba's supposed dictatorial tendencies.[13]

Doctored or not, the private letters of well-known figures like Lumumba fascinated. They promised access to a deeper level of truth about the political process, revealing ramifications and strategies not meant for public disclosure. However, the struggle for independence and the ensuing reconfiguration of state power was also a concern for less prominent letter writers. As a man named Jean Kapita wrote to the UN general secretary, "there [was] not only the Kasa-Vubus, the Lumumbas, the Gizengas, the Tshombes and the Kashamuras in the Congo." The voices of ordinary people like himself mattered as well.[14]

Many people who had learned to type at above-average speed and mastered the codes of professional correspondence felt well-placed to intervene in the political realm. They often experienced independence as a time of opportunities. The massive departure of Belgians left numerous positions in the administration empty, and decolonization in general nourished dreams of a different life. Political scientists have talked of these few months as a decisive moment of class formation, when a national bourgeoisie defined by "its dependency on the state as the source of its social standing" began to emerge.[15] The situation looked different at the time. Independence seemed pregnant with multiple possibilities in 1960. It is only later that high inflation, the strengthening of patronage networks, and the influx of university graduates into the labor market exacerbated inequalities between the emerging bourgeoisie and its petit bourgeois counterparts. In the months that followed the departure of the Belgian colonizers, all Congolese with some education and a decent mastery of French expected to benefit from independence. They expected to benefit not only in terms of personal advancement but also of political participation and as members of a broader human community.

The American ethnomusicologist Alan Merriam noted this optimism for independence among people in rural Kasai, where he conducted fieldwork in 1959 and 1960. One of his informants, for instance, upon learning about the formation of the first government, "began to prepare a letter and its carbon copies to be sent to Lumumba [and] Kasa-Vubu." The letter asked for an "immediate disbursement of funds so that he could study in an American University—[he] had six years of grade school education."[16] The young man's dream of joining an American university sounded delusional to Merriam. However, it appears less ludicrous against the backdrop of the dizzying heights of social elevation that played out in the Congo in the early 1960s. Party affiliations, personal connections, as well as sheer luck played important roles for those who did go places. But properly typed letters and the use of carbon paper could also make a difference. As the Congo entered a cycle of dramatic transformations, bureaucratic codes and routines did not disappear but instead became instruments for navigating the uncertainties of changing regimes of power.

Capital Letters

Postal literacy opened lines of communications that had young men, like Merriam's informant, dreaming of universities in far-off places. It also increased their confidence in their ability to function as political subjects. Would-be political entrepreneurs and activists knew they had to leverage connections with forces outside of the Congo, and decolonization multiplied the opportunities for international correspondences, helping them to extend their networks. Those who wrote about power and politics were virtually all men. All parties interpellated women as key actors in the political process. Yet, they expected them to contribute to local mobilizations, not to the international mediations that young educated men were setting their minds to. With a few exceptions, these young male letter writers corresponded with other men, and their letters often channeled associations of politics with masculinity.

In the months leading to the Congo's independence, many of these young men sent letters to members of the Belgian Communist Party (PCB). Although communism remained the epitome of subversion in the eyes of the colonial state, the progressive opening of the Congolese political field at the end of the 1950s had given the PCB some opportunities to establish contacts in the colony.[17] Socialism and communism had been elusive notions for decades. They now turned into ideological references that elicited desire and curiosity, particularly among the educated youth in urban centers.[18] The PCB was vocal in its denunciation of colonialism, and young Congolese felt grateful that some Belgians were mobilizing on their behalf in the metropole. To them, this proved that "there are other kinds of white people who understand the difficulties of Black people and want to help them."[19] Although the PCB performed only modestly in Belgian elections, to Congolese letter writers it appeared as a powerful force. They perceived the party as a source of knowledge about political theory and methods of activism. Some rising political figures, like Pierre Mulele, for instance, took distance learning classes on ideology and organization through the PCB.[20] But people with no networks or connections also wrote to the party for guidance. "I have read enough Marxist theory," a student with revolutionary leanings wrote at the beginning of 1960. "Now, I need to act. . . . Show me the methods to use, the principles and the rules to fol-low. I am impatiently waiting for your pamphlets."[21]

For some Congolese, the PCB became a relay to interlocutors beyond the metropole, in countries like Guinea, the Soviet Union, and the People's Republic of China. All correspondence could be targeted by postal censor-ship.[22] But the notion prevailed that the postal administration systemati-cally intercepted letters sent from the Congo to socialist countries.[23] For instance, Cléophas Mukeba, a member of a dissident branch of the MNC, used the address of a Belgian communist activist to correspond with a member of the Chinese Committee for Afro-Asian Solidarity.[24] Prior to this correspondence, he had developed sustained contacts with several Belgian communists through the mail. In one of his first letters to the PCB, he had written "WE WANT TO BE MARXISTS" in capitals. His enthusiastic declarations for Marxism helped him built a support network that ad-vanced his political activism. In January 1960, he was able to attend the second All-African People's Conference in Tunis. Conferences like these allowed their participants to connect with like-minded people. And it is in Tunis that Mukeba made the acquaintance of his Chinese correspondent.

Congolese mail to the PCB displayed a logic of self-learning and intel-lectual curiosity similar to that described in the previous chapter, but the goal was no longer personal advancement only. Letter writers now also talked of collective emancipation. Bernard Salamu, a stenographer for an insurance company and an active member of the MNC in Stanleyville, wrote a long letter to the PCB in November 1959 in which he expressed the sense of excitement about politics that so many felt at the time. Salamu narrated his expulsion from school by Catholic missionaries as a young teenager. "I had to educate myself alone *at home*," he wrote, deploring the fact that Belgians "colonized us through and through" by limiting educa-tional opportunities for the colonized and preventing them from traveling abroad. His most profound aspiration was to "open my horizons, in the political domain mostly," and he dreamed of studying in Guinea or at the school that Sékou Touré had attended in Czechoslovakia.[25]

Like Salamu, a growing number of Congolese came to see postal ex-changes as a door into a world that had previously been inaccessible to them. Their letters expressed a wish to make up for lost time: "I have long sought to correspond with COMMUNISTS," one student wrote.[26] Capitalizing this last word, he conveyed urgency and resoluteness. Maybe he also sought to openly provoke colonial censorship. Many correspondents wanted clarifications. Hubert Bokata, a young worker, asked, "Tell me clearly: what is the goal of communism and what should one do to become a member? Are there courses I could follow?"[27] Pontien Tshilenge, a student in Elisabethville, was similarly direct: "So many people talk about communism, either positively or negatively, and I am interested to know what it is about exactly."[28] André Umba, another student from Elisabethville, mentioned that colonial "xenophobia toward communism" had prevented the Congolese from understanding the meaning of this ideology.[29] A lack of theoretical knowledge did not stop François Loola, a bank employee in Stanleyville, from expressing his "total devotion" to the PCB. He was ready to immediately recruit among his fellow countrymen, but he thought it might be necessary for him to be trained properly first.[30] He requested the PCB to sponsor a visit to Belgium. The party turned him down, but Loola insisted: "Without lying, I love communism. This is why I am replying so quickly to your letter."[31]

The aura of communism among the Congolese came in great part from decades of colonial attempts to halt its spread in central Africa. It was not surprising therefore that many letters sent to the PCB sought some balance between attraction and ignorance. Trying to convey an initial bond with their Belgian communist addressees, letter writers had to make do with the information that they could gather. Sometimes they erred when taking guesses. In October 1962, a man named Baudouin Bala sent a letter to Joseph Jacquemotte, whom he referred to as the "founding president" of the PCB. By that point, Jacquemotte had been dead for twenty-six years (Jacquemotte had founded the party's newspaper in 1921 and his name continued to appear on the cover of every issue). Bala's letter requested assistance for a school that he planned to open in Leopoldville, at which girls would be trained in "domestic sciences" and boys in mechanics and carpentry, with all receiving daily lessons in communism. "I am the founding president of that school," he wrote, establishing credentials that would speak to his imagined addressee, "[but] I really created it to facilitate communist actions, which have never had a chance to penetrate this country. So this school will actually be yours to secretly run."[32] Bala declared his enthusiasm for communism, but the arguments he presented to convince the PCB to support him were couched in the language of the Red Scare. This language had circulated widely in the colonial press and during the anti-Lumumbist campaigns of 1960.[33] It appeared in several other letters. A former member of ABAKO who wanted to be taught the theory and practice of historical materialism wrote, for instance, "I ask all the communist parties of the world that are concerned with the liberation of Congo-Kinshasa, central Africa and the world to allow me to participate in a training course to become a RABBLE-ROUSER, AGITATOR and PRO-PAGANDIST of Marxism-Leninism."[34] These words and their typography seemed to borrowed from the register of anti-communism—a register that may have appealed to Congolese letter writers because it associated communism with a form of revolutionary and powerful (even if dangerous and insidious) cosmopolitanism.

Socialist Brides

The Congolese had high expectations about the benefits they could obtain from an association with the PCB, as Eddy Poncelet, a member of the youth branch of the party, discovered when he traveled to Leopoldville a few weeks after independence. In a letter to his Belgian comrades, he expressed his surprise at discovering that there was "*not any* prejudice against us" and that he instead faced "a continuous procession of individuals who, I am not sure how, have heard of my arrival." Countless young Congolese men wanted to shake hands with this similarly young Belgian man. They asked him not only about opportunities to receive fellowships to study abroad but also about "how to easily get a white girl to marry in Belgium!"

Poncelet dared not to venture to some areas of Black Leopoldville, "not because I am afraid of expressions of hostility," he reassured his Belgian comrades, but because he knew that he would be "surrounded by dozens of unemployed young men who would each want to show me their home—how to satisfy everybody?"[35] The overwhelming demonstrations of friendship and homosocial bonding that Poncelet endured with a mix of excitement and apprehensions reflect the affective response of young urban Congolese to communism. Poncelet rejoiced that the desire to engage was mutual. And although he might have dismissed the requests about white brides as odd, he probably sensed that the idea of sexual relationships between Black men and white women, extremely taboo during the colonial period, was a major signifier of decolonization.[36] A few young Congolese who had studied in Europe had already returned to the Congo with white brides. In the eyes of many, international travel became associated with the license to overcome the sexual color bar, while interracial sexuality appeared as a prime accessory in the so-called culture of ambiance—the "mad joie de vivre" that emerged in late-colonial

Leopoldville at the intersection of Congolese rumba, the bar culture, and ideals of a "scandalous" masculinity (at the same time modern and freed from Belgian middle-class moralist expectations).[37]

When the PCB later took charge of sending Congolese students to Czechoslovakia, East Germany, and the Soviet Union, some within the party expressed uneasiness at the type of mutual attraction that connected their fellow party members to young people in the former colony. One of the Belgian activists in charge of fielding requests from the Congolese was anxious that the party's selection of candidates had not always been sufficiently thorough. "You always say yes to smooth-talking Congolese," he wrote in confronting Poncelet. As a result, he added, the PCB had ended up sending "gutter trash" (ramassis de déchets) to socialist countries. Or, as he put in a letter to a leader of the party, "What will the Soviets think if we send them any more of these incompetent or scoundrel types to study in Moscow?"[38]

Preoccupations about gender and allusions to sexuality certainly appeared in letters sent by the Congolese. To succeed politically, you had to be "a man who is called a man," Pierre Kayembe, a young worker, explained to a leader of the Belgian Communist Youth.[39] Although the ideal of the big man informed Congolese approaches to power in the 1960s as Mobutu would soon make clear, Kayembe may have envisioned a masculinity closer to that of the ambianceur—one that suggested international travel, political cosmopolitanism, and access to beautiful suits and ties.[40] In a context in which "the world remains unknown to most of the youth,"[41] a quest for social distinction, material assets, and construction of the self often featured in the Congolese mail, even in letters to Belgian working-class Stalinist party men who constantly emphasized the PCB's "poverty."[42]

Letter writers expressed a strong desire to radically reimagine their place in the world. They related to ideologies that emphasized equality and fraternity and that offered an escape from colonial assignations. Jean-Claude Ilunga, an eighteen-year-old student at the Ford Foundation–sponsored National School of Law and Administration in Leopoldville, sent a series of desperate letters to different Belgian communists in 1962 in which he addressed these questions. "Deep down I have the feeling that I was born a communist," he wrote in one of these letters. However, he did not know anybody who could introduce him to Marxism. "Here we are locked up. The youth lives in obscurity. We are blindfolded by our puppet leaders that do not have any notion of communism." Leaving the Congo seemed to him the only available option: "I am sick of this country, ashamed of bearing its nationality. This is becoming an injurious offense. I would like to escape or, better, to expatriate."[43] Ilunga articulated the ways that ideological identification (and disidentification) caused him suffering. However, he remained hopeful in the face of the Congo's new global connections and the possibility of international support that they offered.

A couple of years later, a series of letters sent to the International Union of Socialist Youth (IUSY) by a high school student named Eugène Gbana Lissasy revealed a different philosophy of postal exchanges.[44] Lissasy opened his letter by explaining how he came to learn about the existence of the IUSY: "One day, close to midday, under the scorching African sun, as I was on my way back from school, I picked up two dirty scraps of paper from the street on which appeared, to my great surprise, the name IUSY." Lissasy was trying to convey the existential implications of internationalization, when new vocabularies and promises of distant connections could interrupt the quotidian walk of a young flaneur: "I read and reread so many times the few lines dotted with dirt but that talked to me about African socialism." Why could the Congo not enjoy the benefits of this vision of the world, Lissasy wondered. The country's authorities tried to maintain the people in their ignorance of African socialism, but Lissasy was convinced that "tyranny, imperialism, and neocolonialism will not live forever."[45]

After the general secretary of the IUSY informed Lissasy that the organization did not accept applications from individuals, the young man wrote a second letter announcing his plan to create a group that could become an affiliate. "The boys and the men" whom he had contacted were "scared by the word 'socialism,' [and by] the cruelty, handcuffs and batons of the police." Yet, if he could take classes on socialism and communism with the help of the IUSY, he believed he could "combat ignorance among the Congolese masses, starting with my closest friends."[46] Whereas Ilunga's letters to Belgian communists imagined salvation in the form of an escape, Lissasy, in his correspondence with the IUSY, expressed his confidence in his ability to help midwife socialism in the Congo. Despite these differences, both sets of letters conveyed a common desire to open up obstructed landscapes and actualize perspective that pointed to a more beautiful elsewhere.

The Benefits of Alignment

Not all Congolese letter writers were as umbrageous and impatient as Ilunga or as starry-eyed and lyrical as Lissasy. Many strove for a pragmatic tone. They appealed to foreign interlocutors for support not out of despair or fantasy but because the crisis of decolonization had interna-tionalized politics in the Congo. The UN's expansive mission in the Congo emblematized the extent of internationalization. The mission shipped tons of resources and hundreds of experts from all continents to the Congo; and interactions with UN personnel enabled the Congolese to connect with various other international organizations and political projects. Among many other prerogatives of governance and statehood, the UN took over the Congolese postal service. Two dozen international experts redrafted postal protocols, streamlined mail distribution operations, and relaunched the postal school in Leopoldville. The head of the expert team boasted that without the UN, there would be no Congolese mail.[47]

Education was another significant field of operation for the UN. Teachers from Haiti, France, and some Eastern European countries were dispatched to secondary schools through UNESCO, while UN programs selected Con-golese students for accelerated training sessions abroad. In less than six months, by the end of 1960, six hundred young Congolese had already been sent to study hydrology, medicine, radio administration, rural devel-opment, and social work in France, Germany, Israel, Italy, Switzerland, Tunisia, and the United States.[48] In parallel, multiple foreign embassies courted students with fellowships to continue their education abroad, and various interlopers lavished advice and money on wooing politicians. Many of the letters that traveled from the Congo to foreign addresses on both sides of the Cold War divide came from the Congolese who wanted to participate in this enlarged political space and imagined that correspon-dence could get them a seat at the table.

Lumumba's assassination unveiled the gruesome persistence of colo-nial violence beyond African independences. It also illustrated the extent of the Congo's internationalization. Not only the Belgians but also the Americans, the British, and the French had exerted pressure to prevent a reconciliation between Kasa-Vubu and Lumumba. Ultimately, in Janu-ary 1961, these pressures as well as the UN's criminal passivity led to Lu-mumba's transfer to the province of Katanga. Lumumba was assassinated the very day he arrived in the mining province in the presence of Tshombe and Belgian police officers who worked for the secession. The fall of Lu-mumba, the prophet of African nationalism and nonalignment, sounded a warning bell to many Congolese political actors: their very survival might depend on their ability to speak the language of the Cold War and secure the protection of powerful patrons on either side of the divide.[49]

In many letters, a pervasive ideological mimetism testified to the grow-ing imprint of this imperative of political alignment. Although political parties had initially tried not to appear dependent on foreign backers, this concern seems to have fallen away after 1960. Political entrepreneurs now named their organizations in ways that hinted at chosen filiation and affiliation with foreign structures. For example, André Lukusa, a minor political figure from the Kasai, took inspiration from the charter of the US Democrats to create a Congolese Democratic Party (Parti Congolais Démocrate), with the ambition of "spreading the Democratic doctrine and saving the Congo from communism." In a letter to John F. Kennedy, Lukusa preposterously claimed that his organization had seven hundred thousand members. According to Lukusa, most of the Congo's provinces had seen "floggings, arbitrary arrests, infringements on freedom of speech and movement, massacres of intellectuals, in a word an unquestionably communist regime"—a situation that his party would successfully oppose.[50] Two years after Lukusa's letter to Kennedy, the leaders of the People's Labor Party (Parti Populaire des Travailleurs) wrote a similar letter to the British Labour Party. Claiming even less credible membership numbers, they mentioned that they had just officially proclaimed Labour as "the MOTHER of our young party" and that the British should "be proud, because your magnificent organization has conquered the spirits of the three million members that our party boasts, out of a total population of fourteen million in our Republic."[51]

Cold War alignments did not only restructure Congolese politics. They also reshaped labor unions. The case of the Syndicat National des Travailleurs du Congo (SNTC) is worth considering in detail, not least because its general secretary, Alphonse-Roger Kithima, played a major role a few years later in the history of student politics as Mobutu's minister of education. The creation of the SNTC followed Lumumba's encounter with Irving Brown, the Paris-based AFL-CIO representative, during the All-African People's Conference in Accra at the end of 1958. Lumumba had talked to Brown about his desire to create a Congolese labor union that would be fully independent from the Belgian labor confederations.[52] Brown, a covert CIA agent who channeled enormous amounts of money to anti-communist unions in Europe, Africa, and Latin America, agreed to fund the project. Lumumba entrusted the leadership of the union to Kithima, a former telecommunications operator in the colonial administration. But when Lumumba's relationship with the United States soured in the summer of 1960, Kithima's proximity with Brown and the AFL-CIO raised suspicions among Congolese nationalists about his true allegiances.[53] Kithima used these rumors to his advantage in his correspondence with AFL-CIO officials, which was primarily focused on financial assistance. One of Kithima's recurrent requests concerned a building in Leopoldville that he hoped to purchase for the SNTC with funds from the AFL-CIO. He brought up the question in at least eight different letters. He also asked for a typewriter, for recording materials for musicians affiliated to the SNTC, for plane tickets to travel to Europe and North America, and for additional personal cash donations.[54] Kithima always introduced these requests by mentioning the sacrifices he had made: "Let me remind you," he wrote to Brown on March 10, 1961, "that I could work as a state employee and earn a living as anyone else."[55] As an ally of the AFL-CIO, he endured suffering and prejudices, he wrote. Would it not be fair to compensate him for his loyalty?

The AFL-CIO did not accede to all of Kithima's demands, but it continued to send him money throughout the 1960s. Maida Springer, one of his interlocutors at the AFL-CIO and a rare female figure in the postal corpus of the Congolese decolonization, valued his commitment to labor unity, and she believed that it was fair to contribute to his financial well-being.[56] She also encouraged his initiatives—his plan to open a soup kitchen for poor workers or a training center where union members would learn how to answer the telephone, keep appointments, and receive visitors.[57] Brown, too, supported Kithima and his organization, seeing them as an alternative to the continuous influence of Belgian labor unions in the Congo. He praised Kithima as being one of his most solid relays in Africa, along with Tom Mboya of Kenya.

Kithima insisted that persuasion, not dollars, changed people's minds. This meant to convey his own importance to his American "brothers and sisters"—to show them that their money would be of no use in the struggle for the Congo without someone who, like him, knew how to speak and to mobilize. He used these very skills of mediation—his ability to persuade— to justify his requests to Brown and Springer. Words mattered. Although not all letter writers were as adept as Kithima at securing powerful foreign supporters, most shared his awareness of how important it was to master the rhetoric of the Cold War.

Postal Values

The letters of the Congo crisis worked as an engine of mobility in two ways. Aerograms and lightweight letter paper traveled far and wide, transporting ideas at a relatively democratic cost. They also blazed a trail for writers, who often aimed to follow their letters to places that colonial regulations had previously rendered inaccessible. Studying abroad presented a major opportunity to travel and to learn about the broader world, and Congolese postal bags were filled with requests for fellowships.

Knowledge and diplomas were intricately linked to the political struggle. Floribert Kabasela, a clerk in Elisabethville, dissected the matter for a Belgian communist correspondent: "Here, it is enough to say that you have studied abroad and that you have a university diploma . . . to attract and recruit all the youth."[58] Kabasela's letter is typical of the mail of the Congo crisis in that it clearly offered to mediate between the Congo's realities—the youth, the masses—and its foreign interlocutors. Kabasela promised ideological alignment and asked for help to study in Eastern Europe. Belgian communists were receptive to this kind of transaction, but not all arguments and justifications used by letter writers resonated with the recipients of requests for fellowships and money. It helped when readers could situate writers within their existing network of friends and acquaintances. Letterheads and the quality of paper, handwriting, syntax, and rhetoric mattered as well. Some arguments carried more weight than others. Requests that emphasized international comradeship, anti-imperialism, and ending "the oppression of man by man" were more likely to be successful than the ones presenting ethnic discrimination or poverty as reasons to seek support. Similarly, disinterestedness was a potent quality to project for letter writers. Some strategically avoided asking for anything that could make them seem mercenary during initial contacts and instead emphasized intellectual curiosity and ideological earnestness. When Joseph Botamba, a postmaster in Coquilhatville, became acquainted with communist activists in Brussels during an internship with the Belgian post, he asked only for political guidance and for books he could send to a group of his comrades in the Congo. "I was struck by the fact that he was telling me that this was the most necessary form of support. Whereas so many Congolese believed that money could save him—for him, it was ideology," one of his Belgian contacts noted positively.[59] A few months later, however, Botamba wrote from Coquilhatville with a request for financial support. He had officially launched a political organization, the Congolese Movement for the Defense of Human Rights, and found out, as he wrote, that "politics is the art of the possible." He pointed out that his political rivals were benefiting from relationships with foreign sponsors—he brought up the example of Justin-Marie Bomboko, the minister of foreign affairs, who was very involved in local politics in Coquilhatville and who had just received a fleet of trucks from the West German government to be used for campaigning purposes. Botamba shared his belief that "the Congolese were purely communists" and that "Marxism corresponds to our Bantu worldviews." But he also said that he would have no chance to win elections without foreign moneys. He should be trusted, he argued, because he had previously proved his pure intentions: "As you know, dear Comrade, I never went to any moneyed circles and I never asked for money during the seven months of my European internship. All I did was simply studying the origins and ideologies of the parties."[60]

A World Republic of Letters

Lumumba had famously prophesied from his prison that Africa would one day write its own history and that this history would not be the one "taught in Brussels, Paris, Washington and the United Nations."[61] But Lumumba had been eliminated and his assassination constrained many Congolese to adopt a pragmatic position as a strategy of survival. When they put pen to airmail writing paper, people like Botamba sought inclusion in a world republic of letters shaped by the Cold War. They were well aware that they were not writing from positions of power.[62] An imbalance in access to resources between these letter writers and their addressees was inherent to their exchanges. Many Congolese were aware of the necessity to play on their own dominated position in the field of world politics, and they used their letter-crafting skills to do so.[63]

Tacit rules governed the circulation of the Congolese mail. The gate-keeping privilege that the Belgians claimed for themselves in relation to the Congo also manifested itself in postal exchanges, for instance. The Belgian establishment argued that the colonial past generated a legitimacy and expertise—giving them a right, and maybe even a moral duty, to intervene and mediate relationships between the Congolese and foreigners. Belgian left politicians did not think differently.[64] The Congolese often refused this state of affairs, however. In 1964, when Alexandre Mavungu launched one of the at least five new political parties created that year in the Congo to have names that directly referenced to socialism, he asked the Socialist International to provide financial backing for his movement. However, Mavungu discovered that instead of responding directly to him, the British secretary general of the Socialist International had contacted the Belgian Socialist Party for advice on Mavungu's organization. Mavungu was indignant: did the Socialist International not know that Belgian colonialism was over, that the Congo was a sovereign state, and that Congolese socialists could be contacted directly through the mail or in person?[65]

Figure 2.1 Lumumba stamps from Guinea, the Republic of Congo, the United Arab Republic, and the Soviet Union, ca. 1961–63 (source: author's collection).

The friction between Mavungu and the Socialist International reflected a strong instability and in-between-ness in the Congo crisis mail. The Congolese correspondents invited foreign interventions to enhance their positions in the harsh struggle for political power. In return, they also offered themselves as mediators.[66] In the act of writing, they stood "intellectually apart" from their environment, coding and recoding Congolese realities for outside interveners.[67] They had to demonstrate a legitimacy to speak for broader communities, while also conveying a sense of individuality and uniqueness that justified their status as interlocutors. These goals were not only achieved through wordsmithing. Writers also used photographs as badges of authenticity, enclosing self-portraits that identified themselves as specific political subjects: young, educated, African men. Many of these photographs were headshots, with formats and visual constructions that evoked the visual conventions of postage stamps. Sitters often dressed formally, with suits and ties that projected respectability and worldliness. Many, implicitly and in some cases explicitly, imitated the "visual embodiments" of Lumumba.[68]

Photographs of Lumumba had been published in newspapers around the world. Immediately after his assassination, Lumumba also appeared on stamps issued in Morocco, the United Arab Republic, Mongolia, Ghana, Guinea, the Seychelles, Egypt, and Congo-Brazzaville, all of which showed him with his signature glasses and goatee, wearing a tie or a bow tie, projecting dignity and confidence (figure 2.1).[69] Connecting visually to Lumumba, ordinary letter writers added precious value to their missives (figure 2.2).

Figure 2.2 Letter from Victor Mafwa to Per Assen, November 20, 1964 (source: International Institute for Social History, Amsterdam, IUSY papers). In 1963, Mafwa had sent three letters to the IUSY asking for financial support. He wrote again at the end of 1964, this time requesting a plane ticket to visit the IUSY in Vienna and plead his case directly with Assen. The headshot he attached to his letter expressed a seriousness and a desire to engage.

Conclusion

In the mid-1950s, many young men in Leopoldville participated in informal study groups. They congregated in private houses or courtyards for regular meetings during which one member "would expose a world problem on which he would have formed an opinion through the reading of newspapers," as a Belgian colonial official who was exceptionally well connected with the burgeoning world of Congolese politics observed in 1957.[70] It is likely that some of the letters discussed in this chapter, and the responses they received, were at times shared in such gatherings. Like the small but growing number of critical pamphlets, newspapers, and books that managed to escape colonial censorship, correspondences contributed to the politicization of key publics. The young men who had benefited from measures that expanded schooling for boys in the 1950s were more aware than most of the structural limitations of colonial education. Mutual self-learning broadened their mental horizons. And because they were tangible objects that materialized distant connections, letters from faraway places reinforced their belief in the possibility of questioning the status quo, encouraging them both to challenge the boundaries of colonial assignations and to circumvent the authority of older évolué men who dominated colonized civic associations.

At the same time, not all correspondence was meant to be shared and further circulated among peers. Letters allowed for a way to connect with distant others that could be much less conspicuous and resonant than other forms of mediation. Letter writers often presented themselves as pensive young men who stood apart from others in the community to reflect critically on the world. Even as some of them boasted of mass political movements with thousands of members, their writing collectively evoked a landscape of atomized subjectivities: nearly each letter writer posed as the source of his own political project and approached writing as a tool for the expression of an individuality.

Letter writing equally brought out introspection and projection. It was an exercise in anticipation. Young correspondents in search of sources of knowledge or fellowships to study abroad had to imagine how their addressees would read and respond to their requests. As the struggle for independence developed, many Congolese became aware of the importance of internationalization, but they were often hesitant about the exact language that could activate the power of foreign ideologies and distant connections. The letters that initially reached foreign political organizations were eclectic in their rhetorical bricolage, and they showed different levels of effectiveness. Yet, all betrayed an urge to search for and explore opportunities in the wider world. In this way, the Congolese mail suggests parallels between the moment of decolonization and earlier eras in the history of central Africa, eras when polities and communities were made and remade by adventurous frontiersmen.[71]

The mad acceleration of the race to independence in 1959 and the crisis that erupted in July 1960 dramatized the stakes in the Congolese's attempts to connect with foreign interlocutors. Decolonization produced multiple kinds of mukanda—paper figments of legality, strategic telegrams among powerful figures, and bottles of hope in the troubled sea of international politics. This chapter presented a mosaic of sources made of fragments that varied in color, pattern, and texture. Different people wrote differently. Some were fully schooled in the codes of correspondence. Others betrayed inexperience or singular personalities. All had to operate in uncharted territory.

This political configuration shifted after a few years. With the end of the Katanga secession in 1963, the UN significantly reduced the size of its

mission in the Congo, eroding the strongest symbol of the internationalization of Congolese affairs. And although Castro's Cuba, Mao's China, or
Ben Bella's Algeria continued to support Lumumba's followers, the Soviet
Union had lost hope in the possibility to wrest the Congo from the sphere
of US influence. Up until the mid-1960s, what had been altered by the political vicissitudes of the previous years, and by the numerous fellowship
programs made available in the wake of independence, was the large number of Congolese expatriates. Thousands of Congolese were now spread
across Africa, Western and Eastern Europe, and North America. At home
and abroad, there were many well-traveled, well-informed, savvy young
Congolese able to engage foreign interlocutors with confidence. Whereas
Congolese letter writers in the late 1950s and early 1960s invested their
energy in largely undisciplined explorations of political possibilities, the
student movement of the mid-1960s, would be dedicated to clarifying its
ideology and fine-tuning its strategy. Yet, the imagination of students (many
of whom had taken part in international postal exchanges as teenagers
during the Congo crisis) still remained deeply extraverted. They strongly
identified with the martyrdom of Lumumba and kept alive an awareness
of the profound exposure of the Congo to the winds of the world.

TO LIVE FOREVER AMONG BOOKS

In 1944, the Haitian anthropologist Suzanne Comhaire-Sylvain decided to research the aspirations of Black children in Leopoldville. She administered a questionnaire to more than three hundred boys in primary and post-primary schools. Prompted to state the professional path they would like to take as adults, the vast majority of these boys responded that they hoped to work as clerks or have some other white-collar job available to men with advanced schooling in French. Many children had their eyes set on the social status conferred by positions in the public administration and the private sector. Some also simply enjoyed the escapism and contemplation of the scholastic world. One little boy said that "he would be happy to live forever among books." When Sylvain asked the same boy if he would like to become a librarian, he answered, "I don't know. Anything so long as I can see books, touch them, and read them from time to time."[1] Books allowed children to travel in a context in which the state was highly invested in controlling the mobility of the colonized. One teenager who dreamed of going to America told Sylvain that Belgians "know that if they gave one of us permission to travel today, the whole of Kinshasa would be empty tomorrow."[2]

Sylvain herself directly embodied the cosmopolitan aspirations of the children she interviewed. She belonged to a family full of trailblazers. Her father had opened his own law school and organized the resistance against the US occupation of Haiti, an uncle convened the first Pan-African conference in London in 1900, one of her sisters was the first obstetrician in

Port-au-Prince, and another pioneered the modern movement for Haitian women's rights. Suzanne's accomplishments did not pale in comparison. After she defended her doctoral dissertation in Paris in 1932, she became the first female Haitian anthropologist. Her work took her to London and New York. She collaborated with Bronislaw Malinowski and Melville Herskovits. Her research initially focused on Haitian folklore, but she turned to African anthropology during World War II after she moved to Leopoldville with her husband, the Belgian anthropologist Jean Comhaire. The couple lived in the Belgian Congo for three years—Comhaire working for the service of information at the general governorate and Sylvain conducting independent ethnographic surveys. She was the first Black anthropologist in a colony that was particularly averse to the form of creole universalism and cosmopolitanism that she represented.[3] It took her a long time to receive the necessary authorization to do research in the cités, Leopoldville's Black neighborhoods. When this authorization finally came, she was forced to comply with a curfew, which to her great regret prevented her from studying the nightlife of the "African town."[4] She had to work with these limitations and focused mostly on childhood. Colonial bureaucrats must have perceived her research project about children and their aspirations to be a relatively innocuous topic and fitting for a female scholar.[5] Regardless, Sylvain asked key questions by studying the urban youth. Children in Leopoldville lived on the bank of a mighty river that flowed into the Atlantic Ocean, in a city that welcomed the sounds and moving images from across the water. They clearly perceived that colonialism was about controlling streams of people and ideas. Although most had integrated the idea that racialized structures would frame their access to full adulthood, they also imagined the possibility of a greater freedom.

Sylvain understood these children as cultural innovators. She studied their French-infused Lingala, their games, and their dreams. She found out that education formed the core of their lifeworld. Boys in particular viewed schooling as a golden door to opportunity. The colonizers had established schools as tools of conversion and control to prepare a limited number of colonized subjects for subaltern positions in the private sector and officialdom, but Sylvain's informants were not beholden to this vision. Some fantasized about escaping as stowaways on a ship. Many fell in love with books and learning. They went to school with goals and ambitions of their own, harboring a curiosity and a desire to learn about the broader world at a time when it otherwise seemed out of reach. The following two chapters register the impact of this desire for education and knowledge on the evolution of the colonial regime and, by the same token, map the progressive politicization of students.

THREE
PATHS TO SCHOOL

The road, of course, was a dangerous place. The danger of and the anxiety about the road to school, was particularly that it might be blocked. Moving on the road to school was an adventure, thrilling and scary largely because it might at a moment be taken away. It was the possibility, first of all, that the journey might be cut short before the goal was reached that made the journey anxious.

Rudolph Mrazek, A Certain Age, 127

Look at the shoes that we are wearing today. For me, it is still a symbol of wealth. Our children were born with shoes on their feet, but we, in our youth, we had to walk 350 kilometers barefoot to go to school.

Daniel Palambwa, personal interview, Kinshasa, August 17, 2010

At the age of six, Patrice [Lumumba]'s parents enrolled him in a Catholic missionary school. Two years later, he revolted against the priests' teachings: "It was then," he said, "that the injustice of the preachers, who were in fact our absolute masters, revealed itself to me."

Frantz Fanon, "Africa Accuses the West," 1961, reproduced
in Frantz Fanon: Alienation and Freedom, 645

In 1955, Martin Ekwa, a young Jesuit, left the Congo to study theology in Belgian and Italian universities. When he returned to Leopoldville in 1960, in the midst of the Congo crisis, he could no longer recognize the city. "The Belgians were gone," he told me during an interview. "They had abandoned their cars in the middle of streets to cross over to Brazzaville. We wondered what we could do. Some people questioned if it was worth governing ourselves. It was terrifying. . . . A void! A void!"[1] This repetition may seem to echo the famous formula from Joseph Conrad's *Heart of Darkness*, "The horror! The horror!" In the early 1960s, Conrad's novel supplied foreign journalists writing about the Congo with easy tropes on the supposed atavistic return to "tribalism" and "savagery."[2] However, the narrative that Ekwa was trying to articulate when we met in 2010 was a very different one.

His return to the Congo fifty years earlier had been precipitated because the church had asked him to take over the presidency of the Bureau for Catholic Education (BEC), the organization that oversaw the network of Catholic schools in the country. A thirty-four-year-old with no experience in education administration, Ekwa found himself in charge of thousands of teachers and more than a million and a half students. He felt that if the Congo was going to survive the turbulences of decolonization, it would only be thanks to the stability of the Catholic Church and its school system. There was a void, but he was ready to fill it.

During our conversation, Ekwa described his role at the BEC as that of a quasi–minister of education. In letters from the period, he preferred to present himself as a diplomat for the church who, when he was not touring the country or attending international conferences abroad, spent all his time "driving in my small car between ministries and foreign embassies."[3] Both comparisons—the minister and the diplomat—underline the strategic dimension of Ekwa's work, and rightly so. When he took the leadership of the BEC, tensions in Leopoldville ran especially high. Lumumba had been placed under house arrest, while Joseph Kasa-Vubu and Joseph Mobutu were sponsoring different governmental teams. One of Ekwa's sisters, herself a Catholic nun training in Belgium, teased him in a letter that his nomination to the BEC was good news because it meant that he had not become a Lumumbist.[4] In reality, the priest strove to maintain relations with politicians of all persuasions, just like a good diplomat might have. He saw the desire for education among the Congolese population as binding together disparate political positions. As he wrote to the superior general of the Jesuit order, grounds for collaboration could be found even with "the most extremist politicians."[5]

Between his numerous daily meetings as the head of the BEC, the obligations of his priestly ministry, and weekly religious lectures for the national radio, Ekwa had little time for correspondence. Quite often, even in his private mail, he simply scribbled quick comments that his secretary transformed into proper responses. Unlike many of the letter writers in the previous chapter, the young priest rarely initiated postal exchanges. But he was the recipient of volumes of correspondence. Many letters arrived from people he had met when he studied in Europe: Belgian priests, nuns, and lay figures alike wrote to encourage him and share their prayers. They talked of parish life, travel plans, their children's successes at school, and the slow coming of springtime. Indulging in the inconsequentiality of the everyday, these correspondents sought to maintain Ekwa's special relationship with Belgium, and they advised him to follow "the government of the Holy Spirit" in his reorganization of Congolese education.[6] Ekwa reassured his Belgian contacts about his affinity with the former metropole. At the same time, he responded to their letters in a much less emotional register than the one they used. Perhaps he did it out of guardedness. Years later, he remembered the hostility he encountered from white missionaries when he attempted to make a Catholic education compatible with the necessities of state building in a newly independent nation.[7] At the start of the 1960s, however, he had not been able to fully escape a rhetoric grounded in the affective and the spiritual. Nor could he have entirely broken the colonial bond.

Ekwa was a Black dignitary in a church that remained dependent on white missionaries, and the contradictions he faced were replicated in the school system he led.[8] Colonial schooling had created an ideological knot that was difficult to untie. As an instrument of social stratification, education allowed some children to move up the social ladder and held others down. Schooling legitimatized colonial domination, but it also unlocked credentials, skills, and vocabularies that the Congolese used to insert themselves into mechanisms of political representation. In other words, schools generated the potential to challenge the same repressive social order that they had engineered in the first place. Education, in this way, resembled the postal service—at once an arm of colonial control and an instrument that the Congolese could use to move more freely in the world.

This chapter investigates the tensions of education from the beginning of the Belgian colonial period to the immediate post-independence era. "The modern passions of education" were acute in colonial spaces, as Rudolf Mrazek has argued in his study of the intellectual elite of colonial Jakarta. Mrazek used the metaphor of the road to figure the structural insecurity of education in the Dutch colony: unschooled commoners and those expelled from the school system were left on the side of the road, while a privileged minority moved along, "pregnant with future," clasping to promises of "safety and even power."[9] Children in the Belgian Congo faced a similar landscape. However, they rarely walked on roads to get to schools and more often had to take narrow and meandering paths, sometimes through forests, and across long distances. Decades later, they looked back nostalgically on the path to school, while also recalling many instances of injustice, racism, bigotry, and boredom. This chapter gives expression to all these affects.

The Specter of Overeducation

Colonial education in the Congo was intimately linked to the missionary movement. Starting in the early 1890s, Leopold contracted Catholic missionaries to manage schools for Congolese soldiers and clerks—the so-called colonies scolaires. Mission societies then established their own schools as instruments of evangelization.[10] If many Congolese initially resisted the missionaries' initiatives, a "craze for education" soon spread across the colony from the awareness of the benefits of literacy.[11] More schools to educate more children were built as Protestants and Catholics competed for pupils and converts. In 1906, the Congo Free State clarified its preference for the Catholics, signing a concordat with the Vatican that formalized subsidies for Catholic missionary schools.[12] At the time, twenty missionary societies were operating close to one hundred "central schools" based in mission stations, with around twenty-six thousand students in Protestant schools and twenty thousand in Catholic-run institutions. The concordat soon changed those numbers, producing an increasing trend toward Catholic domination.[13]

Schools were deliberately established away from villages. They aimed to prepare children for an active life in their churches and to introduce them to a new world. The ringing of the bell punctuated everyday prayers, meals, class time, and chores. Children learned to read and write in languages that often differed significantly from their mother tongues. They interacted with peers whose worldviews, customs, and vernaculars could greatly diverge from their own. Some, after finishing their studies, remained at the mission to teach new generations of students, translate religious texts, conduct ethnographic surveys, or collect oral traditions.[14] Many also moved to urban centers, where they read periodicals, wrote letters, paid to have their photographs taken, decorated their houses with pictures, and patronized bars.[15] Employed by private companies and the state, they became a vital cog in the machine of colonial power. Yet, many Europeans were uneasy with them. They held strong views about how the colonized should dress and speak, and they cringed at the vision of Black people in Sunday-best outfits. They felt that education raised the Congolese above their natural station in life and encouraged them to challenge the colonial order. These fears, suspicions, and prejudices fostered an educational Malthusianism that encouraged basic schooling for the masses, while restricting more-advanced instruction to all but a few.

The colonial magistrate Paul Salkin was an early critique of advanced schooling for the Congolese. "A black man who knows French," he wrote, "rapidly thinks he is the equal of the white man and even superior to him."[16] Other authors claimed that teaching French to the colonized was like serving alcohol to children. Access to gramophones, fountain pens, alarm clocks, and cigarettes had already "fooled" the Congolese into believing in "equality among the races," they argued. Introducing them to the ideas of progress, justice, and self-determination would only aggravate the situation.[17] Missionaries, even if they acted as agents of cultural change, often shared the same views on the need to limit the Congolese's exposure to intoxicating ideas. They wanted to avoid the social type that colonial theorists referred to as the "Europeanized Black" and agreed that education should not spread subversive messages about racial equality. For missionaries, what seemed frightening was not only the perspective of seeing the Congolese use the tools of their education for political goals. They were also careful to preserve their converts from the contagion of European "godless materialism." Some of the stories they shared among themselves triggered their anxieties about the unintended effects of their educational work: they often said, for instance, that students intentionally "mutilated" their own eyes in order to receive medical prescriptions for glasses, an emblem of intellectualism.[18] These anecdotes mocked the students' supposed residual fetishism but also reminded the missionaries that schooling could encourage unwanted mimicry and strategies of distinction.

Prejudices against education among missionaries and administrators did not only emerge from these types of formulaic anecdotes about Congolese children or from actual experience with actual students in the colony. In great part, these prejudices were also comparative constructs, for colonial theorists projected possible Congolese futures by reflecting on what they thought was happening in other imperial locations that had longer histories of "race contact." In the same way that students in the 1960s would imagine themselves as members in an international community of dissent, the colonizers looked at the Congo as part of a continuum that went from the Bengal to the Mississippi. Salkin, for instance, ranted about the dangers of Western education for the Congolese, scoffing at Liberian lawyers, South African communist workers, Indian nationalist students, "unproductive" Haitians, and "depraved Blacks" in the United States.[19]

Not all comparisons were negative. Some colonials looked to the programs of agricultural education for African Americans in the US South as a model to be emulated.[20] Belgians also welcomed American expertise when the New York–based Phelps-Stokes Fund produced a report about education in Africa in the early 1920s. The report commended the focus on character building and manual work in Congolese schools but noted that "in rather striking contrast" with other colonies, mission education in the Congo had fully "overlooked the need for the development of Native leadership." A suggestion was made to create two distinct tracks: one for the mass of school-aged children and another for native teachers and leaders.[21] A couple of years later, echoing these recommendations, the Ministry of Colonies recognized the need to train a small number of semiskilled employees for the state bureaucracy and private enterprises. At the same time, the ministry insisted on the role of education as an instrument for the "stabilization" of a large workforce of peasants in rural areas where they would produce cash and food crops, and it reiterated its opposition to secondary schooling and academic instruction.[22]

Over the next two decades, the numbers of schools grew steadily, and by the end of World War II, there were nearly six thousand primary schools educating more than three hundred thousand students in the Congo.[23] These schools socialized mass numbers of Congolese in the world of the colonizer. Yet, the main effect of education was not colonial control but instead an "aspiration for something more" among the colonized.[24]

Seminaries as Happy Anomalies

Despite a commonly shared reservation about excessive schooling, Catholic missionaries did open a narrow path to male elite education by developing a network of seminaries. Prior to World War I, the colony had only one minor seminary run by the White Fathers.[25] Most other Catholic missionary societies opened their own seminaries in the late 1920s, after the Vatican called for missionary churches to be embedded in African societies through the training of Black priests.[26] These new schools created a wedge that kept the door to academic education in the colony slightly ajar. They welcomed students in brick-building complexes with dormitories, refectories, chapels, galleries, cloisters, and theater halls. Their curriculum included French, mathematics, physics, Latin, and geography, and they encouraged children to play musical instruments, football, and chess.[27]

Minor seminaries aimed to place children on the road to priesthood, but few students went on to study the required philosophy and theology in major seminaries, and only a small fraction made it to ordination. Many more former seminarians ended up as "Europeanized Blacks," sporting suits and ties instead of clerical collars and robes. In Catholic parlance, they returned to the world. The prestige of their training in seminaries fared well on job markets in urban centers. Later, they filled the ranks of the political parties that demanded independence. Many years of close contact with white missionaries prepared them well for negotiations and, eventually, confrontations with colonial authorities in the 1940s and the 1950s.

Many prominent figures in Congolese society first crossed paths in seminaries. Take the example of Kasa-Vubu, Paul Lomami, Joseph Malula, Jacques Massa, and Eugène Moke. They all belonged to a group of children at the Saint François Xavier seminary in Mbata-Kiela, who bonded during a trip over Christmas break in 1932, traveling unaccompanied for two weeks through the hilly, dense Mayombe Forest, which separated Mbata-Kiela from the Atlantic Ocean. Walking for hours every day, often in the rain, dependent for food and lodging on villagers they met on the way, they learned much about perseverance and solidarity. Memories from that trip—the noises of the forest, tasting the saltiness of seawater for the first time—were still with them decades later, long after they had parted ways and followed their own paths.[28] In 1946, Malula, Massa, and Moke became the first Black priests to be ordained in Leopoldville.[29] Around the same time, Lomami penned a newspaper article that put the issue of indigenous political rights on the table for the first time.[30] A few years later, Kasa-Vubu took over the leadership of ABAKO, the Congo's first political party. In 1957, he was elected as the first Black mayor of Dendale, one of Leopoldville's municipalities. Three years later, he was president of the Congo.

Catholic seminaries, like the few Protestant schools that offered similar advanced instruction, shaped the development of an African elite in the Belgian Congo—and not least in reinforcing the idea that interactions with white teachers, Western knowledge, and colonial power happened within a strictly policed male sphere. These advanced schools produced a generation of educated Congolese men who expanded the horizon of possibilities in colonial Congo. Not all the young boys who attended seminaries found their way to key positions of power. Yet, many used what they learned when on the path to school to change the future of their country. Often, they even surpassed the most fearful visions of the colonizers, like Salkin's warning about the dangers of academic instruction during the interwar years.

A More Progressive Pedagogy

In the postwar period, colonial administrators continued to bring up over-education as a political threat. However, the new paradigm of development made the formation of a class of educated Congolese a pressing necessity.[31] In parallel, the growing numbers of Black seminarians eroded part of the racist resistance to academic instruction. If the Congolese could undergo years of Latin, Greek, and theology and if they could be entrusted with the charges of priesthood, why could they not be trained for positions of responsibilities in other sectors? The pedagogical approaches pioneered in seminaries could not be cloistered indefinitely. One advocate for their broader propagation was Father Joseph Guffens. In the 1930s, he established a new congregation, the Congregation of the Josephite Brothers. Based in Kinzambi, a Jesuit mission in the Kwango district, the Josephite congregation was composed of brothers, not priests. As brothers, the Josephites abided by the rules of celibacy and poverty, but unlike ordained priests, they had no sacerdotal responsibilities. Instead, they worked as full-time schoolteachers. In Kinzambi, they received advanced trainings under Guffens, alongside future priests (like Martin Ekwa, the future head of the BEC, who studied there as a minor seminarian in the 1940s) and children who did not intend to embrace religious life.

Guffens felt comfortable with methods that many other missionaries deemed dangerous. He embraced critical thinking, peer learning, and the teaching of modern European languages and sciences.[32] This made Kinzambi stand out in the Catholic landscape, at least until after the war. But the "spirit of Kinzambi" spread as the brothers trained by Guffens took teaching positions in various schools across the Kwango. As V. Y. Mumdimbe argued in an analysis of Guffens's pedagogical breakthrough, it was teachers, more than priests, who acted as the most efficient agents of conversion in the Belgian Congo. And their students looked up to the Josephite teachers as the epitome of educated, sophisticated Black men (figure 3.1). The brothers prided themselves on the quality of their French, having been trained by native speakers like Guffens, rather than by missionaries who hailed from rural Flanders and spoke an accented, corrupted version of the language, as was often the case in other mission stations. What the Josephites taught was distinction—of language, of intellect, of bearing. They believed in intellectual stimulation and the possibility of one's elevation through education. Guffens's project—his promotion of academic-oriented education for the Congolese—remained "rigidly formulated in this colonial, highly elaborated grid of acculturation for a few chosen

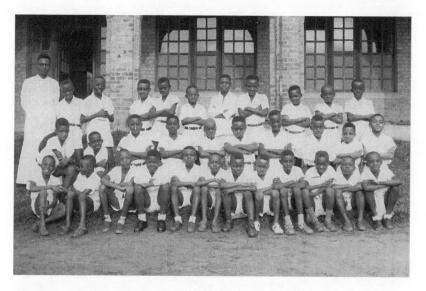

Figure 3.1 First student cohort at the Josephite Brothers' Saint-Dominic Savio Institute in Mikalayi (Kasai). Photograph by A. Maweja-Bajikile, ca. February 1964 (source: Kadoc Documentation and Research Center on Religion, Culture, and Society [Leuven], Brothers of St. Joseph Papers).

ones," as Mudimbe rightly noted.[33] It was nonetheless an emancipatory project, and it produced some of the best-known revolutionary figures of the 1960s—a fact that astonished Father Ekwa when he came back to Leopoldville to take the leadership of the BEC.[34] The two most famous of these alumni were Antoine Gizenga and Pierre Mulele. Both were ministers in Lumumba's government and leaders of the African Solidarity Party (Parti Solidaire Africain), and both had studied with Ekwa at Kinzambi in the 1940s. As many other children trained by the Josephites, Gizenga and Mulele had broken away from the modest emancipation envisioned by Guffens to participate in the most uncompromising faction of the anti-colonial movement. Why did they do so? This question confused Ekwa in 1960. Fifty years later, Daniel Palambwa, a former Josephite brother who had studied and taught at Kinzambi in 1940s and 1950s, offered a response.[35]

Like many educated Congolese of his generation, Palambwa experienced independence as a personal rupture. It marked an end to his work as a brother-teacher at Kinzambi. Although the congregation gave him the opportunity to study pedagogy in Katanga and then in Belgium, the turmoil of decolonization pushed him to reconsider his religious vocation.

He left the church in 1962 and turned to politics. His inclinations were conservative. Independence, he thought, had come too early. In 1964, he ran for and won a seat in the parliament as a candidate of the CONACO, a political party led by Moïse Tshombe, the former leader of the Katanga secession and archenemy of the nationalist left. Palambwa's political career lasted only a few years. He eventually went back to education and moved to Lemba, a part of Kinshasa known as the neighborhood of intellectuals because of its proximity to the university. After Palambwa retired, he started offering daily after-school lessons in classical music and Gregorian chant from the courtyard of his house. Each time I visited him there in 2010, his students were present, busy reading music and rehearsing. During our interviews, the former Josephite often interrupted the conversation to seize teachable moments: walking toward his protégés, he challenged them when they made mistakes, provided encouragement, used humor to make a point, then returned to my audio recorder. He embodied, and maybe performed for my own edification, the generous pedagogy of the old Kinzambi. Critical thinking, he insisted, was a real treasure that Guffens had conferred to his students. In Palambwa's mind, critical thinking was the reason that so many alumni of the Josephite schools embraced revolutionary politics: they stayed true to the spirit of Kinzambi, even when they advocated solutions that Guffens would not have supported.

Palambwa had taught Mulele at Kinzambi, and he shared with me his own interpretation of a well-known episode from Mulele's childhood: his refusal to recognize the virginity of Mary. Palambwa argued that Mulele's dismissal of this central piece of Catholic dogma did not signal his early rejection of Christianity, as some have argued.[36] Mulele simply reasoned that if Mary had given birth to Jesus naturally, her hymen must have broken from the delivery, so she could not be called a virgin. Mulele's opposition was therefore not doctrinal but semantic. In Palambwa's recollection, Kinzambi welcomed rational discussion and encouraged children to think for themselves. Mulele's casuistic reasoning expressed fidelity to Kinzambi's spirit, not a rebellion against it.

Mulele came up again in a group conversation with Palambwa and two other Kinzambi alumni, Augustin Awaka and Julien Ntil.[37] Like Palambwa, Awaka and Ntil were Mbun, and their ethnic compatriots had overwhelmingly endorsed the armed insurrection that Mulele launched in the Kwilu in 1963.[38] Yet, neither Awaka nor Ntil—who both studied in North America at the time—sympathized with the insurrection. They were willing to acknowledge its good intentions but found highly problematic the fact that Mulele was one of the only well-educated persons in his rebel movement. "If he had taken more educated people around him, people who knew politics and the country, maybe he would have succeeded. To launch a war, a rebellion, you need to be organized. It is a system." The violence of the rebellion was easier to set aside decades after the fact.[39] With some temporal distance, educational credentials seemed more relevant to the failure of the rebellion than ideology or power struggles. To Palambwa, Awaka, and Ntil, Mulele remained "one of us"—one of the happy few selected as young children to walk the path of elite education. In their discussions, Kinzambi's alumni envisioned Mulele back within the safe walls of the old mission, in the classrooms where intelligence and analytical skills were valued and different points of view could be civilly debated. Their memories re-created a world, long since gone, that had structured their sense of self.

Urbi et Orbi

The soft voices of children rehearsing Gregorian chants can be heard in the recording of my conversation with Palambwa and his two friends. These voices made the transcription more difficult but not nearly as much as did the distorted music and shouts from the nearby street that drowned out our exchange from time to time. The interference of this urban buzz in the recording is an apt metaphor for the clash between missionary education and urbanity in colonial Congo. Most Catholic missionaries perceived urban centers as spaces of moral turpitude and thus as improper settings for elitist schools.[40] Moving to the Congo had often been their escape from a secularizing Europe that was torn apart by industrial mechanization, consumerism, and violent mass political passions. In the colony, they sought to restore an idealized past. The seclusion of their mission posts and the separation of their students from the world were central to this vision.[41]

The missionary anti-urban bias never fully disappeared. It nonetheless proved difficult to resist the attraction of the cities and numerous alumni from rural elitist schools moved to urban centers without much delay. Some stayed true to the moral precepts they had learned at school, but others diverged from the church's teachings and values.[42] They lived in racially segregated districts that favored forms of sociality and cultural expressions that escaped the control of missionaries and the state. Few Belgians circulated in these areas. In October 1930, when Pierre Ryckmans had the opportunity to visit Black Leopoldville, he marveled at what he saw. A lawyer investigating labor conditions in the colony at the time, Ryckmans wrote to his wife enthusiastically about "*the city* that these people have built with their hands, upon their own initiatives, and after the end of their workday." Ryckmans had been to Leopoldville on multiple occasions, but it was the first time he explored its Black areas in depth. Ryckmans marveled at "the shop counters, photographic studios, hotels, and guesthouses" that the Congolese had created. "Certainly, there is vagrancy, prostitution, and laziness," he wrote in the letter to his wife. "Certainly. But what about all the effort and the many fine examples!"[43]

The visit moved Ryckmans to lobby missionaries to ramp up their efforts toward Black urbanites. Leopoldville had fewer than fifty Catholic priests and nuns for a population of nearly fifty thousand people.[44] One of them was Raphaël de la Kethulle de Ryhove, a Scheutist father who dedicated his ministry to the city's youth and often circulated in the Black cités of Leopoldville.[45] Yet, Tata Raphaël, as he was called, remained an exception. In the 1930s, most missionaries interacted with the Congolese in churches, schools, and hospitals that were located in the white parts of town, where Black people were tolerated during daylight hours only.

Former seminarians often occupied positions of leadership in the cités. They presided over the regional fraternities and alumni associations that were the only outlets for participation in colonial civic life. These community leaders both had reasons and the tools to be critical of Belgian colonialism, as their philosophy courses at the seminary had given them a unique understanding of the crisis of European civilization.[46]

New Paths to and away from School

Once on the path to school, most children dreamed of marching as far as possible. A series of reforms in the postwar era helped many in this regard. Both the Catholic Church and the state registered the évolués' demands for increased educational opportunities. In 1948, taking inspiration from Guffens's experiments at Kinzambi, the Church opened a half dozen secondary schools for Congolese modeled on the so-called collèges that delivered degrees that led to university education in Belgium. A few years later, Auguste Buisseret, the new minister of colonies and a member of the anticlerical Liberal Party, created a network of state-controlled secondary schools that also adopted the curriculum of elite metropolitan educational institutions. Located in urban centers, these athénées catered mostly to white students, only admitting Congolese boys whose families had been vetted by the colonial administrators.[47] The inability of a mother or a little sister to speak French or having a seemingly intemperate father could serve as pretexts to deny a child admission. In one case, a colonial administrator justified the refusal to admit one boy by arguing that "the household of the applicant [was] too well kept to be true."[48] However, a different category of athénées, designed to be "interracial," welcomed mostly Black boys. These schools loosened the grip of the church on the Congolese elite, offering a second chance to the many students who were expelled from missionary schools. In many cases, these students had revolted against their teachers' narrow-mindedness, hypocrisy, and injustices. Expulsion reinforced their dissenting convictions and often proved the initial pull for trajectories of political activism. Without the Buisseret schools, their education would have stopped in its tracks.[49]

Serving as a safety net for these rebellious students, the athénées imported to the colony a "school war" between Catholics and liberals that had raged in the metropole since 1950. These frictions between the church and the state made students aware that education was political through and through. Alienated by the state, missionaries encouraged Congolese Catholics to be critical of the colonial administration; some young Congolese clerics, such as Malula in Leopoldville or Vincent Mulago in Costermansville, began taking positions in favor of self-determination and against the idea of a Belgo-Congolese community in this context.[50]

The school war also accelerated the politicization of laypeople, particularly the évolués. It increased widespread pressures for participation that, combined with external factors such as developments in the French and British colonies on the continent, ultimately resulted in the momentous authorization of political parties in 1958. Politicization also manifested itself within schools, especially in secondary education, as many students became involved with political parties. White teachers certainly cringed when learning of students who had joined the anti-colonial struggle. At the athénée of Ngiri-Ngiri in Léopoldville, Belgian professors bullied Antoine Tshimanga, a cofounder of the Union Nationale des Travailleurs Congolais and leader of ANAJECO, an alliance of the youth branches of various nationalist political parties. "Madame Van Nieuwerbergh, our professor of Latin, was constantly tormenting him," one of Tshimanga's former classmates recalled decades later. "For any small thing, it was: 'Tshimanga, get out! Tshimanga, go stand in the corner!' And he was older than most of us—we were fifteen, sixteen, or seventeen years old and he was over twenty; he must have been twenty-two or twenty-three, or maybe older; he was an adult student—so he felt even more embarrassed."[51] This bullying continued uninterrupted until the colonial authorities jailed Tshimanga for political subversion.[52]

The students' commitment to political activism created friction outside Leopoldville as well. In South Kivu, the athénée of Bagira expelled Albert

Kisonga for having organized a strike and imported subversive politics into the school. Kisonga subsequently became a full-time activist. First, he worked as a militant journalist in Kivu and then, after relocating to Leopoldville, as an adviser to Anicet Kashamura, the minister of information in Lumumba's government. Within a few months, Kisonga had befriended Félix Moumié, met Frantz Fanon, and traveled to Paris and Moscow. He felt that his experience in politics taught him more than all his years at school.[53]

Post-independence Bifurcations

The late 1950s and early 1960s were a time of acceleration, both institutionally and individually. The anti-colonial movement really shook up the education system. Upon independence, the road often became bumpy, but multiple new branches and byways also opened up. Political turbulence diverted many bright students from school. At the same time, the white exodus of July 1960 meant that elite institutions that had once been off-limits to Black children suddenly became accessible, at least to the boys.[54] In Léopoldville, for instance, a small cohort of Congolese pupils transferred to Collège Albert at the beginning of the new school year in September 1960. Most of these children had previously attended Collège Sainte-Anne, a school for Congolese boys run by the Scheutist fathers. Collège Albert, Leopoldville's most prestigious secondary school, was Jesuit, and the differences in pedagogy were striking: "With the Scheutists, it was the chicotte [a type of whip ubiquitous in the colonial Congo]. You felt the spirit of Tata Raphaël," Malonga Miatudila, one of the transfer students recalled several decades after the fact, referring to the Scheutist father Raphaël de la Kethulle, who was reputed for his brutal and authoritarian manners as much as for his dedication to the youth of Leopoldville. In comparison with Sainte-Anne and its "regime of terror," the Jesuit college seemed "much cooler."[55] A few years later, many of the most radical students at Lovanium would be alumni of the Jesuit school; and some of them referenced the Ignatian pedagogy as having played a role in their politicization.[56]

For Miatudila, the transfer to Collège Albert was felicitous, but the game of musical chairs set in motion by independence took place in a troubled context. Despite attempts at reforms by people like Father Ekwa, elite institutions did not accept enough students, failed too many, and proved unable to satisfy the Congo's urgent needs in growing a class of educated citizens. This inadequacy was compounded by the legacies of racial discrimination. Mechanisms of exclusion were not immediately fully erased from the institutions that had been previously reserved to the children of white colonials. Old colonial habits die hard, and some white teachers did make Congolese children feel out of place in Leopoldville's elite schools during the post-independence years.[57]

Clearly, for children who attended schools without the prestige and reputation of institutions like Sainte-Anne or Collège Albert, the situation was far more dire. The disorder that had followed the transition of power in July 1960 loosened state control over education, making it difficult to monitor the independent schools that opened to fill the deficits in educational offerings. Before independence, a lack of places in Leopoldville schools had prevented thousands of students from continuing their education each year.[58] Demographic pressures on educational infrastructures intensified throughout the country after 1960. Between 1962 and 1968, for example, the number of children in primary schools at the national level went from 1,837,132 to 2,338,895. During the same period, the number of students in secondary schools grew from 68,350 to 162,237.[59] As the number of students per class increased, the quality of education decreased, leading to a general feeling that the educational system was in crisis. In 1961, the British consul and MI6 operative Daphne Park told a visiting Ford Foundation official "with categorial vigor that secondary education here does not exist anymore."[60] The following year, when a teenager wrote to ask Ekwa for advice about schools in Leopoldville because he was unhappy with the quality of education in the small town where he lived, the Jesuit's response was blunt: "Don't think about coming to Leo[poldville]. There are no more spots in the schools here."[61] The teachers were desperately overworked and were, as a professional category, the most prone to go on strike. They protested against the many and frequent delays in the payment of their salaries and their deteriorating living conditions. Black teachers had felt as though they belonged to an elite class in colonial society because they "held the key to westernization." But after independence, they found themselves relegated behind the new political class, including people who were much less well educated than them.[62] Many qualified teachers abandoned education altogether for more lucrative positions in politics and in administration, while others neglected their teaching obligations, establishing small businesses to supplement their salaries. Thanks to this, children often experienced significant delays in their education; pupils frequently finished primary school at the age of fifteen or sixteen, instead of twelve.[63] As churches and the state were unable to satisfy the demand for education, other actors moved into the field and set up new schools across the country, despite often lacking the requisite resources and skills. A local union in the lower Congo operated one of these new schools. It had a prestigious

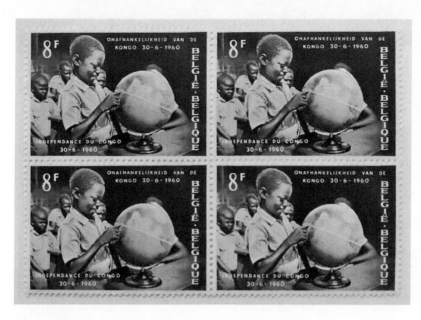

Figure 3.2 "Congo's independence," Belgian stamp, June 1960 (source: author's collection).

sounding name: Collège et Lycée National Saint-Georges. But it lacked proper facilities and took up residence in a dancing bar during its first year and then in cabins built by the students themselves.[64] In Leopoldville, similar schools proliferated in the poorer parts of the city, where many recent migrants with little social and economic capital lived. These schools were often referred to as écoles pamba (worthless schools). The instruction they dispensed was rather rudimentary and failed to deliver the credentials needed to access higher education. However, the people of Leopoldville agreed that a pamba school was better than no school at all.[65]

Conclusion

In May 1960, the Belgian postal service released a stamp to celebrate the Congo's approaching independence (figure 3.2).[66] The stamp portrayed a Black schoolchild standing next to a desk and pointing smilingly at Central Africa on a globe. Belgian colonialism had taught the Congolese to situate themselves in relation to the world, the image suggested. This message may have conformed to the spin that the Belgian authorities put on a decolonization process that had escaped their control. It was nonetheless fully out of step with decades of colonial obsession with enclosure and

separateness. The Belgians had seen schooling as an instrument of mediation in the relation between colonized children and the broader world. Yet,
they chiefly wanted to tie Congolese children to fixed social and gendered
coordinates in the space and time of racial imperialism. Education functioned as a semantic machine: by giving articulation to an order of reality,
it produced both symbolic violence *and* a sense of safety.[67]

There was some built-in mobility in this vision of colonial stabilization,
and education supported this horizon. The path to school allowed individuals to advance into the future, while simultaneously imposing specific
limits on the possibilities of so doing. Missionaries and colonial agents
believed that schooling would set the colonized in motion and keep them
in order. They commissioned photographs and films that showed Black
children standing in line or symmetrically assembled for gymnastic exer-
cises. And they asked students to sing songs that compared the "path to
school" with a military parade.[68] However, colonialism did not fully determine Congolese experiences of education. As in other oppressive regimes,
schoolchildren in the Belgian colony saw schooling as a platform to build
fulfilling lives for themselves.[69] They may have moved along colonial axes
when they traveled to school on trucks, boats, bikes, or foot, but they lived
these journeys as adventures in self-discovery. Later, they used what they
had learned to oppose colonial domination.

Furthermore, not all Belgians regarded education as a form of social
regimentation. Some missionaries prided themselves on their progressive
approaches. They argued that it was "a mistake to think that the Black
has only one ideal: the ideal of the typewriter."[70] Instead, they believed
that theater, the classics, and critical thinking should spread beyond the
minor seminaries. In the 1940s and 1950s, new schools and elite tracks
finally paved the way to university education. Reforms only slowly and
incrementally opened up the horizons of colonial education, but schools
never lacked avid learners who dreamed of social elevation. Students were
also aware that education had far-reaching repercussions for the future
of the Congo, for its association with Belgium, and for the relation between the state and the Catholic Church. This awareness led them to question the intellectual authority of their teachers. Many looked beyond their
classrooms toward the outer world that they wanted to learn about: they
listened to foreign radio stations, sent letters to distant correspondents,
read subversive publications, and joined political parties.

The complexity of Congolese engagements with colonial and early postcolonial education is important to keep in mind, especially when considering the course that student politics took in the 1960s. It was by working

through the contradictions of the education system that Congolese students developed a strong sense of themselves as a national vanguard that could transform the Congo and the world. The degree to which the tensions of colonial education politicized students sometimes escaped otherwise perceptive scholars of Congolese society. In 1972 and 1973, Pierre Erny, a French ethnographer and pedagogue who established the field of psychopedagogy in the Congo, asked four hundred first-year university students in Kisangani to write autobiographical narratives. Analyzing the materials he collected, Erny claimed to have identified "a general bipolarity" among the students, which he described as a cultural pathology caused by the tension between, on the one hand, the values that ruled the Western school system and, on the other hand, "the intellectual and affective acquired characteristics of prime education in village and family environments marked by traditions and paganism."[71] In Erny's eyes, the future-oriented vision that grounded Western education was antithetical to traditional Congolese worldviews, and a conflict of loyalty between these two cognitive worlds produced an existential malaise in his students. What Erny overlooked was the deeply political roots of this specific framing. Having access to education had been a long struggle against the repeated colonial negations of Congolese intellectual capacities and dignity. As the path to academic knowledge slowly widened, tensions remained between two different approaches to emancipation—one that conceived it as a form of incorporation in the colonial order and one that challenged the foundations of that order. This tension is the rootstock on which Erny's theme of mental alienation was grafted. In the 1950s and 1960s, some Congolese may have found it difficult to adhere to the future-oriented vision of Western education, but what many more grappled with was the fact that the Belgians attempted to impose their own definition of this future and to slow Congolese progression toward knowledge, self-rule, and independence.

This struggle continued throughout the 1960s. Colonial schools had trained the generation that successfully led the fight for independence, but education remained an element of continuity in the period that followed the transition to political sovereignty. The Belgians, as someone like Ekwa was deeply made aware, remained strongly invested in Congolese schools after independence. Numerous Belgian missionaries remained active in education across the country, and the Belgian government paid the salaries of hundreds of Belgian lay teachers who worked in Congolese schools.

In the early 1960s, the Belgian authorities set up programs that brought large numbers of Congolese students to Belgian secondary schools and universities because they believed it would create a "psychological benefit" that would enhance their relation with the former colony.[72] In the same way, they considered that the presence of Belgian teachers in the Congo provided them with a strategic advantage. In November 1961, when ninety of these teachers went on strike in the city of Luluabourg, the Belgian Ministry of African Affairs immediately dispatched a special emissary to negotiate with them. The teachers demanded open return tickets to Belgium so that they could escape more easily in the event of a crisis. Pierre Leroy, the ministry's envoy (and the former colonial governor of the Oriental Province, where he had been an early opponent of Lumumba), recommended fully supporting the demand. He saw teachers as a line of defense against the growing influence of communism in Africa: "Our teachers exert a tremendous influence on the country's evolution by educating the next generation of leaders," he noted in his report. Because the Congolese considered education to be sacred, he argued, the presence of Belgian teachers in the former colony was the "greatest means of pressure in our possession."[73]

Like Leroy, many Congolese perceived the strategic and ideological stakes behind Belgian educational efforts in their country, but they resented it. Students in elite schools denounced the persistent colonial character of Congolese education. They clashed with teachers and school administrators whom they saw as attached to an alien system of knowledge and values. This is why the church appointed Father Ekwa as the first Congolese president of the BEC. As Ekwa himself later recalled, his nomination was a symbol of change, but it was also used to maintain continuity and order: "Every time that students began to protest in a school, their missionary teachers would tell them, 'We are not the ones in charge; we just follow the orders of Father Ekwa.' This way, they made me famous: every student in the country knew my name."[74]

FOUR
DANCING THE RUMBA
AT LOVANIUM

Could we call ourselves students if we screamed in the streets, if we raped girls, if we did not carefully pay attention to how we dress for a ballroom dance, if we did not eat properly at a table like well-educated people, if we did not respect the religious and philosophical beliefs of others? If the answer [to these questions] is no, then how can we still call ourselves students when we act as mindless, uneducated people at our campus cine-forum? Why are we applauding political figures during newsreels? Why do we shamelessly moan when there is a kissing scene in a film? Why do we laugh or applaud when a woman is beaten down and molested or when a character has been shot down? Why do we insult images by shouting out loud: "dirty priest," "what an old shit," "whore," "imperialist," etc.?

Cléo Tshibangu, "Lettre ouverte à M. le Président des étudiants de Lovanium,"
Echos de Lovanium (April 1962), 6

Canon Luc Gillon became the rector of Lovanium in 1954. A nuclear physicist by training, Gillon had completed a postdoctoral fellowship at Princeton University with Robert Oppenheimer and, just before moving to the Congo, established his own laboratory at the University of Louvain. The young priest-physicist descended from a line of engineers who had built power plants, railroads, mining installations, and artificial waterways from Chile to China.[1] More than anything else, he took pride in his pragmatism and voluntarism. Leading the Congo's first university through the decolonization era, he faced numerous challenges, but nothing deterred him from turning Lovanium into the most prestigious research and educational institution on the African continent.

At the close of 1961, while the Congo was still torn apart by civil strife, Gillon developed a plan to raise Lovanium's international profile by devising an English-language curriculum that would increase the university's attractiveness outside of francophone Africa.[2] The initiative was quite successful. Catholic bishops in Nigeria, Rhodesia, and several East African countries sent dozens of students to Leopoldville, including several female students, which was particularly meaningful given that Lovanium had only four Congolese women enrolled at the time. Yet, what should have been a reason to celebrate became a crisis for Gillon when the English-speaking newcomers refused to submit to the weeks-long hazing rituals traditionally imposed on first-year students at Lovanium.

The General Assembly of Students (Assemblée générale des étudiants de Lovanium, AGEL) organized this rite of passage. A student government with its president, ministers, and parliament, AGEL considered itself responsible for the cohesion of the student community. Members of the group could not stomach that Gillon seemed to support the English-speaking students' refusal to submit to the hazing rituals. AGEL leaders noted that, in earlier years, when Lovanium had a higher proportion of white students, Gillon had personally attended some of these very rituals.[3] Was the rector now feeling alienated by a campus that looked increasingly blacker?[4]

A violent altercation further escalated the conflict, after a group of senior students—or hangmen (bourreaux) in campus slang—proceed with the hazing by force and cropped the hair of several newcomers they seized at the dining hall. A brawl ensued and one hangman hit a university guard in the face. He apologized almost immediately, but Monsignor Martin-Léonard Bakole, Lovanium's academic secretary and the only Congolese official on campus, lodged a police complaint about the incident.[5]

Student baptism, as the hazing ritual was called, was a direct import from Belgian universities and therefore a typical example of the "invented traditions" that cemented ruling-class culture in colonial Africa.[6] At its core, le baptême estudiantin was a carnival-like appropriation of a religious sacrament that reaffirmed the autonomy of students vis-à-vis their professors; and it resonated distinctively in a mission land like the Congo.

Candidates for religious baptism in the colony were rarely infants like in the metropole but instead teenagers or adults who had been preparing for years to gain entry into the church. As a spectacle, the ceremony addressed the yet-to-be baptized alongside the community of the faithful. Missionaries adapted their ceremonial by incorporating elements from the "heathen traditions" that they sought to supplant, such as the circumcision camp and its initiation rituals.[7] In some cases, for instance, catechumens with their hair shaved off paraded among churchgoers who hit and spit on them.[8]

Like its religious model, student baptism imposed humility on newcomers, through ceremonies that could involve bodily alterations, real or simulated physical abuses, and ritualized humiliation. The "dirty greenhorns" (les sales bleus) presented themselves as symbolically naked in front of their peers by walking shoeless and wearing only shorts, a tie, and no shirt. To be allowed into the cosmopolitan community of Lovanium, they had to perform folkloric dances from their respective ethnic homelands and prove their familiarity with the realm of tradition. Beer featured prominently, even if slightly less so than it did in Belgian universities. Once initiated, the students received a distinct student cap, la penne, a symbol of their esprit de corps, and they wore it with pride every time they ventured outside of campus.

The cheeky appropriation of Catholic rituals through student baptism challenged the symbolic authority of the church. Lovanium was Catholic, but some students, after years of semi-seclusion in missionary boarding schools, arrived at university with a nearly systematic rejection for "anything with a clerical smell" (tout ce qui sent les curés), as a Jesuit complained in 1967.[9] Even staunch churchgoers held dear the principle of student independence vis-à-vis the clerical leadership of the university; and they too adopted the codes, schoolboy humor, and local slang of Lovanium folklore, through which the student community expressed its defiant spirit.[10]

This chapter narrates the colonial origins of Congolese higher education and its gradual contestation by the students. As elements of campus culture, such as the baptism ritual, politicized students and gave them the ammunition they needed to challenge established hierarchies, they appear at different points of articulation in the following pages. The chapter focuses mostly on Lovanium, but the story it tells extends beyond the edges of its campus. The university was a point of dense connectivity: it attracted American funding, French and Belgian faculty, and students from all across Africa. Its prestige radiated throughout the Congo and beyond.[11] Gillon, as much as the students, knew that what happened at Lovanium would not stay at Lovanium. In their confrontations, they performed like actors on a stage, aware that the correspondences between developments on campus and the vicissitudes of the world were many and far-reaching.

In 1928, Hyacinthe Vanderhyst, a Jesuit priest and reputed botanist who had lived in the Congo for close to three decades, published an article calling for the creation of universities to train the colonized in medicine and tropical agriculture.[12] This proposal did not emerge in a void. Just a few years earlier, the Catholic University of Louvain had opened a research and training center in Kisantu, the mission station to which Vanderhyst was attached. This center, known as FOMULAC (Fondation médicale de l'Université de Louvain au Congo), included research facilities, a hospital, and a school for medical assistants. By the time Vanderhyst publicly argued for the necessity to establish a Congolese university, Louvain was already planning to expand its colonial footprints with another center dedicated to agriculture that would be known as CADULAC (Centre agricole de l'Université de Louvain au Congo). These two programs supported by Louvain, FOMULAC and CADULAC, offered a type of advanced technical education that had few equivalents in the colony, but they did not approximate university curriculums: they trained the Congolese not as knowledge producers but instead as subaltern auxiliaries who would assist the colonizers in controlling rural communities through vaccination campaigns and the imposition of production quotas on agricultural crops.[13]

Vanderhyst's dream of a university for the colonized was far removed from the realities of the interwar era, but the idea slowly took hold in various Catholic circles. In 1948, Guy Malengreau, a professor of law at Louvain (whose father, Fernand, had supervised the creation of FOMULAC), oversaw the establishment of a university center (Centre universitaire congolais Lovanium) in Kisantu, which incorporated FOMULAC, CADULAC, and a recently created school of commercial and administrative sciences. This was progress, but some students resented the fact that the new institution would still not confer degrees equivalent to those granted in Belgian universities. Justin-Marie Bomboko, who studied at the university center in the early 1950s, later remembered that he had felt like a guinea pig in Kisantu. In his view, the in-betweenness of the institution (no longer a technical school but not yet a real university) testified to the Belgians' lack of confidence in the Congolese's intellectual abilities.[14]

Malengreau was sensitive to these kinds of feelings. His goal was to turn the university center into a full-fledged university. Several factors crucially advanced this plan: newly created academically oriented secondary schools ensured a supply of prepared candidates for higher education, criticisms expressed in the United Nations of Belgium's insufficient promotion of African elites called for answers, and some Belgians believed that Congolese sacrifices during the war merited a reward, which a university could provide.[15] To obtain the go-ahead from the colonial authorities, Malengreau combined arguments about the timeliness of training the Congolese elite of tomorrow with reassurances about the nonthreatening nature of the project. The University of Lovanium would train "a class of Blacks for whom instruction will not be a factor of moral decay and anarchy, nor a weapon for revolutionary agitation that could compromise our civilizational work," he assured the minister of colonies. The university would inculcate in its students strong moral values and "an acute sense of responsibilities," he also promised.[16] Furthermore, as more Congolese would graduate from secondary schools with qualifications allowing them to attend institutions of higher education, a local university could help reduce the number of Black students in the metropole. As the general governor stated in 1952, sending Congolese students to Belgium was "undesirable for reasons pertaining to morality, domestic policy and general political concerns." Young educated Congolese should instead study in local, "adapted" institutions.[17] Malengreau took a different view on the so-called question of adaptation, telling himself that "we need a real university."[18] He was able to build on the fear of increased Congolese student migration to Belgium to overcome colonial resistance to higher education. His vision prevailed in the end and the colonial state allowed Louvain and the church to transform Lovanium into the Congo's first university. Even officials who expressed doubts about "the intellectual capacities of the Congolese" behind closed doors still supported Lovanium because they believed it could improve the image of Belgian colonialism domestically and abroad.[19]

Kisantu did not seem adequate as a site for the new institution. Some missionaries suggested that choosing Leopoldville instead would reinforce the church's influence at the center of colonial power. Yet, Malengreau and others rejected the idea of an urban university. The compromise was Mount Amba, twenty kilometers outside of Leopoldville, near the Jesuit post of Kimwenza. Construction began in 1952, and the university welcomed its first class of six students in January 1954.[20] The many concrete buildings that rose from the dusty ground of Mount Amba embodied the forward-looking rhetoric of late-colonial developmentalism (see figure 4.1).[21] At the same time, the campus's location recalled the anti-modernist drive of the missionary movement and its dreams of secluded communities of believers.[22] Mount Amba was at a safe distance from urban distractions and "moral threats." As an elevated site that overlooked the Congo River valley, its topography mirrored the configuration of the country's many elitist sec-

Figure 4.1 "View of the auditorium of the Lovanium University in the Republic of Congo (Leopoldville)." Photographer unknown, June 1961 (source: Rockefeller Archive Center, Ford Foundation Papers).

ondary schools.[23] This characteristic was so central to Lovanium's identity that it soon became universally known as la colline inspirée (the inspired hill). To students, the name evoked a studious ivory tower, a place free from the contingencies of pedestrian existence and conducive to intellectual creativity. However, the nickname came from the title of a 1913 novel by the French nationalist writer Maurice Barrès—an ode to mysticism and traditionalism. The readers of Barrès who popularized the nickname in the first place had a specific representation of Lovanium in mind: a place that embodied the temptation of a radical separation from the world.

Oswald Ndeshyo, a student from the Kivu's Masisi plateau who had attended a White Fathers' major seminary on the shore of Lake Tanganyika in northern Katanga just before going to Lovanium, found the campus reassuringly familiar. The language, culinary culture, hustle and bustle of Leopoldville were in many ways foreign to Ndeshyo. But the relative isolation of Lovanium made his transition to the city less abrupt.[24]

The Afro-Club

Notwithstanding the similarities between the Inspired Hill and elitist Catholic secondary schools, the students' lives underwent a dramatic change on arriving at the university. As university students, they reached the highest, most elusive, and most prestigious echelon in colonial society. They also enjoyed more freedom and autonomy on campus than they ever had before. And their desire to protect this freedom and autonomy led to many of their conflicts with Gillon and the university administration.

Aubert Mukendi, a contemporary of Ndeshyo at Lovanium, initially marveled at the new horizon of possibility that his status as universitaire offered. Lovanium gave him a chance to decide what he wanted to become, whereas this had never been an option before. When he had graduated from the Saint Boniface Institute in Elisabethville, professors at the secondary school had pressured him to join a seminary. He had no aspiration to a life in the church, and after a few months, he quit the seminary, moving back to his parents' hometown of Mwene-Ditu in the Kasai. Yet, he remained on Saint Boniface's radar.[25] The school director sent a letter to the territorial administrator in Mwene-Ditu: idleness was not an option for Mukendi, he wrote; the young man had to continue his education, one way or another, and the administration had to help. In 2011, on a cold January afternoon that I spent with him and his Belgian wife, Josée, in their apartment in a suburb of Paris, Mukendi could still recall vividly the dreadful voice of colonial authoritarianism: "The administrator ordered me to go study at the FOMULAC in Kalenda. If I refused, he would draft me into the military for seven years." For Mukendi, medical assistantship was as unattractive an option as priesthood. Lovanium, which had recently opened, appeared a way out, so he applied. The Inspired Hill was not perfect (and Mukendi decided to move to a university in Belgium after a few years), but it presented an array of possibilities that contrasted with the preordained paths previously imposed on him. Mukendi opted to study mathematics, a subject in which he had genuine interest but that he also chose because Belgian colonials thought it was too abstract for Black students.[26]

Lovanium changed the way that young educated Congolese men looked at their place in the world. It "made us less anxious about the future," one of the first graduates in medicine wrote about the moment he and his high

school friends in Elisabethville learned of the creation of the university.[27] Academic qualifications would end the systematic relegation of the Congolese to subaltern positions. Of course, only a few highly select young men could dream of accessing the new institution and obtaining the diplomas that would give them positions of responsibility in their own society. The main bias was gender, as the new status that university education conferred to the colonized excluded Congolese women. Yet, for cohorts of hopeful young men in elite schools across the colony, the news of Lovanium's opening constituted a true promise of independence. The authorities had given their assent to the creation of Lovanium in part to encourage these kinds of feelings among the educated youth. The Inspired Hill proved an exceptional setting for late-colonial propaganda. From the very beginning, it attracted photographers with assignments to improve the image of Belgian colonialism (see figure 4.2); and in 1958, the Ministry of Colonies commissioned a short film by filmmaker Gérard De Boe to further play up the promises of Lovanium. De Boe's film emphasized the high standard of research facilities and the monumentalism of the architecture. But its primary focus was the university's biracial character. Half a dozen shots showed interactions between Black and white students in classrooms or during leisure time while they listened to music, played table football, and drank beer together. Although power relations in the colony were structurally thick with racism, Lovanium seemed to usher in a future unencumbered with the "prejudice of color" in which Blacks and whites could peacefully and convivially live and work together. De Boe's film expressed this transformative sociality of the campus in strongly gendered terms. De Boe was indeed careful to depict Black male students in the same frames as their few white female peers. Such scenes of mixed-gender and mixed-race comradeship were highly unusual. They ran against the specter of sexual relations between Black men and white women that haunted the colonial imagination.[28] In this way, De Boe presented Lovanium as the mark of a rupture.

Although there may have been something daring in scenes of interracial comradeship among male and female students, the idea that Lovanium inaugurated a new era in Belgian-Congolese relations directly served the interests of Belgian propaganda, at a time of increased anticolonial contestations. In contrast with this emphasis on the supposedly bold racial opening of the university, the former students I interviewed rarely shared anecdotes about their white peers. When they referred to the cosmopolitanism of the Inspired Hill, they did not necessarily think about race and instead often meant the social and cultural diversity of the campus. Few other institutions allowed young colonized from such diverse backgrounds to cohabit. For Nestor Mpeye, who came to Lovanium from what he referred to as the "bush" secondary school of Kiniati, it was other Congolese students who represented the quintessential figure of alterity. "One Black student drove an Impala," he told me. "Do you know what the Impala was? It was the Rolls Royce of the time! That student was the son of a great bwana, who was a school director in Leopoldville and therefore an évolué, therefore a darling of the fathers." Mpeye was made immediately aware of his own provincialism at Lovanium, and he identified with other students from petty évolué or peasant backgrounds. He felt intimidated by peers who had grown up in Leopoldville, Stanleyville, and in Katanga's mining towns: "They were urbanisés [lit. urbanized], we were not. I had even never seen an electric iron before coming to Lovanium." Upon graduating from Lovanium, Mpeye pursed a doctoral degree in engineering in Belgium and subsequently served as professor, dean, and rector at the University of Kinshasa. Still, five decades later, he had not forgotten how unsophisticated he felt when he learned that some Lovanium students went out to city bars on Saturdays and that "mind you, they even danced with women."[29]

The students' relationship to Leopoldville nightlife was absent from De Boe's film. However, the nocturnal back and forth between the campus and the cité, between an iconic site of late-colonial modernity and an iconic space of Black cultural sovereignty, was essential to the constitution of the students' identity. These young men aspired to embody a masculinity that did not map onto Catholic moralism but that was cocky and flirtatious and expressed itself on dance floors and in the company of femmes libres—unattached women known for their "scandalous freedom" and aura of hedonism and audacity.[30]

During a long conversation we had in a Congolese bar in Brussels, while loud, madly catchy ndombolo songs played in the background, Thomas Mambo told me the story of Afro-Club, a dancing group that he had created as a freshman at Lovanium in 1963. Mambo had moved to Lovanium at the age of twenty-three after renouncing a life as a Catholic brother. After half a dozen years in a monastery in rural Kivu, he sought to catch up on lost time once at Lovanium: "There was a group of impetuous students, the Ata Ndelists. They were from Leopoldville and they knew how to dance. I befriended some of them and went dancing with them every weekend: to the Phoenix Bleu, the Afro-Milano, the Perruche Bleue, and other clubs."[31] In Leopoldville's famous clubs, those temples of Congolese rumba, with its beautiful aerial sounds, Mambo learned moves that he brought back to campus. With money from the university, he bought a record player, and the Afro-Club was born. It was a place for former seminarians and other inexperienced students to practice the undulating hip movements and footsteps that would accelerate their integration into the cosmopolitan community of the campus, as young men of education and urbanity.[32]

Ata Ndele

The students from Leopoldville who introduced Mambo to dancing bars bridged gaps between the campus and the city at several levels. There had only been a few of them at first. In the first years of its existence, Lovanium recruited predominantly from seminaries and boarding schools located in rural missionary outposts. Elitist secondary education had come somewhat later to urban centers. And the boys who grew up in Leopoldville did not necessarily associate personal success with long scholastic journeys. Jean-Baptiste Mulemba had, for instance, only a vague idea of what a university was when he finished primary school in Leopoldville in 1958. His role models were not priests or university students. Instead, he looked up to his father, a man who had made the best of his little education and knowledge of French, overcame adversity and injustices, and provided for a large family by working as a respected foreman for several companies throughout western Congo. Mulemba also particularly admired one of his older cousins who always dressed well and projected an image of absolute sophistication. To follow in the footsteps of this cousin was Mulemba's dream: he wanted to attend the same trade school as his relative and to take up a clerkship after a few years just as he had. But the missionaries had other plans for the young boy. His grades in primary school ranked him among the best students, and whether he liked it or not, he would continue his education at the elite Saint Joseph School and be groomed for university education.[33]

After a few years, more students from Leopoldville began attending Lovanium (including Mulemba in 1964), and more children in the city came to see university education as the epitome of personal success. On campus, the Leopoldville students formed their own association: Ata Ndele. Whereas most other associations operated along ethnoregional lines, Ata Ndele did not: its members were students from the city, and their pride in being from Leopoldville took precedence over ethnic allegiance. Leopoldville was a city of migrants who hailed from all over the lower and upper Congo, the Kwilu, the Kwango, the Kasai, and from neighboring Angola and the French Congo. As the anthropologist Jean La Fontaine noted, the Bana Lipopo (lit. children of Leopoldville) "tend[ed] to keep together in cliques which ignore[d] the tribal and provincial ties that unite[d] other students in groups of friends."[34] Regionalist tensions periodically surfaced at Lovanium (including among the Bana Lipopo themselves), pitting students from the eastern Swahili-speaking parts of the country against those from the western Lingala-speaking regions, or singling out supposedly tribalist groups like the Lubas who were seen as overrepresented at Lovanium. Yet, the inclusiveness of the Ata Ndelists prevailed. Lovanium students as a whole cherished their shared values: elitism, cosmopolitan sophistication, and a rebellious spirit.

The name Ata Ndele encapsulated the contribution of students from Leopoldville to Lovanium's identity. Meaning "sooner or later," it referred to the lyrics of a 1955 song by Adou Elanga, a young rumba musician from Leopoldville whose father was a migrant from West Africa. "Ata ndele, mokili ekobaluka, . . . ata ndele mundele akosukana" (Sooner or later, the world will change, . . . sooner or later the [domination of the] white man will end). The song was so incendiary that Elanga was briefly detained upon its release.[35] Like him, Lovanium's Ata Ndelists were willing to push against the limits. They liked the pepper of provocation and the sweetness of guitar melodies. They had come of age at a moment of effervescence in the civic life of Leopoldville. One of the first leaders of their association, Paul-Henri

Kabayidi, was a former Bill, the name given to the members of Leopold-ville's youth street gangs who dressed as American cowboys, chased girls, and smoked hemp.[36] Kabayidi also grew up in a house where politics was ever present in the late 1950s. His father was the president of the federation of people from the Kasai in Leopoldville and a prominent member of the Association du Personnel Indigène de la Colonie (APIC), the labor union for Congolese state employees. As a high school student, Paul-Henri ran an in-formal political discussion circle with a group of friends (see also chapter 2). Their guest speakers included several prominent évolué leaders and even the first openly Marxist politician in the city, Alphonse Makwambala.[37]

Students like Kabayidi brought their firsthand knowledge of Leopold-ville's burgeoning political scene and of defiant popular culture to Lova-nium. Their organic connections with the city made the campus open to stronger winds of protest. Politics had been present at the university from the very beginning—students affiliated with the International Movement of Catholic Students (also known as Pax Romana) organized debates about world issues, and several Belgian professors played a role as advisers in the publication of the first évolué manifesto demanding independence in 1956.[38] These positions adopted by students and faculty did not seem to directly challenge the church or Lovanium's authorities. This changed in 1957, 1958, and 1959, when several incidents made Gillon worry about radicalization among segments of the student body.[39] The most serious of these incidents was an open letter demanding salary equality that students circulated in Leopoldville. The language that the students used in the letter was purely inflammatory.[40] "If Blacks and whites do not come to enjoy equal advantages, we are ready to make the Congo a second Algeria," they wrote.[41] The reference to the anti-colonial war between the Front de Libération Nationale and the French state in Algeria unnerved the Belgian colonizers to the utmost. It showed clearly that the students saw the situa-tion in the Congo through the lens of international political developments. In their imagination, Algeria was key. But the Suez crisis, Bandung, or the independence of the Gold Coast they also followed closely.[42]

The Ata Ndelists further developed this awareness of international anti-colonial politics among the Lovanium students. They were also behind memorable shivarees on campus. One happened during the official opening of Lovanium's sport complex at the beginning of 1960. Monsignor Joseph Malula (one of the former Mbata-Kiela seminarians mentioned in the pre-vious chapter) had just joined the board of the university when he insisted that Congolese culture and Bantu customs dictated that female students from a nearby nursing school ought not to use the complex's Olympic-size swimming pool when male students were on-site. "This started a real revolt! A revolt!" as Professor Mpeye later recalled. The Congolese students did not recognize themselves, or their cultures, in Malula's edict: "Which culture is he talking about? Whose customs?" Even students who remained close to the church viewed Lovanium as a space free of determinate cultural assignations, where the only customs and folklore were student-made, worldly, and irreverent. As an act of protest, a group of pleasantly tipsy students in swimming suits invaded Gillon's residence during the reception for the pool's opening. For Mpeye, this "extraordinary episode" encapsulated the spirit of Lovanium.[43] It also showed how fully Leopoldville's rebelliousness had been implanted on the Inspired Hill.

Student Governance

This happening at the pool's opening ceremony foreshadowed many more clashes to come. As the next chapter details, the turmoil of the Congo crisis shifted student politics to the left. Lovanium continued to function nearly normally through the crisis, but the air on campus was thick with the fumes of civil strife, and Congolese students showed a growing distrust for the university's Belgian leadership. This distrust expressed itself through gradual shifts in postures and attitudes, ways of speaking and of occupying space. Some students lamented that their peers did not always live up to their supposed elite status, behaving instead like uneducated urban delinquents. In April 1962, Cléophas Tshibangu, a student in medicine, published an open letter in the student newspaper to denounce abhorrent behaviors that occurred during film screenings on campus. Tshibangu was appalled that fellow students shouted insults at film characters like "dirty priest," "what an old shit," "whore," or "imperialist." The list suggests mental associations between anticlericalism, the rebellious pleasure of uttering profanities, male chauvinism, and the rhetoric of anti-colonialism—the expression of a mindset reminiscent of Leopoldville's youth subculture.[44] In any case, culture at Lovanium had strayed far from the ideal of the well-put-together, responsible, and reasonable gentleman student.

Pace Tshibangu, demographic trends ensured that the new defiant and boisterous mood was not going anywhere. Independence made the production of university graduates an absolute necessity and the overall number of enrolled students grew exponentially each year. In October 1962 (at the beginning of the academic year following the publication of Tshibangu's open letter), the student population nearly doubled in size to 786 students, up from 440 the previous year.[45] The numbers of faculty and staff grew far more slowly, and the student body became more difficult to control, supervise, and reason with. The rapid growth of the student population undermined relations between the university leadership and the students.

The spark that ignited the fire of student protests was the incident around the "baptism" of English-speaking students discussed earlier. Never had students opposed Lovanium's authorities so openly, and never did the latter respond so forcefully. After the administration took a series of measures against the students who had attacked their English-speaking peers, Christophe Mateene, AGEL's president and a senior student in African linguistics, threatened a general strike if these measures were not lifted.[46] Gillon was determined not to give in to the "students' blackmail" and he refused to budge.[47] After Mateene failed to carry out the promised strike, a coalition of "youngsters" within AGEL accused him of being afraid of confronting the rector. They forced him out and ushered in Gérard Kamanda as new student president.

A senior law student, Kamanda was known on campus for his brilliant oratory skills and left tendencies in politics.[48] His mandate was to open discussions about the problem of racism on campus, for Lovanium's authorities did not seem to realize the extent of students' growing frustration.[49] After the hazing incident, Gillon launched a commission on "student problems." The commission, which counted only two Congolese members (Monsignor Bakole and Father Vincent Mulago, a professor of theology), made a few suggestions about possible revisions to Lovanium's curriculum, but it did not otherwise seem to take student discontent very seriously. Members of the commission believed that finding "a myth, a main idea, capable of filling the students with enthusiasm" could suffice to ease tensions.[50] This missed a crucial point: AGEL's defense of campus traditions had morphed into a challenge to Lovanium's colonial legacy. Students now denounced the university as "a Belgian enclave in the Congo, a happy colonial oasis," as a group of seniors wrote in a memorandum to the university board in July 1963. This memorandum referenced the bloody Leopoldville riots of January 1959 that had crucially advanced the cause of Congolese independence, warning that students were ready to fight for the independence of their university. There might be victims and martyrs, but students would "show to the world that [Lovanium's] beautiful concrete buildings—a solid opium supplied by foreign capitalists— have not been built for the happiness of the Congolese youth or to satisfy its aspiration to freedom."[51]

Students were frustrated that Gillon had so little patience for the social demands of his work. He was a rector who clearly preferred to sit in a bulldozer and oversee the construction of laboratories and classrooms than to spend time discussing the soundness of his choices for Lovanium. His antagonizing authoritarian paternalism came into full view around the celebration of the university's tenth anniversary. Gillon wanted a grandiose celebration. There would be bread, circuses, and fireworks to entertain the students, well-catered receptions for a host of prestigious guests, and three commemorative stamps to please philatelists in the Congo and abroad.[52] By contrast, student leaders thought that the anniversary should be an occasion to reflect on shortcomings, not to waste money on misplaced self-congratulations.

An anonymous pamphlet, widely distributed on campus, compared Gillon's plans to the flamboyant celebrations of the fiftieth anniversary of the Union Minière in Elisabethville in 1956—an event that Gillon had attended. Gillon's plans for Lovanium's anniversary shared many similarities with this precedent: "the same splendor, the same colonial atmosphere, and millions spent on charter planes and transporting visitors, on family members and fireworks."[53] It was the students' duty to oppose the rector's megalomania. It was their duty to publicly denounce Lovanium's fundamental colonial nature: its ambition to train "yes men" and its systematic suppression of any student who talked "about African unity, . . . about real and effective independence, and about authentically African leaders like Lumumba, Sékou Touré, Nkrumah, Ben Bella."[54] Protesting Gillon's plans for the anniversary of Lovanium brought out key convergences between campus and world politics. Students looked at the Inspired Hill as a microcosm where forces of decolonization played out similarly to the way that they did on the national and international stages. This view raised the stakes of their grievances against Gillon, but it also reflected their awareness that higher education was at a crossroads: it could either entrench neocolonial relations or help fulfill the promises of independence and emancipation.

When they discussed these points, the members of Lovanium's board considered that the students' politically laden tone delegitimized them. For instance, Albert Ndele, a prominent member of the board who also served as the director of the national bank, believed that the anonymous pamphlet against Gillon showed how immature the students remained and how easily they were manipulated by cynical politicians.[55] Ndele did not see any reason to downscale the celebration. He continued to side with other members of the board in believing that they could make a small concession by canceling the fireworks. As was to be expected, this measure did little for student frustrations, and on the day of the ceremony, protesters welcomed Gillon's distinguished guests with insults and jibes.[56]

Soon after the tenth anniversary, Benoît Verhaegen, a professor of political science at the university, gave a very well-attended talk on campus. Verhaegen was a radical critic of Gillon and of the status quo on campus. To him, Lovanium was not African, not democratic, and also not a real university. Although his talk detailed this critique of the institution, it also argued that students were similarly part of the problem: years of conditioning in Catholic boarding schools had meant that they entered the university "totally sterilized culturally and intellectually, and therefore totally aseptic to revolutionary ideas."

Verhaegen himself was a man of paradoxes. A self-proclaimed Catholic Marxist, he had volunteered as a young man to fight with the Belgian army in the Korean War. Yet, he seemed to find no excuses for the contradictions he saw at play between the students' rhetorical radicality and their continuous abidance to the ethos of the defunct Belgian-Congolese community. Known for his sharp tongue, Verhaegen did not disappoint when he concluded that "Lovanium students are not even denied their freedom of expression, since they have nothing personal or authentic left to express."[57] This was a harsh judgment, but many students in the audience took it as a call for action. A few weeks after the talk, in March 1964, during an extraordinary general assembly, AGEL's new president, Hubert Makanda, declared that students were past the point of polite discussions with the academic authorities, and "the time of resistance and violence starts now."[58]

The same Makanda launched the first successful strike at Lovanium. It was organized as a military operation, with designated "generals" who swore an oath to the student revolution and coordinated a campus blockade, marches, and occupations of administrative buildings. On the morning of the strike's first day, Father Edouard Liétard, the head of student dorms and restaurants, saw that students had blocked all entry points to the campus. Puzzled, he went to Gillon's office to share the news. "The rector immediately sensed that it was serious. I remember very well how struck I felt by the gravity of his reaction," he told me when we met in 2010.[59] While Liétard and Gillon were discussing, a group of students was standing on the other side of the door, planning to take over the rector's office. Pierre Lenoir, Gillon's assistant, physically interposed himself. Tensions quickly mounted and "the whole thing nearly boiled over," as Yvon Bongoy, one of AGEL's leaders recalled during an interview. Ultimately, Makanda convinced everybody to leave the building.[60] Meanwhile, Gillon cabled Malengreau, Lovanium's liaison in Belgium, and asked him to fly to Leopoldville on the very same day so that he could be present at the negotiations with the student strike team. That evening, Makanda gathered the students in the quadrangle between the student dorms known as Lovanium's Red Square. He summed up the students' demands: comanagement of the institution, better living conditions on campus, better judgment in the selection of the faculty, and democratization of the university.

Makanda did not only talk about AGEL's political platform (the three Ds—decolonization, democratization, and decentralization), but he also mentioned the food at Lovanium, forcefully arguing that students "could no longer accept a diet not even worthy of dogs."[61] One of the starting points of the strike had indeed been the university dining hall's frequent serving of Flemish blood sausages (boudin). In most of my discussions with former Lovanium students, they praised the quality of the food there (the living standards of the 1960s compare well with later periods, after a decline in campus life set in), and they struggled to explain how discontent about one specific dish could have played such an important role in the strike. Every time this point was raised, it provoked laughs and smiles. "We didn't like boudin," said José Ndundu, who was a first-year student in Romance languages in 1964. "We didn't like it. I don't know why, but we didn't like boudin. We liked all the rest, even the scrambled eggs. . . . But later, I think, ten years later, we came to miss the food at Lovanium: the catering was really well done."[62] At Lovanium, the students' shared loathing of blood sausages, a typical Belgian dish considered to be a delicacy by many missionaries and expatriate faculty, created unity and cohesion among the Congolese students. These young men came from all parts of this immense country and liked to tease each other about culinary oddities and taboos. They might well have viewed boudin as simply another quirky dish had it not been also a symbol of an enduring colonialism.

The quality of the food offered on campus symbolized the work of social differentiation that students expected from higher education. Perceived discrepancies between the promises of university education and what Lovanium actually delivered angered students. Food brought together the personal and the political in a way that few other issues did so clearly. It notably connected to the self-image of the students as confident and flirtatious young men of the world. Many Lovaniards, riding university buses for weekly visits to the cités, indeed used their food coupons and access to university dining halls to win over the women they met there.

Seven days after the beginning of the strike, a tripartite commission composed of AGEL delegates, professors, and members of the board was created to review student demands. In return, AGEL agreed to stop the strike. The commission met every day for a week, but students walked out when they realized that the administration would never accept one of their key demands: involving AGEL in the selection of any new member to the board. No agreement had been reached, but student leaders felt that it would be impossible to start the strike again.[63] Two weeks after its spectacular initial outbreak, the student revolution had fizzled out.

Although the strike created no immediate changes in university governance, it entered the annals of student politics as a major success because of Makanda's mobilization of the entire student body and because Gillon had agreed to the principle of negotiating with AGEL. Students had a seat at the table, and this emboldened them. As Professor Bongoy later recalled, students from his generation, who grew up under colonialism, had internalized the idea that "deference was automatically due to powerful people like Monsignor Gillon." Standing up to the rector and arguing against his vision for Lovanium was transformative.[64]

Defiance did not recede with the end of the strike. The open hostilities had stopped, but no truce had been signed. To rebuild relations with the students, Lovanium hired Albert Mpase as general secretary for student affairs. Mpase had studied in Kisantu and then in Belgium in the 1950s. He served on the General Commissioners Committee that ruled the Congo after Lumumba's "neutralization" in 1960 and was a close friend of General Joseph Mobutu (see chapter 5). He also connected well with students, and his interpersonal skills helped deescalate several tense situations.[65] Nevertheless, AGEL remained committed to a combative affirmation of student power. In February 1965, it adopted a new charter around the idea that students should act as "intellectual workers animated by the faith and desire to free themselves and their country from any kind of alienation."[66] Despite Mpase's efforts to appease the students, it seemed certain that this discourse would sooner or later produce new moments of open confrontation.

Conclusion

Soon after the strike, Monsignor Malula replaced the outgoing Belgian archbishop of Leopoldville, Félix Scalais, as president of Lovanium's board. Placing a Congolese national in such a key position, the university showed its readiness to embrace a politics of comanagement and Africanization.[67] This was a concession to the student movement, and as such, it probably cost Gillon. The rector dismissed the students' call to decolonize the university as the manifestation of an infantile disorder cropping up across all of Africa. He believed that student radicals had a strategy for taking power in three steps: first, they would try to dominate student life, then they would seek to impose their views on the university leadership, and finally they would aim to seize control of the whole country. According to Gillon, the incident around student baptism was merely the first step; the strike, the second; and if left unopposed, AGEL would probably soon move to the last step and clash with the state. This vision of student politics resonated among many members of the board. Joseph Iléo, a former prime minister, proclaimed that it would be better to shut down Lovanium than "to abandon power" to the students.[68]

Gillon could be condescending. His insinuation that students were being manipulated by politicians or blindly followed the global trend of youth protests was unfair. However, students did relate to people, events, and schools of thought outside the campus. Opening up the Inspired Hill to various horizons was itself a form of resistance. In doing so, students irremediably smashed the Belgian dreams of loyal and obedient Congolese university graduates. They very much acted as the "rabble rousers" that Salkin and other opponents to academic education, discussed in the previous chapter, had fantasized about in the 1920s.

Although the student revolution of 1964 did not succeed in radically transforming Lovanium, it produced an enduring political agenda for further protests around the "three Ds." This agenda resonated with the broader antisystemic passions of the time.[69] But the students also defended a certain gendered and classed idea of themselves. The racism of Belgian professors, the clericalism of the administration, and the censorship of campus folklore posed a threat to this idea. As the nation's elite, students felt entitled to various material gratifications. They viewed themselves as cosmopolitan young men, who were equally nurtured by political discussion groups and the sociability of the rumba. The masculinity they sought to embody was both respectable and defiant. A confidence, even cheekiness, modeled by those among themselves who knew how to dance, how to dress, and how to talk to women, was key in enabling their opposition to the institution. Against Gillon's paternalism, the students defended a collective identity that was anchored both in the vernacular and the cosmopolitan and that also informed how they engaged with the broader world.

To my knowledge, Paul Kabongo Wa Misasa and Kalixte Mukendi Wa Nsanga never met. Yet they lived through a set of related experiences as young, politically active men of the decolonization era. Both embodied the transition from the age of insulated letter writers in the 1950s to the turbulence and new mobilities of the 1960s. They entered into activism around the same moment in 1959 and both lived the lives of revolutionary nomads.

Kabongo grew up in Luluabourg, the son of a successful Luba trader and owner of a popular bar (Joseph Mobutu was a regular during his years at the local military academy). In April 1959, passionate about the struggle for independence that was finally taking off, the sixteen-year-old Kabongo attended a Congress of the Congolese National Movement (MNC) in his hometown. He then decided to abandon everything and follow Patrice Lumumba in Leopoldville. Becoming a permanent fixture at the national headquarters of the MNC, the teenager became something of an adopted son to Lumumba.[1]

The following year, the MNC sent Kabongo to Brazzaville, and Lumumba asked his friend Luis Lopez Alvarez to look after him.[2] Studying at Lopez's Institut d'Etudes Politiques in the capital of the former French Congo, Kabongo encountered many people active in local left groups. In July 1963, he took an active role in the street protests that ousted President Fulbert Youlou from power. Soon after that, he traveled to Moscow as a student, but he quickly became frustrated about what he perceived as a lack of interest for Africa on the part of the Soviets, and he used his contacts with Chinese diplomats in Warsaw to reach Albania. Once in Tirana, he demanded to be treated as a political leader and to study a tailor-made university curriculum in French. Six months later, the Albanians began complaining that Kabongo was spending all his time at the Ghanaian embassy and that he showed no desire to study. "Nothing good can be expected of him," a bureaucrat wrote in a report.[3] Kabongo himself seemed frustrated with the material conditions in Tirana and he told friends that he was thinking about moving to Paris. Events in Central Africa interfered with this plan. After the Simba rebels captured a huge swath of eastern Congo, Kabongo's Lumumbist contacts asked him to come back and take a position as an intelligence officer in the rebellion's Armée Populaire de Libération.[4] His career in the rebellion was rather brief. When the counterinsurgency took back Stanleyville at the end of 1964, Kabongo drifted across communities of exiles, landing successfully in Bujumbura, Kampala, Juba, and Cairo. Then came Paris, a part-time job for the magazine *Jeune Afrique* and an enrollment at the Sorbonne.[5] Lopez Alvarez had put him in touch with the stage director Jean-Marie Serreau, a renowned figure in French third-worldist theater. Serreau offered Kabongo a room in his Parisian apartment, together with a role in his next project: the first French production of Aimé Césaire's theater play about Lumumba's assassination, *Une saison au Congo*. Serreau staged the play at the Théâtre de l'Est Parisien in October 1967, with Kabongo cast as Okito, one of the two politicians assassinated together with Lumumba.[6] May 1968 found the young Congolese on the barricades and coincided with the beginning of his romance with a French Maoist graduate student. Not long after, however, Kabongo relocated to Algiers. Other expatriates provided companionship in his North African exile, but these would be rather difficult years.[7]

Wa Nsanga's trajectory was eventful in its own ways. He was an ethnic Luba like Kabongo, but his background was very different, since he was the son of a migrant worker employed at a refinery owned by the Union Minière du Haut-Katanga in Jadotville. A bright student, Wa Nsanga was admitted to Lovanium in 1958. However, he immediately disliked the uptight atmosphere on the Inspired Hill and instead gravitated to Leopoldville's epicurean nightlife. "Like most boys at the time, I was mostly intent on life, the beautiful ladies of the Congo and ambiance," he later recalled. Politics was never far from the dance floors of Leopoldville, and Wa Nsanga was "a young fellow who sought the

company of his elders and wanted to learn about the world."[8] He min-
gled with foreign journalists and diplomats who were eager to connect
with sociable young Congolese like himself. A visiting journalist for the
Frankfurter Allgemeine who featured Wa Nsanga in an article described
him as an "extremely intelligent young man" who could quote Leibniz or
Voltaire. The piece also had the secretary of the West German embassy
on record as saying that Wa Nsanga had given him "the best analysis
of national politics he had ever heard from a Congolese."[9] While Wa
Nsanga socialized with politicians from his home province of Katanga
and drove them around in a female cousin's Opel whenever they visited
Leopoldville, his conversion to politics, as he called it, took him toward
yet another group: the young nationalists who, like Kabongo, orbited
around Lumumba. A decisive encounter took place at the beginning of
January 1959, on the eve of the riots that deeply shook Leopoldville.
Sitting at the famous O.K. bar in the district of Ruwet, Wa Nsanga chat-
ted with a young man of his age, Antoine Tshimanga (the student we
encountered in chapter 3 who was bullied by his Latin teacher because of
his communist sympathies). Speaking about the future of the Congo and
the world, the two young men hopped from one bar to another. Before
the cock crowed, Wa Nsanga agreed to join the youth organization that
Tshimanga had recently set up.

A year and half later, in the context of the coup against Lumumba,
as the police were rounding up young radical activists throughout Leopoldville, Wa Nsanga was among those arrested. Whereas several of his
comrades were later put to death, the West German embassy interceded
on behalf of Wa Nsanga. He was released and lived. Within a day of his
release, he boarded a plane for Europe with a scholarship to continue his
education at the University of Cologne. He learned about Lumumba's
murder while undergoing an accelerated German-language immersion
in Bavaria. The news shocked him profoundly. Before that, despite his
companionship with Tshimanga and other young nationalists, Wa Nsanga
sometimes expressed doubts about Lumumba's value as a leader. Now
he realized that the former prime minister had been a precursor and an
exceptional figure all along, and he felt committed to help make his vision for the Congo come true. The Simba and Mulelist rebellions' embrace of Lumumba's memory rejoiced him. "The dead Lumumba plays
the role among his people that his murderers did not let him play during
his lifetime," he wrote about the insurrections in 1964, at a time when
he was himself quickly moving toward the left.[10] He soon emerged as an
influential student leader and the main figure behind a clandestine Maoist

organization. An American student who met him at an event in Cologne around that time described him in the following terms: "tall and bearded, self-proclaimed scientific socialist, extreme left, articulate and fairly intelligent, dangerous."[11]

Despite frequent travels to attend political meetings and long nights spent writing pamphlets, Wa Nsanga was a much more diligent student in Cologne than he had been at Lovanium; and in 1968, he received a doctoral degree in geology. By contrast, Kabongo passed through many schools in Brazzaville, Moscow, Tirana, Paris, and Algiers but never graduated. This divergence in their paths was a reflection of a changing student landscape. Independence had enlarged the road to school described earlier in this book. Higher education was no longer confined to a few young men who were granted a place after having toiled away in seminaries and elite secondary schools. Thus, new types of students appeared: some were older, and others received fellowships from political parties or studied at nonuniversity institutions. Despite the differences in their academic trajectories, both Kabongo and Wa Nsanga were representative of a new student generation. It is the emergence of this generation—more politicized, more impatient, in tune with the cadence of a quickly changing world—that is the topic of the next three chapters.

When I interviewed Kabongo in Kinshasa in 2011 and Wa Nsanga in Nouakchott in 2016, both men offered precious insights into the circumstances that had determined their politics. They were, however, certainly not immune to the retrospective projection of coherence that comes up in all biographical interviews.[12] Kabongo and I talked over a bottle of wine at a restaurant located steps away from the Lumumba family's residence and patronized by people active in business and politics. His loud tirades attracted the attention of other parties in the restaurant. At some point, he provocatively stated that only the children of the rich like himself could really be on the left. Elaborating the point, he stated that his family's wealth ensured that he was immune to the lure of profit when he had joined Lumumba half a century earlier, whereas the same could not be said of the people who were now moving through the circles of power.[13] The bitterness was easy to understand: after he moved to Madrid from Algiers in the mid-1970s, Kabongo served as a representative for Laurent-Désiré Kabila's Party for the Popular Revolution and he was a cadre in the Alliance des Forces Démocratiques de Libération (AFDL), the rebel coalition led by the same Kabila that routed Mobutu in 1996. When Kabila became president, he chose Kabongo as the head of the new national state security agency but had him removed and briefly sent to jail a few months later.[14]

Kabongo later returned to the president's good graces and served successively as ambassador to Algeria and as governor of the Kasai. However, like several other historical figures of the AFDL, he was looked over during the rule of Joseph Kabila, Laurent-Désiré's son and successor (see the preface). Speaking loudly about his left credentials in a busy restaurant at the center of Kinshasa's government district, Kabongo set himself apart from people he saw as opportunists without the proper political pedigree.

The mood was different with Wa Nsanga. Nouakchott was a long way from Kinshasa, and distance diluted the somber humors that haunted Kabongo. Wa Nsanga had been away from the Congo for all of his adult life, bar the few years he spent in Lubumbashi in the early 1970s, when he got married and worked as a researcher at the National University. In 1974, he moved to the United States as a visiting professor at the University of Massachusetts in Amherst.[15] He stayed there for six years before relocating to Mauritania as a USAID-funded geological expert. Around the same time, a car accident in which several fellow passengers were killed brought him back toward religion. During my stay in Nouakchott, he insisted on taking me to the Catholic Cathedral of Saint Joseph where he served as a member of the parish council.[16] Our conversations about his student activism ran for hours, but he looked at these years from an intellectual vantage that differed from the intransigent Maoism of his youth.

Kabongo and Wa Nsanga related in contrasted ways to their youth, but they both presented personal aspirations, individual worth, elective affinities, and chosen kinships as factors that guided their journeys through the world. Even if subsequent events filtered their recollections of the 1960s, the stories they shared expressed the subjectivity of the early postcolonial student left. Many students had then felt connected to the revolutionary spirit of independence, when, from one day to the other, realities could be overturned. These were uncertain times, and to many, activism made sense in relation to personal dispositions like courage and curiosity. Kabongo presented his younger years as a journey toward worldliness, one marked by his ability to construct a singular political persona at the intersection of successive chosen kinships—with striking father figures: Lumumba, Lopez, Serreau, Césaire. In Wa Nsanga's narrative, the anti-colonial struggle and the left appeared as an ambiance, both in the word's specific Congolese meaning (indexing urbanity and hedonism, love and joie de vivre, beer and dance) and in its organicist definition (something that "permeates space and time" and "bursts equally out of the universe and of ourselves").[17] Kabongo and Wa Nsanga emphasized trajectories that are shaped by a sense of free will. They talked of left politics as a matter of conviction and as a matter of temperament. Their affective relation to politics evoked regional traditions of mobilization that valued individualism, distinction, and the ability to operate at the frontier of multiple systems of knowledge.[18] And the stories they told about the 1960s resonated with histories of self-making of a longer duration.[19]

FIVE
COLD WAR TRANSCRIPTS

Most of the students I talked with did not like Lumumba although they approved of a national rather than a tribal party to lead the Congo....Above all, the students at Louvanium [*sic*] thought that he was irresponsible and lacked even a basic education....Most of the students ... do not take an active part in national political activity. Instead they have a very elitist attitude (probably justified) and prefer to spend their time laughing at the ministers and their inability to speak French.

James Scott, "Report by NSA Representative on Louvanium [*sic*] University,"
July 1960, p. 6, USNSA International Commission, Box 187, HIA

Finally, I believe that the notion of a hidden transcript helps us understand those rare moments of political electricity when, often for the first time in memory, the hidden transcript is spoken publicly and openly in the teeth of power.

James Scott, *Domination and the Arts of Resistance*, xiii

In the 1980s, the politicians who remained in Mobutu's entourage despite the president's mercurial temper were locally nicknamed the dinosaurs. Joseph N'Singa was one of the most immovable of these political animals. When he first met Mobutu in 1961, N'Singa was president of the student government at Lovanium. As a student leader, he knew everyone in Leopoldville's political establishment, but few figures impressed him more than Mobutu. When the general staged the coup that brought him to power four years later, N'Singa was among his early supporters. He occupied key positions in government over the following decades, including prime minister. His influence was particularly strong on the regime's security services. Maybe not incidentally, a persistent rumor asserted that his mother was the president's main féticheuse.[1] At any rate, N'singa's personal fortune had been tied to the late dictator in deep lasting ways, and he gladly shared anecdotes about this time in his life when I interviewed him in 2010. I was surprised, however, that when I asked questions about Patrice Lumumba, N'Singa began to talk faster, with even more animation and excitement than in his answers about his long companionship with Mobutu.[2]

N'Singa and several other students from Lovanium were in the audience at the independence ceremony in Leopoldville's Palace of the Nation on June 30, 1960. They all enthusiastically cheered when Lumumba famously responded to King Baudouin's glorification of colonialism with a bombastic allocution centered on the suffering of the Congolese people under Belgian rule. Lumumba's intransigent words resonated strongly with them: "We were the revolutionary avant-garde, so, for us, that speech—it was what politics should be."[3]

Talking about Lumumba brought N'Singa back to the exhilarating time of his student years—a period in his life with fewer moral compromises and lighter responsibilities than the decades he spent getting his hands dirty for Mobutu. Yet, the idea that students were naturally drawn toward Lumumba is problematic, even if other interviewees echoed N'Singa's presentation of students as natural-born revolutionaries and even if commentators at the time believed that the more Lumumba radicalized his positions, the more he appealed to the youth.[4] The student movement only moved toward the left after Lumumba's death. In 1960, despite its growing caucus of turbulent Ata Ndelists, Lovanium counted no more than a handful of active leftist students. A so-called nationalist student bloc sent a protest telegram to the United Nations in February 1961, but leftist groups on campus have otherwise not left any traces.[5] Belgian propaganda had convinced many young educated Congolese that évolué politicians demanded immediate independence because they lacked academic credentials and feared that university students would soon be in a position to take the rightful leadership of the country.[6]

In September 1960, less than two months after having applauded Lumumba's independence speech, N'Singa welcomed Mobutu's initiative to endorse the prime minister's removal from office. Responding to pressures from Belgium and the United States, Mobutu replaced Lumumba's government with a team of "apolitical experts" composed of university students and recent graduates. These young "technicians" were charged with putting an end to the alleged communist infiltrations under Lumumba that Western powers had denounced with insistence. Mobutu's move violated the constitution, but at least the colonel had not given the keys to the state to "just anybody"; he had given them to "university men like us," N'Singa reminisced. "And it was better to have such people in power than old guys who had only completed a few years of primary schooling."[7]

This chapter untangles ambiguities and contradictions in the students' relation to power. Although an elitist mindset led some to advocate the suppression of the nationalist camp in 1960, the death of Lumumba and complex Cold War dynamics later pushed others to reinvent themselves as champions of the same nationalist camp. The institutionalization of student politics coincided with a period of reconfiguration in power relations, as the Congo was moving away from formal colonialism, but facing new forces of domination largely in keeping with Cold War rivalries. To account for the fluidity of this moment, I bring together disparate voices and archives throughout the chapter. One character is the political scientist and anthropologist James C. Scott, who as a leader in the United States National Student Association (USNSA) directly intervened in Congolese student politics in the early 1960s. When he visited Lovanium just a few days after the ceremonies of independence in July 1960, Scott did not seek to meet with the "revolutionary avant-garde." He had come to connect with students of a different kind: reasonable, articulate, and little disposed to follow "extremist" positions. N'Singa's excitement about Lumumba's speech would have made Scott unsure about his value, but the young Congolese support for Mobutu's coup in September would probably have reassured him.

Scott's later works as a scholar have shaped understandings of state domination and subaltern resistance across several fields. In a book about infrapolitics, he famously called to approach scenes of power through the restitution of complex transcripts—in the sense of "a complete record of what was said," both openly and behind closed doors.[8] The Congolese drama as it is depicted in these pages does not fully respond to Scott's clear-cut categories of domination and resistance. The notion of an expended transcript, however, is relevant. Many actors in the drama—including Scott and his USNSA comrades—had reasons to hide agendas and opinions. Dissimulation was at different junctures a necessity for Congolese students as well. But what was at stake for many of them was to emancipate themselves from the type of moderation so much valued by Scott in 1960. Thus they slowly built the conditions for "a moment of political electricity" and for a confrontation with forces that were blocking the process of emancipation outlined by Lumumba and other anti-colonial prophets.[9]

Expertise, Nationalism, Extraversion

Few students embraced political competition before independence. Justin-Marie Bomboko, a central figure in the Congolese student community in Belgium, even felt a duty to warn the public about the dangers of electoral politics when he visited his hometown of Coquilhatville in August 1959. Speaking at a public meeting, Bomboko sought to convince his audience not to be lured by "the ideas of democracy, elections, and [immediate] independence."[10] This rejection of politics proved untenable, and in the first place to Bomboko himself. In January 1960, only a few months after his visit to Coquilhatville, he negotiated the terms of the Congo's independence together with a couple dozen other politicians at a roundtable conference in Brussels; in May of the same year, he ran a successful campaign in the Congo's first parliamentary elections; and at the end of June, he became the minister of foreign affairs in Lumumba's coalition government. Whereas Bomboko's initial antipolitical instincts did not resist the fast pace of decolonization, many students continued to criticize democracy, which they saw as constantly at risk of sliding toward demagoguery.[11] Expertise, to these students, seemed a more solid foundation for nation building. They felt confident in their ability to guide the country as universitaires and hoped that politicians would have the wisdom to seek their advice.

Students shared a general uneasiness with regionalism. Safe for Lumumba's Mouvement National Congolais (MNC) and a few other formations, most political parties presented themselves as mouthpieces for ethnically defined constituencies and tended to support federalist or confederalist approaches. By contrast, students generally believed in the idea of a unified Congo, even if some also acted as advocates and brokers for their ethnoregional communities of origin.[12] A strong distaste for factionalism dominated on campuses, and certainly at Lovanium. Even Paul Malimba, a close friend of the confederalist leader Moïse Tshombe, vocally favored unitarism when he headed the Lovanium student government in the year before independence.[13] Students respected the "cultural values of each tribe," but still viewed the nation as a superior entity.[14] As Scott noted when he visited Lovanium, even the students who disapproved of Lumumba's electoral populism agreed with his nationalist and unitarist orientations.[15]

From university campuses, students looked beyond the factionalism of the present. Cementing friendships with peers from all around the country and beyond and accumulating knowledge, students felt that they were concretely building the future of the Congo. Their anti-parochialism directly determined this attachment to the time of the nation. They felt immune to the centrifugal forces in the Congo because they viewed decolonization as a movement for a broader liberation, as a quest to "restore the dignity of the Black man" and re-humanize the world.[16] When they took the streets of Kinshasa for the first time, it was to protest the massacre of sixty-nine Black South Africans in the township of Sharpeville in March 1960.[17] At a moment when political parties were fighting to gain control of a soon-to-be independent Congo, their protest underlined the internationalist and Pan-Africanist vocation of the anti-colonial struggle.

Greater international mobility only increased this tendency to look at nation building through the lens of world politics. By June 1960, eighty Congolese were studying in foreign universities, but their numbers soared a few weeks later, when independence created opportunities for hundreds to study in Belgium, Czechoslovakia, France, the Soviet Union, and the United States.[18] Expatriate Congolese took part in conferences, political rallies, and youth congresses abroad. In Belgium, they attended meetings at Les Amis de Présence Africaine, a club that organized talks with luminaries like Léopold Senghor, Aimé Césaire, Mario de Andrade, Richard Wright, Cheikh Anta Diop, Edouard Glissant, and Alioune Diop.[19] This club and others like it encouraged key conversations about culture, politics, Pan-Africanism, the third world, human rights, and socialism.

Expatriate students gained insights and developed networks that made them valuable to Congolese politicians.[20] In January 1960, when eighty Congolese delegates made the trip to Brussels to attend a roundtable conference about the future of the Congo convened by the Belgian government, students organized an informal welcoming committee and convinced the delegates to create a common front in the negotiations. This strategy panned out, and the Congolese bloc began the conference by forcing the Belgians to agree to endorse the formal end of the colonial regime and to organize the transition of power within a few months. The students' intervention proved fateful for the Congo's independence. Yet, their extraverted dispositions hurt Congolese interests when the Belgians convened a second roundtable conference to negotiate the practical realities of separation. Congolese politicians, busy with parliamentary elections scheduled at the same moment, mandated students to represent them at this conference. These students found themselves unable to stand up to the squad of Belgian experts facing them, including academics under whom they had studied. A few politicians criticized the students for having been unable to escape the spell of their Belgian intellectual formation.[21] However, many did not pay attention to a conference they viewed as purely technical, not realizing that students had agreed to dispositions that would jeopardize Congolese economic independence for years to come.[22]

Lovanium against Lumumba

Lumumba did not openly criticize the delegates at the second roundtable conference, but his relations with students and academics were sometimes tense. In January 1960, when Benoît Verhaegen opened an adult education school for Congolese cadres with funding from the Ford Foundation, Lumumba noticed that the Lovanium professor recruited a dozen politicians who had opposed his rise within the MNC as members of the new institute's board. Lumumba similarly frowned upon the arrival of several professors from Lovanium (including Verhaegen) who came to work as advisers to ministers from rival parties in the coalition government he formed in June.[23] A few weeks later, a state official read on the radio a letter from a mysterious Association of Intellectual Youth that denounced a secret meeting to remove Lumumba from office, supposedly organized by Monsignor Luc Gillon at Lovanium.[24] This gathering likely never happened, but Lumumba found the rumor credible, and it reinforced his conviction of the Inspired Hill's hostility.[25]

Gillon certainly had reasons to want Lumumba gone. Lumumba and Pierre Mulele, the minister of education, had made clear that they intended to nationalize Lovanium.[26] This threat worried church officials at the Vatican, and Cardinal Grégoire-Pierre Agagianian, the prefect of the Sacred Congregation for the Propagation of the Faith, advocated for the replacement of Gillon with a non-Belgian rector who could placate Lumumba. The papal nuncio in Leopoldville agreed with Agagianian. Although the nuncio regarded "Lumumba with the uttermost scorn" and did not want to offer him a political victory, he believed replacing Gillon was a necessary evil to keep Lovanium under the control of the church.[27] With his usual energy, Gillon worked extremely hard to save his head. Early in August, he traveled to New York and secured $500,000 worth of grants from the Rockefeller and Ford Foundations, funds that the university needed to remain afloat in this troubled period. Soon after his return to Leopoldville, he asked to meet with Lumumba and Mulele to change their minds about the nationalization project.[28] In parallel, he also lobbied President Joseph Kasa-Vubu to oppose Lumumba's plans. The rector was one of the several Catholic officials—including most notably Monsignor Joseph Malula—who preached about the dangerous path taken by Lumumba to the former seminarian Kasa-Vubu. These church figures added to the efforts of the American, British, and French diplomatic emissaries who talked to the president about the urgent need to "neutralize" the prime minister. The conjunction of these pressures led to Kasa-Vubu's decision to recall Lumumba on September 5.[29] Quite tellingly, when he denounced Kasa-Vubu's measure as unconstitutional, Lumumba accused Lovanium's students of having orchestrated the smear campaign that led to his revocation.[30]

Mobutu intervened a week later, reinforcing Kasa-Vubu's position and making it difficult for Lumumba to regain control.[31] His intervention was half of a coup. Instead of taking control of the government, Mobutu appealed to the country's young intellectuals to take power from the hands of the politicians, contrasting the superior technical knowledge of the former with the carelessness and destructive abuse of power of the latter. This was a surprising card to pull but one that made sense to Mobutu. At thirty years old, he was close in age to the students (he was fifteen years younger than Kasa-Vabu and five years younger than Lumumba).[32] He had widely networked in student circles when he worked for the colonial information service in Belgium between 1958 and 1960. Speaking in June 1958 to the Congress of the Colonial Press in Brussels, he had advocated that university training be offered to Black journalists.[33] He himself took classes in sociology. Although rumors alleged that the Belgian secret services paid him to report on Congolese expatriates, many students looked up to him.[34]

Three dozen "university men," several of whom had taken part in the Brussels roundtable conference, responded positively to Mobutu's call in September 1960. Operating in a legal limbo, they created a substitute government known as the College of General Commissioners. Bomboko, who had cosigned the act revoking Lumumba from office, served as its president. Members included both recent graduates and students who had not yet completed their degrees. Ambiguities about the exact attributions of the college sometimes strained its relations with Mobutu.[35] It was not clear what level of control the college could aspire to with the colonel acting as his own man, not to mention the two provinces under secession, the dissident Lumumbist government in Stanleyville, and the multi-tentacled United Nations operation that all made the college's claims to imperium theoretical in many domains.[36]

Restoration became the main mission of the college. Early on, Bomboko had announced that the college would preserve the Congo from "communist colonialism" and "Marxist-Leninist imperialism."[37] Even though Lumumba had broken diplomatic relations with Belgium in July, the commissioners attached themselves to the former colonizer. Again, several Lovanium professors, including Verhaegen, served as advisers. And both the representative of the Belgian Sûreté and the Central Intelligence Agency (CIA) chief of station reportedly attended each of the college's daily meetings.[38]

The anti-Lumumbism of the college was visceral, but despite Bomboko's declarations, it was more existential than ideological. After MNC activists attacked members of the college with machetes during a street brawl, the equation seemed simple to the commissioners: it was them or the Lumumbists. Only a "total purging of everything that was Lumumbist," they thought, could guarantee their safety.[39] At the end of the day, what their opponents described as a regime of terror that sanctioned kidnapping, tortures, rapes, and assassinations came to define the student commissioners' short tenure in power.[40] One victim was Lumumba himself. Early on, the commissioners pestered Mobutu with requests to have Lumumba arrested, with the intention of putting him on trial for his alleged responsibility in the massacres committed by the national army during its campaign against the secession of South Kasai in August 1960. Ultimately, Mobutu himself came to play an active role in "neutralizing" Lumumba, while the Belgian and American secret services acted diligently behind the scenes with various plans to assassinate the independence leader. The college knew of these plans, and several commissioners helped with the fateful prisoner transfer to Katanga that cost Lumumba and two of his close allies, Maurice Mpolo and Joseph Okito, their lives on January 17, 1961.[41]

Lumumba Protests

The Congo crisis had been one of the most defining events in the "year of Africa," and the news of Lumumba's death (announced by Katanga officials several weeks after the fact in February 1961) caused a truly global conflagration that affected international relations.[42] People around the world castigated Belgian imperialism for masterminding Lumumba's assassination, but many voices also denounced the Congolese "traitors" who had worked with the "enemies of Africa."[43] In the eyes of nationalist politicians in the Congo, these traitors included the commissioners. And because the college had been established as a government of intellectuals, its actions reverberated on the educated youth in its entirety.[44] Yet, not all young people approved of the part played by the commissioners in the drama of the Congo crisis.

Lumumba's brutal assassination exposed the violence of neocolonialism and changed the worldviews of many students.[45] In Leopoldville, while repression had depleted the ranks of the nationalist left, students at a technical school organized one of the few rallies in the city that publicly mourned for Lumumba.[46] Scott, who then served as the vice president of the USNSA in charge of international affairs, was surprised by how much the event shocked and moved to the left one of his Congolese contacts in the United States—a student at Williams College who had previously defended conservative positions.[47] Like this student, many young educated Congolese took strong heed of the worldwide protests that, from Cairo to Harlem, Moscow, Paris, and Prague, denounced Lumumba's fate.[48] This global outrage imprinted itself powerfully on them. Many who had stayed away from politics began moving toward the cosmopolitan left at this moment. The intense international focus on their country affected how they understood the stakes of the present and their role as their nation's educated elite.

Congolese students in Belgium received news of the murder in a context marked by daily encounters with racism.[49] These personal experiences added to their feelings of revolt against Belgium's participation in Lumumba's murder. Working with left Belgian activists, they organized a street protest in Brussels—the first ever Congolese march in Belgium—and faced hostility from numerous name-calling bystanders.[50] Paul-Henri Kabayidi was one of the event's organizers; he had recently transferred from Lovanium to the University of Brussels. The Lumumba protest happened soon after the murder of his best friend, a young man named Emmanuel Nzuzi. Unlike Kabayidi himself, who had stayed away from party politics when he lived in Leopoldville, Nzuzi was a high-profile and rather impetuous member of a Lumumbist youth organization.[51] In September 1960, he had organized several illegal protests to demand that Lumumba be returned to power, and the police arrested him after the machete attack against the three general commissioners the following month. At the beginning of February 1961, the Leopoldville authorities organized his transfer, together with five other leaders of the Lumumbist movement, to the seceded province of South Kasai. Within hours of their arrival, in a macabre repetition of the treatment of Lumumba, Mpolo, and Okito two weeks earlier in Katanga, Nzuzi and his companions were tortured and put to death.[52] Before leaving Leopoldville, Kabayidi had often helped Nzuzi with writing statements and pamphlets, even if he disagreed with his friend's radical methods. Organizing the street rally in Brussels in February 1961 was a symbolic passing of the baton, and Kabayidi marched with Nzuzi's fate in mind.[53]

In the months that followed, political groups continued to use Lumumba's memory to mobilize students against neocolonialism. At the Free University of Brussels, a "Lumumba Club" was established to promote "fraternity among peoples," "authentic Congolese nationalism," and the "great revolution now breaking out everywhere in Africa."[54] The club's board included Belgian, Congolese, Haitian, Rwandese, and Senegalese students—some but not all of them close to the Belgian Communist Party.[55] At the end of April 1961, the club organized an "African nationalist day." Activities included the screening of a Chinese film on Lumumba, a debate on the anti-colonial struggle in Rwanda and Burundi, and a meeting with the Sudanese vice president of the Prague-based International Union of Students Hassan Bashir.[56] Several professors complained that the club compromised the university's reputation. One argued that honoring Lumumba was obscene and that any students who did so should move to Cairo.[57] The rector of the university agreed with these criticisms and refused all the club's requests to use university facilities, including for a planned symposium with Aimé Césaire in October 1961.[58] Although the club's activities dwindled after a couple of years, anniversaries of Lumumba's assassination remained key moments of political socialization at the Free University of Brussels. Belgian conservative students showed up during such a commemoration in 1963, throwing smoke bombs, breaking windows and furniture, and starting a fight that ended only after police intervention.[59] Some Congolese students later attempted to deescalate antagonisms by arguing that their Lumumbism was not anti-Belgian but anti-tribalist and pro-Congolese national unity.[60] By contrast, other students continued to celebrate Lumumba as a symbol of radical anti-colonial resistance.

The Lumumba days were commemorated every year throughout the world well beyond Brussels. These events reinforced relationships within communities of expatriate Congolese students, while creating opportunities to meet with other foreign students and activists. Socialization also happened over the mail: from Maoist militants in Somalia to anti-colonial activists in Guadeloupe, numerous organizations sent telegrams and letters to Congolese student groups to congratulate them on events commemorating Lumumba's memory and express their solidarity with the struggle of the Congolese people and "all the oppressed peoples in Africa, Asia, and Latin America."[61]

The shock of February 1961 durably transformed student politics. It reverberated to such an extent that when UNESCO surveyed political opinions among students in five African countries a few years later, support for "radical nationalism" appeared strongest in the Congo.[62] The launching of the General Union of Congolese Students (UGEC) in May 1961 was particularly instrumental in this transformation. UGEC emerged as a beacon of left nationalism and resistance to neocolonialism. But its origins lay elsewhere—in the context of the Cold War struggle for dominance over international student politics.

Starting in the late 1940s, the United States had showed its determination to counterbalance the advantage that the Soviet Union enjoyed in this field through its control of the Prague-based International Union of Students (IUS). To do so, the CIA developed an elaborate covert program that allocated generous financial resources to a series of front organizations, which it then activated against Soviet proxies. One such group was the liberal-leaning USNSA.[63] Through the USNSA, the CIA organized and controlled the Leiden-based Coordinating Secretariat of National Unions of Students (COSEC). Weaponized against the IUS, COSEC courted student leaders in the West European noncommunist left, but its priority was to battle communist influence in the developing world.

After Lovanium opened its doors in 1954, students there sought to affiliate themselves with COSEC. They attended several of its conferences in Chile, Nigeria, and India, but formal affiliation required the formation of a national student union. Belgian students at the University of Elisabethville initially opposed the idea of a "national" Congolese organization, but in 1959, they finally agreed to work with their Lovanium peers to create a National Union of Students of the Congo and Ruanda-Urundi (UNECRU).

Following the example of other similar organizations in the third world, UNECRU established formal contacts with both COSEC and the IUS, but its initiators were ideologically closer to the Western bloc.[64] The affinity was mutual: Cold War liberals were more than eager to monitor the developments of Congolese student activism.[65] As early as 1958, COSEC sent two officers to work in Leopoldville and Elisabethville to develop contacts with students in the two cities—the Kenyan student leader Isaac Omolo and the American activist and future political scientist Crawford Young.[66] And in July 1960, the USNSA dispatched James Scott for a one-week visit to Lovanium. Scott was a Williams College graduate with interests in Southeast Asia, development economics, and political science.

Some decades later, while referring to himself in the third person, he would describe 1960 as the year of "the cosmopolitanization of James Scott."[67] His trip to the Congo coincided with the end of his second semester as the American student association's representative in Paris. Only weeks later he would become the USNSA vice president. The report that Scott wrote after his visit in newly independent Congo commented on how UNECRU may behave in the conflict between COSEC and the IUS, an important consideration for determining the opportunity to extend financial support to the Congolese organization. The even more crucial aspect of Scott's mission concerned the assessments of individual Congolese student leaders. One UNECRU member struck Scott as "well oriented but not bright," another was "a little bit too Catholic oriented," yet another was "not so intelligent and carefree," and so forth. The rare bird was Venant Ngoie, a student who had recently secured a scholarship for a one-year study program in the United States: "He is the conservative, intelligent, French speaking African [whom] people have been looking for. A year in the States should do him a tremendous amount of good and we will be able to give him a closer look."[68]

The same type of character evaluation proceeded page after page in memos and reports on Congolese students composed over the following years by Scott and other American activists—many of whom had been briefed about the secret relationship between their student association and the CIA, with a few working directly as covert CIA agents. These USNSA officers showed up at Congolese student meetings in Leopoldville, Cologne, and Detroit. They talked over beer or coffee with young Congolese expatriates in Zurich, Los Angeles, and Brussels. They occasionally argued with their counterparts, questioning their definitions of imperialism and debating US policies in Africa. Yet, their goal was to let their Congolese contacts speak their minds and to collect any relevant observations (that a student's apartment "included an expensive radio-phonograph and several pictures of Lumumba," for instance).[69] The USNSA officers classified Congolese students according to three different categories: those they could work with (the moderates, the pro-West, a student who was "more like a Nigerian than a French African"), those they should worry about and try to undermine (the extremists, the Marxist-Leninists, the anti-Americans who remained "close-minded about us"), and those without any sort of leadership potential. Some students were deemed sophisticated, intelligent, dynamic, likable, and articulate; others were painted as naive, unreliable, shifty, not talkative, emotional, brutal, and "ideologically gelled." Young educated men were evaluating other young educated men, and an ideal of cosmopolitan masculinity unsurprisingly informed their judgments.

Few Congolese seem to have imagined that the anti-racist, liberal, pro–civil rights young Americans who were taking an interest in them worked so closely with the CIA.[70] In June 1964, the young Harvard graduate Duncan Kennedy noted with relief that students at a UGEC congress in Detroit had "heard nothing bad about us, and seemed very willing to believe that we are the good guys."[71] Many Congolese appreciated the attention they received from the American activists. The plane tickets, typewriters, and scholarships that came from the USNSA or COSEC (like those sent by the IUS and other communist-aligned organizations) were precious for a movement that remained resource-poor. The Congolese also recognized themselves and their aspirations to worldliness and cosmopolitanism in the USNSA mirror.

These aspirations were prominent features for the establishment of UGEC in 1961. From the very beginning, the Congolese Student Union presented itself as a response to the failure of the general commissioners. As Ernest Wamba, then a student at Kalamazoo College, would write later, the students who created the organization believed that they "could teach the older generation of those who crucified Lumumba how to breathe the new air of unity."[72] Henri Takizala, the first president of the new student union, had refused to participate in the college as commissioner for education.[73] Political divergences may have motivated his decision to stay away from the college and dedicate his time to student organizing, but he still shared many of the commissioners' views and certainly the idea that only students could stand above tribal considerations because university campuses were unique spaces that brought young people from all the regions of the country together. Like the commissioners, Takizala also evolved in a world in which US intelligence operatives pulled many strings, pushing for the assassination of Lumumba on the one side and helping launch a platform for Congolese nationalist students on the other.[74]

Takizala's frenetic travel schedule in the fall of 1960 influenced the thought process that led to the creation of UGEC. In less than four months, Takizala attended events organized by COSEC and the IUS in Belgium, Czechoslovakia, England, Germany, Iraq, Sweden, Switzerland, and Yugoslavia. He then traveled to the United States for a one-month tour that included various meetings (with NAACP leaders, CORE activists, Ford Foundation executives, Department of State officials, or Democrat senators like Hubert Humphrey and Chester Bowles), as well as a dozen presentations about the Congo crisis at various colleges. At Harvard, Takizala's talk attracted the largest crowd the local USNSA chapter had seen in a long time. Alexander Korns, a history major and USNSA officer, felt "terribly impressed" by Takizala's performance. He appreciated how Takizala handled a question on US race politics asked by "a pockmarked and bitter American negro," as well as his refreshing "plague on both houses attitudes" in addressing the political situation in Leopoldville. "This guy ought to be watched," Korns wrote to Scott. "He is the kind of fellow who could give truly responsible leadership not only to the Congolese students, but to the Congo itself."[75]

In the middle of this tour, Takizala set his mind on transforming UN-ECRU into a union that would bring together the Congolese studying at home and the growing number of their peers studying outside of the country. This would "make students in the Congo benefit from the experiences of those abroad while those abroad, in turn, would have a framework on which to relate their experiences with the fundamentally national interests in the Congo."[76]

When Takizala organized the founding congress of UGEC in May 1961, American students did not fail to encourage a movement that promised to "remain above factional rivalry." The USNSA tapped into its pot of CIA money to pay for plane tickets that allowed Congolese students in the United States, France, and Belgium to attend the congress. The event displayed the deep internationalist fabric of the new organization. In his opening speech, Takizala explained how contacts with student organizations in Algeria, Turkey, Japan, and diverse Latin American countries had been key to the process that led to the UGEC's creation, and he called on his peers to "prove to our African friends and to the entire world that you are definitively men of your times." He added, "Do not forget that the eyes of students from across the world are fixed on you. Do not disappoint the trust they have placed in you. And show to our people that, far from being bourgeois students, you are at their side, sharing their sorrows and their joys."[77]

Takizala called his peers to embrace an intransigent anti-colonial nationalism as a fulfillment of their international responsibility. Despite this kind of exhortation, UGEC did not break at once with the old rhetoric of responsibility and expertise (which so much reassured Scott, Korns, and other members of the USNSA leadership). This rhetoric, for instance, did clearly emerge when the union publicly endorsed Cyrille Adoula as new prime minister in August 1961. A former labor organizer, Adoula promised to work for reconciliation with Lumumba's supporters and to end the Katanga secession. But he also belonged to the Binza group and benefited from the CIA's largesse in his accession to power. The fact that UGEC threw its weight behind Adoula's coalition government must have delighted the USNSA.[78] However, the students' support for Adoula was not unconditional. When the prime minister's nationalist profession of faith unraveled, UGEC organized a protest rally in front of his residence to demand that he publicly reaffirm his commitment to force Katanga into line and denounce French and British enablers of the secession.[79] Antagonism grew over the following months. Students condemned the arrest of the Lumumbist leader Antoine Gizenga, and they battled to free labor organizers imprisoned by the government after a wave of wage protests.[80] As UGEC activists multiplied their contacts with opponents to Adoula, they also embraced more radical actions, culminating in a memorable street demonstration—once again, concerning the question of Katanga—during which students occupied and completely sacked the British embassy in Leopoldville.[81] A striking sign of the radicalizing tone among students appeared in their denunciation of Adoula's dependence on the United States, as a symptom of an "imperialist cancer that threatened to kill the Congo."[82]

The USNSA did not necessarily mind this anti-imperialist rhetoric. During a visit to Leopoldville in 1963, Korns approvingly commented on UGEC's "impressively principled approach of international problems." His Congolese interlocutors brought up "early US anti-Lumumba interference," but they also publicly protested against "racist incidents in Prague against African students there."[83] A few Congolese students maintained this neutralist line through the following years: they placed imperialists from the West on par with imperialists from the East and presented their nationalism as a contribution to a "world civilization of man."[84] Yet, the balance of student indignation increasingly tilted toward a focus on US interventionism—with the Gulf of Tonkin incident in Vietnam and the counterinsurgency campaign against the Simba rebellion in eastern Congo being two ominous moments in this development. Despite their willingness to show flexibility in the face of criticism, American Cold War liberals were losing Congolese students.

The shift in student political sensibilities appeared with clarity at the second congress of UGEC in August 1963. Delegates from across the Congo, Europe, and America attended. Photographs of the event showed young men in suits and ties, carrying folders as they went from one session to another and posing with gravitas as respectable elite subjects, not dissimilarly to earlier cohorts of students (see figure 5.1). By contrast, the motions voted on during the congress attested to political positions that broke with the injunction to moderation that had dominated in previous years. One of these motions accused former general commissioners of having participated in an illegal government that served the interests of foreign powers and that was "partly responsible" for the assassination of Lumumba. These commissioners had discredited the entirety of the Congolese educated youth, and the congress delegates felt compelled to "finally

Figure 5.1 Students watching a masquerade performance during the second UGEC congress. Photographer unknown, August 1963 (source: author's collection).

denounce their ill-fated action in front of national and international public opinions."[85] Another statement called for the eradication of "alienation and exploitation" in Africa in general and the abolition of South African apartheid and Portuguese colonialism in particular. N'Kanza Dolomingu, a delegate from UGEC's North American branch, shared his experience of racial discrimination at Princeton. Other students denounced the American embassy as the main source of neocolonialism in the Congo and accused John F. Kennedy of transplanting his Latin American policies to Africa. Delegates criticized Congolese politicians as corrupt. They denounced the army as a tool of oppression. They called for the suppression of "the imperialists' occult forces that . . . alienated Adoula's government." And they demanded an investigation into Lumumba's murder, the erection of a large monument to his memory, and his proclamation as national hero. Finally, UGEC decided on a new motto: "All for the people and its revolution." Embracing a radical left rhetoric, students broke their attachments to colonial conservatism and Cold War liberalism. Not surprisingly, Lumumba's memory was in keeping with this move from a liberal to a revolutionary cosmopolitan imaginary. Congolese students still felt, as Takizala had solemnly phrased it in his speech at the first UGEC Congress in 1961, that

Figure 5.2 Zénon Mibamba (center) with other participants to the second UGEC congress. Photographer unknown, August 1963 (source: author's collection).

foreign students from across the world had their eyes on them; and they now more clearly perceived in this gaze a strong hope for them to prove worthy of Lumumba's legacy.

Conclusion

Zénon Mibamba, a student at the Plekhanov Institute of Rural Development in Moscow, presided over the last session of the UGEC congress in 1963 (see figure 5.2). Even though the conservative press in Leopoldville denounced him as communist infiltrator, two employees at the US embassy—CIA agents, he supposed—approached him with an offer to study Sovietology in the United States and the promise to make him the head of a future Soviet studies department set to open at the University of Lubumbashi. This department never materialized, and it may just have been part of a bluff on the part of the embassy employees. In any case, Mibamba was not interested in following the American path that earlier UGEC leaders like Takizala had taken.[86]

More than most students, Mibamba proved steadfast in his commitment to third world Marxism and the Congolese revolution. He joined the political struggle in 1959, at a time when he was a happily married young accountant who worked for Unilever, owned a car, and enjoyed access to facilities reserved for the company's white employees. Upon hearing Lumumba speak at a public rally, he risked putting his career prospects on hold and turned himself into an active propagandist for the MNC. At the begin of 1961, he quit his job and managed to reach Stanleyville, where partisans of Lumumba had proclaimed a Popular Republic of Congo in the aftermath of the prime minister's unconstitutional dismissal by Kasa-Vubu. It was there that he received a fellowship to study in Moscow from Lumumba's minister of education, Mulele. Leaving the Congo alone, without his wife and young son, the former accountant embarked on a new journey both as a university student *and* a revolutionary.

A few weeks after the 1963 congress, Mibamba joined the Committee of National Liberation (CNL), a newly created group among exiled Lumumbist politicians in Brazzaville. After Mulele launched an armed insurrection in the Kwilu, the CNL followed in his footsteps and opened fronts in central and eastern Congo. Mibamba served the rebellion movement as a military cadre on various front lines and became an envoy to ally countries such as Egypt, China, and North Korea. Despite some support from their Afro-Asian friends and from Cuba, the Congolese rebellions collapsed after 1965, in great part due to the counterinsurgency campaign orchestrated by Belgium and the United States. In October 1968, when Mobutu promised him a full amnesty, Mulele felt compelled to accept and he returned to Kinshasa together with four other militants, one of whom was Mibamba. Breaking Mobutu's promise, the army arrested the former rebels on their arrival. Some soldiers tortured Mulele and dismembered his body, disposing of his corpse in the Congo River. Mibamba escaped this fate but remained imprisoned until Mobutu had him released in 1973 together with a group of radical students from Lovanium—Mobutu's act was a gesture of goodwill before his first visit to Mao's China (see chapter 9). Decades later, when Laurent-Désiré Kabila took power, Mibamba returned to active politics, serving as a member of parliament for a couple of years. In 2001, after Kabila's murder, the relative clout that Mibamba had enjoyed as a former rebel leader disappeared. When I met him at the end of the decade, he was working in government but in a relatively subaltern position. He did not own a car and lived in Masina, a poor district of Kinshasa known as the People's Republic of China owing to its overpopulation (not because of its political sympathies).

In the 1960s, Mibamba contributed to turning the student movement toward the left. He had not wavered much in his political opinions when we met. An ascetic man whose goatee, baldness, and half-laughing eyes called to mind photographs of Lenin, he embodied a fidelity to the spirit of 1960s' student activism. The following chapters explore further the embrace of socialism and militant politics that Mibamba and other students performed in the 1960s. But outlining this trajectory of radicalization does not mean erasing the ideological complexities behind student politics. The episode of the general commissioners in 1960 is certainly key; it was the original sin that would haunt the students' collective mind for the rest of the decade. The close association between UGEC's founders and the USNSA, while nearly completely forgotten, is no less important to an understanding of the stakes of Congolese student politics.

The American shadow cast over the creation of UGEC illuminates the complex Cold War entanglements that hovered over the Congo. Lumumba's murder, as a cold war event, may have figured an "appropriated trajectory of nationhood," an attempt at derailing a project of sovereignty and dignity among the formerly colonized.[87] Nonetheless, the US government's understanding of its interest in the Congo involved supporting a process of nation building that would result in a credible and legible nationhood. This policy involved building relationships of influence across interlocutors who embodied the nation in different fields—as transpired in CIA-mediated contacts with students, labor activists, and politicians. It also involved knowledge production, including the Congo's establishment as an object of knowledge thanks to the generous financial backing given to institutions of higher education like Lovanium. Congolese students did not realize it, but US Cold War warriors envisioned the creation of UGEC as part of a broader process of control and legibility, to use two key terms in James Scott's later analysis of high-modernist state governance.[88]

Quite remarkably, the renowned political scientist and Congo specialist Crawford Young served as a witting USNSA delegate in the 1950s.[89] In 1958, his first trip to the Congo was as associate secretary of COSEC. Four years later, he enjoyed generous support from the US authorities in Leopoldville when he conducted his doctoral fieldwork on Congolese politics.[90] And when he then returned to the United States, he wrote up his dissertation while working as a consultant for the African desk of the Bureau of Intelligence and Research, one of the Department of State's intelligence agencies.[91] In 1965, his revised dissertation came out as a book, *Politics in Congo*; Lovanium published a French translation of it three years later. Young's volume is a remarkable book, a foundational reading of elite politics and the "challenges of nation-building." Scores of Congolese students revered it, without fully realizing the hidden transcripts that provided the foundations for Young's initial work. Many of these students thought of themselves as radical nationalists and they dreamed of returning the Congo to the path of emancipation outlined by Lumumba. Still, they evolved in intellectual milieus and relied on schemes of knowledge shaped by cold war entanglements in more ways than they knew.

SIX
REVOLUTION IN THE
(COUNTER)REVOLUTION

When I asked a former student of mine how he planned his return trip from New York to the Congo, he said he was flying on Sabena Airlines, which would cost more and take longer. When I asked why, he simply said that he was more familiar with the Belgians and felt most comfortable on their airline.

Tamar Golan, *Educating the Bureaucracy in a New Polity*, 44

To make the education system truly ours, we will have to submit it to our nation's philosophical, sociological and economical characteristics. This entails profound changes that should be realized along the lines of the Congolese revolution that recently began.

Auguste Mabika Kalanda, speech at the opening ceremony for the new academic year at the Ecole nationale de droit et d'administration, 1967

Established in Leopoldville in 1961, the Ecole Nationale de Droit et d'Administration (ENDA) trained future civil servants and magistrates for positions vacated by Belgian colonials throughout the Congo.[1] The Ford Foundation subsidized the school and appointed its staff, including the first director-general, James T. Harris. A former president of the National Student Association, Harris had been a central player in the Central Intelligence Agency's (CIA's) infiltration of the American student movement as recounted in the previous chapter.[2] People at ENDA, however, had no inkling of Harris's background with US intelligence. What was crucial for many was that Harris was African American. His appointment reinforced the image of ENDA as an instrument in the decolonization of the Congo that moved the country away from the age of colonial racism. The faculty at the school was more diverse than at Lovanium and other institutions of higher education. Tamar Golan, a young Israeli socialist who taught there in 1962 and 1963, noted the presence of some Belgian and French professors, whom she described as colonial in their mentality, rigid in their pedagogy, and obtuse in their relationship to anything African. But ENDA also had what Golan called an international brigade of American, Chinese, Syrian, Haitian, Israeli, and Swiss faculty members—people whose motivations "ranged from idealism to neuroses" but who were willing to Africanize their teaching and engage students outside of rigid authoritarian models.[3] Unfortunately, according to Golan, many students rejected the progressive pedagogy of the international brigade: "They felt it lacked dignity, and dignity, to these students, was synonymous with formality. They had learned to over-appreciate authority and felt the symbols of authority to be impersonality and distance."[4]

When a Ford Foundation official visited ENDA in 1961, he appreciated that the school admitted "somewhat older and more experienced" students who were "rather more interesting than the untried products of *petits seminaires* that Lovanium has."[5] By contrast, the intellectual vivacity that ENDA students prided themselves on (see figure 6.1) did not impress Golan. Instead, she found the student body at the school to be mostly conformist and captive to colonial worldviews. Student conservativism was real, but what Golan ignored was the fact that many young Congolese reacted against it.[6] She also failed to mention the strong influence of Auguste Mabika Kalanda, one of the only Congolese professors at the school. A thirty-year-old Lovanium graduate, Mabika served both as a faculty member at ENDA and as the minister of foreign affairs in Cyrille Adoula's government. In 1960, he had occupied the position of commissioner for the civil service for two months (and the creation of ENDA had been the main item in his portfolio). Thanks to his charisma and image as a radical nationalist, he avoided the stigma that attached to other former members of the college.[7] A book he wrote entirely in Tshiluba about the negative impact of colonialism on ethnic tensions in the Kasai reinforced his aura as an intellectual maverick and moral authority in student circles.[8] In his courses at ENDA or during informal encounters with students, he continuously emphasized the necessity to decolonize consciousnesses. There was not much hope with the older generation, he said, but the youth could undergo this mental decolonization, and it was urgent to "shield our children from the influence of foreigners who often present a distorted image of

Figure 6.1 "Students from the National School of Law and Administration, Leopoldville, the Congo, debate some points between classes." Photography Jacques Surbez, ca. 1963 (source: Rockefeller Archive Center, Ford Foundation Papers).

Africa."[9] ENDA students echoed these preoccupations. Around the time of Golan's departure from the Congo, the student journal at the school featured a long article on Patrice Lumumba, "the man that all Africa is grieving for." This combative call for real independence opposed the Congolese government's repression of democratic and nationalist forces "under the pressure of foreigners."[10] Other pieces in the same issue targeted Belgian interests in the Congo and announced that nationalist students would soon replace the corrupt bourgeois politicians in power.[11] Two months later, a former Lumumbist militant from northern Katanga (and childhood friend of Laurent-Désiré Kabila) was elected vice president of the student government, running on a platform aligned with these criticisms.[12]

Golan overlooked them, but seeds of radicalism were germinating at ENDA by 1963. They soon blossomed, as they did in other schools around the country, in great part because of the insurrectionary movement launched by Pierre Mulele and other followers of Lumumba. By forcefully and often violently evoking the fact that the work of decolonization remained unfinished, the rebels encouraged a collective reassessment of the meaning of independence. Their movement, maybe the largest insurrection in an independent African country,[13] brought back the popular energies of the late 1950s' anti-colonial struggle and older episodes of resistance to colonialism. Popular uprisings unmasked the untenable nature of growing social inequalities. Uhuru (independence) had become utumwa (slavery); equality turned into a myth; exploitation continued unabated. The rebels and their supporters refused to accept the failure of Lumumba's vision of independence, sovereignty, freedom, and justice.[14] The certainty that a revolution was the ultimate horizon of the young Congolese nation-state legitimated the insurrection. The futurity of the struggle resonated far and wide within the country. Among student circles, it spoke both to left activists and to their reputedly conservative peers. These students did not fit Golan's typecasting of them as alienated elitists that remained prisoners of a colonial mindset. Instead, they sought to reconcile their colonial upbringing with the movement to liberate Africa. They related to the debates about mental decolonization that animated ENDA and other campuses. Their synthesis between revolution and counterrevolution suggested new paths of emancipation but also paved the way to the remaking of the political landscape under the aegis of General Joseph Mobutu later in the decade.

This chapter revisits the history of the so-called struggle for the Congo's second independence initiated by Mulele. It analyzes the reverberations of this struggle on two sets of students: a group of Catholic students at Lovanium who launched a humanitarian operation in areas affected by the Lumumbist rebellions in 1965 and the authors of a mysterious utopian manifesto sent to the French publisher François Maspero in 1969.[15] The destructive violence of the rebellions marked many people at the time and for years after.[16] Yet, the rebellions were not only defined by this violence. Presenting themselves as a movement of liberation from colonialism and its legacy, they also encouraged a radical transformation in how people imagined their collective destiny. As a young Pierre Bourdieu noted in relation to Algeria, liberation struggles ushered in a broader revolutionary processes when they "awaken[ed] political consciousness and by the same token the thirst to learn, understand, and be informed."[17] A key argument in this chapter is that in the Congo, the impetus to embrace revolutionary thinking transformed the terms of the political debate well beyond the core of left militants. It certainly affected students and intellectuals much more deeply than social scientists like Golan perceived at the time.[18]

Revolution

Mulele refused to take part in Adoula's government in August 1961. Instead, he traveled to China with his friend Théodore Bengila, a former student of the Josephites like himself. The two men studied Marxism and guerilla warfare at the military academy of Nanking, planning an armed insurrection that would continue Lumumba's struggle for real independence. In March 1963, Bengila returned clandestinely to Leopoldville to work with a group of young activists around the redaction of a manifesto that would officially launch the struggle. Two of his interlocutors worked for Mabika at the ministry of foreign affairs: Emmanuel Lonji, a member of a small Marxist group that recruited mostly among students and labor activists, and Léonard Mitudidi, a graduate in natural sciences from the University of Nancy who had cut his teeth in the Fédération des étudiants d'Afrique noire en France (FEANF) and reportedly "brought an intellectualist dimension to Mulele's insurrection."[19] Mabika himself, despite his position in Adoula's government, was associated with the genesis of the rebellion, and he secretly met Mulele several times after the latter returned clandestinely to Leopoldville a few weeks after Bengila.[20] In August, while Mitudidi and a few others took advantage of the second General Union of Congolese Students (UGEC) congress to further develop contacts with students, Mulele and a small team relocated to rural Kwilu, where popular discontent and dissensions among various political factions had been particularly high in the preceding months.[21] Reaching out to local members of Mulele's Parti Solidaire Africain, they quickly recruited over five hundred young men and women, most of them ethnic Pende and Mbunda, to begin their maquis. High school students, teachers, seminarians, and Josephite brothers joined as well. They fulfilled different roles but often took charge of teaching the rudiments of Marxism in political education classes for the peasant recruits.[22]

The state reacted with brutality to the rebellion. The police stormed villages suspected of supporting Mulele, while the government suspended Parliament and proclaimed a state of emergency in Leopoldville.[23] Adoula conferred extraordinary powers on the head of the Sûreté, Victor Nendaka, the Congo's J. Edgar Hoover, as the *New York Times* nicknamed him. Nendaka's agents arrested and detained political opponents and labor activists they suspected of planning insurrectionary strikes.[24] This aggressive suppression of dissent pushed numerous nationalist politicians to exile themselves in Brazzaville, where an insurrectionary movement had just overthrown President Fulbert Youlou and turned the former French colony into a beacon for progressive Africa.[25] The newspaper *Dipanda*, the mouthpiece for the left-wingers within the new regime, was particularly supportive of the movement for a second independence across the Congo River. Articles regularly hailed Mulele as the new Lumumba and attacked Leopoldville's authorities as "running dogs of imperialism," "dollarized Africans," "anti-people crocodiles."[26] Abdoulaye Yerodia, a regular contributor to *Dipanda* who had studied philosophy at the Sorbonne and had roots in both Congos (as well as in Senegal), helped connect the exiled Lumumbists with the Brazzavillois left.[27] The Algerian, Chinese, and Cuban embassies, together with guerilla operatives from Angola and Cameroon that operated bases in the former French Congo, also provided assistance. This political environment sustained the establishment of a Conseil National de Libération (CNL) that grouped all the Lumumbist politicians exiled in Brazzaville.

Mulele was anxious for the CNL to open new military fronts that could eventually be connected with his landlocked maquis in the Kwilu. Yet, infighting among the Lumumbists in Brazzaville slowed down preparation. One wing within the CNL focused on urban guerilla operations in Leopoldville, but their plans quickly folded.[28] The other main wing, led by Christophe Gbenye, proved much more successful ultimately. Starting in April 1964, members of this faction launched attacks against governmental positions in northern Katanga and the Kivu. Thanks to veterans of the anticolonial struggle like Kabila and Gaston Soumialot who had maintained bases in eastern Congo, the CNL conquered several towns right away. Their troops of young peasants and child soldiers were called the Simba (the lions). They possessed rudimentary weapons but made abundant use of magic rituals. "Mulele mayi," their combat cry, reportedly turned their opponents' bullets into water. Soldiers from the national army were scared of this power, and they often preferred to escape rather than fight back when Simba troops showed up. In just a few months, the Simba conquered a third of the national territory. Their relatively easy capture of Stanleyville in August surprised everybody. Numerous CNL activists moved to this city, the Congo's third most important urban center, which became the capital of the Popular Republic of Congo with Gbenye as its self-proclaimed president.

The revolution had spread like a bushfire in the east. Whereas Mulele had theorized an armed struggle that would develop gradually and organically out of profound relationships with the masses, Gbenye and his associates only exercised loose control over their Simba fighters. Episodes of arbitrary violence against civilians in "liberated areas" were frequent, including torture, rape, and murder. Rebel leaders constantly opposed each other. Corruption and lack of discipline were rampant. The bureaucratic apparatus—the paper trail of the Popular Republic—served as a bulwark for some revolutionaries who felt threatened by the regime of arbitrariness and decentered violence in which they participated. It failed to ensure efficiency, but it sometimes succeeded in creating impressions of order.[29] Ultimately, foreign intervention brought the Popular Republic to its end in November 1964. The United States, which had already taken care of an aerial counterinsurgency operation in the Kwilu (using anti-Castro Cuban exile pilots paid through a CIA-cover organization), convinced Belgium to take the lead in military campaigns (Operation Red Dragon and Operation Ommegang) to liberate Stanleyville, rescue the hundreds of whites who lived as hostages of the Simba in the city, and "cleanse" other rebel areas.[30] Soldiers from the Congolese national army, together with Belgian officers and a motley crew of white mercenaries, captured Stanleyville and nearly wiped out the rebellion's eastern front within a few weeks.

The fall of Stanleyville pushed columns of insurgents into exile. It also further increased tensions within the CNL, to the great displeasure of foreign backers of the Congolese insurrection. In April 1965, President Gamal Abdel Nasser of the United Arab Republic pressured rebel leaders—many of whom had sought refuge in Cairo—to create a common front. Around forty of them agreed to join a Supreme Council of the Revolution (CSR) that would be led by Soumialot, Mulele, Kabila, and Yerodia.[31] Yet, five months after the conference that created the CSR, Victor Pakassa, a colonel in the rebel army, and Michel Botike, a student, were killed during a fight among Congolese exiles in Cairo. Pakassa had been a vocal advocate for restoring unity in the insurgency.[32] His murder produced the opposite effect, unveiling the impossibility to reconcile the various rebel factions and making the Egyptian authorities decide to withdraw their support.

Despite the failure of the leadership to reconcile their differences, a few pockets of resistance remained active in eastern Congo, most notably in the region of Lake Tanganyika. For a few months in 1965, the Simba rebels there were joined by a large contingent of Black Cuban volunteers led by Che Guevara.[33] The Congolese revolution, if it succeeded, would create a formidable impetus for the liberation of Southern Africa from colonialism and white-minority rule, Guevara believed. However, the mission proved more difficult than expected: the Cubans and the Simba had difficulties communicating, Guevara's relations with his own men were sometimes strained, tensions mounted between the Congolese fighters and their many Rwandese allies, and leaders like Mitudidi and Kabila remained isolated or inaccessible.[34] By the end of 1965, as the noose of counterinsurgency was tightening, Guevara exited the maquis together with the Cuban volunteers.

"This is the history of a failure," Guevara wrote when he put to paper the narrative of his adventures with the Simba. Many Congolese rebels refused this framing. Three years after Guevara's retreat from the Simba maquis, Joseph Sébastien Ramazani, a former insurgent leader who had found refuge in Khartoum, announced in a letter to Belgian Maoists that "a new phase in the struggle against American imperialism in the Congo" was starting. To make this phase a success, it was key to educate activists who then would mobilize the masses, and Ramazani was hoping that his Belgian contacts would find him a fellowship to study political sociology in Eastern Europe.[35] Ramazani's words were strategic and aspirational, but they were indicative of the strong imagined connection between revolution and higher education. Still, it was doubtful that the struggle could be revived in the short term. As Thomas Kanza had already noted when he renounced his position as ambassador for the CNL in 1966, mutations in the international context—the assassination of Malcolm X, the overthrow of Ahmed Ben Bella, and the coup against Kwame Nkrumah—made an immediate comeback of the Congolese insurrection unlikely.[36]

A Congolese Peace Corps

As rebel leaders scattered in exile, the "pacification" of eastern Congo was steaming ahead. Counterinsurgency operations matched and often exceeded the violence of the Simba.[37] Mass executions were frequent. The presence of CIA-recruited anti-Castroist Cuban plane pilots and of mercenary battalions that included former Nazi officers outraged public opinion throughout Africa and beyond. White mercenaries were unutterably cruel in hunting the Simba, and images of their violent methods circulated on posters, militant publications, and films.[38] The fact that Moïse Tshombe replaced Adoula as prime minister in July 1964 also shaped reactions to the counterinsurgency. The former leader of the Katanga secession, Tshombe was seen as a figure of abjection outside of the Congo: a traitor to African independence and a neocolonial stooge.[39] In Leopoldville, even if he managed to gain acceptance among various sectors of the population, Tshombe failed in his efforts at co-opting the student movement. He recruited the UGEC leader Ferdinand Kayukwa as his main adviser, but he found no one else to put on the council of students and intellectuals he had promised to establish to guide him.[40] Most students could simply not conceive working with a man they viewed as Lumumba's murderer. In fact, Tshombe's accession to power encouraged further radicalization in student circles.[41] And two months into his tenure as prime minister, he ordered the censorship of UGEC and had three prominent student leaders (André N'Kanza Dolomingu, Hubert Makanda, and Gérard Kamanda) arrested.[42]

While the UGEC leadership frontally opposed Tshombe, some Lovanium students took part in humanitarian operations connected to the pacification campaign. The American embassy in the Congo had strongly encouraged their involvement. For the embassy, it was crucial that Congolese authorities not only "physically put down the rebellions" but also "give the liberated Congolese hope for a prosperous, tranquil and non-communist future."[43] The diplomats believed that students could contribute to these goals through "a Congolese Peace-Corps type project."[44] The relief mission, known as Debout Stan, was carried out by Lovanium's Catholic student association, Pax Romana, and led by Isidore Ndaywel, a student in romance languages and the president of the group.

Pax Romana could count on the strong awareness among students about the impact of the rebellions in the Kwilu and in eastern Congo. Catholic students had been particularly sensitive to the targeted assassinations of missionaries and members of the national clergy. Even left students opposed to Adoula and Tshombe came to reject the Simba for their use of violence. They denounced the rebel leaders as évolué politicians no different from the ministers in Leopoldville's government and who, like them, caused suffering among the Congolese people.[45]

Debout Stan recruited eighty students from Lovanium who traveled to the former capital of the Popular Republic for several weeks in July and August 1965. The volunteers worked on agricultural, medical, and educational projects. General Mobutu covered the costs of the operation, and according to the label on the check that he handed out to Ndaywel, he viewed the operation as part of the "psychological actions of the National Army."[46] After Debout Stan, Pax Romana continued to collaborate with the government by sending students for one year to Stanleyville as secondary school teachers, while an operation Debout Idiofa brought volunteers to the Kwilu during school vacations in 1966.[47]

Many students at Lovanium referred to Pax Romana as a conservative and reactionary group. Ndaywel and his comrades rejected this rightist reputation. They wished to erase the politicized image of Pax Romana and to instead emphasize its role as an instrument of social action.[48] Debout Stan and Debout Idiofa, they hoped, would reinforce this aura of social engagement. Their new vision for Pax Romana built on previous projects by the Belgian sociologist Paul Raymaekers and his Office for Rural Programs at Lovanium (which academic authorities nicknamed the Office for the Revolutionary Programs).[49] Raymaekers aimed to overcome the "disastrous dualism between traditional academic training and the idea of development" through summer activities with student volunteers like archeological excavations and camps for the "idle youth."[50] The same desire to challenge academic conventions motivated Pax Romana's participation in pacification operations: the goal was to render Pax Romana "less clerical" and "more respectable" in the eyes of the General Assembly of Students (AGEL) and of UGEC activists.[51] Since 1960, frequent discussions in the group had interrogated the meaning of decolonization. Early on, most Catholic students conceived political independence as just a stage in a longer process of liberation in which the spiritual dimension was central.[52] Over time, these discussions took an increasingly critical tone. Some Pax Romana students argued for the necessity to free the Congo from cultural colonialism. They called on their peers to promote a radical African humanism and rejected politicians who served foreign interests.[53] These debates about the political and social duties of African intellectuals also entered into the establishment of the Debout Stan campaign.

Despite the group's efforts, radical students derided Pax Romana's humanitarian initiative as a "counter-revolutionary attempt at bribing" the poor with "dog food from Yankee surplus."[54] And the Debout Stan volunteers' stories about the human cost of the rebellions did not move those students who had expressed sympathy for the insurrection in the past.[55] Regardless, general perceptions of Pax Romana did shift. In 1968, the students elected Hubert Tshimpumpu, a member of the group and Ndaywel's second in command in Debout Stan and Debout Idiofa, as the new president of the student government.

The anticonformist impulse behind Pax Romana's actions in 1965 and 1966 indicates the pervasiveness of rebellious sentiments on campus, including among supposedly more conservative students. The insurrection's revolutionary rhetoric touched even the students who never sympathized with the CNL or its armed struggle. As the enthusiasm for the "student revolution" of April 1964 (see chapter 4) showed well, the language of guerilla warfare resonated with students who saw themselves as rebels of their own kind.

Counterrevolution

The same type of diffuse rebelliousness and occasional posturing that dominated at Lovanium also drove Leopoldville's circles of power. Even Tshombe played the popular tune of disavowing the political class when he became prime minister in July 1964. The former secessionist leader promised both an end to the corruption and insecurity that had defined

Adoula's tenure and the beginning of a new era of prosperity and real independence. Yet, the same Tshombe also recruited white mercenaries to eradicate the remaining pockets of the Simba rebellion, and his image as "an imperialists' puppet" stuck more than ever. When Joseph Kasa-Vubu began suspecting that Tshombe would try to oust him from the presidency, he availed himself of the language of anti-imperialism to contain his prime minister. In October 1965, he replaced Tshombe with Evariste Kimba as prime minister, while making sure that the new government included politicians who favored his turn to the left. The president also publicly opposed the presence of mercenaries in the eastern Congo, he encouraged the holding of a popular rally against Belgian neocolonialism, and he indicated that he may vote for the membership bid of Maoist China at the United Nations.[56]

Into this fraught context of growing antagonisms between Kasa-Vubu and Tshombe, the military coup of November 24, 1965 exploded like a bomb. Mobutu proclaimed himself president and suspended all existing institutions. The general justified the coup by referring to the politicians' inability to work together. Even though he had been closely involved with the counterinsurgency campaign, and even though Western countries welcomed his takeover as a timely reaction to Kasa-Vubu's leftward turn, Mobutu also capitalized on anti-Tshombe feelings. Some people on the radical left looked favorably on Mobutu's coup (and some may have helped to organize it) because the general's accession to power ensured that Tshombe would not stage a comeback.[57]

At Lovanium, the enthusiasm for the general and his marginalization of the political class dominated. Two weeks after the coup, the whole student community welcomed Mobutu in an official ceremony on campus. In a warm welcoming speech, Tharcisse Mwamba, the president of AGEL, promised the new head of state that students were ready to assist him in his program of national renewal. Mwamba hoped that Mobutu, unlike the politicians who had occupied power until then, would "replace the old semi-colonial structures by well-fitting, authentically democratic and more efficient new ones," including in education.[58] Mwamba visibly took advantage of Mobutu's visit to make a show of AGEL's rebelliousness and upset Lovanium's authorities.[59] Photographs taken of the day show Rector Luc Gillon dressed in full academic regalia, while Mwamba and his second, the Cameroonian student Samuel Belinga, wore plain shirts with no ties—a clear break from the campus dress code, a refusal of bourgeois and Western norms, and a symbolic act toward the decolonization of the institution. Mobutu's coup enabled these kinds of statements. A few years later, he famously outlawed Western clothing and instead imposed the so-called abacost, a Mao suit-like national costume. The importance of the sarto-rial already appeared clearly in 1965: in his first public meeting after the coup, Mobutu turned the phrase "Let's roll up our sleeves" (Retroussons nos manches) into the slogan of the military regime, literally rolling up the sleeves of his army shirt onstage as he said it. The slogan became ubiqui-tous in various media, including the first postage stamps issued after the coup. The phrase called the Congolese to "get back to work," criticizing the "all talk, no action" politicians who had previously ruled the country. By asking male citizens to drop their jackets and neckties and get their hands dirty, Mobutu tapped into a discourse about cultural alienation that resonated deeply within the educated class. His words landed well with students who saw themselves as breaking away from the évolué genera-tion and its assimilationist relation to Europe.[60]

Mobutu may have betrayed Lumumba in 1960, but he did not back away from presenting himself as a champion of Congolese independence. While overseeing the counterinsurgency campaign against the Mulelists, he kept an ear out for the rhetorical radicalism emerging from rebel camps. The few CNL members who explicitly refused to align themselves with com-munism and presented nationalism as an ideological alternative to the bi-nary of the Cold War became an important source of inspiration.[61] Mobutu also rephrased his opposition to the politicians: he did not only point toward their incompetency as he had done in 1960; he also rejected the arrogance of their class distinction and excessive dependence on European values. Meant to stand in stark contrast to the corruption of the political class were the plebeian ethos of the army and Mobutu's own self-professed righteousness, simplicity, and proximity with the people. This voluntarism appealed to students who embraced the spirit of the revolution and radical national-ism or simply sought for ways to exit the ivory tower.

The Proletarian Brotherhood

In July 1969, a package mailed from Kinshasa landed on the desk of François Maspero, the Parisian editor of Frantz Fanon, Régis Debray, Che Guevara, Louis Althusser, and countless other Marxist and anarchist writ-ers. In it, there were six school notebooks that contained a handwritten text with the intriguing title of *Manifesto of the Proletarian Brotherhood of Revolutionary and Conscious Peasants, Workers, Intellectuals and Stu-dents of the Congo.* The manifesto's authors, of unknown identity, hoped that Maspero would publish their text, a detailed program for a new phase in the Congolese revolution.[62] Maspero, the authors urged, should also arrange for an English translation, organize its worldwide circulation (notably in China, Cuba, and the Soviet Union), and collect money for a recently established "clandestine government of the Brotherhood."

What did this mysterious brotherhood want to share with the world? The authors claimed that their manifesto offered "a correct and fair adaptation of Mao Tse-Tung's Marxism-Leninism," but this description failed to capture the originality of their text, which composed a unique collage of anti-imperialist, socialist, Christian, Pan-African, Afrocentrist, Fanonian, and Gandhian references. The manifesto called for a new revolutionary movement, encouraging Congolese people to create independent cells, organize village communities, and send letters of application to the "government of the Proletarian Brotherhood." A "pacific and non-violent armed revolution" would soon overthrow the ruling national bourgeoisie and its "imperialist American devil" masters. The new society would affirm the value of "the men of the Black race" and their capacity to redeem humanity, but it would also welcome tourists from around the world and encourage real friendship among people of all races. The revolutionary government's program explicitly promoted love and sexual hygiene as core dimensions to be developed in the new society. The brotherhood would fight against adultery and ensure that women were recognized as "the summit of all preoccupations and all human activities." Happiness would be guaranteed to all, and love between husbands and wives would become the basis for the construction of a fraternal society. At the same time, a constant iron discipline would also be expected from spouses—perhaps an attempt by the manifesto's authors to radicalize the contemporary visions on the family expressed in Julius Nyerere's Ujamaa policy.[63] The manifesto's sexual language reflected the male-centered configuration of the Congolese intellectual left, but it also testified to a willingness to engage with gender and masculinity more critically than had been done in other similar programmatic interventions.

The authors explicitly stated at different moments that Congolese students constituted their first public. They warned them against the reign of "the whiskey and the dollar" and against the "decadence" of foreign universities. Because students had a unique responsibility to lead the revolutionary struggle, it was urgent that they abandon their nice clothes, reject their foreign books, dress with "blue jeans and . . . working jackets," and return to their villages to learn from nature and the popular masses.

The manifesto's self-professed Maoism echoed the Mulele and Simba rebellions. But the text stood the insurrectionary movement on its head in a number of ways. Although it referred to Lumumba as a hero who had chased white devils in 1960, it did not include any direct mention of Mulele or the Simba—and it is doubtful that the authors had been part of the rebellions. Their insistence on the dignity of all human beings and their oxymoronic mantra of a nonviolent armed revolution were clear signs of a disavowal of the mid-1960s insurrections. The manifesto's authors believed that most people in the Congolese ruling class, because they were children of peasants, could be convinced to stop following the "Yankee imperialist Satanists" and reconnect with their people.

Education featured at the center of the brotherhood's program. The authors referred to their leader as the "chief-guide-educator." Schools and universities would multiply in their utopian future. And they would even teach white imperialists the justice of their movement to help them understand that "their negro is dead and that the man of the Black race is firmly and steadfastly standing."[64] The text magnified the universal vocation of the Congolese revolution. It situated it in relation with the long history of the liberation of Black people—the "most oppressed and humiliated in the world." The second independence, a true messianic coming, would engender an "absolutely new human being" and a civilization based on simplicity, beauty, and harmony with nature.

Conclusion

The intensity of the manifesto struck Maspero when he first read it in 1969. The anthropologist Gérard Althabe, who worked with Maspero on the text's publication, reacted as passionately. Several people—the physicist Abdou Moumouni, the filmmaker Chris Marker, and the third-worldist activist Yves Benot—strongly encouraged the project. Yet, while the three thousand copies of the book quickly sold out after its publication, Maspero later deplored that there had been a "*total* absence of reactions, critiques, or commentaries" from readers and from the press.[65] This silence may be indicative of the difficulty for the French public to apprehend the text beyond its strong singularity and to make full sense of its logic of enunciation. Althabe's introduction to the book offered a detailed reading of the Congolese political situation, but it failed to show how the manifesto, far from being unique, belonged to a broader collective reappraisal of independence among Congolese students and intellectuals in the aftermath of Lumumba's murder and of the Mulelist and Simba uprisings. It is this broader space of ideological experimentation that this chapter has revisited.

Like the ENDA students of 1963 and the Pax Romana activists of 1965, the authors of the manifesto questioned the colonial nature of elite production and urged their educated peers to get off their pedestals. One section in the text explicitly called on students "to go to the field to feel the . . . salutary work of the peasant, to go to the factory to feel and live the creating genius of the worker, to write in Swahili and ancestral ethnic languages after having sweated at work and dirtied their intellectual's clothes."[66] These were the words of self-identified radical anti-capitalists, but Catholic students at Lovanium could have signed them just as easily despite their conservative reputation. These students, like the manifesto's authors, were painfully aware that independence had not improved the everyday life of the population, and they reacted to the context of the rebellions by thinking about ways in which education could radically transform social relations.

Responses to the mid-1960s rebellions created a paradoxical overlap between revolution and counterrevolution—an overlap that Mobutu attempted to extend to the point of rupture, as is further analyzed in the final part of this book.[67] Yet, the rebellions also encouraged a more dogmatic and therefore less pliable form of political radicalization among some Congolese students, in particular among those who studied abroad. The next chapter centers on these students.

SEVEN
A STUDENT FRONT

The disastrous management of the res publica that characterized the College of the General Commissioners created great distrust [of the educated
elite] among the Congolese people. But that time is over and the orientation
of the Congolese intellectual youth has changed wonderfully, as it forms now
an avant-garde force in the urban anti-imperialist struggle.

Edouard-Marcel Sumbu, *Il sangue dei leoni*, 61–62

It seems like there are few if any doctrinaire Congolese Communists. This
would require an intellectual sophistication and discipline that is lacking in
the Congo.   G. Mennen Williams, memo to Governor Harriman,
June 3, 1964 (Records of the US Bureau of African Affairs)

In January 1969, the Milanese publisher Giangiacomo Feltrinelli released
Il sangue dei leoni, a new title in his book series on revolutionary movements in Africa. The volume gathered three texts, all translated from French,
on the Simba rebellion. These texts differed radically from the utopian vision of the Proletarian Brotherhood's manifesto discussed in the previous
chapter. Their author was Edouard-Marcel Sumbu, a former Simba who
had served as the Conseil National de Libération (CNL) liaison in Cuba
since 1965.[1] Along with Sumbu's apologetical stories about the Congolese
revolution, *Il sangue* reproduced a fifty-page-long training manual for
secret counterinsurgency operations used at the US Army Special Warfare
Center at Fort Bragg in North Carolina.[2] The leaked manual offered de-

tailed, practical instructions on how to make bombs and other techniques for operating in nonconventional conflict zones. How did stories about the Simba rebellion end up bundled together with this literally explosive handbook? The transactions behind the making of *Il sangue* remain elusive, but it reportedly ended up on the bedside table of every member of the Italian Red Brigade and was read in Arabic translation by Al Fatah fighters in Palestine.[3] Intersecting revolutionary struggles in Africa, the Caribbean, Europe, and the Middle East, Sumbu's book emblematized the broad entanglements of the radical post-Lumumbist left.[4]

Sumbu, writing from Cuba, sought to increase international support for the Congolese revolutionary movement. Through Feltrinelli, he hoped to reach Congolese students in Europe. He had found inspiration in the global youth uprisings of 1968 and believed that the educated youth could revive the movement started by Pierre Mulele. His book reminded readers of the role played in previous years by Congolese students—both those in the maquis and those who "opened a real war on another front: that of ideological education." Creating propaganda that "taught patriotism to the Congolese people" and "attracted the attention of world opinion," these students, Sumbu explained, laid the groundwork for critical international connections.[5]

This chapter builds on Sumbu's intuition of the importance of students in the Congolese revolution. As the previous chapter showed, the insurrections created a feverish political climate that led many young educated Congolese to redefine the meaning of independence and envision decolonization as a mental process. Yet, a specific focus on the students who did not simply respond to this revolutionary climate but championed the insurrections is in order because these students traced a distinctive and highly influential path within the landscape of Congolese politics.

Former student leaders like Zénon Mibamba, Thomas Kanza, Antoine Mandungu, Thomas Mukwidi, and Etienne Mbala emerged as figures of their own in the various maquis and rear bases of the insurrections. These highly educated and well-traveled young men rerouted their lives to become militants of the second independence. They felt compelled to answer the revolution's call because they believed that their help and good knowledge of questions of ideology and strategy were needed to ensure that the CNL lived up to Patrice Lumumba's legacy "in the eyes of the whole world."[6] Far from the blood and the mud of the combat zones, other students acted as propagandists for the uprising. These students, too, mattered, for the revolution was also a war of words. Despite public statements that officially presented the Congolese rebels as pawns of the Eastern Bloc, many US officials appeared to have been convinced that global Cold War ideologies did not apply in Central Africa; in the words of a CIA operative who had served in the secret US operation in Laos before being sent to the Congo, the Simba only amounted to a "ragtag bunch of illiterate dissidents," and they "certainly weren't communists."[7] By contrast, the students who supported the insurrections defended the ideological dignity of the struggle. The particularization of the Congolese rebels was anathema to them. Instead, they saw the events in the Congo as part of an epochal revolutionary movement that would overturn regimes of oppression the world over. Although the propaganda front to which these students contributed was unable to reverse a balance of power on the ground that favored the counterinsurgency, it radicalized many of their peers in Congolese universities and abroad. As it moved to the left, the student movement augmented its authority and imposed itself as a major player. And when Joseph Mobutu began to reinvent the identity of the Congolese nation after taking power in November 1965, the students constituted a force he could not ignore.

Students Go Underground

During the first months of the armed insurrections in late 1963 and early 1964, many student activists expressed reservations about militancy and the recourse to violence. They refused to choose between the government and the rebels, equally opposing their actions and the impact of their confrontation on the Congolese people. However, in July and August 1964, when the CNL's spectacular military successes captured the world's attention, the students' neutrality threatened to make them irrelevant. This became even more the case in November with the deployment of a Belgian and American counterinsurgency campaign throughout eastern Congo. The recourse to white mercenaries to put an end to the rebellion's advance in particular sparked international condemnations, in a way that recalled the reactions that followed Lumumba's assassination in 1961. Demonstrations were staged in multiple countries, but nowhere with the same intensity as in China, where hundreds of thousands of people—eight million according to the government—shouted their solidarity with the Congo and their hatred of US imperialism during rallies in Shanghai, Peking, Sian, Kunming, and Canton.[8]

Cold War polarization altered and simplified the intelligibility of the insurrection, pushing an increasing number of students to challenge the General Union of Congolese Students' (UGEC's) neutral stance, most markedly abroad as student expatriates enjoyed a greater freedom of expression than their peers in the Congo. Many of these students considered that the insurrection imposed an "either-or dialectic" typical of revolutionary situations: they could either get their hands dirty in active support of the rebellion, or they could contribute to the defeat of the revolutionary project by inaction.[9]

Many discontented activists organized themselves in informal groups to act as factions within UGEC. A few friends in Brussels—all of them men—created one such groupuscule in January 1964, the Congolese Patriots Front (FPC). The FPC functioned as a study group. Members read newspapers, carried out their own research, and produced various analyses. The group discussed topics as diverse as the "psycho-sociological condition of the Congolese today," the situation of labor activism, the political and moral duties of African intellectuals, and their views on the role of women in the life of the nation. All members agreed that the Congo needed a revolution, and they used their nightly meetings to debate its modalities and goals. The detailed minutes of these meetings intimate various sensibilities: some members argued that the memory of Lumumba constituted the principal revolutionary force in the Congo; others believed that poverty would leverage radical change. Accordingly, the former pushed for popular antagonisms against the anti-Lumumbist establishment to be capitalized on; the latter, by contrast, called to co-opt as many members of the establishment as possible, even politicians who had opposed Lumumba, as long as they were ready to align themselves with a progressive populist agenda.[10]

The more cautious FPC members warned against measures that could alienate Congolese Catholics and Belgian interests, which a revolutionary movement would not have enough firepower to counter. They considered that they could not turn their back on capitalism and believed that Maoism, because it called for the abolition of existing family structures, was not adapted to the Congo.[11] The same members favored the "moderate" option of African socialism over the "scientific" approach of orthodox Marxism.[12] Yet, within a few months, the more militant Marxist vision dominated. The caution and prudent tactical considerations of the first meetings faded as a result of a dynamic of conviction and radicalization within the group, but also in the face of the acceleration of events in the Congo. In April 1964, the group began collaborating with the editors of the Maoist journal *Révolution*, the French lawyer Jacques Vergès, and the Vietnamese anti-colonial activist Ngô Manh Lân.[13] A few months later, Antoine Robert, a mixed-race Lumumbist student from Katanga and one of the most radical FPC members, enlisted in the armed struggle. Robert had been living in Belgium for four years by that time. He was married and had a young daughter. But he could not stand continuing to have theoretical debates in Europe while people were fighting in the Congo. After several trips to Prague, Leipzig, Berlin, and Algiers to collect paratrooper uniforms, machine guns, books, letterhead paper, and typewriters, he reached the front in eastern Congo toward the end of 1964.[14]

Robert's departure for the front added substance to the FPC's revolutionary rhetoric. The FPC, in his view, should turn into a school for Congolese Marxist-Leninist militants abroad and form the roots of a self-disciplined party of the proletarian avant-garde. The goal was to build "the perfect machinery to ensure the triumph of the Congolese nation's liberation" and "prove to the whole world that the Black from Africa is also an organizer and a maker of things."[15] Robert thought that infiltrating UGEC could be a first step in the construction of his dreamed proletarian avant-garde. In September 1964, several FPC members ran in elections for leadership positions within UGEC-Belgium. Although personal charisma and ethnic alliances usually decided student elections, the FPC members used campaign language that was combative and politicized, presenting themselves as nationalist, progressive candidates and portraying their opponents as "fascist conspirators."[16] This aggressive approach paid off, as four of them—Pontien Tshilenge, François Beltchika, Théo Tango, and Oswald Ndeshyo—were elected to the executive committee of UGEC-Belgium, with Ndeshyo as the new president.[17]

In November 1964, the Belgian and American military operation against the Simba offered an opportunity for the FPC activists to use their position within UGEC. Ndeshyo, Tshilenge, Tango, and Beltchika circulated a long statement printed on the student union's letterhead in which they accused the Belgian army of massacring civilians in eastern Congo.[18] The Belgian government was outraged by UGEC's declaration. They arrested Ndeshyo and Tshilenge, arguing that they had failed to respect the silence on domestic political matters expected of foreign students. Numerous voices in Belgium and abroad interceded in defense of the two students. As a minor concession, the Belgian authorities agreed to put them on a plane to Algiers instead of to Leopoldville, as they had initially planned.[19] When Ndeshyo and Tshilenge landed in Algiers, President Ahmed Ben Bella welcomed them at the airport, and the National Union of Algerian Students offered them financial aid so they could continue their education in the country.[20]

The arrest of Tshilenge and Ndeshyo caused a profound commotion in student circles and deepened the fracture between reformists and revolutionaries.[21] Students disagreed on strategies and ideologies to the point that a UGEC officer at the University of Louvain, Gérard Buakasa, pushed for a three-year suspension of all UGEC's public activities, during which time the union would have to transform itself from the inside. Buakasa was a graduate student in sociology at this moment. His research focused on the question of cultural authenticity, and he was appalled that despite all the talks about revolution, too many Congolese students remained captive to a colonial mindset and to bourgeois aspirations. In the past, he had shared his views about the necessity to invent a radical form of African socialism, based on the clan system and an Africanized Christian theology, as a platform for the total suppression of all forms of oppression on the continent.[22] The dominance of the revolutionary wing within UGEC was fragile, he believed. Most political labels had become misleading: students "who yesterday were on the Left are today on the Right; and those who were on the Right say they underwent a conversion and are now in the Center." The solution to the confusion, Buakasa argued, was to train the UGEC membership through workshops on Pan-Africanism, international student politics, and avant-garde political doctrines. "Let's build first a strong UGEC before involving ourselves in political adventures. No more inconsiderate public statements, but actions inside the movement."[23]

Frontline Intellectuals

Who could Buakasa hope to convince with this plan? On the one hand, "moderates" within UGEC were asking for less focus, not more, on ideology. On the other hand, many of the "radicals" had lost all hope of transforming the union from within. Kalixte Mukendi Wa Nsanga, the former ambianceur who had discovered activism on the dance floors of Leopoldville (see interlude III), was a major force among those who pushed for a revolutionary alternative to UGEC. Wa Nsanga had been isolated at first when he moved to the University of Cologne in 1960. Germany was a terra incognita on the map of the Congolese student diaspora then, and the press became a lifeline to the world for Wa Nsanga. His strict daily reading routine involved scanning *Die Welt*, the *Frankfurter Allgemeine*, the *Kölner Stadt-Anzeiger*, *Le Monde*, *Le Figaro*, and various French news magazines for articles about Africa, while keeping tabs on books that could help him to advance politically. He also made numerous contacts throughout Europe, traveling regularly to Belgium, Czechoslovakia, France, East Germany, and Poland. The apathy and provincialism he sometimes perceived among many Congolese students in Europe, and particularly in Belgium, outraged Wa Nsanga.[24] As he told a journalist a few years later, young people did not show enough interest in the world's problems: they were aware of the necessity of liberation and decolonization but preferred to focus on their personal comfort rather than educate themselves and invest in the future.[25] In his eyes, political engagement demanded self-discipline— almost asceticism. It also required compartmentalizing, a game at which he excelled.

At the end of 1961, the Belgian Communist Party had reached out to Wa Nsanga with an astonishing request: would he agree to transport a large sum of money on behalf of Mulele, who was still in Cairo then, to his supporters in Leopoldville? Wa Nsanga had known several of Mulele's close party associates quite well in Leopoldville and answered yes.[26] Although he only acted as a courier, he felt emboldened by the trust placed in him. After this risky trip, the idea of doing something concrete for the revolution, of helping the Congolese people *now* rather than promising to save them in a distant future, came to obsess him. He came up with a detailed program for developing workers' cooperatives, which he submitted to his Belgian communist contacts, mentioning in a cover letter that he had worked "day and night, in my student bedroom, through the hubbub of Cologne's bourgeoisie" to write up this political project.[27] Opportunities to reconnect with Congolese realities were priceless, he wrote after another trip during which he visited his parents and met with Laurent-Désiré Kabila and Gabriel Sumbu. The Congo was a country inhabited by "men, women, and children that we love," and it was this affective bond that kept the young student up at night.[28]

Wa Nsanga's insomnia was existential. He felt out of sync with his host society but even more fundamentally with the Congolese student expatriates who located change in the future, imagining they would transform their country only after completing their education and returning home with their university credentials. By contrast, Wa Nsanga was moved by an urgency to fill a gap that was both spatial—the distance between the Congo and his Western European location—and temporal—the lag between a present of oppression and a future of emancipation. Although he quickly familiarized himself with Marxism around the time of his correspondence with Belgian communists, voluntarism remained his personal religion, and calls for sacrifice and militaristic organization, his main credo.

Wa Nsanga was a close friend of Antoine Robert and he shared his revolutionary mysticism. When Robert decided to join the Simba rebellion at the end of summer 1964, Wa Nsanga traveled with him to East Berlin to facilitate contacts with Chinese diplomats and East German officials. Already by then he had retired his ideas about using cooperatives as instruments of a bottom-up transformation, and he supported the turn to violence advocated by his Mulelist contacts in Brazzaville, the Kwilu, and eastern Congo. It was around the same time that Wa Nsanga began making plans for a new political organization that would ultimately supplant UGEC. He worked together with Luc-Daniel Dupire, a student at the University of Brussels and member of Robert's FPC. Dupire was a white Belgian who had simply happened upon his involvement in Congolese politics.[29] Although some members of the FPC had objected to having someone not Congolese in the group,[30] Dupire proved himself a valuable contributor and was assigned a strategic role as the group's contact person with the pro-Chinese split of the Belgian Communist Party led by Jacques Grippa.[31] In Dupire, Wa Nsanga found an interlocutor who shared his methodic dedication to activism and his conviction that students had a role to play in the revolutionary process.

The de facto dislocation of the FPC in November 1964 reinforced Wa Nsanga's belief in the necessity to create a new clandestine student group that would progressively replace the UGEC. In January 1965, together with Dupire, he flew to Algiers to convene with Ndeshyo and Tshilenge, the two exiled FPC members. They all agreed to launch a new organization under the name of Union de la Jeunesse Révolutonnaire du Congo (UJRC). A few months later, a UGEC seminar that Wa Nsanga had long been scheduled to convene offered a convenient cover for members of the new group to gather together in Cologne—Ndeshyo who landed in Munich without a proper visa was denied entry into Germany and missed the meeting, but several students who would become active participants in the UJRC, such as Théo Tango from Brussels and Symphorien N'Kita Kabongo and J. R. Benza from East Berlin, made it to the seminar.[32] A large group of UGEC activists from across Europe also attended the seminar, and Wa Nsanga seized the opportunity to clearly and publicly articulate his violent critiques of the student union. The UGEC's tradition of "ultra-democratism" and its fear of offending, he argued, translated into a vain search for consensus and neutralism. In his eyes, the only purpose of the student union was to help its members to "sleep better at night."[33]

Wa Nsanga had no qualms about offending the sensibility of people who feared sleeplessness. He saw the UJRC as a vanguard. His intransigence proved crucial in prolonging attention to the movement within the student diaspora when rebel positions in the Congo were fast receding. Whereas Mulele found himself increasingly isolated and Simba fighters rushed into exile, the UJRC maintained momentum around their struggle. Wa Nsanga and his comrades ignored the rhetoric of decline. Their idea of the Congolese revolution as an ineluctable historical process transcended the contingency of the balance of power on Congolese battlegrounds. Over and over, they compared the Congolese movement to other major struggles of the time, from Cuba to Vietnam. Their anti-defeatist stance helped to sustain political radicalization in student circles. It gave a sense of purpose to young Congolese expatriates by emphasizing that their mobilization mattered for the success of the revolution.

Wa Nsanga's impatient voluntarism fashioned the UJRC. The group was born out of a conviction that students' immediate involvement in the revolution was in order. Yet, beyond this clear rhetoric, the UJRC was also able to strategically shift registers when necessary. It remained a student organization and did not fully break with the logic of the autonomy of the intellectual field. When the East German authorities decided to send back five Congolese students who had finished their cursus at the East German Trade Union School in Bernau in 1965, the two leaders of the UJRC in the country, N'Kita Kabongo and Benza, wrote to Walter Ulbricht, the head of the Socialist Unified Party, to advocate for them. These students should be allowed to stay and continue their education in Germany, the two activists wrote, because Congo most urgently needed carefully trained cadres who could lead the way in building a classless socialist society. They argued that the knowledge that the students would acquire in Germany could form an essential contribution to the ongoing armed struggle. This was particularly important, they said, because the armed struggle differed from a war of liberation that would end simply by making changes at the top. Instead, a war led by patriots "against social injustice and for the building of a new order," it called for "a complete and fundamental change in the economic organization and political orientation of our country."[34] This required cadres, students, and intellectuals.

Revolutionary Correspondence

UJRC activists envisioned different ways of contributing to the political struggle. Many of these contributions mobilized the students' ability to cross borders and travel long distances. Wa Nsanga and his comrades made short trips to the eastern Congo maquis to directly liaise with the rebels; they traveled to Kampala, Khartoum, and Cairo to mediate among opposed factions within exiled Simba communities; they sought guidance about military strategy and Maoist theory in China; and they established contacts with Albanian officials who pushed for the Congo's full "Vietnamization."[35] As they traveled the world, UJRC activists engaged in transactions that sustained the rebellions. Yet, the group's significance lay mostly in its impact on the political imagination of a generation of students, not in the practical organization of the struggle. In this regard, its journal, *L'Eclair*, was central. It circulated in multiple countries and disseminated a revolutionary language that encouraged students to imagine themselves as part of the struggle. The journal called on readers to create autonomous UJRC cells. One place where this happened was in Lyon. The members of this cell corresponded with Dupire and Wa Nsanga, without knowing their real identity since the UJRC used pseudonyms and post office boxes.[36] The Lyonnais' affiliation to the UJRC was loose; it never went beyond the occasional bit of postal correspondence and the reading of *L'Eclair*. Nevertheless, the idea that they belonged to a self-professed revolutionary group mattered quite a lot for these young men. Most of them had left the Congo as young teenagers. Under the UJRC umbrella, they felt intensely connected to the nationalist armed struggle in their distant homeland. By choosing to stand with the Congolese revolution, they claimed a political identity that served as a compass while they were coming of age as African expatriates in Europe, negotiating their relations to French society, positioning themselves in relation to the challenges of the present, and figuring out their place in the world.[37]

Wa Nsanga highly valued the kind of conscientization that happened among the Lyonnais. Each cell should evolve separately, he believed; unification would come later.[38] Meanwhile, the journal in its materiality created a paper community and space of projection for the readers.[39] Like E. D. Morel's *West African Mail* had done at the time of the red rubber campaign, *L'Eclair* dedicated a prominent place to readers' contributions. "Your articles, your information, all your news about every aspect of our revolutionary struggle," the editors enthusiastically declared, "must pile up on our desk."[40] Letters arrived from Algeria, Belgium, the two Congos, France, the two Germanys, Hungary, Italy, Poland, the Soviet Union, and Tanzania. The routes of the UJRC's mail mapped out an otherwise invisible transnational space of protest. Readers at home and in the diaspora saw their own political inclinations reflected in the writings of like-minded young revolutionary sympathizers. Photographs and manuscripts sent to *L'Eclair* from the Congo provided information to faraway readers about the "puppet regime" in Leopoldville, recent developments on the front, and testimonies of student involvement in the rebellions (see, e.g., figure 7.1); while articles about revolutionary ideology, anti-imperialist struggles, and social conquests in places like Albania, the Dominican Republic, Tanzania, or Vietnam contributed to the edification of all subscribers. The UJRC saw itself as bringing together "fighting young revolutionaries, soldiers,

Figure 7.1 "Four leaders from the eastern front (Congo-Leopoldville)," including Julien François Matutu (third from the right), a graduate from Lincoln University in Pennsylvania who collaborated with Malcolm X around his advocacy for the Congolese rebellion. Photographer unknown, ca. 1967 (source: author's collection).

workers, and students." For Wa Nsanga, this meant not simply creating a line of communication between the front and the rear but opening up a front that extended the combat zone of the revolution, the "information front."[41]

Antoine Robert, the former member of the FPC who had returned to the Congo to join the rebellion at the end of 1964, contributed several articles for *L'Eclair* under the pseudonym of Imani Mwana Lukale.[42] Initially, Robert presented the revolution as a transformative and educational process—one that would quickly "chase the ignorance in the spirits of our fighting peasants" and open "new horizons to thousands of patriots who had never considered them."[43] However, he was also realizing that the realities of the struggle did not fully align with his expectations and that he had much learning of his own to do. In a fifty-page essay he shared with his UJRC comrades, Robert wrote of his new vision of the revolution, which aimed to harmonize Marxist scientism with Congolese epistemologies, returning in a way to the position advocated by people like Gérard Buakasa within UGEC-Belgium.[44] *L'Eclair* did not publish the essay.[45] Although Wa Nsanga had defended the use of magic during the anti-colonial struggle in 1960,[46] he did not seem to sympathize with Robert's efforts to seriously engage the centrality of invisible agency among Simba fighters. Probably because Western journalists kept describing the rebels as irrational peasants, and also because he believed in the absolute necessity of universalizing the Congolese struggle, Wa Nsanga instead downplayed the articulation of the revolution with local histories and practices of insurgency.

L'Eclair did not bother much with the specificities of the struggle. Its discourse about the rebellion was both abstract and direct: it targeted readers that mostly resided far away from the front line, with a clear strategic goal to increase the antagonisms between conservatives and radical students. Articles talked of the "hypocritical notions like pacifism, humanitarianism, and love for humanity [that] blur[red] the distinction between friend and enemy,"[47] and urged students "to CHOOSE, to decide *once and for all.*" As Wa Nsanga repeated over and over, young Congolese could be on the side of the oppressors or on the side of the oppressed—there was no third option.[48] "We can either embark on the puppets' absurd dead end or we can become fighters and put ourselves at the service of the people who will judge, in total sovereignty, whether it is appropriate to accept us in the ranks of the Revolution."[49]

Readers of *L'Eclair* talked about sharing their theoretical knowledge with the masses by becoming "the books in which these popular masses will learn many things."[50] But their first battleground was within the student milieu itself. The task, a correspondent from Kinshasa explained, was "to decolonize our compatriots' mentality, to win thousands of undecided comrades to our cause, and to put an end to the arrogance of our pseudo-universitaires who are a shame to the Congolese elite."[51] *L'Eclair* contrasted these corrupted bourgeois students with intellectuals like Léonard Mitudidi who were active in the rebellions and could inspire their readers.[52] An article written by N'Kita Kabongo after a visit to eastern Congo sought to dismiss the idea that the Simba opposed students. "On the contrary, they want to be with intellectuals," N'Kita argued. "But revolutionary intellectuals, of course, and not petit-bourgeois reactionaries who only think about growing rich." N'Kita reported a conversation with the chief of the eastern front: "Kabila told me that comrades who don't want to directly commit themselves in the Revolution by coming to the front might be nationalists, but they are not revolutionaries." After listing the many functions students could fulfill on the front (as teachers, secretaries, information officers, or in other capacities), N'Kita concluded with a provocative question: "When will those who are outside of the country take this revolution seriously?"[53]

The Guevarist tone of Kabila's remarks to N'Kita contrasts with the UJRC's initial calls to build a student front around information and advocacy. And indeed, the more the situation deteriorated on the ground, the more *L'Eclair* advocated for a more direct involvement of students in the armed struggle. Dupire argued that students could not just look at the revolution from afar anymore: they should master both "the pen and

Figure 7.2 "Mobutu, Tshombe, Assassins de Lumumba," UJRC pamphlet, ca. 1967 (source: author's collection). French and Lingala slogans celebrate Marxism-Leninism, Mao's thoughts, Albania, and the union between Congolese and Vietnamese revolutionaries, while denouncing US imperialism and "fake communists" in Moscow, Prague, and Belgrade.

the gun" and "participate in the Revolution, arms in hands."[54] A strategic posture, this combat rhetoric widened the split in the student left—a split that Mobutu's coup and his attempt at co-opting student radicalism aggravated.[55] To the UJRC, the students who called themselves socialists and revolutionaries but refused to back the armed struggle proved their inability to unify "revolutionary theory and practice."[56]

From its inception, the UJRC strove to map a global ideological and theoretical framework onto the Congolese situation. This meant in particular connecting Lumumba to Marxism. As Wa Nsanga and his comrades reckoned, Lumumba may not have openly embraced Marx, but his thinking showed affinities with "the science of Marxism-Leninism" and, in all logic, he would have ended up a Marxist had he not been assassinated.[57] Some readers of *L'Eclair* may have perceived in this reasoning resonances of Catholic missionary theology and its notion of stepping-stones (pierres d'attente), which sought out aspects of "pagan" African societies seen as compatible with Christianity. In the same way that missionaries presented these stepping-stones as deeds of grace, as evidence that the divine had prepared the way for missionary work, young Marxist enthusiasts saw predetermination in the affinity between Lumumbism and Marxism. *L'Eclair* expressed this genealogical connection visually, bringing together portraits of Lumumba and Mao Zedong, as they did in a red-inked bilingual French-Lingala poster from 1967 (figure 7.2). Over time, however, references to images of Lumumba seemed to decrease, while portraits of Mao became more ubiquitous, as if the latter figure slowly absorbed the former.[58]

The Poetry of Insurrection

L'Eclair circulated clandestinely from hand to hand in the Congo.[59] In Europe as well, the UJRC had an aura of danger and mystery. Its ideological irredentism appealed to many. Students participated vicariously in the struggle for the second independence by the act of reading. Secrecy around the journal's production and circulation reinforced their feelings of fraternal intimacy and conspiratorial kinship. The journal had no proper network of distribution: it was sent to subscribers and was made available in the cafés and cultural centers patronized by Congolese students.

Joseph Mbelolo, a frequent reader, later remembered how the journal appeared in the *Maison africaine* in Liège nearly "miraculously," without anyone knowing who dropped the journal there.[60] Unlike the aforementioned students in Lyon, Mbelolo did not create a UJRC cell. Neither was he very interested in Maoism or the Hoxha regime in Albania. It was the fervor of *L'Eclair* that attracted him when he became engrossed in the journal. A student in Romance languages at the University of Liège, Mbelolo viewed the performing arts as a privileged platform for cultivating a revolutionary spirit among his peers. The main editor of the literary magazine of the Belgian section of UGEC, he also composed music, wrote poetry, and directed theater plays. Before joining the University of Liège, he had studied at a teachers' training school close to Brussels, where one of his professors, Raoul Vaneigem, introduced him to the Situationist International (SI). The illegitimate child of Dadaism and surrealism, the SI had made itself known throughout Europe with a series of provocative happenings that criticized the separation between art and life and denounced the reign of the spectacle—a term that Guy Debord, the Situationist journal's editor, defined as a social relationship mediated by images. The events in the Congo fascinated Vaneigem, Debord, and several other members of the SI. They believed that European revolutionaries could learn much from what Western journalists had denounced as the chaotic and irrational nature of the Lumumbist and Mulelist movement, which they considered instead as a poetic radical refusal of the world as it was.[61] Mbelolo and a few of his friends therefore appeared as precious interlocutors. Reading *L'Eclair* connected them to the revolution in the

Congo, which in turn informed many of their interactions with the SI and other left European groups.

L'Eclair mattered for students like Mbelolo because it provided a rhetoric of radicality unencumbered by the elitist etiquette and consensual tone that still dominated within the UGEC. Many students related to the search for a language that could express and translate the violence and passion of their political affects. More literally than the Situationists, they associated politics with poetry, a genre that several of them practiced assiduously in a way that resembled the reading of incendiary revolutionary publications like *L'Eclair*. One name emerged among the many student poets: Matala Mukadi. A close friend of Mbelolo, Matala had encountered his share of racial discriminations as a student in Belgium and he had turned to poetry and activism as ways to repair his assaulted dignity.[62] His poems truly made him the voice of a generation.[63] He dedicated these texts, which chronicled the revolutionary struggle through the filter of student expatriation, to figures such as Ndeshyo, Tshilenge, Lumumba, Padmore, Fanon, Malcolm X, Um N'Yobe, Ben Barka, Nguyen Van Troi, and Cienfuegos. In "Manzambi," his most famous poem—a quasi-national hymn for Congolese students in Belgium—he portrayed a dying rebel fighter in eastern Congo.[64]

Matala used a broad range of colors and emotions to transpose the aesthetic experience of the Congolese revolution into words. He echoed the Manichean order depicted in the pages of *L'Eclair* and looked at politics as a moral enterprise and internal struggle. His poems explored the intimate and nearly existential ramifications of revolutionary politics. In one of them, "*Echo du maquisard*," he juxtaposed the voice of a male combatant, insistent on sacrifice and dignity, with the voice of his female companion, whom he had left behind. This gendering of the struggle—through the lonely male fighter in the forest and his longing female lover left in the village—was belied by the fact that many women lived in Mulele's maquis. But Matala's lament reflected the demographic makeup of the student diaspora, where female students were a minority, often actively excluded from student politics by their male peers. The poem talked to how young Congolese in Europe who read *L'Eclair* and fantasized about joining the insurrection commingled their visions of the world and the self. These themes also appeared in "*Poète, ton silence est un crime*," a text written from the perspective of a student migrant who is longing about the Congo while strolling along a Belgian beach and looking at the sea. Matala wrote the text as a reflection on distance, describing the student's torment as he thinks about the struggle in faraway Congo and feels guilty for the pleasures he is able to enjoy in Europe—"love, dream, dance, . . . the embrace of a woman's body, . . . the immersion in the absinthes of life"—while others are struggling in maquis and forests. Matala, however, ended the poem with a clear call—"your silence is a crime"—that transcended the powerlessness of the expatriate revolutionary dreamer and claimed the virtue of testimony.[65]

Conclusion

The propaganda front of the Mulelist insurrection did not change the balance of power on Congolese battlefields. Still, the war of words and visions mattered. It may have enlarged the gulf between the distant intellectual construction of the revolution and the struggle's actual development in the maquis, but it did manage to establish the global significance of the Congo as a site of resistance against imperialism and neocolonialism. As the insurgents and their supporters soldiered on in shaping discussions about the moral and ideological superiority of their cause, they affirmed their struggle's relevance in the eyes of foreign backers and allies and mitigated the effects of the military retreat on the ground.

The UJRC's success mostly came from its ability to maintain a literary act of political shadow puppetry, achieved through the mystique of anonymity and secrecy. L'Eclair gave its readers the illusion that the UJRC was a more important force than it actually was, which encouraged students (both at home and in the diaspora) to believe in their collective political capacity. The UJRC forged ahead on the path of radicalization that had begun after the assassination of Lumumba. Until its demise in 1967, the group kept the feelings of rebelliousness among Congolese students simmering, and these feelings would soon erupt in a spectacular turn against the Mobutu regime.

In 1966, Thomas Mukwidi, one of the UJRC's closest allies in the CNL, offered a powerful self-critique of the Mulelist insurrection that explicitly sought to make room for revolutionary intellectuals in the struggle. Mukwidi wrote this booklet, L'an 3 de la révolution, immediately after attending the first Solidarity Conference of the Peoples of Africa, Asia, and Latin America (also known as the Tricontinental Conference) in Havana. His main criticisms centered on the bourgeois tendencies of the CNL leadership, a lack of proper training for cadres, and the near-total absence of action in cities. Student mobilizations against the regime, Mukwidi argued, could infuse new blood into the revolution and a switch from rural to urban guerilla tactics. That vision, which suggested challenges to both student politics and the revolutionary struggle, also became essential to the project of *L'Eclair* as the possibility of rapid military successes in the Kwilu and eastern Congo rapidly evaporated.

Sumbu's *Il sangue dei leoni* similarly envisioned the junction between radicalized students and the Mulelist insurgency as the way forward for the Congolese revolution. His text called for cinemas, "where we are intoxicated psychologically," to be bombed.[66] It also baldly announced that "the time for tyranny" had come and called "the African man [to] show the whole world his power."[67] Like the UJRC, Sumbu outlined a revised revolutionary strategy that would take the struggle to the cities and mobilize the student movement "as a catalyst for the silenced working class."[68]

While contested sensibilities emerged within Congolese engagements with revolutionary politics—Sumbu's nihilism differed from Mukadi's romanticism—the various textual interventions discussed above all rewrote the Congo into global revolutionary narratives. They offered young Congolese ways to engage with fresh cosmopolitan horizons. And they built bridges between the twin mystiques of peasant insurgency and of campus radicalism.

Jacques Bongoma's eyes shone with a youthful, mischievous sparkle when he talked to me about his life over several long sessions at his Kinshasa house in July and August 2011. Yet, he had been sick for several years by that point, and he was visibly frail and weak. Often, he stumbled in the middle of sentences, as if lost in time. As I later realized, these bouts of silence amplified ambient sounds in the recordings of our conversation. Most audible were the regular pounding of hammers in a shoemaking workshop that occupied half of the house where he lived, and the loud devout timbre of praying congregants at a nearby evangelical church that occurred around the clock. Strikingly, Bongoma's memories evoked a temporality that contrasted with the chronometric and eschatological tonalities of these background sounds. Nostalgia surfaced at times, but it did not dominate; it came up most notably when Bongoma talked of the palatial villa with a swimming pool, a view of the Congo River, and a ten-thousand-volume library that he lost at the fall of the Mobutu regime in 1997. The temporality that dominated as Bongoma faced up to dissonances between past and present was both more specific and more elusive: it was the long-gone futurity of the early postcolonial years.

The range of possibilities seemed particularly broad when Joseph Mobutu appointed Bongoma as one of his advisers after seizing the presidency in November 1965. The pair had met during Mobutu's visit to the United Kingdom the previous year. Bongoma was then a student at the

London School of Economics (LSE). He talked for an hour with Mobutu after a press conference that the general had given at the Savoy Hotel and was wooed by his humor, brilliance, and generosity (the meeting ended with a cash gift).[1] The admiration must have been mutual, as the general called the young economist to his side at the presidency on the morning that followed his coup. Bongoma occupied Joseph Kasa-Vubu's former office at the presidential palace. Although rumors claimed that Kasa-Vubu had hidden invisible and harmful magical objects in the room, it was exciting for Bongoma, barely twenty-seven years old at the time, to sit at the desk of the former president. Putting the Congo on the path of real independence was part of his job description. This was a daunting task, but Bongoma worked for a chief of state for whom military fiat was a natural form of public action, and he saw a historical opportunity to implement truly nationalist policies.

A dozen young university graduates worked at Mobutu's side in those years. The general chose them for their association with the student left, in marked contrast with his insistence on the apolitical nature of his College of General Commissioners in 1960.[2] Bongoma and a young lawyer named Gérard Kamanda, the two most influential of these advisers,[3] were reportedly as thick as thieves, but their temperaments differed markedly. Kamanda had been a campus radical and formidable orator at Lovanium. He did not fear direct action, and he served time in jail in 1965 for his intransigent opposition to then–prime minister Moïse Tshombe.[4] Bongoma, on the other hand, had learned to navigate between worlds and adapt to new circumstances from a young age. His life had been a succession of lateral moves: as a young teenager, he had left the remote upriver town of Bolobo so that he could continue his secondary education in Leopoldville. When being a Catholic was required to access a more prestigious school, he abandoned the Salvation Army Church of his parents and converted. In 1958, he was part of the first sizable cohort of young Congolese allowed to relocate to Europe as university students. Before going to LSE, he first studied at the Institut Catholique des Hautes Etudes Commerciales in Brussels. A personable, mild-mannered, handsome young man, he easily picked up new languages, attracted beautiful girls, enjoyed Baroque music, and spent time in the old bourgeois cafés in Sablon Square. Politics entered his everyday life at this time. "With all these people I was around, I too had . . . *naughty left ideas* . . . as my English friends said," he later recounted.[5] In 1959, a series of memorable trips—to the Second Congress of Negro Writers and Artists, to Vienna for the Seventh World Festival of Youth and Students, and to Crimea for a road trip—shaped his views in the long term. Most notably he returned from the Soviet Union convinced that socialism held the key to Africa's development, and in the years that followed, he took night classes with the Trotskyist economist Ernest Mandel, befriended the Communist Youth leader Eddy Poncelet, and took a leadership position in the General Union of Congolese Students (UGEC). Yet, all along, he remained as committed to urbanity as he was to the left.

When he served as an adviser to Mobutu, Bongoma was well known for his sense of humor and the dashing MGB sports car he drove. He spoke English well and played tennis even better, and many foreign residents sought his company.[6] His charm, however, operated on Western diplomats only for so long. These foreigners initially welcomed the presence of young intellectuals like Bongoma at the side of the president, even when these advisers "tend[ed] to speak the language of Marxism." In general, they felt that Mobutu struck the right balance by "assum[ing] the leadership of the left without making demagogic appeals to the extreme left."[7] They could understand decisions to Africanize city names or reduce the role of white mercenaries in the army. But when Bongoma and Kamanda convinced Mobutu to partially nationalize the Union minière du Haut-Katanga, Westerners found it a hard pill to swallow.[8] The public affair officer at the US embassy thought that the American government should "insist as quid pro quo for our assistance that Kamanda and perhaps Bongoma be fired, since they [are the] persons responsible for the [government of Congo]'s recent mistakes and are working against US interests."[9] Mobutu complied. At the end of 1967, he put a few thousand kilometers between him and Kamanda, sending the young man to work as a high-ranking official at the Organization of African Unity headquarters in Addis Ababa. A few months later, the president indicated that Bongoma also had stopped being essential and he encouraged him to go on a monthlong tour of the United States. Bongoma's relationship with Mobutu was not permanently broken, and he kept using his business cards from the presidency for months after this trip. Still, he had lost his position in the innermost circle of power. He attempted to mitigate his reputation as a radical by writing a book on African development that praised Mobutu's pragmatism.[10] This was to no avail. Bongoma's star continued to decline, and in 1971, a prosecutor built a case of treason against him that saw him arrested.[11]

Bongoma's proximity to power before his downfall was so intense that a persistent rumor had it that he was Mobutu's lover. Bongoma dismissed the rumor as a simple expression of jealousy, but his retelling of this period in his life does go from infatuation to broken romance. This emotional story line, as well as the journey from having a prime office in the presidential palace to being shut in a crowded yard in Kinshasa's central prison, paralleled the ups and downs in the relationship between Mobutu and the student movement during the same period. The presence of figures like Bongoma and Kamanda in the presidential team helped make Mobutu attractive to student activists; and their marginalization coincided with the growing disillusionment of many of the students about the limits of Mobutism.[12] During one of our conversations, Bongoma also placed himself at the center of a key episode in the relationship between the dictator and the students: the decision to proclaim Lumumba a national hero in June 1966. The story he told is worth quoting at length:

> This is how it happened. One day in June 1966—it must have been the 12th, a Sunday—Mobutu arrived at my place: "Jacques, June 30 is coming soon and I want to make a great speech. Write a draft and we'll discuss it." After Mobutu left, I prayed a lot. The next morning, I told him, "I would like to take inspiration from [Lumumba's Independence Day] speech. Do you have objections to that?" He replied, "Come over home next Sunday morning and I will tell you what I think of Lumumba."
>
> I knew he was an early riser and I arrived at seven thirty on the following Sunday. I waited in the living room with the minister of information, Jean-Jacques Kande, a former UGEC member who had studied in Prague. At seven fifty, [Mobutu] invited us to have breakfast with him and his wife. Then he took me by the hand—he often made affectionate gestures—and we walked down to the end of the garden. He first sat down on the lawn, and then I did as well, like in the movie *Breakfast at Tiffany's*! And then he said, "I am going to tell you the truth about Lumumba. If I am president today, it is thanks to him. He had a lot of trust in the intellectual youth like I have trust in you. The first time I met Lumumba, it was *love at first sight*, a coup de foudre. When he asked me to work with him, I was like the Apostles with Jesus: I said yes immediately. And I gave up everything to become his private secretary." Mobutu indeed read the Bible a lot and often made biblical references—he truly was a phenomenal man, Mobutu! He told me Lumumba knew he was going to die because of his extremist nationalist politics: "I warned Patrice"—he always said simply Patrice—"and Patrice answered, like in the Bible, like Jesus, 'There is no greater love than giving one's life for others.'" When Mobutu said that Lumumba accepted to die for the freedom of the Congo, I told him, "He was like a national hero who died for the fatherland." So Mobutu said, "Write

that down in the speech. Here is what we are going to do: we are going to proclaim him a national hero." . . . He then put his hands in his *boubou*'s pocket and took out photographs to show to Jean-Jacques and me, telling us that they were pictures of the house where Lumumba was killed in Katanga: "We will turn this house into a memorial that people who come to the country, African nationalists and others, will be able to visit."[13]

Visualizing Mobutu as a character in *Breakfast at Tiffany's* may require a great effort of imagination.[14] Still, Bongoma's recollection is precious for the multiple affective associations it contains. In Bongoma's retelling, Lumumba and Mobutu overlapped as Christlike figures, appearing both as subjects and objects of love. Indeed, when Mobutu proclaimed his former mentor a national hero, he was well aware of the emotional capital this would generate for him. The speech that Bongoma wrote for Mobutu, which had been announced on the radio for days before the ceremony as an exceptional allocution, created a level of popular support for the president that he had never had before. Reportedly, the "crowd of 25,000 cheered every mention of Mr. Lumumba's name, although they were silent through most of a 5,000-word speech in which the president promised prosperity and an end to all the vestiges of Belgium's economic control."[15]

Ultimately, Mobutu's proclaiming of Lumumba as a national hero, like other measures suggested by his progressive young advisers, gave him traction with the student left for only a short time. The general had enjoyed parading in his Lumumbist attire, but he had no clothes. Enthusiasm for Mobutu dramatically declined in student circles and a new cadre of activists worked to initiate a confrontation with the regime. The following two chapters explore how, when the president's broken promises alienated more and more students, he made increasingly clear that although he had cajoled before, he would not hesitate to crack down now. Like Bongoma, many students endured imprisonment. Some were exiled. Others suffered an even more tragic fate when a student protest in June 1969 turned into the first state massacre in postcolonial Kinshasa.

EIGHT
(UN)NATURAL ALLIANCES

UGEC has no obligation to define itself in relation to any given regime, since it constitutes the country's avant-garde. Instead it is up to the present regime and those that will come after it to adopt and apply the ideology that the recent UGEC congress has determined to be the only path of salvation for the Congo: scientific socialism.

UGEC-Belgium, "Réponse à l'article paru dans la Voix du Peuple," February 7, 1967, 2

Our revolution does not have anything to do with revolutions in Pekin, Moscow or Cuba. It is not based on ready-made theories nor on borrowed doctrines. It is . . . a truly national revolution, inherently pragmatic, nurtured by experience, and tailored to the specific characteristics of the country. It rejects capitalism as it does communism.

J. D. Mobutu, *Manifeste de la N'Sele*, May 20, 1967

This book has been arguing that students positioned themselves at the interface of the Congo and the world through the 1960s. They continued but also transcended the intellectual and ideological transactions that earlier generations could only conduct through postal correspondences. Well-stocked university libraries, contacts with peers of various backgrounds, and scholarships to study abroad offered resources to mediate the politics of distance. The ability to manipulate and deploy the rhetoric of sovereignty, liberation, and development, as well as the capacity to critically reflect on global interconnections proved even more crucial in light of the general internationalization of Congolese affairs in the aftermath of independence. In 1961, reckoning with the assassination of Patrice Lumumba and the role of the General Commissioners in the Congo crisis moved students to denounce the colonial matrix of higher education. The late-colonial language of elitism did not fully disappear, but it now coexisted with claims of political vanguardism. The General Union of Congolese Students (UGEC) took the mantle of nationalism, as a commitment to a united and fully independent Congo, and a response to what the world expected from the Congo's educated youth. Quickly, the same students embraced the idea that a revolution was both necessary and ineluctable. Students disagreed about what this revolution should concretely accomplish, but they all believed it had to address the Congo's place in Africa and the world. Joseph Mobutu's coup happened in this context.

On Pentecost in 1966, five months into the new regime, four politicians accused of conspiracy, including former prime minister Evariste Kimba, were hanged in front of a crowd of several thousand people in Leopoldville. This violent spectacle shocked, but it also symbolized a willingness to level the political field. While Mobutu initially chose to keep the old political establishment at bay, he relied on a squad of young university-trained advisers. The new president was convinced he could use the students' political energies to his own advantage, and he encouraged them to think that their time to shape national politics had finally come.[1] In reality, this alliance was unstable and indeed untenable. Both Mobutu and the students believed they would emerge as the dominant partner in the relationship, but a fallout was bound to happen. This chapter retraces the gradual illumination of the antagonisms that had always existed between the dictator and the students (both at Lovanium and within the national committee of UGEC). The chapter also shows how, in the long term, the difficulty to harness the student left forced Mobutu to invent his own ideological dressing.

From Scientific Socialism to Authentic Nationalism

Mobutu intended the stadium ceremony that proclaimed Lumumba a national hero in June 1966 as a momentous show of strength (figure 8.1). Parades, musical performances, and a theatrical reenactment of the floggings that were dealt to the Congolese for petty offenses in the colonial period all served to stage the new regime's nationalist creed. The presence of prominent foreign guests like Kenneth Kaunda and Julius Nyerere symbolized the Congo's return to the rank of progressive African nations

Figure 8.1 CVR members dressed in Mobutu shirts are carrying a portrait of Lumumba during a street rally. Photographer unknown, June 1966 (source: ARNACO, MPR Papers).

after a period of banishment under Tshombe.[2] One speech at the event also certainly caused Mobutu a great deal of satisfaction. André N'Kanza Dolomingu, the national president of UGEC, took the stage during the ceremony to solemnly thank the new authorities for "their clear understanding that the youth had a key role to play as an intellectual avant-garde in a country like ours, which is fighting against various forms of alienation and domination."[3] This remarkable endorsement contrasted with UGEC's near-systematic opposition to previous governments.

A few months earlier, N'Kanza and other UGEC officers had already agreed to help launch the Corps des Volontaires de la République (the Republic's Volunteer Corps, CVR), an organization created by two journalists, Gaston Nsengi-Biembe and Paul-Henri Kabayidi, to assist Mobutu in his crusade against "the diabolical maneuvers orchestrated by the enemies of the Congo."[4] Kabayidi had been active in the student movement earlier in the decade (see chapter 5). Not less crucially, he had also been a well-known figure in the world of the Bills, Leopoldville's youth gangs. His connections to former "street cowboys" and to left intellectuals allowed him to mobilize the muscles and the brains that the Mobutu regime needed.[5]

Kabayidi and Nsengi-Biembe also looked across the Congo River for ideas about state building: in presenting the CVR as a radical anti-imperialist organization, they drew much inspiration from the rhetoric and strategies of popular mobilization of the Jeunesse du Mouvement National de la Révolution (JMNR), the youth branch of the one-party state established in the aftermath of the 1963 revolution in Congo-Brazzaville.[6] The similarities between the CVR and the JMNR in turn attracted people like N'Kanza to the new Mobutist organization.

Although N'Kanza attended several meetings of the CVR and spoke at the June ceremony, he was careful not to immerse himself fully in the Mobutist bath. He refused an official position within the CVR, arguing that the student union needed to maintain its independence from the new regime.[7] UGEC responded with reasoned enthusiasm to the progressive measures taken by the government, but it remained fixated on developing and fostering its own agenda. Many students could have been described with the terms that an American visitor used to situate politically Yvon Bongoy, a member of the UGEC bureau: "pro-Lumumba, strongly nationalistic, moderately pro-Mobutu but unwilling to commit."[8]

Pragmatically, UGEC took advantage of Mobutu's goodwill and organized its third congress, which had been postponed several times because of the hostility of previous governments (so much so that the students even considered organizing it in Algiers).[9] By contrast with Adoula and Tshombe, Mobutu authorized UGEC to hold the meeting in Kinshasa and bring delegates from across the Congo and the student diaspora. The most important item on their agenda was the question of ideological clarification, which had been pushed forward by the ardor for the idea of revolution in student circles in the past few years. After tense discussions but in line with the views of N'Kanza and most other members of the bureau, the congress officially proclaimed scientific socialism as the sole and unique path for the Congo.[10]

This was a delicate move to make. N'Kanza opened the congress by acknowledging the authorities' open-mindedness. He claimed that the student union wished to help the government find "the right path to lead the Congolese people to its final victory in the struggle against exploitation and alienation."[11] He also quoted from speeches by Mobutu that expressed promises to firmly oppose imperialism and fight against the Congo's recolonization. Using Mobutu's own words was an astute and careful rhetorical strategy, but N'Kanza also more bluntly complained that the state did not do enough to Africanize universities and he insisted that only socialism could bring durable peace and authentic democracy. A few weeks after the congress, N'Kanza traveled to Lubumbashi to explain UGEC's recent resolutions to students there. During a two-hour talk that focused in great part on explaining the tenets of Marxism-Leninism, he presented the Second Republic as "a necessary historical stage in the Congo's evolution towards socialism."[12] Dialectics served N'Kanza well, allowing him to simultaneously legitimize the Mobutu regime and announce its future replacement by a more advanced system (even more so since Mobutu had not yet reneged on his promise to occupy the presidency for only five years). Some people reacted strongly against this form of intellectual gymnastics. US diplomats called UGEC's embrace of scientific socialism "crazy" and a sign of "communist infiltration."[13] In December 1966, Colonel Alexandre Singa, the head of the Sûreté, announced the arrest of labor activists suspected of communist allegiance.[14] This was a warning that UGEC activists could not fail to register. Still, they decided to ignore it. N'Kanza continued to vocally promote the new Marxist orientation. He argued that socialism could be developed in the Congo through a transformation of higher education, which would force the universities to open their doors to the masses, to abandon elitism, and to initiate students into methodic observation, analytic dialectics, and innovation.[15] This went far beyond the reforms that the state was willing to promote. In March 1967, the government's decision not to authorize an international conference on Lumumba's legacy, which UGEC hoped to organize, offered a confirmation that N'Kanza's radical positions rubbed many people in Mobutu's entourage the wrong way. The students had looked at this conference, to which they had planned to invite Jean-Paul Sartre and Aimé Césaire, as a platform to increase their pressure vis-à-vis the regime's ideological orientation.[16] Yet, with the event being called off, entryism seemed it had reached an impasse. A few weeks later, N'Kanza openly criticized the president for the first time, while attending a meeting of the International Union of Students (IUS) in Ulan Bator. N'Kanza notably put his name under motions that called Mobutu a lackey of the Americans and criticized "the measures of intimidation now being inflected" on UGEC.[17]

Students had forged ahead when embracing scientific socialism.[18] For all of his audacity, Mobutu could not go down their path. His pushback against UGEC coincided with an effort to reposition himself within the ideological battlefield. Soon after N'Kanza's return from Mongolia, Mobutu replaced the CVR with a new organization better tailored to his regime, the Mouvement Populaire de la République (MPR).[19] The MPR would evolve into a state party that absorbed the administration and organized a personality cult around the figure of the autocrat.[20] But it was initially designed to counter Mobutu's dependence on the left and reinforce his image as a progressive leader.[21] In May 1967, Justin-Marie Bomboko, Joseph N'Singa, and Etienne Tshisekedi—three collaborators of Mobutu who had entered politics as student leaders in the late 1950s and early 1960s—authored a manifesto for the MPR that articulated these priorities, and promised to restore the Congo's prestige in the world. Mirroring other state ideologies that embraced populism and rejected Cold War binaries, the Mobutist manifesto "establish[ed] itself outside of the signifying system itself."[22] It rejected both capitalism and communism as sources for "the sorrows of the Congolese people," and it promised that the principles of Congolese nationalism would guide all economic policies.[23]

Appropriating the left's signifiers, the MPR claimed the idea of revolution for itself. Still, its version of revolution did not go much beyond the "cosmetics of power."[24] What mattered was to break Mobutu's dependency on left students. The competition focused not only on words and symbols. The MPR intended to cut the ground out from under UGEC's feet. To do so, it created its own youth branch, the Jeunesse du Mouvement Populaire de la Révolution (JMPR), and poached Guillaume Sampassa, a UGEC leader in Lubumbashi, who had been a proponent of the Marxist line.[25] Sampassa's mission at the JMPR was to establish the movement's presence in schools and universities and root UGEC out from the landscape. Sampassa's former comrades in the student union experienced his departure for the JMPR as a trauma.[26] It added to other recent defections, which had turned the national committee of UGEC into an embattled fortress, at a moment when it faced criticisms for its lack of ethnic representativity.[27] Yet, UGEC's influence remained strong thanks to school protests that multiplied around the country and validated its combative orientation.

The Inspired Hill Occupied

Conflicts were on the rise in 1967. The problematic implementation of a civic service that required hundreds of students to interrupt their education and teach for two years in secondary schools created resentment against the government.[28] But student protests did not necessarily challenge the state. Many strikes started over the food served in school restaurants or the obtuse authoritarianism of professors and school authorities. This was the case at Lovanium in February 1967.

As we saw in a previous chapter, Mobutu had visited the Inspired Hill very quickly after his coup in 1965. The president of the student government at the time, Tharcisse Mwamba, warmly welcomed the general and expressed his willingness to help the regime's program of national renewal. Weeks later, when Mwamba refused invitations from the authorities to discuss concrete collaborations between the student government and the state, many students on campus expressed their incomprehension.[29] In parallel, members of the General Assembly of Students (AGEL) revealed that Mwamba had selectively shared information about fellowship opportunities with students from his native Katanga. Challenged both for his inconsistency vis-à-vis Mobutu and for his supposed tribalism, he was forced to resign in December 1966.[30] Mathieu Nzanda-Buana succeeded him at the presidency of AGEL. The new president was particularly careful to distinguish himself from his predecessor, including from Mwamba's close alignment with the UGEC's national committee. Although his campaign promise was to be as radical as Fidel Castro, Nzanda-Buana had also claimed to be a free thinker who would not blindly follow the new Marxist line in fashion.[31] Once elected, he wanted no ambiguity in the relation between the Inspired Hill and Mount Ngaliema (the spot on the Congo River where Mobutu had established his residency). In January 1967, he mobilized students for a street demonstration to celebrate the regime's nationalization of the Union Minière du Haut Katanga. A few days later, he organized a salongo—a state-sponsored voluntary cleaning of public space—in Mobutu's presence. Mwamba seized the occasion to offer to the president the distinctive cap that only "baptized" Lovanium students could wear, making him an honorary member of the student community.

Less than a week after the salongo, a fateful incident happened at Lovanium. A nurse at the university hospital refused to assist a student's distressed pregnant wife. When the woman lost her pregnancy a few days later, her husband and four of his friends from the married students union returned to the hospital to retaliate, beating up the nurse as well as two agents from the university police.[32] The university expelled the five married students and pressed charges against them. Many of their peers on campus found these measures upsetting. They saw the incident at the hospital as emblematic of everyday infringements on their dignity. The campus was still overwhelmingly male, and the university continued to regiment the sexual life of unmarried students, so the gender dimensions of the incident—the fact that the university refused to consider the married student's duty to protect and defend his wife as mitigated circumstances—resonated. AGEL threatened to block the campus if the married students were not immediately reintegrated. Nzanda-Buana was convinced he could twist Rector Luc Gillon's arm thanks to the support of the government. He had discussed the situation with Gérard Kamanda, the former student activist who had become one of Mobutu's closest advisers. Kamanda told him that he absolutely agreed that the expelled students should be reintegrated, but he also asked him to temporize. Yet, Nzanda-Buana's desire to act was too strong. On the morning of February 20, two weeks after the beginning of the crisis, AGEL carried out its threat, launching the first major strike at Lovanium since the black pudding revolution of 1964. Students imposed a full blockade of the campus, occupied most of the administrative buildings, and demanded nothing less than Gillon's departure.[33] This intransigence annoyed the government, and Mobutu sent in the army to put a forceful end to the strike. Soldiers reopened the campus and remained at Lovanium for several days. This was the first time that the army had intervened on the Inspired Hill. The transgression upset AGEL students, even more so since, only a few weeks earlier, they had made Mobutu a honorary "old wolf" (as upper-class students were called). A graffiti appeared nocturnally on the wall of a campus building: "Long live Karl Marx and Lenin! Down with Mobutu!"[34]

Despite the campus reopening, Gillon responded aggressively to the strike. An internal memo released on February 22 insisted that spoiled students should not be allowed any significant power in the governance of Lovanium.[35] The university announced the immediate expulsion of Nzanda-Buana and three other AGEL activists. Gillon also demanded that all the other students individually sign a document pledging respect for Lovanium's bylaws before being allowed back in class. The rector may have had in mind the criticisms from church officials in Kinshasa and Rome who believed he had been too soft in dealing with Marxist students.[36] In any case, he was convinced that Mobutu had disavowed the students by sending in the army to stop the strike.[37] What Gillon did not realize was that the president had other chess moves up his sleeve. If AGEL's precipitous intervention and Nzanda-Buana's overconfidence had bothered Mobutu, the general remained aware that many Congolese looked at Lovanium as the "last stronghold of colonialism in the Congo."[38] The crisis on campus had offered the authorities an opportunity to tame student agitators, but it could also add to the regime's effort at building up its nationalist credentials.

On April 5, the minister of education wrote a short letter ordering Gillon to reintegrate Nzanda-Buana and his fellow AGEL activists at Lovanium.[39] This was a grievous blow to the university leadership. Gillon thought the decision unfair to him, but he also believed that sanctioning a student power that could one day be turned against Mobutu was dangerously shortsighted on the part of the government.[40] The rector only obtained a couple of formal concessions: a new letter from the minister of education presented the reintegration of Nzanda-Buana as a recommendation rather than as a demand and claimed it had been made in the spirit of de-escalating tensions and keeping student protests from destabilizing the whole country.[41] Nzanda-Buana himself wrote a half-hearted apology that Gillon ungraciously accepted. Nonetheless, the Belgian priest's hand had been forced, and two months later, he tendered his resignation from Lovanium. His successor at the rectorship was Tharcisse Tshibangu, a Congolese priest and theologian. The new rector had made a name for himself in 1960 when, as a young doctoral student, he had challenged the universalist dogma that dominated at Lovanium, arguing that it was necessary to develop a specific African theological tradition.[42] A few years later, he had also served as theological expert on the Second Vatican Council. He was only thirty-four when he became rector, but he was already a renowned intellectual, whose approach to African theology owed much to his friendship with Alioune Diop, the Parisian-based editor of *Présence africaine*.[43] Mobutu knew Tshibangu's views about the necessity of combining Christianity with African authenticity and he took much satisfaction in his appointment to Lovanium's rectorship.[44] When a dozen heads of state came to Kinshasa for a meeting of the Organization of African Unity in September 1967, Mobutu organized only two outings for them: one being the inauguration of the Lumumba monument on the road to the airport and another a guided tour of the Inspired Hill.[45]

Student activists applauded Gillon's fall from power. However, they wanted more steps taken toward the decolonization and democratization of higher education. A ten-page memorandum released by the Lovanium branch of UGEC in November 1967 highlighted the new tone of student demands in the aftermath of the February strike. The text combined campus activism, nationalist politics, and world ideologies. It presented the fight against the students' tribalism and disconnection from the proletariat as concrete steps toward opposing neocolonialism and undermining the "comprador bourgeoisie" that had captured the benefits of the Congo's independence for itself. Similarly, to these UGEC activists, democratizing the university mattered as much as professing solidarity with the Vietnamese people.[46] Some of the points they were making echoed the systemic critique of higher education that Benoit Verhaegen had developed for several years.[47] Yet, their memorandum offered students' own take on these questions. Discourse was not an aside for them. They perceived intellectual labor—the "discreet and quiet work" of "meditating and communicating one's knowledge"—as central to their political practice.[48] Giving expression to diffuse feelings among the student body, texts like the UGEC memorandum reinterpreted past events and kept pushing for new struggles. They also cleared up any lingering ambiguity about the antagonisms that existed between the students and the authorities. When the minister of education Bernardin Mungul-Diaka visited Lovanium to attend a theater performance on December 30, 1967, students greeted him with whistles and hisses—the honeymoon was unequivocally over.[49] Five days later, Hubert Humphrey landed in Kinshasa and received a similar reception from the students.

1968

As already made clear in this book's introduction, the US vice president's brief stopover dramatically affected relations between the student activists and the Mobutu regime. The night before Humphrey's arrival, UGEC activists at Lovanium quickly drafted and distributed posters against American imperialism in Vietnam, calling on fellow students to demonstrate in front of the Lumumba monument at which they believed Humphrey would stop on his way from the airport.[50] The framing of the protest appealed to the students' internationalist spirit. It also clearly signaled defiance against Mobutu. The following morning, the police brutally quashed the anti-American gathering, beating up and arresting more than two hundred students. In the aftermath of this event, pamphlets portraying Mobutu as a stooge of American imperialism circulated at the Ecole Nationale de Droit et d'Administration and other schools in Kinshasa.[51] As UGEC activists asked bluntly in a public statement: how could Mobutu claim to oppose imperialism when he was friends with "the country that most embodied imperialism?"[52]

This statement unnerved the authorities. Police reports had shown that these kinds of criticisms of the president began producing some echoes among the masses.[53] And UGEC was adding fuel to the fire with plans for a conference to address Mobutu's role in the Congo crisis, which they scheduled for the anniversary of Lumumba's death. The general lashed out against N'Kanza in the press, calling him "a brainless loser who has never done anything for his country . . . , an outcast and bitter madman who can only distinguish himself through unwarranted and grouchy criticisms."[54] The president's indictment started a chain of repression: the police arrested N'Kanza and other members of the national committee, the army occupied different schools around Kinshasa, the Universities of Kisangani and Lubumbashi expelled activists, and Mobutu summoned Rector Tshibangu to demand his full cooperation in the offensive against the student movement.[55] A few weeks later, the Sûreté stormed Lovanium and arrested a sociology student named François Kalonji. They tortured the young man and brought him before Mobutu to confess that he had been a correspondent for the Maoist student publication *L'Eclair* (see chapter 6). The national radio reported on his arrest and called him "the head of a subservice network."[56] On the same day, the political bureau of the MPR announced the dissolution of UGEC's national committee.

In the eyes of the regime, UGEC de facto ceased to exist from that moment on. Many Congolese students abroad vehemently protested these repressive measures and some lost their state scholarships as a result. In Belgium, the immigration services gladly collaborated with the Congolese embassy by suppressing open dissent among expatriate students and canceling the residency permits of the most vocal opponents.[57] Repression forced several activists to turn to illegal ways to make ends meet, while some also experienced imprisonment and deportation.[58] However, many expatriate students successfully resisted the attempt at silencing. The revolutionary energies of the 1968 protest movements in Europe stimulated them, encouraging them to reject incorporation into the JMPR, to keep UGEC alive or even launch new organizations to oppose the Mobutu regime and its "tribalo-fascisme."[59] In the Congo, by contrast, a combination of police repression and a systematic campaign of harsh attacks against "subversive" students in newspapers and on the radio actively lowered the volume of student rage. Some saw a silver lining in the repression (as Jean Ilunga Kabese, a senior student at Lovanium, wrote in a long letter to the publishers of *L'Eclair* two days after the arrest of N'Kanza, "our morale remains very good because, as Chairman Mao teaches us, being attacked by the enemy is a sign that we have traced a clear line of demarcation between the enemy and us").[60] Many students, however, were afraid that they, like N'Kanza or Kalonji, may well forever vanish in the Second Republic's prison system if they continued to confront the state.[61]

Hubert Tshimpumpu had to be cautious. As the new president of AGEL, he was particularly exposed. Yet, he believed that students should convince Mobutu that it was in his best interests to allow freedom of expression on university campuses, since free speech was a necessary condition for the emergence of a critical discourse able to fully decolonize Congolese culture and society.[62] In this context of repression, imposed self-censorship, and restraint, Tshimpumpu offered a new vision of student politics that diverged from the language of scientific socialism and instead privileged a language of rights that would increasingly resonate in the political opposition to the dictatorship in the decades that followed.

It is doubtful that Mobutu gave any consideration to Tshimpumpu's arguments, but he was not opposed to mending his relationship with the students and the intellectual left in general. The government, for instance, reiterated its support for Afro-Monde, a group that operated a "House of Friendship" in Kinshasa, which had served as a meeting place between student activists and young Mobutist operatives.[63] In July, the president also launched a series of consultations with various "constituted bodies," including student representatives, dedicating 136 hours to these listening sessions. The French ambassador reported that these consultations were a sign that Mobutu was drifting leftward again. He mentioned "a strange end of mourning ceremony *à la mode locale*" organized by the president to commemorate Lumumba in the presence of the dead prime minister's widow and numerous politicians, military officials, and foreign diplomats.[64] Around the same time, the Congolese government released a "Little Green Book" of quotations from Mobutu that copied the format and aesthetic of Mao Zedong's Little Red Book and attempted to reengage the left.[65] However, this all remained tactical maneuvering on the part of a skillful chess player. Mobutu was after complete dominance, not consensus.

Conclusion

Nearly three years into his presidency, Mobutu's cyclothymic temperament, like his paternal manipulation of the forces of punishment and pardon, ceased to surprise.[66] His treatment of student activists suggested a pattern to the way he managed his political personnel: collaborators were kept on their toes, but opponents never had the door permanently shut on them. In the case of N'Kanza, for instance, the general first tried to woo and use, but when this failed, he threatened and cracked down. Finally, he absolved the UGEC leader and ordered his release from prison at the end of August 1968.[67]

Unpredictability and violence were pillars of the Second Republic. Political opponents often underwent physical abuses and torture in prison.[68] Some, like Pierre Mulele, disappeared forever (see chapter 5). His murder in October 1968 recalled the public hangings of 1966 and the assassination of Lumumba in 1961. It fully exposed the darkest side of Mobutu's power.[69] The students perceived and problematized this aspect of Mobutu's rule, even if many had initially rejoiced at his coup. Those who ended up working for the general were willing to trade protest for influence and participation. But approval of the new regime did not last. As Mobutu's actions increasingly marginalized the students, marooning them in an uncomfortable zone where they had to fight for their political survival, they began to craft their demands using the rhetoric of human rights. The main point in the memorandum they presented to Mobutu in July 1968 concerned the "right to speak and create freely." They polemically asserted that governments in developed countries responded to student dissenters with "subtle constraints," whereas brutally repressive responses in Africa "dulled man and prevented him from producing intellectual work."[70] The comparison was debatable and certainly did not tally with the experience of state repression by expatriate Congolese students in Belgium or France. Yet, this trenchant critique of the postcolony—a critique of the impasse of authoritarian nationalism—testified to the productivity of the students' political quest to decolonize Congolese higher education.

NINE
A POSTCOLONIAL MASSACRE AND CAPORALISATION IN MOBUTU'S CONGO

The athénée of Kalina was one of the most leftist secondary schools in Kin-shasa. We listened to "La voix de la révolution" on Radio-Brazzaville; Marien Ngouabi, Ho Chi Min, Castro, Mao and the Soviets were well known among us; and students in our group Sovietized and "Vietcong-ized" their names: Mukunovich, Kumbalev, Mpo Hin, Tung Dan Nga, Kam bung Pang'i etc.

Shungu Tundanonga-Dikunda, "4 juin 1969: Il y a 43 ans.
Ne pas oublier," unpublished, 2012

We want cultural revolution Mao style not imperialist style.

Student slogan, Institut national des arts, Kinshasa, January 1969

Our country is about to adopt governing methods defined by Marx, applied by Lenin and perfected by Stalin. But do not be mistaken: our Party and the Congolese people will not convert to the Marxist ideology; instead we will sim-ply apply principles of rigorous discipline that characterize [those who] follow Marx, Lenin and Castro. . . . From now on, no one—no students, no workers, no state employees, no ministers—no one will trifle with discipline and with the orders from the Party, which has chosen for its basic doctrine a nationalism that is neither right nor left. Opinion piece, Congolese National Radio, June 16, 1969

At the end of May 1968, a fight among some students at the University of Lubumbashi led to what the authorities described as a night of riot. The context around the clash remained somewhat unclear, but it did not prevent the local US consulate from coming up with an easy explanation for the "flare-up": campus agitators had simply been looking for "excuses to act up like students everywhere this Spring."[1] The consulate officer who provided this reading was not alone in articulating relations of causality between youth rebelliousness in the Congo and elsewhere in the world. Not all commentators denigrated students as mere imitators of foreign movements, but the feeling prevailed that a worldwide chain of protests informed events in Central Africa. As we saw, the students themselves time and time again situated their politics within a cosmopolitan horizon and framed their actions by referring to the global context of youth rebelliousness.

The anti-Humphrey rally of January 1968 of course reinforced this framing, while also marking the end of the peaceful coexistence between Joseph Mobutu and the students. This chapter hones in on the three years of confrontations that ensued—from mid-1968 to mid-1971. The intense repression that marked this period unmasked the colonial atavism of the Mobutu regime: its dependence on sheer violence and on caporalisation, a term that, referring to the imposed submission to petty authoritarianism, had a specific valence at the time of global 1968.[2] Colonial shadows were made dramatically manifest when soldiers opened fire on a peaceful protest in June 1969 and when the government conscripted Lovanium students into the army two years later. More diffuse attempts at circumscribing, containing, and neutralizing the students' political imagination were no less important. As the chapter argues, what was at stake at the close of the 1960s was the mental ligature that tied Congolese students to a worldwide community of dissent—a ligature that the Mobutu regime was resolute on cutting.

Contested Political Geographies

Student internationalism bothered the Congolese authorities because it always shed light on the unfinished nature of decolonization. For instance, when students at the Free University of Kisangani walked out of their classrooms after Martin Luther King's assassination in Memphis, they wished to express solidarity with African Americans *and* denounce episodes of racism on their own campus—an institution sponsored by American Protestant churches and staffed with many white American professors.[3] Like Malcolm X a few years earlier, they considered that the Congo and the Mississippi were one and the same.[4] The making visible of broader geographies of race and imperialism empowered these students, while the blockades, occupations, and street battles that multiplied in the United States and elsewhere validated their own turn toward confrontation.

People around Mobutu perceived very well the stakes of the global framing of student politics, and, for this very reason, they resolutely sought to undermine it. The minister of education, Alphonse-Roger Kithima, made this much clear at the opening of the academic year in 1968. In a speech at Lovanium, the former labor activist claimed that because President Mobutu was a revolutionary figure, the types of protests against "conservative social and political structures" that may be valid in socialist and capitalist countries were unnecessary in the Congo. Kithima even suggested that Mobutu's radicality far surpassed that of the students and that the Congolese government had ambition "to decolonize and fully demystify the young Congolese man in his mentality and behavior, so he can become a man who only has hatred and contempt for imperialism and colonialism of any kind."[5] This rhetoric mirrored the student movement's semantics (including its gendered language), but it failed to convince. The students booed the speech. Even worse, they laughed loudly, leaving Kithima feeling humiliated.[6] When the minister gave another version of his speech a week later at the University of Lubumbashi, his tone was less accommodating: any imitation of the uprisings in Europe and Latin America would be violently repressed, he solemnly warned.[7]

The wide-open imagination of the student movement unsettled academic authorities as well. Although pockets of progressive faculty at the universities of Lovanium, Lubumbashi, and Kisangani sympathized with student demands,[8] the professors and administrators—most of them still foreigners— who led these institutions felt threatened by the Congo's permeability to the increasing radicalization of youth politics around the world. At Lovanium, one member of the board suggested a riposte: if professors acted as real-life Catholic role models, could they not counter the influence of the Lumumbas, Césaires, Nkrumahs, and other radical icons whose posters adorned the walls of student dorms?[9] René Deckers, the Belgian rector of the University of Lubumbashi, reasoned in somewhat similar terms, believing that students rebelled first and foremost against the alienating tendencies of a soulless global industrial civilization. Coming from an anticlerical background, Deckers did not view the Catholic faith as the antidote to the growing dominance of the student left, but he suggested that a return to the corporatist spirit of medieval European universities could satisfy the thirst for meaning among the Congolese educated youth. As the rector also said to his students, if they reconnected with the spirit of "Bantu solidarity," they could even offer the world with a "counter-poison to save humanity from its growing egoism."[10]

Congolese officials and academic authorities drew on various references— from Negritude, African humanism, social Catholicism, and even "revolutionary authenticity"—but they shared a common goal: to counter the appeal of left internationalist imaginaries. And lying behind their different responses was a similar strategy: to neutralize subversive ideologies and bring Congolese youths back within mental enclosures policed by religious institutions and the nation-state.[11]

Identity Politics at Lovanium

In December 1968, the South African singer Miriam Makeba gave a concert at Lovanium. Most in attendance experienced her performance as a near-magical moment of pure enjoyment in an otherwise tumultuous year. Members of Mobutu's entourage had facilitated the event to appease the increasingly disgruntled students.[12] Makeba, because of her biography and style, occupied a special place in the pantheon of the Congolese youth.[13] Images of the singer rivaled with posters of Patrice Lumumba, Kwame Nkrumah, and Che Guevara for prime exposure on the walls of their bedrooms. She was an icon of Pan-African resistance who built bridges between the anti-apartheid struggle in South Africa and Black power in North America, but she was also a musical innovator who expanded the reach of African dance music. Everybody—even Monsignor Joseph Malula reportedly—stood up and danced when she played "Pata Pata" at Lovanium. Her ability to reconcile authenticity, cosmopolitanism, and radicality was unique. Yet, while her magnetic personality and performance brought a divided community together, the brevity of this moment of communion underlined the intensity of tensions on campus.

Some of these tensions were deeply gendered. A sex symbol and an icon of modern African style, Makeba captivated men and women alike.[14] Her concert at Lovanium took place at a moment of transition in the demographic makeup of Congolese higher education. It was the first year that a sizable group of Congolese women featured in the new class of students admitted to universities. At Lovanium, only a few women, most of them foreigners, had attended the university until then, but the new freshman class raised their proportion in the student body to nearly 10 percent.[15] This shift added to the climate of volatility at Lovanium. The increased visibility of women antagonized some male students. The misogynist thrust of student culture was so pronounced that the simple presence of women in campus spaces could be a cause of shivaree. One male student in history actually found it surprising that no such uproar happened when his girlfriend, chaperoned by a female cousin, visited him for the first time on campus. "I was struck by the way all my friends respectfully welcomed these two young girls," the student wrote in his diary. "Nobody whistled at them, and nobody made a racket and banged their plates on the table when they entered the restaurant."[16] The history student noted that his peers later commented positively on his girlfriend's mastery of French. In general, students claimed to want modern educated girlfriends. However, many thought that their female peers on campus—arguably the most educated women in the country—were too independent and competitive to be suitable partners.[17] Yet other Lovaniards, by contrast, worried that the increase of female students would result in more engagements on campus and therefore threaten the ideal of the epicurean womanizing male student. The satirical student magazine Le Furet chronicled the activities of a fictional General Association of Confirmed Bachelors (Association générale des célibataires endurcis), which it imaged as a group that saved male students from themselves by making sure they did not become romantically involved with female peers and lose their sexual freedom as lifelong bachelors.[18] Moreover, male students felt threatened by their female peers' exercise of their own sexuality. They resented the idea that these women could have relationships with older, established men with the means to offer them expensive clothes unaffordable for students living on state scholarships. Stories about female students spotted at night while returning to their dorms in ministerial limousines haunted the campus imagination.[19] Male students were concerned that these women would spy on them.[20] After all, a mixed-race, first-year student from Katanga was known to be the girlfriend of Major Mika, a central figure in Mobutu's security services. The young woman had to run away from the campus during a meeting of the General Assembly of Students (AGEL), when activists claimed that she was secretly recording them with a device hidden in her hair.[21] In general, and even if female students were not easily impressed and could carve out spaces for themselves in male-dominated groups, many endured instances of discrimination that effectively marginalized them on the scene of student politics.[22]

Mobutu's discourse on female emancipation surely added to these antagonisms. The president claimed credit for allowing women to serve in the army, work as high-level public servants, and study at the university level.[23] His favorite example was his minister of social affairs, Sophie Kanza, the first Congolese woman to occupy a position in government. Kanza was also the first Congolese female university graduate and a major source of inspiration for female students.[24] The state's active promotion of female education may have increased anxieties among young men that they were being denied opportunities. Women arrived at university at the moment of a rapid, nationwide expansion of higher education. At Lovanium alone, the total number of students increased from 2,137 in 1967 to 2,988 the following year.[25] Concretely, this meant a packed campus, competition for resources, and demographic transformations that challenged Lovanium's elitism and unsettled its students. These developments informed how students related to the global context of the 1968 protests and how they perceived their relation with the Mobutu regime.

By Any Means Necessary

Despite these tensions, the language of decolonization maintained a common ground and ensured a modicum of goodwill between the government and the students. The political elite frowned upon the continuous domination of foreign faculty, pedagogies, and research agendas in Congolese universities.[26] And to many students, the state appeared as a potential ally against institutional resistances to Africanization. Many called for more, not less, government intervention in higher education. Even after the poor reception he had received at Lovanium in October 1968, Kithima still hoped to capitalize on these feelings.[27] At the beginning of 1969, he hosted a meeting with all education ministers from francophone African countries on the question of student participation in school management. He then organized a five-day conference on the same theme in the town of Goma with delegates from the Congo's twenty-six institutions of higher education (including both universities and technical tertiary schools).[28] The minister opened the conference with a statement about the urgent need to solve the higher education crisis, for which he blamed the aristocratic mentalities of foreign professors and the lack of interest in the Congo for "social and human tensions" on campuses.[29] Implementing the principle of co-responsibility across the country, Kithima believed, could turn the lead of student discontent into the gold of positive participation. This fell short of the co-gestion (joint management) demanded by students, which included their integration as voting members on all school committees and decision-making bodies, as well as a veto right in all nonacademic sectors that concerned them directly, such as transport, catering, and housing. Regardless, Kithima's plan to systematize student representations in school governance was a first step, and student delegates at the conference supported the solemn adoption of a charter along these lines.

Whereas the students had to accept that the charter did not meet all their demands, some university administrators thought the text went too far. After the conference, they voiced their hostility to any form of co-gestion to Mobutu in person. They argued that giving voting rights to student delegates in schools' councils and committees would undermine the hierarchy that education demanded. Moreover, the spirit of the Goma Charter, they predicted, would encourage students to challenge state authority and to demand democratic reforms of the political system—an argument that echoed predictions that Luc Gillon had made back in 1964 and 1967.[30] This language seems to have struck a nerve with Mobutu this time: he fired Kithima and declared the Goma Charter null and void. The president then chose Mario Cardoso, a research assistant at Lovanium and former member of the College of General Commissioners, to succeed Kithima. The new minister set the tone straightaway: the democratic ideas of co-responsibility and co-gestion, he declared, were simply incompatible with Congolese "philosophical and ideological conceptions."[31]

Mobutu valued conservative university administrators more than he feared the students. The rejection of the charter coincided with a move away from the lexicon of left nationalism that he had borrowed from the students. Instead, the president now embraced an authoritarian version of African humanism, one centered on invocations of Bantu notions of power and a looming rhetoric of authenticity—ideological constructs moored in the colonial library but that also corresponded to the lived experiences of many Congolese.[32] In any case, the failure of Goma made student activists realize they had become dispensable in the eyes of the government. François Kandolo, the president of AGEL, was determined to reverse this situation through a show of force. The anti-Humphrey protest of the previous year, in which he had participated, had convinced him of the importance of direct action. His deputy at AGEL, Valérien Milingo, also believed in the urgency of confrontation.[33] The two young men worked together to restore unity in students ranks. Too much energy had been spent in conflicts that had pitted male against female students, under- against upperclassmen, students who attended universities against those who studied in less prestigious technical schools. In mid-April, AGEL initiated discussions with student leaders from a half-dozen tertiary schools in Kinshasa, including the National School of Law and Administration (ENDA), the National Pedagogical Institute (IPN), and the National Institute of Building and Public Works (INBTP). A new committee, the Kinshasa Student Circle (CEK), emerged from these discussions. Against the usual exclusion of women from student politics, the CEK initiators associated delegates from an all-female Catholic teacher training school to the group. Students in that school, the Lycée Régence, had recently mobilized against a code of conduct that obliged them to attend mass every morning before class. This experience emboldened them to fight for the ideals of co-gestion and they gladly joined the new attempt at reviving student opposition to Mobutu.[34]

The CEK came along because of the need for a common response to the government's reversal on Goma, but it also demanded the valorization of state scholarships, a sensitive question with the potential to amplify participation in the protest movement. As V. Y. Mudimbe wrote a few years later, "generosity [and] idealism" dominated in student politics, even when protests focused on material conditions.[35] Students defended a certain vision of education and society in the demands they formulated around their living standards. Against politicians who denounced them as privileged and spoiled, they claimed that intellectual growth and learning required a certain level of comfort. State scholarships allowed them to spend money—to buy clothes, books, beer, or presents for friends and family—in ways that contributed both to the gendered selves they aimed to project and to the political role they aspired to play. Yet, the massification of higher education caused a sharp decline in on-campus living conditions. At Lovanium, students complained about the cost of food at the cafeteria.[36] And whereas students were supposed to be one or two per dorm bedroom, some now slept in basement rooms that they had to share with several other students.[37]

This erosion of living standards increased the urgency of the comanagement measures discussed at Goma and gave a strong mandate to the CEK. Anxieties about social status combined with an awareness of worldwide youth rebelliousness to legitimize a rhetoric of radicality. In its first public statement, the CEK declared its duty to defend the interests of Congolese students "by any means necessary, including revolutionary violence, with the same determination as our comrades from Africa, Latin America, Europe, and Asia."[38] The statement's terminology evoked Jean-Paul Sartre and Malcolm X, while its content referred to concrete everyday realities on campuses. This must have seemed an indomitable alliance in the eyes of the students. Yet, Mobutu would certainly not have shown himself impressed easily.

A Postcolonial Massacre

The CEK called for a strike. A march from the Central Station to the Ministry of Education would serve as the launching event. The rally would be the first street protest in Kinshasa since Mobutu's arrival to power. The government had warned students not to import the repertoire of international youth contestation. The activists knew that Mobutu would interpret the street rally as a provocation and tried to keep their plan secret until the last minute.[39] Most students learned about the march only hours before it took place on June 4. Participation was still massive. Chanting revolution-

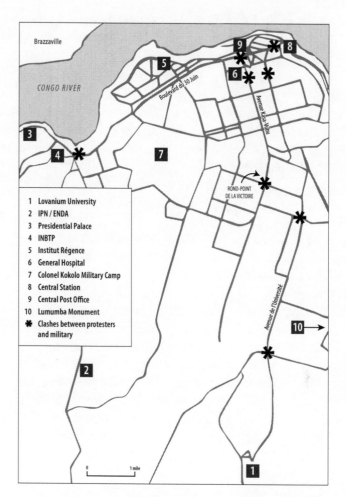

Map 9.1 Map of Kinshasa, with the main locations of clashes between the army and the students during the June 4, 1969, protest.

ary slogans, students requisitioned school buses and took the direction of the city center. When the group coming from Lovanium reached the district of Ngaba, they were stopped by tear gas and an army roadblock that forced them to disembark from their buses. Most of the students managed to outflank the assault and they continued their progression toward the city center on foot. Further encounters with the military happened on the way and scattered students. Some sought to hide in the cité, others attempted to return to campus, and still others forged ahead until reaching downtown Kinshasa.

After various groups arrived at the Central Station, Valérien Milingo read out a memorandum with the CEK's demands and the march toward the Ministry of Education began. The soldiers attacked the students again. They badly hurt several women from the female teacher training school. And Milingo had his mouth smashed with the butt of a machine gun.[40] The students ran to escape beatings and arrest. Some even rushed into a nearby post office and tried to hide among the employees but to no avail.[41] The army fully locked down Kinshasa and, by the day's end, detained hundreds of students in military camps.

Blood had been shed. Soldiers had fired to kill. They took dozens of lives, with the greater number of casualties being on avenue de l'Université in the Yolo district and on place de la Victoire in Kalamu. Most students were convinced that there had been a deliberate plan, that this was not, as some government officials later argued, the panicked act of poorly trained soldiers.[42] Mika, Mobutu's security adviser (whose lover had been caught spying on an AGEL meeting at Lovanium), was present alongside firing soldiers at place de la Victoire—a sign for many that the use of lethal violence had followed orders from high up.[43] After the march, the authorities falsely claimed that soldiers had opened fire to stop the sacking of public buildings. The press widely relayed these misreports, talking of "a hysterical crowd of students, yelling Maoist slogans, and armed with Molotov cocktails and grenades," as one Belgian journalist did.[44] Besides blaming the violence on students, the government also actively concealed the extent of the massacre, announcing that six students had died while the actual number was probably higher than forty.

The authorities made sure to erase all traces of the dead.[45] On the night of June 5, Pius Sapwe, the general inspector of the police, led a team of policemen who snatched the bodies of dead students from the mortuary of Kinshasa's general hospital so they could be buried in an anonymous mass grave.[46] Sapwe had been the chief of police in Elisabethville during the Katanga secession. He had personally participated in the torturing and assassination of Lumumba and supervised the destruction of his body, working directly with the two Belgian policemen who dismembered Lumumba's corpse and dissolved the remains in acid. A few years later, Sapwe took part in a counterinsurgency campaign against the Simba revolt in northern Katanga.[47] His presence at the center of the state's repressive apparatus in Kinshasa in 1969 shows the structuring role of the "work of death" in instituting the Congolese postcolonial state.[48]

Repressive Opportunities

The authorities carried out the work of repression in the days and weeks that followed. They sent the army to Lovanium and repatriated all students to their provinces of origin on military planes. Force and massive arrests were used when students in Kinshasa's other schools continued to strike after June 4, or when some of their peers organized sit-ins or burned photographs of Mobutu in Lubumbashi, Kisangani, Goma, and Mbuji-mai.[49] In Brussels, when students demonstrated in front of the Congolese embassy, several men attacked the protesters with iron rods.[50]

The regime announced that it would track "the enemies from within and the enemies from without."[51] Mobutu called students demented and dunces (cancres), and hammered on about their alleged contacts with Maoist China, the Soviet Union, and Congo-Brazzaville (where Mobutu believed students had undergone military training under the supervision of exiled Lumumbist leader Antoine Gizenga).[52] State officials considered sanctions against Benoît Verhaegen.[53] One of his recent talks at Lovanium had denounced the university as an absurd and useless institution. He had called for a new type of university, freed from pretensions to elitism, open to all, and entirely focused on knowing and transforming the world. Mentioning the French events from the spring of 1968, Verhaegen had shared his belief that students had become the new revolutionary class, and that by transforming higher education they could have a deep impact on Congolese society in its globality.[54] The Belgian professor was ultimately let off the hook, but the government's resoluteness in countering alternative views to its own revolutionary rhetoric was clear to everybody. Daniel Gambembo, one of the few Congolese professors at Lovanium, certainly understood it. On the morrow of the June protest, during which he had been briefly detained in one of the military camps, he buried in his garden the several copies of Mao Zedong's Little Red Book he owned in his personal library.[55]

The question of foreign allegiances, of a communist fifth column, featured prominently when the state put the CEK organizers on trial in July and August.[56] "The magistrates had one obsession: we had to confess that it was foreigners who pushed us to organize the march," Alice Kuseke, one of the two female students in the group that was brought to court, later recalled.[57] The students were found guilty of conspiracy against the state's security and attracted sentences ranging from two to twenty years in prison. Mobutu needed their guilt to justify a series of measures that limited the freedoms of students and academics alike, and that, beyond higher education, engineered a broader authoritarian turn. The president stopped presenting his hold on power as temporary. Instead, he was now openly cementing his one-party state and asserting control over all sectors of Congolese society.

Rebels and Revolutionaries Unite

In a measure typical of his general attempt at projecting the image of a father chief, one capable of both violence and clemency, Mobutu pardoned all the student leaders only a few months after their trial; and journalists were charged with publicizing this act of mercy (see figures 9.1 and 9.2).[58] Regardless, nuclei of resistance developed on all campuses when students returned to school for a new academic year in October 1969. One group at Lovanium took the name Comité Clandestin des Cancres (Clandestine Committee of Dunces). These cancres likened themselves to the Uruguayan Tupamaros National Liberation Movement and the German Red Army Faction, even if their militancy remained mostly fantasy.[59] Some members had known each other since their high school years at the Jesuit Collège Albert in Kinshasa or the Benedictine Collège de la Karavia in Lubumbashi. Other students came into contact with the group in university classrooms, the medicine and law faculties being two privileged sites of recruitment.[60] In the words of one former member, two types of students joined the cancres: the revolutionaries and the rebels.[61] The revolutionaries came to the group already well-versed in Marxism. These were students like Jean Tshinkuela, whom everybody on campus called Mao, or Jean-Baptiste Pondja, who could reportedly recite entire pages of Lenin by heart.[62] Within the committee, the revolutionaries saw their role as helping with the ideological training of their peers. They supervised reading groups to discuss Marxist theory and history. Their ambition was to push for a "dialectical overcoming" within the student movement, which they believed would only come through more engagement with theory.[63] The rebels, on the other hand, became active in the student underground out of a visceral opposition to Mobutu. Having lived through the havoc of the Congo crisis as young teenagers, they had believed in the promises of restored order and reconciliation made first by Tshombe in 1964 and then by Mobutu in 1965. When state violence turned against them, they felt betrayed, disillusioned, and willing to take the regime down.[64] They focused their energies on campus agitation, distributing leaflets, and publishing a popular gazette that combined schoolboy humor with violent jabs at the authorities. They also organized happenings: most memorably, at the end

Figure 9.1 François Kandolo exits the Ndolo prison in Kinshasa. Photographer unknown, October 1969 (source: Valérien Milingo).

of June 1970, they managed to spray Mobutu and King Baudouin of Belgium with a hose as the two were concluding a short tour of Lovanium.[65]

The traumatic resonances of the June 4 catastrophe united the revolutionaries and the rebels. One of their most meaningful initiatives was the organization of a nocturnal vigil to commemorate the massacre's first anniversary. Hundreds of students gathered and kept each other company late into the night, listening to poems, songs from Miriam Makeba, Rochereau and Grand Kalle, and records of speeches from Lumumba, Guevara, and

Figure 9.2 Sister Félicitée Niapudre, together with fellow organizers Alice Kuseke and Joséphine Mumbala, during an interview following their amnesty by Joseph Mobutu. Photographer unknown, October 1969 (source: Valérien Milingo).

Nkrumah. Attendance was similarly massive, and the mood, equally solemn, when students walked in a procession across campus the following morning. All displayed signs of mourning: wearing no shoes and no shirts, with their hair unkempt and red ribbons wrapped around the head. The procession ended at the campus church, where Father Raymond Thysman, Lovanium's Belgian chaplain, officiated a mass in memory of the martyrs of June 4.[66]

A few months later, the cancres convinced dozens of their peers to send a clear message on the occasion of the first presidential elections since the coup. Mobutu was the only candidate, and voters could in theory either cast a green ballot, expressing a vote for the general, or a red ballot, expressing a vote against him. With active pressures from party officials in all precincts, virtually everybody in the country voted green. Some students, however, ignored the pressures and voted against the president. Nearly all of the 156 red ballots that were counted for the whole country were cast in the precinct directly attendant to Lovanium. This act of defiance galvanized the student underground. In 1969, students had rejected the government's attempt at dividing the movement along ethnoregional lines, arguing that they all belonged to the same province: Lovanium.[67] Now they proudly claimed that Mobutu was the president of all the Congo, except for the Inspired Hill.[68]

Mobutu's massive electoral win did not produce the boost he expected. In fact, the president entered a period of unpredictability. Rumors of conspiracies spread with even more virulence than before, and several key personalities of the regime fell into disgrace, including longtime allies like Justin-Marie Bomboko and Victor Nendaka. The country faced a sharp decrease in copper prices. As state policies kept agricultural prices low and more people were migrating from rural areas to urban centers, unemployment rates spiked and the quality of urban public services collapsed. In Kinshasa, whereas around fifteen thousand children had entered primary schools for the first time in 1967, they were forty thousand in 1970, with no significant changes in governmental spending to match the spectacular increase in enrollment.[69] Living conditions in most parts of the city were generally deteriorating. Kinois also complained about insecurity. At the same time, Mobutu traveled abroad a lot and seemed uninterested in the business of the country's daily management. As the Belgian secret services wrote in a note, the general was preoccupied by the health of Mama Yemo, his beloved mother, and "it is a fact that when the Chief of State finds himself in a particular state of nervousness and irritation, his reactions tend to be brutal and somewhat unpredictable."[70]

The nationwide hum of anti-government discontent found echo chambers on university campuses well beyond the revolutionaries and the rebels. Even some students active in the Jeunesse du Mouvement Populaire de la Révolution (JMPR) took positions critical of the authorities. At Lovanium, for instance, the JMPR section commemorated the anniversary of Lumumba's death in January 1971, and it made demands about increasing student scholarships the following month.[71] In several other schools, members of the state party's youth branch relayed demands about the decolonization, democratization, and Africanization of higher education.[72] Young Congolese professors whose own research directly addressed the question of the decolonization of knowledge, like V. Y. Mudimbe or Victor Bol, led study groups that pushed for reforms.[73] Similar conversations happened outside of the humanities as well. At Lovanium, six faculty members and thirty-five students in the Faculty of Sciences created a study group on pedagogy and research practices. They discussed issues such as harmonizing relations between the university and society at large, as putting the sciences at the service of national development and as encouraging students to attend "the school of the people."[74]

Kisangani students used a similar lexicon when they staged a strike in December 1970. Their main demand was to oust the white American missionary Ben Hogbood from his position as the university's acting rector.

They denounced a climate of "negrophobia" and organized a rally during which they paraded a coffin for Hogbood's mock burial. Congolese faculty and the campus section of the Mouvement Populaire de la Révolution (MPR) supported their movement. The university board surrendered and announced the American-trained Congolese vice-rector Jean-Félix Koli would replace Hogbood.[75] The new acting rector had been a prominent leader of the North American section of the General Union of Congolese Students (UGEC) when he studied in Detroit a few years earlier. He now adopted Mobutu's fashion style and publicly called himself a dictator. The students soon clashed with him as well when he refused to fire a Dutch professor they believed did not have the proper qualifications to teach at the university.[76] After a series of skirmishes between Koli and some students, Mobutu sent two of his ministers to Kisangani to stop the protest movement in March 1971. Dozens of students were dismissed, and the authorities forcefully removed Stephen Weissman, a young political science professor whom they accused of being a Maoist agitator.[77]

A Symbolic Burial

As they got closer to the second anniversary of June 4, the cancres decided to repeat the commemorations of the previous year at Lovanium—the nocturnal vigil with poems, songs, and speeches, the day of fasting, the barefoot-shirtless procession through campus, and the mass at Our Lady of Wisdom Chapel. They began preparations weeks in advance, including with a clandestine symposium that celebrated the anniversary of the Paris Commune.[78] In parallel, activists released numerous pamphlets aiming to rile the student community ahead of the commemoration of the 1969 massacre. One fateful pamphlet denounced the Mobutu-decreed period of mourning introduced after the president's mother passed away at the beginning of May 1971. Brutal in its language, the text called Mama Yemo a whore unworthy of any honor.[79] Drawings and graffiti in campus toilets echoed the same slanderous rhetoric.[80] The attack evoked the sexual and gender crux of student politics. Its vulgarity meant to underline the contrast between Mama Yemo's pompous official funeral and the denial of proper burials for the students killed on June 4.

It was unlikely that Mobutu would leave this provocation unanswered.[81] The regime's ill-famed new secret police, known as Centre National de Documentation (CND), kidnapped two cancres in downtown Kinshasa on June 2. The following night, a senior CND officer drove to campus to hand to Rector Tharcisse Tshibangu a list of other students who were to

Figure 9.3 Student procession during the commemoration of the second anniversary of the June 4 massacre. Photographer unknown, June 4, 1971 (source: Alexandre Luba).

be arrested. The agent arrived in the middle of the nocturnal commemoration of the 1969 massacre. Some students recognized him, set his car on fire, and detained him in a dorm bedroom.[82] They let him go after several hours, but a rumor was already circulating that they had killed him.

The following morning, several thousand students turned out for the scheduled mourning procession and Catholic mass (figure 9.3). Father Thysman later described the mass as the most fervent celebration he had officiated in years. The cancres solemnized the event by exposing in the church an empty coffin (stolen from the university hospital's mortuary). After the religious service, they invited attendants to gather on the square facing the university's main administrative building for a symbolic burial. Two students lowered the coffin into a pit that had been dug during the night, as Thysman and his assistant, the Congolese Jesuit father Christophe Munzihirwa, blessed the grave.[83] After the two priests returned to their chapel, the students remained at the tomb. The ceremony took a more militant tone. The students replaced the Congolese flag from a nearby pole with a red banner; they sang "The Internationale"; and they proclaimed that the square would from now on be known as the place des Martyrs.[84]

In the middle of this dramatized declaration of student autonomy, the army's commander in chief, General Séraphin Bosango, barged onto the campus. He wanted to see what was in the tomb, but students protested that excavating it would be an unacceptable violation of their dead comrades. Some shouted that the soldiers would first have to shoot and kill them. Thysman and Munzihirwa intervened. They convinced Bosango that the tomb was empty, and the soldiers departed without causing further commotion. It is unclear what Mobutu expected from Bosango's raid, but he was not satisfied with how things went. Bosango returned the following day to campus. His soldiers destroyed a monument that students from the engineering school had begun erecting on top of the tomb, and they forced Thysman and Munzihirwa to dig up the casket. Once this was done, Bosango has the two priests thrown in a car that was to drive them to Mobutu's presidential palace for questioning.[85] Meanwhile, a large group of students had seized Rector Tshibangu and announced they would not release him unless the soldiers freed Thysman and Munzihirwa.[86] Unwilling to negotiate, General Bosango rescued the rector by force. Soldiers fired their guns. One student sustained a gunshot wound and three others were seriously hurt in the panic that followed.

The students had crossed too many lines. They had insulted Mobutu's dead mother, mistreated Tshibangu, and threatened to secede from the MPR's party state. As in the aftermath of the massacre in 1969, Mobutu faced both a challenge to his rule and an opportunity to strengthen his hold on power. Toward the end of the afternoon on June 6, the radio announced that an extraordinary meeting of the MPR's bureau had decided to discipline Lovanium students by drafting them into the army for a period of two years. The measure concerned all of the 2,850 Congolese students on campus—male and female, single and married, lay and religious.[87]

The news caused mayhem at Lovanium. Students looted the bedrooms of JMPR activists, helped themselves to beers at the university grocery store, and cursed the regime. However, soldiers invaded the campus the following morning, and they did not leave students much choice but to comply and board the trucks that took them to various military camps located across the city. Some students continued to show defiance as they left Lovanium, but the humiliations that awaited them in the camps stamped out all their bravado. Years later, several women recalled the cruel collective punishments meted out at Mobutu's newly built party state's headquarters in Nsele, where they were stationed. Men sent to a paratroopers' military camp near the airport also recalled beatings and mistreatments.[88]

After a few weeks, conditions improved, but the exhausting physical drills and the dull ideological indoctrination remained the daily routine of the student soldiers. The young recruits were dumbfounded to have to learn military instructions by heart from a "catechism for new recruits" that included the lyrics of colonial hymns and rules about proper ways to salute co-lonial officials or the king of Belgium. Among other acts of anti-intellectual pettiness, students resented the ban of newspapers and taunts against those of them who wore glasses.[89] Whereas French dominated on campus, it was replaced by Lingala in the army, which not all students could speak. Vul-garities, often sexual in nature, pervaded their learning of the language.[90]

The idea of conscripting students did not come from nowhere. During the colonial period, local authorities punished troublemakers by sending them for seven-year terms in the Force publique. Mobutu himself had been forced to enroll at the military training academy of Luluabourg in 1950 after performing misdeeds at a missionary school.[91] In 1971, the army ended protests by subjecting students to a rigid structure of command. In a press conference held directly after the forced draft, Mobutu announced that military doctors had identified multiple cases of syphilis among the new recruits. The students were "morally and physically rotten," he said.[92] Turning the stigma of the insult to his mother back onto the students, the general presented the conscription as a way to transform the student body, both literally and metaphorically.

Conclusion

The world of the Lovaniards collapsed in less than forty-eight hours. Gone were the suits and ties, the working toilets, the well-stocked restaurant, the swimming pool, and the long nights of discussion on the Inspired Hill. In their place were ill-fitted military uniforms, leaking tents, rationed food portions, and the exhausting alternation of running, crawling, and climbing drills. Pervasive disciplinary controls and quotidian punishments numbed the students into submission and reminded them of the danger of dissent. The MPR had used the draft both as a collective punishment and as a shock measure that outlined a specific vision of society. Collapsing the boundaries between higher education and the military, between the campus and the camp, the draft turned the nation's educated elite into sub-altern agents in the machine of state violence. The elitism of the students had to be eliminated because it encouraged a form of distinction rooted in inauthentic colonial values, so the authorities claimed. To the unfinished decolonization of the student mindset, the state's solution was simple: removing students from the elevated site chosen by the church to shape a new class of educated Congolese, they relocated them to mosquito-infected swamps in the alluvial plain of the Congo River where they were told to obey, chant, and not to think (see figure 9.4).[93]

Accusations of collusion with foreign powers featured prominently when the government put a dozen suspected cancres on trial in August.[94] Sentenced to life imprisonment, these students overlapped on the prison island of Mbula-Mbemba and at the Luzumu penitentiary center with several political prisoners who had been arrested in a series of raids conducted by the CND in the aftermath of the Lovanium events. These other inmates had not necessarily been in direct relation with students, but their anti-imperialist visions had also clashed with Mobutu's alignments.[95] At the same time that the police rounded up dissenters, the government announced a seemingly eclectic set of resolutions: it expelled a dozen Soviet and Eastern European diplomats, suspended all state scholarships to young Congolese who studied abroad for degrees offered locally, and banned Freemasonry and Rosicrucianism. Anybody who possessed publications and documents about these latter organizations, as well as about the Templars, the Grail Message, Gnosis, Martinism, Subud, or Caodaism, was required to hand them over to the Ministry of the Interior.[96] The connection between anti-occultism and political repression was clear: the authorities sought to ban any source of knowledge that could mobilize outside forces against the Mobutist order.[97]

Mobutu's repressive nationalist measures constituted the affirmation of a power. It was a power set on destroying, displacing, and confining. The draft participated in the MPR's ambition to erase the boundaries between state and society.[98] It was the most literal incarnation of a politics of caporalisation, insofar as it sought to regiment all the country's vital forces and activate their corporal energies in a performance of autocratic power.[99]

The crisis of June 1971 ushered in a radical reform that brought universities once and for all under the control of the state. A first step came on June 16 when the MPR decided to "de-Westernize" the names of the Congo's three universities.[100] Instead of names that evoked foreign institutions or reminded Belgian ideological markers, each university would now bear the name of the city where it was located. The second step, two months later, announced a more dramatic leap: the government nationalized all private institutions of higher education and merged them with the ones that were already state controlled to create a new single, integrated National University of the Congo (UNACO). The new institution made the choice not to duplicate any department across the various campuses: instead, polytechnics, science, and medicine would be centralized in Kinshasa; Kisangani would host pedagogy and psychology; and the humanities and social sciences would go to Lubumbashi. The creation

Figure 9.4 Student soldiers at the CETA camp, Kinshasa.
Photographer unknown, ca. June–October 1971
(source: Mbuyi Kapuya).

of UNACO therefore launched an extraordinary process of dismembering and repatching, as students, professors, libraries, and research facilities had to be moved across the three sites.[101] At the end of October, just days before the opening of the first academic year in the post-reform era, the MPR spokesman, Prospère Madrandele, announced another spectacular measure: the country would from now on be known as the Republic of Zaire, its inhabitants as Zairians (Zaïrois), and the Congo River as the Zaire River.[102] A break with the colonial past, the act of renaming marked the coronation of Mobutu's so-called politics of authenticity, which he had introduced as a method of governance inspired by Bantu humanism a few months earlier during an official visit to Senegal.[103] For the national university, the last-minute shredding of its UNACO letterhead only weeks before the opening of the new institution's first academic year, was the icing on the cake of a much broader logistical ordeal. When students resumed their education in November 1971, they returned to a permanently altered landscape.

THE GAZE OF THE DEAD

Students have two weapons that are much more powerful than the gun or the club of the soldiers: their capacity to make people think and their social prestige.   E. W. Lamy, "La mort de Lovanium," 369-70

In August 1971, Jean-Paul Sartre's journal *Les Temps Modernes* published an article on the recent nationalization of Congolese higher education, written under a pseudonym by the young Belgian political scientist Jean-Claude Willame. While the article rejoiced at the death of Lovanium, it also expressed skepticism at the Congolese government's action. The university "should neither be reformed, redesigned or adjusted"; rather, it should "be destroyed," Willame argued, using a famous slogan of the time.[1] For better or worse, Mobutu actually shared this rhetoric of destruction. Multiple Congolese and foreigners later talked of his university reform as a disastrous and authoritarian takeover that ruined Congolese higher education forever—with the historian Jan Vansina going as far as comparing the measure to the Nazification of German universities in the 1930s.[2] By contrast, different voices celebrated the creative dimension in Mobutu's destructive gesture. The former Jesuit and philosopher Kangafu Gudumbagana described the creation of the National University of Zaire (UNAZA) as part of a Marcuse-inspired project of radical liberation.[3] And many other people, although less dithyrambic, praised Mobutu for having cut the umbilical cord between Louvain and Lovanium. The nationalization certainly ended years of ambivalence on the question of Africanization and empowered a generation of Congolese academics.[4] Like the students, these academics had demanded the realignment of university education with the priorities of national development for years, advocating, in the words of Mabika Kalanda, for a relationship of "political, philosophical, sociological, and economic dependency" between the education system and the nation.[5] Still, the reform was a pyrrhic victory at best. Many of those who initially applauded then grew disillusioned.

Authenticité

The state's response to the student movement combined repression and revolution, destruction and innovation. Mobutu abolished a precious tenet of the students' political imagination by brutally thwarting its international ramifications. At the same time, he also connected eclectically to the spirit and energies of global 1968. Zairian ideology, despite its own insistence on cultural self-sufficiency, combined elements borrowed from foreign currents of ideas and systems of rule. Kangafu mentioned Herbert Marcuse; Maoism was another obvious reference. Mobutu had repeatedly denounced student agitators as Maoist puppets. Even so, he ended up normalizing his relationship with mainland China and drawing inspiration from Chinese approaches to popular mobilization. In an ironic twist, he pardoned the Lovanium cancres in 1973 because he was set to travel to China and meet with Chairman Mao.

Within Zairian academia, Mobutu's ideological bricolage encouraged intellectual creativity. The president needed scholars to flesh out his discourse about cultural decolonization and place authenticité on the map of African ideological trademarks, on a par with negritude, Ujamaa, the common man's charter, and African humanism.[6] In June 1971, as the government was shutting down Lovanium, it commissioned the first major publication on authenticity, assigning it to the sociologist Ferdinand Kazadi, the political scientist Honoré Mpinga, and the philosopher Daniel Gambembo.[7] Whereas Kazadi (an alumnus of the General Commissioners Committee of 1960) had been working with Mobutu for years, the other two had not. Gambembo had even actively encouraged student dissenters when he taught at Lovanium. As a philosopher, he had written about Aristotle's ontology, the Kongo cosmogony, and Africa's cultural renaissance—all intellectual references that arose in his work for the Mouvement populaire de la révolution (MPR).[8]

The government explicitly presented the national university as an institution dedicated to ending "all indoctrination on the order of ideology other than that of authentic nationalism."[9] Many academics followed in the footsteps of Kazadi, Mpinga, and Gambembo and contributed works on authenticity (most notably at the Lubumbashi campus, which hosted the humanities and the social sciences). A few professors embraced obsequious sloganeering in their exegeses of Mobutu's thought.[10] But the scholarly conversations around authenticity went beyond the immediate propaganda needs of the party state. Contributions were often intellectually robust. In some cases, they could even be read between the lines as critical of the regime.[11] For many scholars, the stakes involved nothing less than "the foundation of a new African discourse about the world."[12] The plasticity of authenticity made it a particularly useful concept for this kind of foundational project: it spoke to the Afrocentric enthusiasts who received Cheikh Anta Diop as an intellectual hero when he came to Lubumbashi for a series of lectures in 1972, and to scholars who considered that Afrocentrism was blind to its own essentializations. V. Y. Mudimbe, now a dean in Lubumbashi, was the most prominent figure in the latter group. His Sartrean approach to authenticity—as a reckoning with one's real sociohistorical determinations to enable the subject's liberation—launched his critical exploration of the colonial library.[13]

Profound intellectual shifts followed the creation of UNAZA. The 1971 reform also informed the work that expatriate researchers were conducting in the country. It abolished the colonial rigidity that had reigned hitherto, improving social relations and facilitating collaborations among professors and students. The historian Bogumil Jewsiewicki recalled how the transition from Lovanium to UNAZA allowed him to connect differently with Zairian society. At Lovanium, professors lived among themselves in campus residences but not so at Lubumbashi, where Jewsiewicki moved after the reform. Having an immediate relation to the city was affectively and intellectually generative.[14] Like several of his colleagues in Lubumbashi, Jewsiewicki socialized with artists and became newly attuned to histories from below and to popular culture.[15]

Students were instrumental in transforming the affective environment of university campuses. When UNAZA opened its doors at the end of 1971, the government authorized Lovanium draftees to resume their education (mostly out of fear of a growing fraternizing between students and regular soldiers in military camps). The condition was that the former Lovanium students would remain conscripted and continue their military service

REGLEMENT MILITAIRE
(à l'intention des Etudiants de l'ex-Université de Kinshasa)

UNIVERSITE NATIONALE DU CONGO
Campus de Kinshasa

Figure E.1 "UNACO Kinshasa campus, military regulations for the students of the former University of Kinshasa." 1971 (source: ARNACO, MPR Papers).

from their respective campuses. In practical terms, it meant that they had to attend military drills every morning and that they went to class in military uniform (figure E.1). After months in camps, the students returned to school imbued with the soldiers' plebeian mindset. The army clashed with their elitist habitus, but it encouraged a powerful esprit de corps (figure E.2). In Lubumbashi, the student soldiers saw their role as that of abolishing the remnants of colonial racism in the copper capital. Making the desegregation of the city their patriotic duty, they purposely went dancing in white-owned nightclubs that had hitherto succeeded in keeping Black patrons out.[16]

Relations among men and women also altered somewhat in the era of the national university. Mobutu had not discriminated among students at

Figure E.2 Student soldiers at UNAZA in Kinshasa. Photographer unknown, ca. 1971–72 (source: Mbuyi Kapuya).

the time of the forced conscription. Female students, even while stationed separately from their male peers, were also obliged to undergo weeks of military training. The experience marked them all. As a result, many felt more confident and willing to assert themselves when they returned to school. And although women would remain a minority on UNAZA campuses for many years to come, they found slightly enlarged spaces for expressing themselves in the new institution.

The 1971 reform eroded the colonial matrix of the university at the level of class, race, and gender, but it also led to politicization, to repeated arbitrary arrests of students and faculty, and to a lack of resources that quickly crippled the whole UNAZA system.[17] In a comment about the reform's effects, the Kisangani-based French ethnologist Pierre Erny argued that "the poverty of the university is nothing to be ashamed of in a poor country . . . and it is an act of realism to maintain it in [this] state."[18] Many other professors, by contrast, looked at the pauperization of UNAZA as a dramatic development and worried about the institution's inability to cope with a vertiginous rise in student numbers, which went from around fifteen thousand in 1971 to more than one hundred thousand ten years later.

Cosmopolitan Imaginaries

The repression of student dissent altered relations of power in Mobutu's postcolony. Willame, the political scientist who wrote the aforementioned article for *Les Temps Modernes*, developed this argument in a book published in January 1972. *Patrimonialism and Political Change in the Congo* was the first monograph to theorize postcolonial state formation in the Congo-Zaire and one of the first studies to apply Max Weber's concept of patrimonialism to an African context.[19] This concept, according to Willame, captured the dynamics of fragmentation and military competition in play during the Congo crisis of the early 1960s. Willame also argued that Mobutu's 1965 coup marked the end of this patrimonialist period. The Congo then turned into a centralized Caesarist bureaucracy. Mobutu paid as much attention to reinforcing his image as an authoritarian figure as he did to strengthening his alliance with a bureaucratic administrative structure in which students and intellectuals occupied key positions. Willame interpreted the massacre of June 4, 1969 as another moment of transition. A crisis in the bureaucratic Caesarism of the previous years, the event suggested that the coalition behind Mobutu had fallen apart and that the regime was shifting toward pure dictatorial Caesarism.[20] Willame's Weberian elaborations received contrasting responses from reviewers.[21] Other political scientists writing after him—many of them US-trained faculty at UNAZA like Willame—produced resolutely different interpretations. They questioned the idea that the 1965 coup had put an end to the patrimonialist characteristics of the First Republic. And they did not perceive June 4, 1969, as a momentous rupture in Mobutu's presidency. Instead, the event that attracted their attention was the so-called Zairianization of 1973, when the MPR seized the near totality of economic assets that had belonged to foreigners throughout the country and redistributed them to hundreds of "acquirers" connected to the party leadership. This massive upheaval in the Zairian economy evoked the patrimonialist strategies of the First Republic, but it also indicated Mobutu's willingness to strengthen the broad coalition behind his regime—and several university professors featured among the apparatchiks who received Zairianized factories, plantations, and stores. Scholars diverged in their assessments of Mobutu's power. Some talked of Zaire as an "integral state" that verged on absolutism. Others argued that the president had no effective control over society. They agreed, however, in seeing the "creation of inequality" as the defining political process in post-independent Congo-Zaire. The gap indeed widened between workers and peasants, on the one hand, and

Mobutu's coalition of First Republic politicians, intellectuals, and comprador bourgeois, on the other hand.[22]

Mobutu certainly carefully attended to solidifying his power coalition in the early 1970s. Many of the measures taken in 1972 and 1973—animation (the organizing of daily singing and dancing sessions in praise of the autocrat), the ban on Christian names, or the imposition of national costumes for men and women—participated in the forging of intimacy between "those who command and those who are assumed to obey."[23] These measures were also in many ways directly conceived to help with elite reproduction, as widely circulating images of abacost-wearing, leopard-hatted imitators of Mobutu attested.[24] What the political scientists who focused on the seemingly relentless ideological inventiveness of Mobutu sometimes downplayed was the destructive nature of his politics. As the history of the student movement reveals, the regime invented new traditions, rituals, and myths, but it also destroyed lives and ways of being in the world. Accounting for what was lost and for the technologies of power that produced these losses, fiction often proved more apt than the social sciences.[25] It also appears clearly that the reinstitutionalization of students within the disciplinarian nationalist structures of the army and UNAZA eroded most of their capacity to rebel.[26] Violence, co-optation, and institutional decay eliminated the students' cosmopolitan distinction. This spirit of distinction had been rife with gender and class tensions. It had excluded women from active participation in student politics and had fostered a permanent ambiguity in the students' relationship to power. Yet, it had also sustained specific forms of intellectual autonomy and political resistance that disappeared along with the old higher education apparatus.

Writing about global imaginaries, Arjun Appadurai recalls what it was that constituted modernity for young Indians of his class and generation in the 1960s: Hollywood films, *Life* magazine, jeans sent by an older sibling who was studying in America. According to Appadurai, thirty years later, electronic mediations and mass migrations made a similar type of "experiential engagement with vernacular globalization" part of daily life for much broader sectors of the population in the postcolonial world.[27] This genealogy resonates in the Congolese case as well: to a certain extent, the students' experience with the enlarged mental horizon of the 1960s prefigured the more widespread globalization of imaginaries in the 1980s and beyond (which therefore suggests a relative reopening of the horizon that Mobutu had tried to block).

Comparisons can be made between the students' appetites for the world in the 1960s and the post-1980s figure of the mikiliste (after the term *mokili*, meaning "world" in Lingala)—that is, Congolese-Zairian migrants who lived at the margins of legality and used their access to Europe (in particular to exclusive designer clothes valued by the sapeurs) for their personal advancement in Kinshasa's economy of reputation.[28] A small but growing interest in new religious movements from East Asia (and esoteric knowledge in general) also recalls the passion that young letter writers in the decolonization era had for learning about communism.[29] The figure of China, which for the student left and then for Mobutu himself counted so much, has resonated with a new force ever since the People's Republic of China spectacularly increased its economic presence in the Congo in the 2000s.[30]

People in Kinshasa perceive their city as a deeply cosmopolitan space. They value the ideals of elegance, education, and emancipation from ethnic assignations.[31] Both the rich and the poor project themselves within a globalized world. Translocal aspirations reshape their here and now. Electronic media, posters, ubiquitous billboards create junctions with multiple elsewheres.[32]

In some ways, the political adventures of the first generations of Congolese students continue to reverberate in the present. Through the massacre of June 1969, the student movement now belongs to a reading of the Congolese 1960s as a time of oppression, as a time when state violence indiscriminately targeted rebel figures like Patrice Lumumba and Pierre Mulele, insurrectionary peasants, and young urbanized intellectuals. In the present context of intense political violence, young activists often turn back to this earlier period as the moment of an unfinished history of oppression and struggle.[33] As the late historian T. K. Biaya argued, students from the 1960s played a key role in the constitution of an "antineocolonial nationalism"—that is, in developing a multipolar political identity that has accommodated both ethnic identification and national pride and that, abiding for decades now, has fueled multiple movements of political contestation, including several that resulted in episodes of state repression reminiscent of the 1969 protest.[34]

Still, despite these legacies, something unique—a distinct worldedness—has been lost. It had been directly connected to the specific constellation of the 1960s, when cold war dynamics intersected with nation-building and intense dreams of revolution. The Congo found itself at the center of global frictions. It was both a site of neocolonial interventions *and* a battleground over antagonistic visions of a decolonizing world. Keen and skilled, the students operated mediations that the Congo's new centrality authorized and demanded. More than others, they fought against a colonial temporality that had denied the Congolese the right to act as political subjects in charge of their collective destiny. They knew that the Belgians had attempted to isolate the Congo from the rest of the world to prevent the dreams and aspirations for the future that long-distance connections could encourage.[35] Through what they learned, the conversations they initiated, the vocabularies they introduced, these students changed the Congo and vitally prolonged the yearning for radical independence that Lumumba had so powerfully expressed. Connecting the Congo to the world, they kept the door of radical emancipation ajar for a decade. Interweaving the postal and the ethnographic, moving from campuses to rebel camps, mining diplomatic archives and affective memories, following itineraries that cut across national borders and ideological boundaries, exploring the many resonances of the Congolese 1960s, this book has sought to account for a specific experience of decolonization as a pedagogy of the world.

For Betty and Symphorien

Decades after Lumumba's assassination, in the post–Cold War, post-Mobutu, post–Mze Kabila era, the revolutionary imagination of the students seems decoupled from the world of active politics. Nevertheless, it still lived on for many of the people whom I met while researching this book, if only in the space of memory, through the stories they told. Different modes of emplotment have organized their rendering of their youth in the 1960s. Many naturally embraced the structure of the tragedy, a genre to which they had been exposed in late-colonial elite school curriculums that emphasized the Greco-Roman classics. In June 1969, the student theater club staged a performance of Jean Anouilh's *Antigone*.[36] After they themselves faced the murderous violence of the state just a few days later, the students were denied the possibility of mourning their dead comrades, and many students felt a painful resonance with Antigone's struggle to provide her dead brother Polynices a burial. Decades later, many persons to whom I talked told me of their own Polynices. The name of Symphorien Mwamba, a member of the student theater club who died on June 4, often came up in these conversations. Although virtually no images of the protest exist, the moment of Mwamba's death emerged with a near-photographic quality in multiple interviews.[37] A known member of the campus left who had been elected as the "mayor" of one of the student residences, Mwamba was a student in romance languages. He had only a small part in *Antigone*, but former students remembered that he played the main character in *Montserrat*, a play by the Algerian French writer Emmanuel Roblès, which the theater club performed to packed audiences in May 1969. The existentialism of *Montserrat*—the story of a Spanish officer who sides with Latin American revolutionaries in 1812 and, after his capture, choses death over betrayal—resonated with a prevalent structure of feelings among students.[38] Looking at revolts and liberation struggles in the Congo and in the world, students had perceived an urgency to take sides, to act, to leave the comfort of campus radicalism. To his peers, Mwamba's death appeared a tragic sacrifice, a heroic proof of the consistency between their words and their deeds.

Elisabeth Mweya described Mwamba as "someone who wrote poems, who was confident, who believed in freedom and free speech, who believed in love and who loved, who was tender."[39] The two of them were engaged; Mwamba indeed had renounced the life of Lovanium's lifelong bachelors. The relationship between Mwamba and Mweya, like many of the political connections described in this book, had started through the post. Mweya, at the time, was a twenty-year-old aspiring nun. As the author of an advice column, "Betty et ses amies," in the Catholic weekly magazine *Afrique Chrétienne*, she was also a national celebrity. The column consisted mostly of responses by Mweya to letters from the magazine's young readers about personal relationships. Mweya regularly criticized parents who used the authority of tradition to regiment the lives of their daughters, especially concerning marriage. She preached the superiority of love and advocated for more direct interactions among young people from both genders, encouraging her female readers "to be bold" and "to dare to speak French" in front of their male comrades.[40] When a young male reader wrote to regret that Congolese women did not like to correspond with men, Mweya answered that even if men sometimes used letters to seduce, letter writing in itself was "in no way scandalous" and that it could "contribute to broadening young people's views of the world."[41] She herself received a massive personal correspondence from readers, but the letter that Mwamba sent touched her in a way she could not explain. Mwamba was asking to meet her, and she accepted. They became romantically involved, and Mweya left the convent.

Mweya and Mwamba rarely discussed politics. "Betty would probably not understand," is what Mweya later imagined Mwamba told himself. Yet, they shared a common love for theater and literature. Monsignor Joseph Malula, who had founded the Catholic congregation in which Mweya was being trained, nicknamed her la Senghorine. Poetry had been an important part of her life since she was a teenager. After Mwamba's death, she turned to writing to work through her grief. And her first collection of poems, published in 1970 by Mudimbe, opened with a dedication to Mwamba:

Nous nous taisons
On nous croit morts et vaincus
Tant pis
Nos regards, eux,
N'ont pas cessé de vivre

We fall silent
And are believed to be dead and defeated
Never mind
Because our gazes
Keep on living.[42]

Preface

1 François Mayala, personal interview, unrecorded, Kinshasa, August 10, 2010.
2 On the Congo and the figure of state collapse, see Trefon, *Reinventing Order*; Reno, "From State Collapse"; Autesserre, *Trouble with Congo*, 41–83.
3 See Yoka, *Kinshasa, signes de vie*, 24–28, 119–26; De Boeck and Plissart, *Tales of the Invisible City*, 75–138; De Boeck and Baloji, *Suturing the City*, 153–90.
4 See Davis, *Planet of Slums*.
5 François Mayala, personal interview, unrecorded, Kinshasa, December 3, 2010.
6 But see Mamdani, "African University," and Mbembe, "Decolonizing the University."
7 Humanitarianism is certainly neither foreign to ideology nor to the history of the third-worldist left. See Mann, *Empires to NGOs*, 165–242. Similarly, the "relation of the self to the world" that Liisa Malkki sees as a central motivation in the professional trajectory of today's aid workers is in keeping with the psychological determinations of Western third worldism in the 1960s. Malkki, *Need to Help*.
8 See Roessler and Verhoeven, *When Comrades*.
9 On Kinshasa's memoryscape in the late 1990s and 2000s, see Jewsiewicki, "Reading in Kinshasa."
10 As president, Laurent-Désiré Kabila had to compromise with the cluster of political forces that constituted the AFDL and with an international

context hostile to his revolutionary rhetoric. His claimed loyalty to the left nationalism of the 1960s coexisted with a pragmatic embrace of the social market economy. See, for instance, Mukendi and Kasonga, *Kabila*, 68–71.

11 See, for instance, De Villers, *Histoire du politique*, 165–89, and White, "Political Undead." The creation of the Rassemblement congolais pour la démocratie (RCD) in 1998 was a first important moment in the dissolution of the ideological markers initially reasserted by the Kabila regime. A rebel group created to give a Congolese face to the Rwandese and Ugandan war against Kabila, the RCD gathered prominent Mobutists and radicals from the Congolese diaspora, including many former left student activists. See Stearns, *Dancing in the Glory*, 201–16.

12 See Pype, "Political Billboards."

13 See De Boeck, "Inhabiting Ocular Ground."

14 Richard Mugaruka, personal interview, unrecorded, Kinshasa, November 3, 2009. For detailed self-critiques of the role played by this generation in postcolonial Congolese politics, see the various interventions in Sabakinu, *Elites et démocratie*.

15 Jean-Claude Tammaire, preface to Dikonda, *Face à face*, 12. Dikonda's own trajectory illustrates the versatility he himself once denounced. Before positioning himself on the left in the mid-1960s, he had been closely associated with Albert Kalonji, an arch-opponent of the left nationalist orientations of then–prime minister Patrice Lumumba. Decades later, he cofounded a major party opposed to Mobutu and was forced into exile but ultimately changed allegiance and joined the Mobutu regime as a provincial governor after having been found guilty of misappropriating funds from his party. See Colette Braeckman, "Il avait été un des fondateurs de l'UDPS: Mort du Professeur Dikonda," *Le soir*, March 24, 1992, as well as Patrick Wenda Tshilumba, personal interview, recorded, Kisangani, October 11, 2010.

16 On "practical nostalgia" among older Kinois, see Pype, "Dancing to the Rhythm."

17 On Dar, see Ivaska, "Movement Youth."

18 Kabeya Tshikuku, personal interview, recorded, Kinshasa, August 3, 2010.

19 See De Sousa Santos, *Epistemologies of the South*.

Introduction

1 On the impact of the civil rights movement on Johnson's foreign policy in Africa, see Lerner, "Climbing off the Back Burner."

2 Simeon Booker, "Humphrey's African Safari: Nine Country Tour Reveals Store of Respect for US, but Smoldering Resentment in Some Places," *Ebony* 23, no. 5 (March 1968): 51.

3 See Solberg, *Hubert Humphrey*, 355–75; King, *History of New Zealand*, 548; Klimke, *The Other Alliance*, 155–56; Rikir, *Le P.C.B.*, 19; and Temkin, "American Internationalists."

4 "La tournée 'triomphale' de Himmler Humphrey," *Dipanda*, February 19, 1966, 5.
5 Benjamin Welles, "Humphrey, after African Tour, Seeking Changes in Policy," *New York Times*, January 13, 1968, 12.
6 "Humphrey's Car Blocked by Congolese," *International Herald Tribune*, January 5, 1968, 3. On broader reactions to the Vietnam War in Africa, see Hodgkinson and Melchiorre, "Vietnam War."
7 The 1975 US Senate's Church Committee provided many revelations about the CIA's part in destabilizing the Congo in 1960. See Kalb, *Congo Cables*. For more details on the events that led to Lumumba's assassination, see De Witte, *Assassination of Lumumba*, as well as Gerard and Kuklick, *Death in Congo*. What the students had probably not known was that Humphrey had defended Lumumba in 1961 against widespread allegations that the Congolese prime minister was a communist sympathizer. *Executive Sessions of the Senate Foreign Relations Committee (Historical Series): Volume XIII, Eighty-Seventh Congress, First Session, 1961* (Washington, DC: US Government Printing Office, 1984), 643–46.
8 UGEC-Lovanium, "A l'attention des camarades qui ont manifesté le 4 janvier 1968," 4 January 1968, Jules Gérard-Libois Papers, Africa Museum, Tervuren.
9 "L'UGEC et le nouveau régime," *Courrier africain* (*Travaux Africains du CRISP*) 77 (March 1968): 5.
10 H. A. Ryan, "Lovanium Student Participation in Anti-American Demonstration, U.S. Information Agency Memorandum of Conversation," January 9, 1968, Central Foreign Policy Files 1967–69 [hereafter CFP], Box 356, NARA. French sources argued that the Congolese government knew of the student protest ahead of time and informed local CIA agents (Vaïsse, *Documents diplomatiques: 1968*, 1:57).
11 When officials in Washington, DC had considered reducing their support for the Congolese army, the US ambassador in Kinshasa argued that air defense was absolutely necessary in the struggle against "anti-Western rebels" (George McMurtrie Godley, telegram to Dean Rusk, March 14, 1966, LOC, Averell Harriman Papers, Box 448). See also "Telegram from the Embassy in the Congo to the Department of State," January 5, 1968, reproduced in Howland et al., *Foreign Relations*, 823–26. On Mobutu's leveraging strategies, see Rich, "Manufacturing Sovereignty."
12 Kamitatu, *La grande mystification*, 238–89. In 1974, the *Washington Post* revealed that Muriel kept the diamond despite regulations mandating officials to return to the state any gifts worth more than US$100,000. Maxine Cheshire, "Humphrey Turns in Gift Gem," *Washington Post*, June 13, 1974, A1.
13 "Le vice-président des Etats-Unis à Kinshasa," *Congo-Magazine* (January 1968): 26.
14 I borrow this phrase from David Scott's work on the failure of the 1983 revolution in Grenada. Scott, *Omens of Adversity*, 99.

15 Early studies of higher education in Africa tended to focus on social stratification and processes of class formation, but they rarely engaged with
questions of political imagination. See, for instance, Wallerstein, *Africa*;
Coleman, *Education and Political Development*; Arrighi and Saul, *Essays
on Political Economy*, 44–103; and Hanna, *University Students*. Important works about Congolese higher education and student politics in a
similar vein include Verhaegen, *L'enseignement universitaire*; Kasongo-
Ngoy, *Capital scolaire*; and Bongeli, *Université contre développement*.
16 Pursley, "Stage of Adolescence."
17 See, for instance, Straker, *Youth*, 19–55; and Ahlman, *Living with
Nkrumahism*, 84–114.
18 See Ivaska, *Cultured States*, 124–65; and Blum, *Révolutions africaines*,
79–98.
19 Like Sarah Van Beurden, I look at the 1960s and the first few years of the
Mobutu regime as a critical period in the decolonization of the Congo, a
process that continued to unfold well beyond the colonial regime formally
ended on June 30, 1960 (see Van Beurden, "Art of (Re)possession," 144).
20 For an approach to postcolonial African cosmopolitanism that similarly
emphasizes generational dynamics, see Callaci, *Street Archives*, 18–58.
Parallels can also be drawn in the way students and "vernacular cosmopolitan" devotees in dissident churches used colonial infrastructures of
mobility and communication to craft political identities that set them
apart from others in their own society (see Cabrita, *People's Zion*, 18–21,
197–228; and Peterson, *Ethnic Patriots*, 37–49). Yet, the students' liminal
position vis-à-vis the world of expertise and elitism placed them at odds
with religious dissidents and reformers. Likewise, students did not necessarily embrace the views of the elite political actors who favored federalist
alternatives to the nation-state, a position associated with cosmopolitanism
in the recent scholarship on African decolonization (see Fejzula, "Cosmopolitan Historiography"). Some students questioned the "global political
scenario" of decolonization and its focus on nation-stateness (see Lee,
"Between a Moment," 19), but many did not. Instead, they simultaneously
and unproblematically embraced nationalism, Pan-African internationalism, tricontinentalism, and world socialism (for an argument about the
imbrication of cosmopolitanism with nationalism and internationalism in
a different context, see Clark, *Moscow*, 1–5; see also Glassman, "Creole Nationalists" for a critique of the opposition between nativism and
cosmopolitanism in an East African context). Crucially, their cosmopolitanism politicized the students at the same time that it remained politically
undetermined. It was visceral and existential first and foremost—emerging,
as it did, from the experience of higher education and its promises of intellectual advancement, personal emancipation, and social mobility.
21 On late-colonial educational policy toward women, see Hunt, "Domesticity and Colonialism"; Mianda, "Colonialism"; Bandeira Jeronimo,
"Restoring Order"; and Lauro, "Women in Congo."

22 See the parallels with Lumumba's own ambivalences about the status of women as political subjects in Bouwer, *Gender and Decolonization*, 13–37.

23 On the impact of colonialism on the "sur-masculinization" of power in the Congo, see Biaya, "La culture urbaine," 348.

24 On the genealogy of Mobutu's authenticity project, see Van Beurden, *Authentically African*, 107–14.

25 Nkrumah, *Neocolonialism*.

26 For a recent article mentioning the Czechoslovakian intelligence service's interest in the Congo, see Telepneva, "Code Name Sekretar," 10. On interferences from other countries, see chapters 2 and 6.

27 Di Capua, *No Exit*, 182; O'Malley, *Diplomacy of Decolonisation*, 2.

28 Ambar, *Malcolm X*, 3, 142. On the significance of the Congo crisis on Dutschke and the German student movement, see Brown, *West Germany*, 24.

29 See colonial police reports on listeners of Radio Cairo in "Sécurité, confidentiels divers" (1953–59), GG6150, AA; and Michel Elesse, personal interview, unrecorded, Kinshasa, July 28, 2015.

30 Kadima Nzuji, personal interview, recorded, Brazzaville, September 22, 2010.

31 A few months earlier, West German student radicals had staged a well-publicized protest against Senghor at the Frankfurt Book Fair for the same reasons. See Brown, *West Germany*, 116–21. For a detailed account of the "Senegalese May," see Gueye, *Mai 68*.

32 Afraid that Senghor would end up speaking to an empty room, Lovanium's academic secretary reportedly requested that the university's janitors and custodians attend the speech. Polydor Muboyayi Mubanga, personal interview, recorded, Kinshasa, July 25, 2011.

33 Senghor, *De la négritude*. The speech responded to Wole Soyinka's criticisms of Negritude as an incarnation of French cultural imperialism. Recalling his long-term dialogue with the Harlem Renaissance, Senghor argued that the imperialism of Negritude, if there was one, was "negro-African, not French."

34 See Diagne, *Bergson postcolonial*, 37–64.

35 See Wilder, *Freedom Time*, 64–68, 206–40.

36 See Byrne, *Mecca of Revolution*, 5; and Lee, "Between a Moment," 26. On the history of futures and reverie in colonial Congo and on the role of imaginary futures in 1930s South Asian anti-colonial internationalisms, see Hunt, "Espace, temporalité"; and Goswami, "Colonial Internationalisms."

37 See Mobe, "Intellectualités estudiantines."

38 Negritude was not universally appreciated among Congolese students. Some rejected it as false consciousness and as a romanticizing discourse. And although more nuanced in his critique, Mudimbe—who had been a student at Lovanium before he emerged as a major Congolese intellectual

in the late 1960s—developed his understanding of Africa in tension with Senghor's Negritude. See Kasereka, "Mudimbe Senghorien."

39 Anastase Nzeza, personal interview, recorded, Kinshasa, October 10, 2010.

40 Mudimbe famously referred to Sartre as an African philosopher to acknowledge his deep impact on his generation of African intellectuals. Mudimbe, *Invention of Africa*, 83–87. See also Young, "Sartre"; and Di-Capua, *No Exit*, 11–13.

41 Worldedness should be understood in relation both to the Sartrean existential "presence to the world" and to the Senghorian framing of decolonization as human reconciliation on a planetary scale. See Sartre, *Being and Nothingness*; and Wilder, *Freedom Time*, 206–41. On worldedness in the context of the global 1960s, see also Connery, "World Sixties."

42 Hubert Humphrey, "The Vice-President's Trip to Africa: Report to the President," January 1968, Hubert Humphrey Papers, Vice-Presidential Foreign Affairs Files, Box 916, MHSL.

43 Maurice Tempelsman, "Report to the Vice-President," January 1968, Hubert Humphrey Papers, Vice-Presidential Foreign Affairs Files, Box 916, MHSL. On Tempelsman's personal business dealings in the Congo at the time of the visit, see "Humphrey Dumphrey," *Ramparts*, November 17, 1968, 41–46.

44 Besides Kinshasa, Humphrey also faced manifestations of hostility in Addis Ababa and Tunis where students organized pro-Vietnam and anti-American street rallies. See Zewde, *Documenting*, 33–44; and Hendrickson, "March 1968."

45 On the report's reception by the Johnson administration (including Humphrey, National Security Adviser Walt Rostow and Secretary of State Dean Rusk), see Klimke, *The Other Alliance*, 194–213. The report's conclusion is reprinted in Suri, *Global Revolutions*, 216–37.

46 See notably Christiansen and Scarlett, *The Third World*; Blum et al., *Etudiants africains*; Jian et al., *Routledge Handbook*; Hodgkinson and Melchiorre, "Student Activism." Monographs that identify "sixties moments" in Africa and develop histories of student protests at the time of global 1968 notably include Ivaska, *Cultured States*; Blum, *Révolutions africaines*; Zeleke, *Ethiopia in Theory*; and Zewde, *Quest for Socialist Utopia*. On the postcolonial dimension of 1968 in the francophone world, see Blum, "Années 68"; Hendrickson, "Imperial Fragments"; and Ross, *May '68*. See also Slobodian, *Foreign Front*; and Dedieu and Mbodj-Pouye, "Fabric of Transnational Activism," on the contribution of third world students to new far-left movements in both France and Germany.

47 "Communiqué de la FEANF," May 11, 1968, Jacques Foccart Papers, AG/5(F)/2610, AN.

48 On African students in Eastern Europe and the Soviet Union, see notably Katsakioris, "The Lumumba University"; and Burton, "Journeys of Education."

49 Revel, *Un parcours critique*, 54
50 Central Intelligence Agency, "Restless Youth," 1970, n.p., Freedom of Information Act Electronic Reading Room, Central Intelligence Agency, https://www.cia.gov/library/readingroom/document/0002987248. For the CIA's vision of Congolese history, see the memoir of its first chief of station in independent Congo: Devlin, *Chief of Station*. As further elaborated in chapter 5, the CIA, working with young liberal activists, including future academic luminaries James Scott and Duncan Kennedy, played a crucial role in the creation of Congolese student politics in the early 1960s.
51 Using Jacques Rancière's work on ideology, Kristin Ross theorized a police conception of history in relation to May '68 in France that she equates with a refusal to recognize the singularity of the event by reducing it to its sociological determination and refusing to look at the novel forms of political imagination it produced: Ross, *May '68*.
52 Holt, "Bread or Freedom." See also Rubin, *Archives of Authority*; and "The CIA as an Equal Opportunity Employer," *Ramparts* 7, no. 13 (June 1969).
53 Wallerstein, "1968."
54 See Getachew, *Worldmaking after Empire*.
55 See Featherstone, *Solidarity*, 1–12.
56 Ferdinand Kayukwa, speech at the International Union of Students' 7th Congress in Leningrad, August 1962, IUS archival collections, IISH. Cuba was a particularly important reference as the Cuban revolution shaped US perceptions of Lumumba in 1960. A few years later, while Che Guevara joined Congolese rebels in eastern Congo, the CIA employed Cuban exiles as pilots in counterinsurgencies in the Congo. Weiner, *Legacy of Ashes*, 87–198, 323–24.
57 Duncan Kennedy, "Report on the 2nd Congress of the US Section of the Union of Congolese Students," June 1964, USNSA International Commission, Box 188, HIA. Incidentally, Averell Harriman, who redefined the US engagement in Vietnam as John F. Kennedy's and Johnson's ambassador at large in the mid-1960s, saw himself "as the toughest Congo-fighter" in the US administration (Robert Komer, "Memo for Governor Harriman," October 21, 1965, A. Harriman Papers, Box 448, LOC). Increased involvement in Vietnam made the stabilization of the Congo more pressing for the US government. See Namikas, *Battleground Africa*, 186–222; and O'Malley, *Diplomacy of Decolonisation*. On US interventionism in the Congo, see Gibbs, *Political Economy*; Schmidt, *Foreign Intervention*, 56–77; and De Witte, *L'ascension de Mobutu*.
58 Tsing, *Friction*, 85–86. On the antagonism between African "freedom dreams" and Cold War realities, see Allman, "The Fate of All of Us." On the power of foreign discursive constructs in shaping the Congo's position in international relations, see Dunn, *Imagining the Congo*, 61–104. On US one-worldedness, see Apter, "On Oneworldedness," 386.

59 Sorensen, "Alternative Geographic Mappings." For a typology of trans-national connections in the global 1960s, see Langland, "Transnational Connections"; and Langland, *Speaking of Flowers*.

60 See Matera, *Black London*; Goebel, *Anti-Imperial Metropolis*; and Ray, *Crossing the Color Line*.

61 Hunt, *Nervous State*.

62 Jewsiewicki, "African Peasants"; Jewsiewicki, "Political Consciousness"; Likaka, *Rural Society*; Higginson, *Working Class*; Henriet, "Concession Experience"; Seibert, "More Continuity." See also Gray, "Territoriality"; and Stanard, "Revisiting Bula Matari."

63 Hodgkin, *Nationalism*, 55.

64 A handful of Congolese had studied in non-university higher education institutions in Europe before Kanza. The most famous was Paul Panda Farnana, who studied at a school of tropical agriculture in France and then at an institute of commercial and consular sciences in Belgium a few years before World War I. See Bontinck, "Mfumu Paul Panda Farnana," 594–95.

65 See, for instance, Chafer, "Students and Nationalism." People in Por-tuguese African colonies also enjoyed a rather limited access to higher education before the 1960s, but there, the opening-up of educational possibilities (notably through scholarships from socialist countries) started years before the ultimate downfall of colonial rule in 1974. See, for instance, Katsakioris, "Students from Portuguese Africa."

66 On the évolués and elite politics in the Belgian Congo, see Mutamba, *Du Congo belge au Congo indépendant*; and Tödt, *Lumumba Generation*.

67 The students' frustrated expectations can be compared to the dynamics around the labor question, whereby increased rights and welfare re-sulted in more, not fewer, protests and claims from workers. See Cooper, *Decolonization*.

68 On Congolese student politics, see Tshimanga, "La jeunesse étudiante"; and Mobe, "Intellectualités estudiantines."

69 Boyle, *Class Formation*, 114–16.

70 See Paul-Lomami Tshibamba, "Quel sera notre place dans le monde de demain?," *La voix du congolais* 1, no. 2 (1945).

71 Gikandi, "*Arrow of God.*"

72 Vansina, *Paths in the Rainforests*, 239–48. Vansina contrasts this cogni-tive insecurity with the social and intellectual constructions that allowed people to generate institutions and bodies of thoughts in previous eras. These constructions included the model of big man leadership, the use of wealth to accumulate power, and the ability to attract dependents with specific knowledge that allowed to adapt to difficult and changing envi-ronments (see also Guyer and Belinga, "Wealth in People"). According to Vansina, this political tradition died in the 1920s because of the violence and cognitive challenges of the colonial conquest, which left people in the region disoriented and unsecure. Several scholars have questioned

Vansina's diagnosis, showing how Congolese continued through the colonial and postcolonial periods to function as cultural bricoleurs, mixing the old with the new, and using central elements of the tradition—from therapeutic lexicons to idioms of witchcraft and bigmanship—as tools to engage with alien epistemologies. See Hunt, *Colonial Lexicon*; Gondola, *Tropical Cowboys*; and MacGaffey, *Kongo Political Culture*. See also Bernault, *Colonial Transactions*.

73 See Vellut, *Congo*, 461–62. Some of these students later produced major works that recovered oral traditions, epics, and material artifacts that could reactualize elements of an ancient cultural patrimony in the present. For a paradigmatic example, see Biebuyck and Mateene, *The Mwindo Epic*. The culturalist bent of Flemish missionary Catholicism often informed the intellectual genealogy of the Congolese intellectuals who worked on reviving local traditions. See Hunt, "Rewriting the Soul."

74 Kalixte Mukendi Wa Nsanga, personal interview, recorded, Nouakchott, May 20, 2016.

75 See Dhimiter Mandro, "Relacion takimi me Kalikst Mudendi," August 11, 1965, Foreign Affairs collection, 14/15/612, GDA.

76 Manjpara, "Third World Humanities."

77 See Mudimbe, *Invention of Africa*; Fraiture and Orrells, *Mudimbe Reader*; Nzongola-Ntalaja, *The Congo*; and Buakasa, *L'impensé du discours*. See also Mudimbe, *Les corps glorieux*, 147–53; and Mobe, "Intellectualités estudiantines."

78 Another relevant literality in the Congolese context lay in the fact that educated Congolese were often referred to as "the lettered" in colonial parlance. See, for instance, Hunt, "Camouflaged Polygamy."

79 Mbembe, *Sortir de la grande nuit*, 68.

80 Foucault, *Dits et écrits*, 417.

81 On the foundations of these two traditions, see discussions of W. E. B. Du Bois's *The World and Africa* (1946) and Darryl Forde's *African Worlds* (1954) in Cooper, *Africa in the World*, 1–10; and Mudimbe, *Invention of Africa*, 135–86.

82 Bayart, "Africa in the World," 218, 234.

83 See, for instance, Bostoen and Brinkman, *Kongo Kingdom* on the longue durée of cosmopolitan dispositions in west central Africa.

84 Amin, *Le développement*.

85 Hountondji, *Struggle for Meaning*, 140.

86 Hountondji, *Struggle for Meaning*, 141.

87 Prestholdt, *Icons of Dissent*, 40.

88 On the use of the Habermasian notion of the public sphere in a midtwentieth century African context, see Hunter, *Political Thought*, 21–30. See also Calhoun, "Public Sphere."

89 See Fraiture, *Mudimbe*, 83–89.

90 On mediation and appropriation, see Krings, *African Appropriations*, 1–27.

91 Getachew, *Worldmaking after Empire*, 1–3.
92 On intersubjectivity, see Jackson, *Lifeworlds*, 5–6.
93 See Malkki, "Citizens of Humanity."
94 See Karagiannis and Wagner, "Globalization or World-Making?"
95 On archival dispersion and the writing of African postcolonial histories, see Allman, "Phantoms of the Archive"; and White, "Hodgepodge Historiography."
96 See Hountondji, *Struggle for Meaning*; and Verdery, *Political Lives*, 24.
97 Mazrui, *Political Values*, 1–20. See also Abiola, "In Praise of Alienation."
98 Cited in Findlay, *Caring for the Soul*, 15–50. See also Bernard, "Le monde comme problème."

Interlude I. Postal Musings

1 See MacGaffey, "Zamenga of Zaire"; Ngoma-Binda, *Zamenga Batuke-zanga*; and Hunt, "Tintin."
2 And letters were also often involved in connecting reading and listening publics to newspapers and radio stations, helping to cross the line between the production and consumption of information and cultural content in print and radio communications. See, for instance, Moorman, *Powerful Frequencies*, 89–92; and Newell, *Power to Name*, 59–60.
3 Zamenga, *La carte postale*. By the mid-1970s, novels about sub-Saharan students in France had already become a subgenre in African francophone literature, but *La carte postale* was one of the first literary works by a Congolese writer on the experience of studying in the former metropole. Despite its title, the book was not an epistolary novel. Zamenga adopted this genre in several other of his books in a self-proclaimed act of filiation with Montesquieu's *Persian Letters*. Djungu-Simba, "Ce sorcier de Zamenga," 10.

One. Distance Learning and the Production of Politics

1 De Quincey, *English Mail-Coach*. De Quincey was not unknown in the Belgian colony. Pierre Ryckmans, the governor general from 1934 to 1946, was an avid reader of his works. See Vanderlinden, *Pierre Ryckmans*, 227. The text's first French translation was published in a literary journal from Lyon in 1943.
2 "A Black who quotes Montesquieu had better be watched. Please understand me: watched in the sense that he is starting something" (Fanon, *Peau noire*, 52). Echoing Fanon, a Belgian colonial legal scholar in 1952 argued that thinking about political participation in the Congo was premature because "Bantus are still far from having read and understood Montesquieu" ("Procès-verbal de la reunion extraordinaire du CEPSI," *Bulletin du Centre d'étude des problèmes sociaux indigènes* 18–19 [1952]: 163).

3   Bennington, "Postal Politics."
4   On the text's engagement with time-space compression, see Valtat, "Vitesse, réseau."
5   Love and conjugality were also important questions debated by letter writers. See Breckenridge, "Reasons for Writing"; Prichard, "Let Us Swim"; and Mutongi "Dear Dolly."
6   Ernest Wamba dia Wamba, personal interview, recorded, Kinshasa, November 7, 2010. Wamba shared the same anecdote with Jason Stearns. See Stearns, *Dancing in the Glory*, 201–16.
7   See Derrida, *La carte postale*.
8   Achebe, *Home and Exile*, 76.
9   See, for instance, Tagore's "The Postmaster."
10 I borrow this phrase from Prita Meier's study of Swahili stone architecture. Meier, *Swahili Port Cities*, 2.
11 See Chalux, *Un an*, 393–95. As noted by Chalux, colonizers attempted to segregate postal offices early on. Yet, they were never able to make these spaces unavailable to the colonized altogether.
12 Word of mouth, rumors, and direct interactions were much more efficient at engineering mobilizations and forms of collective action. See, for instance, Henriet, "Elusive Natives"; and Eggers, "Kitawala in Congo."
13 On delay and strategic deferral as constitutive dimensions in long-distance correspondence and circulation of images, see Roberts, *Transporting Visions*, 7–9.
14 See Hunt, *Colonial Lexicon*, 159–95.
15 Sandrine Colard notes a similar ambivalence in relation to photography, which functioned both as an early instrument of colonial conquest and order and as a powerful medium in the denunciation of Leopoldian violence. See Colard, "Photography in Congo," 39–70. On the history of rubber atrocities in the CFS, see also Hunt, *Nervous State*, 27–60.
16 "Postal Service in Interior Africa," *Scientific American* 69, no. 25 (December 16, 1893): 389.
17 This rhetoric recalls Conrad's description of the CFS mail in his first short story about the Congo. See Conrad, "An Outpost of Progress," in *Almayer's Folly*, 86–117.
18 See Schmitt, *Nomos of the Earth*, 214–15. Like the Congo Conference, the UPU had a strong German imprint, as it was very much designed by the former Prussian postmaster general D. R. von Stephan. See Williamson, "International Postal Service."
19 Louis, *Ends of British Imperialism*, 123; Craven, "Between Law and History," 39.
20 See, among many other works, Siegert, *Relays*; Henkin, *Postal Age*; and Thomas, *Postal Pleasures*. See also Laborie, "Global Commerce." Despite his focus on the press and print capitalism, Benedict Anderson pays little attention to postal communications in *Imagined Communities*. Yet, he still alludes to the importance of postal capacities by noting the dependence

of printer-journalists on postmasters in eighteenth-century North America. Anderson, *Imagined Communities*, 61.

21 The participation of colonial territories was debated at all the congresses of the UPU from 1924 to 1938. A few territories, like the CFS and later the Belgian Congo, participated in the UPU as full members with voting rights, while other colonial possessions did not. Some argued for the abolition of voting rights for colonial territories in the name of equality among nations and "because the UPU had been created to serve the interests of Humanity and not those of individual countries." By contrast, others claimed that a truly universal union—one that would participate in the abolition of borders and ensure the "primordial conditions of universal civilization"—demanded the inclusion of all territories, regardless of their status of sovereignty. See "Congrès postal universel de Londres, procès-verbal de la 3e séance de la 1ère commission," May 15, 1929 and "Rapport de la 1ère commission," February 20, 1934, AA, 3DG310. See also Codding, *Universal Postal Union*, 79–85.

22 Joyce, "Filling the Raj," 105.

23 On Belgium's role in the emergence of European liberal internationalism, see Laqua, *Age of Internationalism*.

24 See Burbank and Cooper, *Empires in World History*.

25 For instance, the African Steamship Company, a Liverpool-based shipping line that had been central to the development of British imperialism in West Africa since the 1850s, acted as a recruitment agency for the CFS in Lagos, while also enjoying a decade-long monopoly in the transport of the Congolese mail. See Cookey, "West African Immigrants."

26 "Our Postal Deficit," *The Postal Record: A Journal for Postal Employees* 8, no. 10 (October 1895): 153.

27 There were then twenty-three post offices for the whole territory, and around 370,000 letters and printed materials circulated yearly. Wack, *Story of Congo Free State*, 243–45.

28 Wack, *Story of Congo Free State*, 245. The practice was officially banned in 1903 but may have continued for several years after that.

29 *Le martyr des congolais*, 54.

30 Casement, *Correspondence and Report*, 62. The same people who told Casement about local white agents' disregard for official orders still believed in the power of the written word, as Casement noted in the preface to the transcription of his interview with them: "The fact of my writing down and asking for names, &c., seemed to impress them, and they spoke with what certainly impressed me as being great sincerity."

31 On the notion of colonial sublime, see Larkin, *Signal and Noise*. On the colonial state postal rhetoric in the Congo, see "Rapport de la commission d'enquête," *Bulletin officiel* 21, no. 9–10 (September–October 1905): 144; and Du Four, *Cinquante ans*.

32 Dworkin, *Congo Love Song*, 19–48.

33 See Zimmerman, *Alabama in Africa*, 173–204.

34 On shock photographs, their framing of the discourse on Leopoldian atrocities, and their long-term impact on the development of a specific form of representational ideal, see Hunt, *Nervous State*, 27–60; Hunt, "Acoustic Register"; Grant, "Limits of Exposure," 64–88; and Colard, "Photography in Congo," 39–70.

35 Pavlakis, *British Humanitarianism*, 26. As noted by Isabel Hofmeyr, correspondence played a prominent role in the work of missionaries who aimed at creating a "continuous evangelic field" between imperial metropoles and peripheries. Hofmeyr, *The Portable Bunyan*, 45–55.

36 Twain, *King Leopold's Soliloquy*, 14, 23. On the collaboration and friction between Morel and the missionaries, see Grant, *A Civilised Savagery*, 39–78.

37 On the very frequent occurrence in the lexicon of the imperial press of the word *mail*, a shorthand term for the frequent exchanges of articles among newspapers that established "a common link between post and news as common institutions," see Hofmeyr, *Gandhi's Printing Press*, 75–76.

38 Twain imagined the Belgian king's annoyance with italicization in the publications of the Congo Reform Association: "M. Morel intrudes at this point, and contributes a comment which he could just as well have kept to himself—and throws in some italics, of course; these people can never get along without italics" (Twain, *King Leopold*, 38).

39 Vandewoude, *Voyage du Prince Albert*, 25.

40 Several telegraphy students had been recruited at the state school for clerks in Boma. Robert Goldschmidt, letter to the Minister of Colonies, August 20, 1912, Fonds Belgacom, AGR.

41 See Zana, *Het land van de Banoko*.

42 Goldschmidt and Braillard, *La télégraphie sans fil*, 7.

43 Goldschmidt and Braillard, *La télégraphie sans fil*, 65, 100. Goldschmidt, who directed the school for Congolese telegraphers that operated in King Albert's palace, conducted the first successful experiment in wireless communication between Belgium and the Congo in 1913. After the war put an end to his work, Congolese radiotelegraphy only really took off again in the 1930s.

44 Segaert, *Un terme au Congo*, 123.

45 "La T. S. F. au Congo," *L'Indépendance Belge*, March 23, 1930, 15. On the slow and difficult development of wireless telegraphy in the lower Congo after World War I, see Counet, *Deux ans au service*.

46 "Note au Gouverneur Général," February 8, 1922; "Note pour le Ministre," September 22, 1921; and "Utilisation du personnel noir," March 12, 1921, 3e DG 1648, AA.

47 Hill, *Marcus Garvey Papers*, 9:42–50.

48 Booker T. Washington was one of the most prominent members of the Congo Reform Association in the United States, and Belgian suspicions about the dangers of African Americans for Congolese affairs remained very strong throughout the 1920s and 1930s. See Dworkin, *Congo Love*

Song, 132–38. On Belgian fears of Garveyism in the Belgian Congo, see also Ewing, *The Age of Garvey,* 94–95.

49 Hill, *Marcus Garvey Papers,* 97–100, 233–35. On Panda and colonial fears of pan-Africanist conspiracies in the Congo, see also Vellut, *Simon Kimbangu,* 2:56–65.

50 See Eggers, "Kitawala in Congo." On postal censorship targeted at Black mineworkers in Katanga during World War II, see Higginson, *Working Class in Making,* 167–68.

51 Hunt, *Nervous State,* 95–134. See also Zana, "L'armée du salut."

52 Stoler, "In Cold Blood," 153.

53 See, for instance, the notice on André Yengo in Vellut, *Simon Kimbangu,* 1(2):352–53.

54 In 1928, the list included the Garveyist publications *Negro World* and *African World,* as well as the Belgian communist newspapers *Le Drapeau Rouge* and *De Rood Van.* "Questionnaire destiné à être utilisé pour la publication d'une nouvelle liste d'objets interdits," August 20, 1928, 3eDG 1592, AA.

55 Surveillance also concerned correspondence exchanged by Europeans. In the late 1950s, a Belgian socialist senator questioned the minister of colonies about the existence of a cabinet noir that allegedly screened all correspondence being sent from the Congo to Belgium. "Question parlementaire n°6 de monsieur le sénateur Yernaux en date du 30.9.1958," 3eDG 339, AA. On the colonial sureté's surveillance of Europeans in the Congo during World War II, see Williams, *Spies in Congo.*

56 Hunt, "Letter-Writing." See also Nzuji Mukala, *La littérature zaïroise,* 20–33.

57 See Lauro, "J'ai l'honneur."

58 The term *mukanda* also referred to male circumcision and initiation rituals into manhood among a variety of people in central Africa's southern savanna, in the Congo, Angola, and northern Rhodesia. See, for example, Lengel, *Mukanda.*

59 See Mudimbe-Boyi, "Le français, langue paternelle," 87.

60 Johannes Fabian defines mukanda as "the kind of 'texts' that colonial (and postcolonial) administration and enterprises produce to ensure their control over the population or labor force" and terrorize illiterate people. See Fabian, "Text as Terror."

61 Vellut, "Le Katanga industriel." See also Mutamba, *De Congo belge au Congo indépendant,* 36–37.

62 This may not have been the first letter to do so. For instance, according to a Songye political activist interviewed in 1993 by historian Donatien Dibwe, the colonizers decided to hang Chief Kamanda Ya Kaumbu in 1936, not because he had killed a young woman as was alleged, but because he had sent a letter to King Leopold III demanding independence for the Congo. Dibwe, "Popular Memories," 68–69. On the canonization

of the mid-1950s' manifestos as the starting point for Congolese politics, see Monaville, "Histoires politiques congolaises."

63 On similar exchanges in Cameroon, see Terretta, *Nation of Outlaws*, 112–14. See also Pedersen, *The Guardians*, 77–104. While the Congolese in the late 1940s and early 1950s did not enjoy direct lines of communication with international addressees who could have supported claims about political rights or poor living conditions, they could easily write to the colonial authorities. As Amandine Lauro has noted, anonymous letter writing to the state bureaucracy was a common practice to express grievances at the time. Lauro, "Suspect Cities."

64 In comparison, the same metric was 1.5 letters in French Equatorial Africa, 7.4 in India, 7.7 in the Gold Coast, 48 in South Africa, 58 in France, and 116 in Switzerland. Around 1955, there were 248 postal offices in the Congo, seven times less than in Belgium; on average, each Congolese office covered an area of 9,672 square kilometers. Only six of the then ninety-four members of the UPU fared worse: Ethiopia, French West Africa, French East Africa, Aden, Somaliland, and Dutch New Guinea.

65 André Coine, "Le service des postes au Congo belge et Ruanda-Urundi," September 5, 1959, 3eDG 334.

66 Depaepe, *Between Educationalization and Appropriation*, 215.

67 On Lumumba's youth, see Mutamba, "La destinée de Patrice Lumumba," 11–52; Omasombo and Verhaegen, *Patrice Lumumba, jeunesse*; and Omasombo and Verhaegen, *Patrice Lumumba, acteur politique*.

68 On the role of the print media in creating an évolué public sphere in colonial Congo, see Tödt, *Lumumba Generation*.

69 Quoted in Verhaegen and Omasombo, *Patrice Lumumba, jeunesse*, 123.

70 Gazi, *Culture, littérature et enseignement*, 24.

71 Paul Nyssens, the eighty-year-old director of the institute, was a self-professed specialist of phrenology, vegetarianism, and autosuggestion. Nyssens was the author of dozens of books about happiness and the importance of daily laughter, self-knowledge, the development of memory, success, and willpower. A half brother of a close collaborator of Leopold II who had remained very involved with Congolese affairs until his death in 1901, Nyssens seemed to have been aware early on of the potential of finding readers in colonial territories and had his books advertised in colonial publications starting in the 1900s.

72 "Procès-verbal," April 14, 1951, Colonial Postal Administration Papers, 3 DG 336, AA.

73 Paul Nyssens, letter to the Minister of Colonies, May 26, 1950, Colonial Postal Administration Papers, 3 DG 336, AA.

74 Paul Nyssens, letter to Port Franqui's Postmaster, March 20, 1950, Colonial Postal Administration collections, 3 DG 336, AA. On the selling of talismans by French merchants to correspondents in colonial Africa, see Bernault, *Colonial Transactions*, 94.

75 O. Vevloet, "Procès-verbal administratif," April 18, 1951, Colonial Postal Administration Papers, 3 DG 336, AA.

76 Kingansi carefully kept Nyssens's courses in a tin trunk that stayed with him through more than half a dozen moves until his death in 2000. Soon after his run-in with "postal paternalism" at Port Franqui, Kingansi left his work with Lever and became an employee of the State Institute for Agronomical Studies. In 1958, he was part of the large cohort of évolués who visited Belgium to attend the Brussels World Fair. Around the same time, he joined the anti-colonial struggle. In 1960, he was elected as a provincial member of parliament for the Parti solidaire africain and became a member of the state territorial administration after 1965 (Marie-Léonie Kingansi, phone conversation with author, December 2, 2017).

77 Labrique, *Congo politique*, 55.

78 Patrice Lumumba, "Editorial," *L'Echo Postal* 1, no. 1 (1955): 1. A Belgian journalist argued in a biography of Lumumba that white postal employees forced their way into the organization in order to control Lumumba and restrain the politicization of APIPO. De Vos, *Vie et mort de Lumumba*, 42.

79 Patrice Lumumba, "Rapport de fin d'exercice, année 1954," *L'Echo Postal* 1, no. 1 (1955): 2–5.

80 Patrice Hemery Lumumba, "Vous faîtes-vous aisément des amis?" See also Patrice Hemery Lumumba, "L'action est base de tout progrès," *L'Echo Postal* 1, no. 2 (1955): 35–37.

81 Tead, *What Is a Race?*

82 Patrice Hemery Lumumba, "Les races humaines," *L'Echo Postal* 1, no. 1 (1955): 17–20; 1, no. 2 (1955): 40–42; 1, no. 3 (1955): 69–72; 1, no. 4 (1955): 88–91.

83 R. Tavernier, "Histoire de la poste," *L'Echo Postal* 1, no. 1 (1955): 5–6; R. Tavernier, "Histoire de la poste: Suite," *L'Echo Postal* 1, no. 2 (1955): 45; L. Delfosse, "Histoire de la poste," *L'Echo Postal* 2, no. 1 (1956): 7–9; L. Delfosse, "L'Union Postale Universelle," *L'Echo Postal* 1, no. 3 (1955): 59.

84 R. Tavernier, "Réflexions sur notre activité administrative," *L'Echo Postal* 1, no. 2 (1955): 33–34.

85 R. Tavernier, "Réflexions au sujet du comportement du postier," *L'Echo Postal* 1, no. 4 (1955): 78.

86 Patrice Hemery Lumumba, "Postiers, soyons dévoués," *L'Echo Postal* 1, no. 3 (1955): 53.

87 L. Delfosse, "Buts à atteindre," *L'Echo Postal* 1, no. 4 (1955): 83–85. See also L. Delfosse, "Famille," *L'Echo Postal* 1, no. 2 (1955): 47–48.

88 Patrice Lumumba, "Quelques règles de politesse et de savoir-vivre," *L'Echo Postal* 1, no. 2 (1955): 46. On the specific framing of an évolué respectability in late colonial Congo, see Tödt, *Lumumba Generation*, 231–41.

89 Patrice Hemery Lumumba, "Quelques devoirs des agents des services publics et plus spécialement des postiers," *L'Echo Postal* 1, no. 1 (1955):

9–12. See also Patrice Hemery Lumumba, "Quelques devoirs d'un homme civilisé," *L'Echo Postal* 1, no. 2 (1955): 44.

90 Mutamba, *Du Congo belge au Congo indépendant*, 313–15. Lumumba had hoped to spend time observing postmen in Brussels and in rural areas and to visit the postal museum in Brussels while in Belgium ("Un beau voyage," *L'Echo Postal* 2, no. 2 [1956]: n.p.). However, the program was already full and the Ministry of Colonies did not grant a lot of room to Congolese visitors in determining their agenda. In the end, Lumumba visited the office of postal checks on May 8 and Brussels's main post office on May 9. See Zana, "Lumumba en Belgique," 211.

91 Patrice-Emery Lumumba, "L'acheminement d'une lettre," *La Croix du Congo* 18, no. 32 (August 27, 1950): 4 (reproduced in Mutamba, *Patrice Lumumba correspondant*, 78).

92 On the politics of colonial enclosure, see Bernault, "Politics of Enclosure."

93 Paul Cornil, "Prisons congolaises," *Bulletin de l'Administration des prisons* 7, no. 2 (February 1953): 361–69. Not surprisingly, a few decades later, images of colonial prison life became one of the best-selling subjects in urban popular painting. See Fabian, *Remembering the Present*, 68–70; Jewsiewicki, *Mami wata*; and Verbeek, "D'une thèse de doctorat."

94 "Envoi vélo détenu Kasandji," September 29, 1956, G. G. Papers, AA, Brussels; "Effets Paul Simba," January 30, 1956, G. G. Papers, AA.

95 Cornil, "Prisons congolaises."

96 B. S. Lupaka, "Le système pénitencier congolais tel que nous l'avons vu," *L'Afrique et le Monde*, December 13, 1956, 7.

97 "Prison Divers," n.d., G. G. Papers, AA.

98 After an intervention by the government in Brussels, Lumumba's sentence was reduced to fourteen months. Considering the time he had already spent in prison, he was finally freed on September 7, 1957.

99 Lumumba, *Le Congo, terre d'avenir*, 13.

100 On the symbolism of deliverance in postal transactions in a different context, see Robbins, "Fugitive Mail."

101 See Gondola, *Tropical Cowboys*, 53–67; Grabli, "La ville des auditeurs"; and Fierens, "Reporting on Independence."

102 Larkin, *Signal and Noise*, 75.

103 Foucault, *Technologies of Self*.

104 Sartre, *Colonialism and Neocolonialism*, 95–96.

Two. Friendly Correspondence with the Whole World

1 "The Stamp Explosion: Philatelists Welcome Boom in Stamps by and of Blacks," *Ebony* 25, no. 2 (December 1969): 142–43.

2 The literature on the Congo crisis, notably on the role of the United States, is quite extensive. See, among others, Weissman, *American Foreign Policy*; Ilunga, "Catastrophe of Belgian Decolonization"; Gibbs, *Political*

Economy of Third World; De Witte, *Assassination of Lumumba*; and Hill and Keller, *Trustee for the Human Community*.

3 To add to this already flourishing production, the UN mission in the Congo issued its own stamps and postmarks. These multiple peculiarities would later fill several generations of philatelists with enthusiasm, but it initially made their heads spin. They did not know what to collect and how to properly catalog their new acquisitions. See Charles Jonker, "Congo," *Le Philatéliste Belge* 107 (July–September 1961): 56.

4 See various reports and an array of correspondence in the folder "Question des déficits postaux," 3e DG 382, AA.

5 Devlin, *Chief of Station*, 100. The postal administration recovered in subsequent months and years, notably thanks to technical support from the UN, until it underwent an even more dramatic downfall in the age of structural adjustment in the 1980s and 1990s.

6 On Lumumba and Fanon in Accra, see Cherki, *Fanon*, 142, 146.

7 Lopez, *Lumumba ou l'Afrique*, 45.

8 The institute delivered evening courses and public lectures to the Congolese state employees who had replaced the departed Belgian colonials. The Ford Foundation, one of its main sponsors, later described it as an "oasis during the post-independence tumult" (*Two African Patterns* [New York: Ford Foundation, 1966], 13).

9 Pierre Wangata, letters to Louis Mandala, September 21 and 25, 1960, Jean Van Lierde Papers, CEGES.

10 This has emerged most clearly in the forensic historical investigations into the murder of Patrice Lumumba. Historians have now closely read the diplomatic paper trail to determine the respective degrees of responsibility of all the actors involved, locally and internationally. See De Witte, *Assassination of Lumumba*; De Vos et al., *Les secrets de l'affaire*; and Gerard and Kuklick, *Death in Congo*.

11 Quoted in Willame, *Patrice Lumumba*, 78.

12 Van Lierde, *La pensée politique*, 393.

13 See I. D. Scott, letter to Basil, September 29, 1960, Foreign Office, Political Departments, General Correspondences, NA; and *Courrier Africain*, October 2, 1960, 1, 3, 5, 6. Later on, Jean Van Lierde included many letters in his anthology of Lumumba's political thoughts, while Kwame Nkrumah published most of his abundant correspondence with the dead Congolese hero. See Van Lierde, *La pensée politique*; and Nkrumah, *Challenge of the Congo*.

14 Jean Kapita, letter to the General Secretary, February 4, 1961, S-0841-1-8, UNA.

15 See Young and Turner, *Rise and Decline*, 111.

16 Merriam, *Congo*, 178–79.

17 However, the censorship of communist pamphlets and periodicals persisted in some places until the very last days of the Belgian regime.

Albert Onkonyi, letter to Marcel Levaux, August 8, 1960, Levaux Papers [hereafter LP], CARCOB. See also, Gijs, *Pouvoir de l'absent*, 1:483–94.

18 A report by the Belgian Communist Youth from June 1960 estimated that twenty-five political youth organizations were active in the Congo, noting that half of them were corresponding with the Belgian Communist Youth, and that six were Marxist in inspiration. "Les organisations de jeunesse de création africaine en République du Congo," June 1960, LP, CARCOB.

19 Gerard Gifondja, letter to Madame Jaelens, October 9, 1959, LP, CARCOB. The PCB revived its anti-colonialism at the beginning of the 1950s, intensifying its propaganda activities in central Africa with the publication of a periodical, *L'éveil du Congo*, which published translations of the Socialist International in Lingala, Kikongo, and Swahili, points of view on the socialist world, letters by Congolese correspondents, and criticisms of colonial domination.

20 Pierre Mulele to Marcel Levaux (?), June 4, 1959, LP, CARCOB.

21 Théodore Nanshakale, letter to Levaux, February 19, 1960, LP, CARCOB.

22 See Gijs, *Pouvoir de l'absent*, 2:23–68.

23 Beyond the state, other actors took it upon themselves to censor postal exchanges. In boarding schools most notably, missionaries felt it their duty to control the correspondence of their students, even after independence. For instance, when Grégoire Mukengechay arrived in Poland to study law, he started to write regularly to his brother Antoine, who was a high school student in Luluabourg. Yet, after a couple of letters, the Belgian priests at the school told Antoine that if he received any more mail from socialist countries, they would have to expel him (Grégoire Mukengechay, personal interview, unrecorded, Berlin, July 30, 2014).

24 Marcel Levaux, letter to Tcheu Tse Tchi, May 10, 1960, LP, CARCOB. When the provincial government of Katanga was created, Mukeba became the minister of health. He was the only member of the executive who did not belong to Tshombe's CONAKAT. He was still in this position when Lumumba was assassinated in Katanga in January 1961.

25 Bernard Salamu, letter to Marcel Levaux, November 25, 1959, LP, CARCOB. Salamu later served as Lumumba's private secretary. In 1964, he participated in the Popular Republic established by the Simba rebellion in Stanleyville. After the military defeat of the rebellion, he sought asylum in Sudan, where he became one of the leaders of the large Congolese refugee population in Juba.

26 Alphonse Londa, April 3, 1960, LP, CARCOB.

27 Hubert Bokata, letter to Marcel Levaux, May 13, 1960, LP, CARCOB. Not all correspondents were happy with the answers they received from the PCB. A high school student from Elisabethville wrote that after having looked at the literature he had received, he came to realize that communism was not something he could adhere to as a fervent Catholic

who supported the actions of missionaries. Jean Nguza, letter to Marcel Levaux, July 18, 1960, LP, CARCOB.

28 Pontien Tshilenge, letter to Marcel Levaux, April 28, 1960, LP, CARCOB, Brussels. Tshilenge later transferred to the Free University of Brussels, where he became a leader in the student left. In 1964, he organized protests against a Belgian military operation in the Congo and was expelled to Ben Bella's Algeria (see chapter 5).

29 Andre Umba, letter to Marcel Levaux, May 7, 1960, LP, CARCOB.

30 Francois Loola, letter to Marcel Levaux, June 6, 1960, LP, CARCOB.

31 Francois Loola, letter to Marcel Levaux, July 6, 1960, LP, CARCOB.

32 Baudouin Bala, letter to Joseph Jacquemotte, October 15, 1962, LP, CARCOB.

33 On Belgian colonial anti-communism, see Gijs, *Pouvoir de l'absent*, 2:423–34.

34 Bernard Loubikou Matuvanga, letter to *La voix du peuple*, December 16, 1966, DP.

35 Eddy Poncelet, letter to the Belgian Communist Youth, August 17, 1960, Terfve Papers [hereafter TP], CARCOB. Poncelet had been previously in charge of establishing contacts with Congolese students in Belgium and notably organized the participation of a few of them to the international youth festival of Vienna in 1959. He had developed friendships with many young Congolese and claimed to be close to at least half of the ministers in Lumumba's government: Eddy Poncelet, personal interview, unrecorded, Ostend, September 7, 2011. On Poncelet's activities in relation to the independence of Congo, see also Gijs, *Pouvoir de l'absent*, 2:75–77.

36 See Monaville, "La crise congolaise."

37 See Biaya, "La culture urbaine," 350–51.

38 Jacques Deleu, letter to Eddy Poncelet, October 11, 1961 and letter to Maitre Terfve, August 7, 1961, TP, CARCOB.

39 Pierre Kayembe, letter to Marcel Levaux, May 19, 1960, LP, CARCOB.

40 On Mobutu's relation to gendered bigmanship and to Kinshasa's street masculinity, see Gondola, *Tropical Cowboys*, 175–76.

41 S. Muya, letter to Levaux, May 22, 1960, LP, CARCOB.

42 Books and political texts were also often discussed in terms of their capacity to enhance forms of cosmopolitan identity. Take Joachim Massena's words to Belgian communist writer Pierre Joye in a letter from 1961 that requested books about Marxism: "Our times being placed under the sign of the socialist revolution, it would absolutely inconceivable for a leftist minister like myself not have in his personal library books about Marxism-Leninism." Joachim Massena, letter to Pierre Joye, May 17, 1961, TP, CARCOB. A member of the Parti Solidaire Africain, Massena served as minister of labor in Lumumba's government in July 1960 and in the government of the Popular Republic of Congo established in Stanleyville in October under the leadership of Gizenga. He was assassinated in Leopoldville at the beginning of 1964.

43 Jean-Claude Ilunga, letter to Robert Mathys, September 2, 1962, TP, CARCOB.

44 The IUSY, the Vienna-based youth wing of the Second International, disseminated its literature right across the African continent in an attempt to limit the influence of communist organization over the African youth. On the IUSY in East Africa, see Millford, "More than Cold War."

45 Eugène Gbana Lissasy, letter to Monsieur le Président de l'IUSY, June 5, 1965, IUSY Papers, IISH.

46 Eugène Gbana Lissasy, letter to Miguel Angel Martinez, June 25, 1965, IUSY Papers, IISH.

47 Franz Emmenegger, "Opération des Nations unies au Congo, services postaux: Rapport final," March 1963, S-0728-6-4, UNA.

48 "Fellowships Offered during 1960," n.d., S-07839-30-1, UNA.

49 This meant sometimes being cautious about whom you decided to send letters to. At the beginning of January 1961, the East German authorities expelled a young Congolese student in Leipzig, after other Congolese at the school he attended exposed him for corresponding with people in "reactionary circles" in Belgium. The student tried to defend himself by arguing that he had started this correspondence to collect evidence about Belgian duplicity in relation to the Congo, and that in all of his other letters, he "had always praised the actions of socialist countries" (Pierre Ngoma, letter, Leipzig, February 7, 1961, Freier Deutscher Gewerkschaftsbund files, BA). Yet, after he left Germany, his discourse switched and he began denouncing life in communist countries as a "nightmare" ("Un Congolais intercepté," *Horizons Nouveaux Est & Ouest* 15, no. 1 [January 1963]: 21).

50 André Lukusa, letter to John Fitzgerald Kennedy, February 24, 1962, Documents Related to the Congo and the Congo Working Group, 1960–64, NARA.

51 I. R. Musampa, H. F. Nuba, and E. B. Kabuya, letter to the Labour Party, July 16, 1964, Socialist International Papers, IISH.

52 See Antoine Ngweza and Patrice-Emery Lumumba, letter to Irving Brown, December 20, 1958, Irving Brown Papers, GMMA. Although it is well known that the PCB supported the MNC, by printing pamphlets and producing electoral propaganda material for example, Lumumba's party also benefited from AFL-CIO's largesse in the form of two Volkswagen cars that the party used during the electoral campaign in May 1960. See "Prévisions budgétaires pour le lancement du Syndicat national des travailleurs Congolais," April 14, 1960, Irving Brown Files, GMMA.

53 On Kithima's supposed CIA affiliation, see notably Kashamura, "Le labyrinthe congolais," *Rencontres Méditerranéennes* 4, no. 12 (December 1963): 307. In several interviews with me conducted in 2009 and in 2010, Kithima reiterated his admiration for Lumumba and denied ever having turned on him (Alphonse-Roger Kithima, personal interviews, unrecorded, Kinshasa, November 2, 2009, April 6, 2010, April 22,

2010, and April 30, 2010). Yet, recent evidence from the British archives suggests that he might have been associated with an assassination plot against Lumumba devised by the British secret service in December 1960. See Williams, *Who Killed Hammarksjöld*, 134–35. Brown himself has been described as an active anti-Lumumbist who bribed Congolese members of parliament with CIA money during trips to Leopoldville in August and September 1960. See Willame, *Patrice Lumumba*, 379. However, the AFL-CIO archives show that Brown opposed the vilification of Lumumba, as it would be counter to US interests, a topic on which he disagreed with Jay Lovestone, another AFL-CIO activist also involved with the CIA. See Richards, *Maida Springer*, 212.

54 See A. R. Kithima, letter to Irving Brown, November 3, 1960; A. R. Kithima, letter to Maida Springer, November 30, 1960; A. R. Kithima, letter to Irving Brown, December 8, 1960; A. R. Kithima, letter to Irving Brown, December 15, 1960, Irving Brown Papers, GMMA.

55 In the same vein, he wrote a week later to Springer (directly in English this time), "You must admire my mind of sacrifice. . . . I hope to receive a present from my colleagues of USA perhaps I'll be invited on congress AFL-CIO at Miami in April." A. R. Kithima, letter to Maida Springer, March 15, 1961, Irving Brown Papers, GMMA.

56 Springer visited the Congo several times. She narrates the circumstances of her first visit in 1957 and the high level of surveillance she was placed under as a Black anti-colonial labor activist. See Richards, *Conversations with Maida Springer*, 216–18.

57 Maida Springer, letter to Jay Lovestone, March 22, 1962, Irving Brown Papers, GMMA.

58 Floribert Kabasela, letter to Marcel Levaux, March 19, 1960, LP, CARCOB.

59 Jean Terfve, "Congo," undated manuscript note, TP, CARCOB.

60 Joseph Botamba, letter to dear Comrade Albert De Coninck, July 16, 1962, TP, CARCOB. The rhetoric of human rights appeared regularly in correspondence about the Congo crisis, with slightly more occurrences appearing among nonsocialist organizations. One group that was particularly invested in it was the Luluabourg-based Association des détenus politiques du Congo. See P. Mykengeshayi and E. Kayembe, letter to the Confédération internationale des syndicats libres, ICFTU Papers, IISH.

61 Van Lierde, *Lumumba Speaks*.

62 Parallels are imperfect with the world literary space analyzed by Pascale Casanova, but her work provides evocative images that can be transposed in this context. Casanova, *World Republic of Letters*.

63 Their letters show that the "recognition of a kind of global supranational belonging" and claims to "equal rights of membership in a spectacularly unequal global society" that James Ferguson describes as typical of the post–Cold War era were already part of the experience of decolonization in the 1960s. See Ferguson, *Global Shadows*, 156–75.

64 A telling incident occurred when Albert De Coninck and Jean Terfve, two leaders of the Belgian Communist Party, secretly traveled to consult with Congolese politicians in Leopoldville in September 1960. The Chinese ambassador to the United Arab Republic, Ch'en Chia-k'ang, and one of his aides happened to be in Leopoldville on a similar mission at the same time. The Cameroonian anti-colonial activist Félix Moumié organized a meeting in a hotel room between the Belgian and Chinese apparatchiks. The Belgians came to the meeting with confidence in their expertise in all things Congolese, and they were taken aback when their interlocutors did not seem to acknowledge it. "We were stuck by the deep ignorance of the Congolese situation that characterized the Chinese ambassador's comments," Terfve mentioned in notes taken after the meeting. Ch'en misunderstood the sociology of the Congo, according to Terfve: "He did not understand that the Congolese proletariat is not playing a leading role" and "refused to accept the non-existence of a Congolese communist party." The ambassador challenged the information presented by De Coninck and Terfve and "for an hour he endeavored to lecture us on theoretical Marxism and its repercussions on the necessary conditions to the liberation of the Congo" (Jean Terfve, "Note sur le contact réalisé à Léopoldville en septembre 1960 avec l'ambassadeur de chine au Caire en mission au Congo," September 1960, TP, CARCOB). It did not seem to occur to Terfve that Chinese communists might have had more legitimate claims to supporting the anti-imperialist struggle or that they might have had valuable material and ideological resources to offer (on China in the Congo, see Shinn and Eisenman, *China and Africa*, 471; see also Namikas, *Battleground Africa*, 33–47).

65 Alexandre Mavungu, letter to His Excellency the General Secretary of the Workers' International of London, April 1, 1964, Socialist International Papers, IISH.

66 The contexts differ, but there are interesting parallels and continuities with Nigerian scam letters and 419 emails. As Matthias Krings writes, "Scam letters contain local interpretations of African social reality *and* the mimicry of Western representations of African reality precisely because they need to connect two systems of knowledge—that of those penning the letters and that of their recipients. Scammers are mediators between two different life-worlds and their dominant imaginaries. Letters that consciously mediate between the two must surely have the greatest chance of success; hence they carry imprints of both" (Krings, *African Appropriations*, 209).

67 On coding, recoding, transmission, and the shift from geographical to informational colonialism, see Collier, *Repainting Walls of Lunda*.

68 On the "visual genealogy" of Lumumba, see De Rezende, "Visuality and Colonialism." See also De Groof, *Lumumba in the Arts*. During the electoral campaign in April 1960, MNC activists planned to cover a significant part of the propaganda expenses by the benefits generated from selling photographs of Lumumba: "We have recently attempted to put

personal photographs of Mister Lumumba on the market. As a test, we ordered 30,000 photographs, which were sold in 8 days. Not only were these photographs bought at the price that we proposed, i.e., 10 francs a piece, but some merchants bought rather large numbers of these photographs and resold them at three times that price" ("Commentaires sur les prévisions budgétaires du MNC," April 14, 1960, p. 2, GMMA).

69 See Petit, *Patrice Lumumba*.

70 Labrique, *Congo politique*, 73. A press attaché at the General Governorate, Labrique was expelled from the Congo in 1957 following the publication of his book and his involvement with *Quinze* and *Congo*, the first independent Congolese periodicals (see Young, *Politics in Congo*, 55).

71 On frontiersmen and border epistemologies in regional epics and oral traditions, see De Luna, "Hunting Reputations."

Interlude II. To Live Forever among Books

1 Comhaire-Sylvain, *Food and Leisure*, 119–21.

2 Comhaire-Sylvain, *Food and Leisure*, 117. On the cult of America among young men in Leopoldville during that period, see Gondola, *Tropical Cowboys*.

3 On creole universalist cosmopolitanism, see Vergès, "Vertigo and Emancipation."

4 Suzanne Comhaire-Sylvain, letter to Edwin W. Smith, August 7, 1945, Suzanne Sylvain-Comhaire papers, SUL.

5 Sylvain also conducted research among African women in Leopoldville. She completed this research upon returning to the city two decades later in 1965. See Comhaire-Sylvain, *Femmes de Kinshasa*.

Three. Paths to School

1 Martin Ekwa, personal interview, recorded, Kinshasa, December 7, 2010.

2 See Dunn, *Imagining the Congo*.

3 Martin Ekwa, letter to Simon [Decloux], January 22, 1962, Martin Ekwa Personal Papers, ACIA.

4 Sister Marie-Gertrude, letter to Martin [Ekwa], October 20, 1960, Ekwa Papers, ACIA.

5 Martin Ekwa, letter to Jean-Baptiste Janssens, January 3, 1962, Ekwa Papers, ACIA. However, in March 1961, in the aftermath of Lumumba's assassination, he wrote to a Belgian nun that "few countries have been able to resist the communist current. The Congo, with its little resources, seems to resist it. Should we not see here Divine Providence's finger and an answer to our prayers and sacrifices?" (Martin Ekwa, letter to Mother Claire, March 3, 1961, Ekwa Papers, ACIA).

6 Jacques Libois, letter to Martin [Ekwa], October 22, 1960, Ekwa Papers, ACIA.

7 Ekwa, *La RD Congo contée*, 57–79. See also Ekwa, *L'école trahie*.

8 Despite his frustrations with the conservatism of some missionaries, Ekwa was aware of the necessity to preserve Belgian support for Congolese Catholic education. The former colonizer could notably serve as an ally against UNESCO, which exerted a strong influence on the Congolese ministry of education at the time. UNESCO experts advocated for reforms that meant to democratize secondary education by reducing the importance of Greco-Latin humanities, which many Catholics perceived as an attack against them: Martin Ekwa, personal interview, recorded, Kinshasa, December 7, 2010; and Valentin Kimoni, personal interview, recorded, Kikwit, May 31, 2010.

9 Mrazek, *A Certain Age*, 128, 130–31.

10 On the beginning of Scheutist schools in the Kasai region, see Van Keerberghen, *Histoire de l'enseignement*, 11–45.

11 See different occurrences of this idea: Yates, "Missions and Educational Development," 133, 171, 177, 308–21. Some Congolese viewed missionary stations as sanctuaries where they could escape heavy and violent demands in labor from the state and private enterprises, even if many missionaries collaborated closely with private companies in exchange for subsidies. See, for example, Nkay Malu, *La mission chrétienne*, 33–53.

12 On the concordat and on Catholic-Protestant rivalries, see Markowitz, *Cross and Sword*, 38–51.

13 Yates, "Missions and Educational Development," 86–102.

14 See MacGaffey, *Kongo Political Culture*, 18–42; and Mudimbe-Boyi, "Vivre (à) la mission."

15 On the cultural and material life of these évolué figures in the post-1945 period, see Tödt, *Elitenbildung und Dekolonisierung*; and Hunt, *Nervous State*, 207–35.

16 Salkin, *Etudes africaines*, 15.

17 See Gaston Moulaert, "L'effort colonial de la Belgique," *Revue économique internationale*, July 1930, 13–50; A. Houyet, "L'organisation politique, administrative et judiciaire de l'Afrique française du Nord," *Congo* 11, no. 1 (1930): 221–49; and Hédo, *Mosselmans*.

18 Biaya, "Ethnopsychologie," 169.

19 Salkin, *Le problème de l'évolution*. On the use of India as a counterexample of what should be done in the Congo in terms of education, see Yates, "Missions and Educational Development," 271–77.

20 Booker T. Washington's Tuskegee Institute in particular became a reference for European colonizers in Africa. For more, see Zimmerman, *Alabama in Africa*; Serufuri, "Les Etats-Unis d'Amérique et l'enseignement"; as well as Markowitz, *Cross and Sword*, 52–54.

21 Jones, *Education in Africa*, 286–87. The report partly excused the limitations of Belgian colonial education by pointing to the "backwardness" of the Congolese population and the size of the country: "The task of supplying any kind of education to eleven million primitive and, in some

instances, barbarous people, distributed . . . over a territory almost a million square miles in extent, cannot be fully appreciated even by a student of education" (Jones, *Education in Africa*, 257).

22 On colonial education in the Congo, see Depaepe and Van Rompaey, *In het teken van de bevoogding*.

23 Kita, *Colonisation et enseignement*, 167–91.

24 Depaepe, "Parallélisme belge-congolais," 27.

25 See Zana, "Stefano Kaoze." On the United Congo Evangelical Institution of Kimpese, one of the few Protestant equivalents to Catholic seminars, see Yates, "Missions and Educational Development," 86–102.

26 Yates notes that the Vatican already pressured the Jesuits in 1922 to open a seminary at Lemfu. See Yates, "Missions and Educational Development," 110. Pope Benedict XV had affirmed the necessity to train an African clergy in *Maximum illud*, issued in 1919. See Mudimbe, *Tales of Faith*, 110.

27 See, for instance, Murairi, *Le festin des vautours*, 72–94.

28 See Moke, *Itinéraire et mémoires*; and Eugène Moke Motsüri, personal interview, unrecorded, Kinshasa, October 14, 2007.

29 Massa later renounced priesthood and became an organizer in Christian trade unionism, while Moke and Malula progressed up the church hierarchy, the latter becoming Leopoldville's first Black bishop in 1959, the only African member of the liturgical commission during the Second Vatican Council between 1962 and 1965, and the Congo's first cardinal in 1969. On Malula, see De Saint Moulin, *Oeuvres complètes*.

30 Lomami Tshibamba had been hired as the first editor in chief of *La voix du congolais*, a state-sponsored periodical created after the war to connect évolués across the whole colony. His political articles earned him the hostility of colonial authorities, and he chose to emigrate to Brazzaville at the end of the 1940s. See Bodart, "Entretiens avec Lomami." On Lomami, see also Tödt, *Lumumba Generation*, 118–30.

31 On the connection between postwar development and secondary education in northeastern Katanga, see Loffman, *Church, Sate and Colonialism*, 189–211.

32 See Kiangu, *Préparer un peuple*; and Kiangu, *Le Kwilu à l'épreuve*. Despite its more progressive pedagogy, Kinzambi also shared with other colonial elitist schools a focus on manual labor, a high attrition rate, and a strict separation of children from their families. See Daniel Palambwa Andzwa Empak, "L'école de mon patelin: Notes autobiographique présentées par Kiangu Sindani," unpublished manuscript, pp. 34, 36, 61.

33 Mudimbe, *Tales of Faith*, 115–17. Mudimbe contrasted Guffens's experiment with what he considered to be the more advanced approach used in Protestant schools, and their promotion of "a new type of consciousness: acculturated but capable of functioning in the civil society as in the Church on the basis of merits, competence and cultural integration." Some Protestant schools did indeed play important roles in the emer-

gence of the Congolese intellectual elite, but they trained a much smaller number of students.

34 Martin Ekwa, letter to "Little Mother" [Sister Marie-Gertrude], November 10, 1960; and letter to Octave, January 23, 1961, Ekwa Papers, ACIA.

35 Daniel Palambwa, personal interviews, recorded, Kinshasa, August 9, 10, and 17, 2010. See also Daniel Palambwa Andzwa Empak, "L'école de mon patelin: Notes autobiographiques présentées par Kiangu Sindani," unpublished manuscript.

36 Martens, *Pierre Mulele*.

37 Daniel Palambwa, Augustin Awaka, and Julien Ntil, personal interview (together with Daniel Tödt and Cécile Michel), recorded, Kinshasa, August 17, 2010.

38 Kiangu, *Le Kwilu à l'épreuve*.

39 This was not the case for everybody, however, as shown by Emery Kalema's work on the trauma of Mulele's insurgency and the government's suppression of it. Kalema, "Scars, Marked Bodies."

40 The desire for seclusion—to stay away from pagan villages and corrupted urban communities alike—was strongest when it came to establishing seminaries. Even small towns were seen as undesirable settings for the training of future priests. In the mid-1920s, for instance, the director of the major seminary in Mikalayi petitioned his bishop to have the school moved to the most remote location of Kabwe. As he wrote, "Every day, I become more aware of the inappropriate location of the seminary, here, at the heart of the mission. We are unable to transform the mentality of the seminarians: everything we say or do is directly neutralized by the environment in which they find themselves" (cited in Van Keerberghen, *Histoire de l'enseignement*, 56).

41 The phrase comes from Mudimbe's reflection on the years he spent during his youth in the ascetic atmosphere of Benedictine seminaries and monasteries in Katanga and Rwanda. Mudimbe, *Le corps glorieux*, 26.

42 See Hunt, "Noise over Camouflaged Polygamy," 477–85.

43 Vanderlinden, *Main d'oeuvre*, 135. Four years after his tour of Leopoldville, Ryckmans became the general governor of the Belgian Congo. On his long colonial career, see Vanderlinden, *Pierre Ryckmans*.

44 Bontinck, "Les missions catholiques."

45 Raphaël de la Kethulle de Ryhove, "Le vagabondage à Kinshasa," *Congo* 3, no. 2 (1922): 727–30; Bontinck, "Le directeur d'école," 64.

46 See Mudimbe, *Tales of Faith*, 118.

47 Jules Lubuele, who joined the athénée of Kalina in Leopoldville, remembered very well the various inspections and tests he had to submit to before being admitted. His father, an évolué who worked for the Banque du Congo Belge, had written multiple letters to the colony's general governor to support Jules's application to the athénée: Jules Lubuele, personal interview, unrecorded, Kinshasa, March 17, 2010.

48 Henry Bruyheel, "Admission des enfants autochtones dans les écoles pour enfants européens. Dossier: Siya-Siya Nestor," June 26, 1956, ARNACO-K.

49 Jean-Baptiste Mulemba, personal interview, recorded, Kinshasa, July 21, 2015; Elikia M'Bokolo, personal interview, unrecorded, Kinshasa, July 12, 2010; Anastase Nzeza, personal interview, recorded, Kinshasa, June 1, 2010; Germain Mukendi, personal interview, unrecorded, Liège, April 22, 2011. Some students transferred from Catholic to Protestant schools, but few of the latter were as academically advanced as the Catholic collèges created in 1948.

50 See, for instance, Kalulambi, "Le manifeste." On the school war, see also Tödt, *Lumumba Generation*, 308–18.

51 Anastase Nzeza, personal interview, recorded, Kinshasa, June 1, 2010.

52 Tshimanga had been in contact with Belgian communists since 1958 and the first Russian-language book on the Congo (published in 1959) referred to him as one of the leaders of the anti-colonial movement. In 1961, he briefly served as deputy minister of defense in the government established by Antoine Gizenga in Stanleyville. He later found his way back to Leopoldville where he was kidnapped from his home in 1965 and never seen again. See Houart, *La pénétration communiste*, 40; Namikas, *Battleground Africa*, 40; Kamitatu, *La grande mystification*, 214; and Gijs, *Pouvoir de l'absent*, 2:33–49.

53 Kisonga's course through the education system was particularly bumpy: before Bagira, he successively studied at two different schools in the lower Congo—one Catholic, one Protestant—then moved to Leopoldville, where he studied at the athénée of Ngiri-Ngiri and at the Salvation Army school. In his memoirs, he wrote how, a year after independence, he was given the honor of conducting a troop inspection during a public ceremony in Bukavu. Students from the athénée of Bagira attended the ceremony and cheered enthusiastically when they recognized their former comrade and strike leader. Yet, a Belgian professor, also in attendance, was less thrilled to see how quickly this recently expelled student had become a notability. He reportedly packed his suitcase and returned to Belgium the following day. Kisonga, *45 ans d'histoire*, 39.

54 One of the few exceptions was the Lycée du Sacré-Coeur in Leopoldville, which took in half a dozen Black female students after independence—most of whom joined Lovanium a few years later: Yvonne Nsansa, personal interview, recorded, Kinshasa, December 2, 2010.

55 Malonga Miatudila, personal interview, recorded, Rockville, Maryland, April 3, 2012. Many spits of laughter punctuate that recording, as if in recognition of the inescapable oddity of a school system that was so remote in time and space when recalled from the vantage point of suburban Maryland in the 2010s.

56 Jean-Baptiste Sondji, personal interview, recorded, Kinshasa, October 4, 2007; André Yoka, personal interview, unrecorded, Kinshasa, July 21, 2015.

57 Suzanne Sylvain-Comhaire, *Femmes de Kinshasa,* book manuscript, pp. 169–71, Suzanne Comhaire-Sylvain Papers, SUL.

58 Association des parents d'élèves de l'enseignement catholique, Léopoldville, July 22, 1958, Miscellaneous Papers, ACIA.

59 Bitoma and Ntil, *Enquête sur les professeurs,* 7. That increase was caused, in part, because girls gained broader access to school—this was one of Ekwa's priorities when he took the leadership of the BEC. Between 1959 and 1963, the number of female students already nearly tripled, going from five thousand to fourteen thousand. Comhaire-Sylvain, *Femmes de Kinshasa,* 243.

60 Francis Sutton, "General Memorandum on the Congo," May 9, 1961, p. 5, Ford Foundation Records, International Division, Box 10, RAC.

61 Martin Ekwa, letter to Romain Kimpwena, February 27, 1969, Ekwa Papers, ACIA.

62 Bernard, *Ville africaine,* 20–21. Bernard notes that teachers in Leopoldville lost more than half of their purchasing power between 1961 and 1963 (pp. 112–15).

63 Comhaire-Sylvain, *Femmes de Kinshasa,* book manuscript, pp. 234–36, Suzanne Sylvain-Comhaire Papers, SUL.

64 The union unsuccessfully applied for funding to the AFL-CIO to support its school in 1961 and already then claimed to have more than five hundred students. See Hector-Georges Massianga-Foundou, letter to Irving Brown, August 31, 1961; and Maida Springer, letter to Hector-Georges Massianga-Foundou, October 27, 1961, Irving Brown Papers, GMMA.

65 On pamba schools and Leopoldville's shantytowns (known as squatting zones), see Raymaekers, *L'organisation des zônes de squatting.*

66 *Emission de timbres-poste spéciaux: Indépendance du Congo* (Brussels: Administration des Postes de Belgique, n.d.), 1.

67 See Boltanski, *De la critique.*

68 Kita and Depaepe, *La chanson scolaire,* 193.

69 See Magaziner, *The Art of Life.*

70 Dom Rombaut Steenberghen, "A l'Institut Saint-Boniface d'Elisabethville, le milieu scolaire, la vie familiale et les élèves," *Bulletin trimestriel d'étude des problèmes sociaux indigènes* 24 (1954): 56. On the status of typewriting students as the most eligible bachelors in the Kivu in the 1950s, see Murairi, *Le festin des vautours,* 58–59.

71 Erny, *Sur les sentiers,* 430.

72 See "Rapport sur les activités du servie des bourses d'études pour Congolais," March 1961, p. 9, Harold d'Aspremont Lynden Papers, AGR.

73 Pierre Leroy, "Compte-rendu de mission à Luluabourg (du 13 au 17 novembre 1961)," p. 23, Assistance Technique Papers, AD. On Belgium's foreign policy in the Congo in the early 1960s, see Vanthemsche, *La Belgique et le Congo,* 213–96.

74 Martin Ekwa, personal interview, recorded, Kinshasa, December 7, 2010.

1   See Gillon, *Servir en actes*, 19–27, 31–32.
2   "Université Lovanium. Procès-verbal de la réunion du conseil d'administration," October 30, 1961, p. 5, Van Der Schueren Papers [hereafter VSP], LUA.
3   On an earlier incident around an attempt at segregating hazing around racial lines in 1958, see Mantels, *Geleerd in de tropen*, 56.
4   "Malaise sur la colline inspirée," *Présence universitaire* 11 (January 1963): 59–61.
5   Edouard Liétard, personal interview, recorded, Kinshasa, August 17, 2010.
6   Ranger, "The Invention of Tradition."
7   For similar dynamics among Protestant missionaries, see Hunt's *Colonial Lexicon*, 27–79.
8   Erny, *Sur les sentiers*, 394. These Catholic borrowings from local registers of initiation were sometimes counterproductive. For instance, shaving one's hair was associated with mourning rituals in many local contexts and could cause confusion among catechumens about its meaning in the context of baptism. See Murairi, *Le festin des vautours*, 42–44.
9   Quoted in Erny, *Sur les sentiers*, 394.
10 See Nyunda, "De Lovanium à la Kasapa." See also Nyunda, "Mémoires de la colonie"; and Nyunda, "Tango ya Ba-Papa Bol."
11 The fact that Gillon was able to acquire a nuclear reactor for Lovanium in 1959, a first in Africa, was an important element in the international aura of the university. See, for instance, Osseo-Asare, *Atomic Junction*, 80–81.
12 See, notably, Hyacinthe Vanderhyst, "Les futures universités catholiques au Congo: Leurs rapports avec l'enseignement secondaire," *Bulletin des missions* (November–December 1928): 254–59. On Vanderhyst, see Nkay, *La mission chrétienne*, 135–36; and Markowitz, *Cross and Sword*, 67.
13 See Likaka, *Rural Society*; and Hunt, *Nervous State*.
14 Justin-Marie Bomboko, personal interview, recorded, Kinshasa, November 6, 2009. Bomboko later transferred to the Free University of Brussels, where he was the first Congolese student to attend the university. In 1960, he became minister of foreign affairs in Patrice Lumumba's government and remained a fixture in Congolese politics in subsequent decades.
15 On the latter, see Markowitz, *Cross and Sword*, 68.
16 Guy Malengreau, letter to Pierre Wigny, January 1, 1949, Lovania Papers, ACIA. Scholars have at times failed to account for the importance of these conservative considerations in the development of Congolese higher education, instead adopting a whiggish reading. For a recent example, see Mantels, *Geleerd in de tropen*.
17 "Etudiants congolais en Belgique," November 30, 1952, Fonds gouvernorat général, GG13887, AA.

18 Guy Malengreau, "Diaire du secrétaire général du 2 septembre 1952 au 24 juillet 1954," p. 75, Malengreau Files, FI 341, UCL.

19 "Lovania: Procès-verbal de la réunion du comité central du 4 novembre 1953 au Cercle Ablert Ier," Lovania Papers, ACIA, Kinshasa.

20 See Mantels, *Geleerd in de tropen*; and Yakemtchouk, *L'Université Lovanium*.

21 The campus associated monumentalism and austerity in a way that was also clearly meant to inspire respect for order and hierarchies. Its architect, P. Boulangier, was a former officer in the Force Publique who was mostly known for having designed a major military camp in Luluabourg (Toulier, Lagae, and Gemoets, *Kinshasa*, 101).

22 There was ambivalence, however, as the location of Lovanium also reflected the impulse toward isolation in the planning of new university campuses in postwar Europe and North America (see Malengreau, *L'Université Lovanium*, 39).

23 On the physical, affective, and social isolation of Catholic colleges and seminaries, see Mudimbe, *Le corps glorieux*; Sampassa, *Conscience et politique*, 17–18; and Kabemba, *Le destin de Biabululu*, 15. Filip De Boeck talks of Mount Amba as "the last mountain site that the Belgians converted into a glorification of their colonial endeavor" and notes that the site had been used as an ancestral burial ground before the colonizers' arrival (De Boeck and Baloji, *Suturing the City*, 11).

24 Oswald Ndeshyo, personal interview, recorded, Kinshasa, June 7, 2010. A former dean of the law department at the University of Kinshasa, Professor Ndeshyo played an important role in the "political transition" and the military rebellions of the 1990s and early 2000s, first as part of Laurent-Désiré Kabila's Alliance des Forces Démocratiques de Libération military coalition and then in the armed movement that opposed its presidency. In the 1960s, after he transferred from Lovanium to the University of Brussels, Ndeshyo became one of the leaders of the Congolese student movement in Belgium.

25 The attrition rate at the school was so abysmal—there were around three thousand students when Mukendi left the school in 1954, but only eight other boys graduated that year—that the institution maintained an intense investment in the pathways of the few students who completed the curriculum (Dom Rombaut Steenberghen, "A l'Institut Saint-Boniface d'Elisabethville, le milieu scolaire, la vie familiale des élèves," *Bulletin trimestriel du centre d'étude des problèmes sociaux indigènes* 24 [1954]: 54).

26 Aubert Mukendi, personal interview, recorded, Paris, January 15, 2011. Mukendi later transferred to a Belgian university, returning to the Congo in 1960 to serve as a member of the College of General Commissioners. In the mid-1960s, while he worked as the general director of Air Congo, he was arrested and jailed for several months. In 1968, he left the Congo for France, where he acted as an early opponent to Mobutu and representative of Kabila's People's Revolutionary Party. He returned to the

Congo in the 1980s and joined local opponents to the regime in Etienne Tshisekedi's Union for Democracy and Social Progress. After Kabila's victory in 1997, he served as the first chief of staff of the new president for two years before relocating to France again.

27 Kabemba, *Le destin de Biabululu*, 34. He joined as a medical student in 1956.

28 On Belgian anxieties about intimate relations between white women and Black men, see Lauro "Violence, Anxieties." See also Monaville, "La crise congolaise"; and Halen, *"Le petit Belge,"* 78–84.

29 Nestor Mpeye, personal interview, recorded, Kinshasa, April 10, 2010.

30 See Biaya, "La culture urbaine," 350–51; and Lauro, "Women in Congo."

31 Thomas Mambo Santos, personal interview, recorded, Brussels, February 26, 2011. Mambo was born Thomas Santos (the last name of his Portuguese grandfather) and became Mambo Elanga when Mobutu ordered the Congolese to give up foreign names. When the authenticity policy was abandoned, he decided to combine the two names.

32 On Congolese colonial urbanity, see Hunt, *Nervous State*, 207–35.

33 Jean-Baptiste Mulemba, personal interviews, recorded, Kinshasa, July 18 and 27, 2011.

34 La Fontaine, *City Politics*, 133.

35 See Stewart, *Rumba on the River*, 71; Gondola, *Villes miroirs*, 274; Gondola, "Bisengo ya la joie"; and Gondola, "Ata Ndele."

36 On Kabayidi's career as a Bill, see Gondola, *Tropical Cowboys*, 89–90, 175–76. According to Tshungu Bamesa, another former Bill who became a student at Lovanium, the impact of "Billism" on the campus also included a stronger sensibility of social inequalities in Leopoldville: Tshungu Bamesa, personal interview, recorded, Kinshasa, September 22, 2007.

37 Paul-Henri Kabayidi, personal interview, recorded, Brussels, February 12, 2011.

38 See Mutamba, "Les auteurs du manifeste"; and Kalulambi, "Le manifeste."

39 See Mantels, *Geleerd in de tropen*, 256–58; Young, *Introduction à la politique*, 63; and Kabemba, *Le destin de Biabululu*, 49.

40 The letter followed a controversy around the refusal of the colonial state to treat Thomas Kanza as equal to Belgian employees with similar qualifications. Kanza had returned to Leopoldville to take a position in the administration after being the first Congolese to graduate from a Belgian university in 1956. See Kanza, *Rise and Fall*.

41 See Tshimanga, *Jeunesse, formation et société*, 245.

42 Gillon, *Servir en actes*, 150–51.

43 Nestor Mpeye, personal interview, recorded, Kinshasa, April 6, 2010. For a slightly different recollection of that event, see Gillon, *Servir en actes*, 117.

44 Cléo Tshibangu, "Lettre ouverte à M. le Président des étudiants de Lovanium," *Echos de Lovanium* (April 1962): 6. On youth subculture

in Leopoldville, see Gondola, *Tropical Cowboys*. See also Raymaekers, *Prédélinquance et délinquance.*

45 "Situation du budget ordinaire de l'université de l'année civile 1959 à 1963," VSP, LUA.

46 Christophe Mateene, letter to Rector Gillon, December 19, 1962, AGEL Papers, UNIKIN.

47 Charles de Kerchove de Denterghem, telex to the Ministry of Foreign Affairs, December 20, 1962, Consular correspondences, AD.

48 Willame, "The Congo," 54–55. Mateene graduated a few months later and moved to the United States to work with the anthropologist Daniel Biebuyck on the translation and edition of the *Mwindo Epic*, which the two published in 1969. The same year, Mateene defended a doctoral dissertation at the Sorbonne on the grammar of the Nyanga language. A professor at Lovanium and then Lubumbashi, Mateene served for two decades as head of the division of language policy at the Organization of African Unity. In 1962, rivalries between students in the faculty of law and students in the faculty of philosophy and letters may also have played a role in his removal from the presidency of AGEL (Jean-Baptiste Murairi, personal interview, recorded, Brussels, December 30, 2019).

49 "Le malaise continue . . . ," *Présence universitaire* 12 (April 1963): 49–50.

50 Maurice Plevoets, "Conclusions de la commission chargée d'étudier les problèmes estudiantins," May 28, 1963, VSP, LUA.

51 "Mémorandum des étudiants aux membres du conseil d'administration," reproduced in Kabongo, *Crise à Lovanium*, 19–28.

52 He had been able to procure a modicum of social peace by buying one thousand costumes specially shipped from Italy so that students could buy them at a discount. See Gillon, *Servir en actes*, 181.

53 Cited in Mabika, *La remise en question*, 61–63.

54 Cited in Kabongo, *Crise à Lovanium*, 7.

55 "Procès-verbal de la 73ᵉ réunion du conseil d'administration," January 31, 1964, p. 7, VSP, LUA.

56 Gillon, *Servir en actes*, 219.

57 The talk, titled "Lovanium, Year Zero," is reprinted in Verhaegen, *L'enseignement universitaire*, 27–33.

58 Quoted in Kabongo, *Crise à Lovanium*, 8.

59 Edouard Liétard, personal interview, recorded, Kinshasa, August 17, 2010.

60 Yvon Bongoy, personal interview, recorded, Kinshasa, December 12, 2010.

61 Kabongo, *Crise à Lovanium*, 32.

62 José Ndundu, personal interview, recorded, Kinshasa, June 10, 2010.

63 Gillon was grateful that student leaders did not revive the campus blockade. In his memoir, he praised their sense of responsibility, while dismissing the validity of their demands. The decision not to continue with the strike meant that AGEL leaders did not burn their bridges with

the administration and that, the following year, Lovanium funded three of them to pursue graduate studies in the United States: Bongoy and Ilunga Kabongo went to Berkeley and Makanda went to the University of Pittsburgh.

64 Yvon Bongoy, personal interview, recorded, Kinshasa, December 12, 2010.

65 Mpase, "Vivre le devenir," 261–64.

66 "AGEL: Feuille de route n.91," n.d., AGEL Papers, UNIKIN. See also Ndaywel, "La première écriture," 423.

67 "Procès-verbal de la séance du 24 octobre 1964 du conseil d'administration," pp. 7–10, VSP, LUA.

68 "Procès-verbal de la 75e réunion du conseil d'administration," May 25, 1964, pp. 2–3, VSP, LUA.

69 See Wallerstein, "1968."

Interlude III. To the Left

1 Paul Kabongo, personal interview, recorded, Kinshasa, July 8, 2011.

2 Lopez, Lumumba ou l'Afrique, 133.

3 Kole Paparisto, "Información për Studentin Kongoles Paul Kabongo," July 1, 1964; see also Kahreman Yli, "Información mbi Studentin Kongolez që erdhi pranë universitetit me 14-1-1964," January 15, 1964, Foreign Affairs collection, GDA, 14/20/588.

4 Yambuya, Le néocolonialisme au Congo, 150.

5 See Signaté, L'Afrique entre ombre, 35–38.

6 Césaire, Une saison au Congo. Kabongo used the pseudonym Jackson Shindi for the play's production and a few appearances in other plays staged by Serreau. On Serreau, see Challaye, "Jean-Marie Serreau."

7 See Kasa-Vubu, Douze mois chez Kabila, 51, 71.

8 Kalixte Mukendi Wa Nsanga, personal interviews, recorded, Nouakchott, May 19–21, 2016.

9 Hans Jürgen Krüger, "Aus tausend Flüssen strömt der Kongo," Frankfurter Allgemeine Zeitung, October 8, 1960, 18. The article called Wa Nsanga "Zébédée Mukeni" (using his middle name and an altered version of the last name he used before opting for Wa Nsanga later in the decade).

10 Kalixte Mukendi, "Das Erbe Lumumbas und die Tragödie der Freiheit im Kongo," Blätter für deutsche und international Politik, September 9, 1964, 734.

11 Thomas Turner, "Preparatory Seminar for 3rd UGEC (Congo) Congress," Cologne, April 17–20, 1965, p. 2, USNSA International Commission, HIA.

12 Bourdieu, "L'illusion biographique."

13 Paul Kabongo, personal interview, recorded, Kinshasa, July 8, 2011.

14 See Kennes and Munkana, Essai biographique, 269, 315–16; and Kasa-Vubu, Douze mois chez Kabila.

15 Wa Nsanga was then very active in Congolese political circles around Boston. See Ernest Wamba dia Wamba, *Profil de courage: Une courte autobiographie*. See also "Statement of Wa Nsanga Mukendi," in United States Senate, *U.S. Loans to Zaire: Hearing before the Subcommittee on International Finance of the Committee on Banking, Housing, and Urban Affairs* (Washington, DC: US Government Printing Office, 1979), 31–42.

16 See "Un congolais à Nouakchott," *Jeune Afrique*, May 29, 2010, 17.

17 Biaya, "La culture urbaine"; Leon Daudet, *Melancholia* (1928), quoted in Griferro, *Atmospheres*, 76.

18 See Guyer and Belinga, "Wealth in People"; De Luna, "Hunting Reputations"; and De Luna, "Affect and Society." More recent Congolese migrants to Europe have explicitly drawn from a precolonial register to express their transnational identity. See, for instance, Pype, "Bolingo ya face," and Trapido, *Breaking Rocks*. (On p. 32, Trapido also makes an interesting point about the parallels between ambiance and forms of "cultural validated 'madness'" in precolonial traditions.)

19 See Magaziner, "Two Stories about Art."

Five. Cold War Transcripts

1 Isidore Kabongo, personal interview, unrecorded, Kinshasa, February 15, 2010.

2 Joseph N'Singa Udjuu, personal interview, recorded, Kinshasa, December 2, 2010. Born in a family of village chiefs in the district of Lake Leopold II (Lake Mai-Ndombe today) in 1934, N'Singa entered the colonial school system quite late. His maternal family opposed sending him to the school of the whites, but his father insisted that he should receive a Catholic education and walked with him the hundred kilometers that separated their village from the closest primary school run by missionaries. A bright student, N'Singa was encouraged to follow the path toward priesthood. He graduated from the minor seminary of Bokoro and then studied for four years at the major seminary of Kabwe. He changed path in 1958 and joined Lovanium as a first-year student in law. His tenure as president of the General Assembly of Students (AGEL) was an important moment in the formulation of the grudges that led to the strike described in chapter 4.

3 Joseph N'Singa Udjuu, personal interview, recorded, Kinshasa, December 2, 2010. See also Kabemba, *Le destin de Biabilulu*, 59; and Nzongola-Ntalaja, *Patrice Lumumba*.

4 Jef Van Bilsen, letter to Joseph Kasavubu, November 16, 1960, KADOC.

5 Groupe d'étudiants nationalistes de Lovanium, telegram to Dag Hammarskjöld, February 14, 1961, S-0730-6-5, UNA.

6 Sampassa, *Conscience et politique*, 18. On generational tensions between évolués and students, see Young, *Politics in the Congo*, 412–17. See also "Politiciens contre universitaires?," *Présence universitaire* 3 (April 1960): 67.

7 N'Singa Udjuu, personal interview, recorded, Kinshasa, December 2, 2010.

8   Scott, *Arts of Resistance*, 2.

9   On Lumumba as prophet, see Peck, "It's about the Image."

10 [Jacques] Paulus, "Réflexions d'un voyageur," *Présence universitaire* 2 (December 1959): 10. Bomboko had been a former student at the University Center in Kisantu as we saw previously; he transferred to the Free University of Brussels in 1955.

11 Etienne Tshisekedi, "Editorial," *Présence universitaire* 4 (July 1960): 4–5.

12 "Editorial," *Présence universitaire* 2 (December 1959): 4. See also Vellut, *Congo*, 462; and Young, *Politics in the Congo*, 568.

13 Paul Kabayidi, personal interview, recorded, Brussels, February 12, 2011. Young made the same observation about Malimba, noting that Lovanium was "the only level at which communication was taking place" between individuals from different ethnic backgrounds. Young, *Politics in the Congo*, 516–17.

14 This was a position notably articulated by Thomas Kanza, the first Congolese to study at a Belgian university. As other activists across Africa, Kanza envisioned anti-colonial nationalism as a step toward greater goals (Kanza, *Eloge de la révolution*, 8).

15 The Congolese understood the term *nationalisme* as relating specifically to the support for a centralized state and for a maximalist version of self-determination.

16 Kanza, *Eloge de la révolution*, 1–33.

17 Nestor Mpeye, personal interview, recorded, Kinshasa, April 6, 2010.

18 By comparison, Lovanium and the University of Elisabethville combined, then enrolled 466 students. See Mutamba, *Du Congo belge au Congo indépendant*, 154.

19 See Van Lierde and De Bosschère, *La guerre sans armes*, 55–70.

20 Kanza, *The Rise and Fall*, 93.

21 Mutamba, *Du Congo belge au Congo indépendance*, 450; Gérard-Libois and Verhaegen, *Congo 1960*, 1:99.

22 The conference defined the framework for future Belgian assistance to the Congo, decided a program of scholarships for Congolese students in Belgium, and enacted measures to protect private capital and the free market economy in the future independent nation. Most critically, it allowed Belgian private companies in the Congo to repatriate the totality of their capital to Belgium before independence. That measure undermined the financial stability of the new independent state and created a thirty-year dispute between Belgium and its former colony.

23 Verhaegen became the adviser of Alphonse Nguvulu, the vice-minister for economic planning, while another Lovanium professor, Hugues Leclerc, occupied a similar position at the Ministry of Finance, where two recent graduates from Lovanium had been given important responsibilities: André Tshibangu as vice-minister and Albert Ndele as a special adviser (Willame, *Patrice Lumumba*, 375–76). Although he later became known as a fervent supporter of the Congolese left, Verhaegen was associated

with anti-Lumumba politicians throughout the period of the Congo crisis in 1960 and 1961.

24 See Gérard-Libois and Verhaegen, *Congo 1960*, 2:693–94. See also "A Congo Bishop Accused," *Catholic Herald*, July 29, 1960, 6; and "Communist Sympathisers in Congolese Cabinet: Threat to a Catholic University," *Catholic Herald*, August 5, 1960, 8.

25 The rumors may have originated after an improvised assembly during which finishing students at Lovanium evoked the idea of taking power out of the hands of politicians to end the Congo crisis. See Kabemba, *Le destin de Biabululu*, 65–66.

26 Kashamura, *De Lumumba aux colonels*, 101.

27 See Poswick to Wigny, July 13, 1960; Poswick to Wigny, July 29, 1960; and Poswick to Wigny, August 3, 1960, consular correspondence, AD.

28 Gillon, *Servir en actes*, 163–64.

29 Willame, *Patrice Lumumba*, 388–96.

30 See Van Lierde, *La pensée politique*, 361.

31 See Gérard Libois and Verhaegen, *Congo 1960*, 2:868–69.

32 A few months later, when he was promoted by Kasa-Vubu, he reportedly became the "youngest general on earth" (Francis Monheim, "Joseph Mobutu, le plus jeune général du monde," *Le phare-dimanche*, May 10, 1964, 1).

33 Joseph Mobutu, "Discours de M. Mobutu au congrès international de la Presse coloniale belge," 1958, Désiré Denuit Papers, UCL. On Mobutu's work as a journalist, see Langellier, *Mobutu*, 27–44.

34 See Chomé, *L'ascension de Mobutu*, 68–70. In 1959, when Aubert Mukendi contemplated quitting his studies after a racist incident with a professor at the University of Louvain, his friend Jonas Mukamba insisted that he meet Mobutu. "I know who you are," Mobutu told Mukendi. "You must graduate. If you go back to the Congo without a degree, the colonialists will have you crushed." Mukendi credited this pep talk for his decision to continue his studies. In September 1960, both he and Mukamba joined the new government initiated by Mobutu. Aubert Mukendi, personal interview, recorded, Paris, January 15, 2011.

35 In interviews, former commissioners argued that the college prevented Mobutu from capturing the entirety of power and talked about Mobutu's visible inferiority complex in his dealings with them. Justin-Marie Bomboko, personal interview, unrecorded, Kinshasa, November 6, 2009 and Mario Losembe-Cardoso, personal interview, recorded, Kinshasa, July 23, 2015. See also Mutamba, *Autopsie du gouvernement*, 37–39, 87–90.

36 Internal tensions undermined the college, as a few members developed direct relations with Mobutu and with him created the so-called Binza group, an informal alliance that would act as a shadow government for the next five years. See Nzongola-Ntalaja, *The Congo from Leopold*, 125–26.

37 Quoted in Gérard-Libois and Verhaegen, *Congo 1960*, 2:871–72.

38 Willame, *Patrice Lumumba*, 426; Mutamba Makombo, *Autopsie du gouvernement*, 7. It seems likely that some commissioners featured among the early Congolese CIA recruits made by Larry Devlin in the fall of 1960. See Devlin, *Chief of Station*, 97, 111.

39 Mutamba, *Autopsie d'un gouvernement*, 34.

40 P. Julien Dema, "Comment la guerre civile a failli éclater à Léopoldville en fin d'année 1960," *Remarques congolaises* 4, no. 9–10 (1962): 82–84; Kamitatu, *La grande mystification*, 86–91.

41 See Kabamba and Kasulula, *Rapport sur les assassinats et violations des droits de l'homme*, 1:44–45; Omasombo, "Lumumba, drame sans fin"; and De Vos et al., *Les secrets de l'affaire*.

42 See, for instance, Ahlman, *Living with Nkrumahism*, 152–57; Byrne, *Mecca of Revolution*, 85–99; and Tolliver, *Of Vagabonds and Fellow Travelers*, 158–83.

43 See Fanon, *Toward the African Revolution*, 192–94; and Lopez, *Lumumba ou l'Afrique*, 126.

44 Kamitatu, *La grande mystification*, 74.

45 See also Monaville, "Political Life."

46 Jean-Baptiste Mulemba, personal interview, recorded, Kinshasa, July 21, 2015; François Beltchika, personal interview, recorded, Kinshasa, July 22, 2011.

47 James Scott, Memorandum to the COSEC staff regarding Venant Ngoie, June 1961, USNSA International Commission, Box 92, HIA.

48 Both the CIA-funded Coordinating Secretariat of Nation Union of Students and the Soviet-aligned IUS called on their members to organize events to denounce Lumumba's assassination (Norman Kingsbury, "International Student Mourning Day: Death of Lumumba," February 16, 1961, USNSA Box 92, HIA; "Students Firmly on Side of Congo," *World Student News* 15, no. 2 [March 1961]: 1, 4).

49 See Henri Hockins Kadiebo, "Quelques recherches sur le rôle de l'U.G.E.C. et sur ce que pensent de son action des étudiants Congolais effectuant des études en Belgique" (unpublished MA thesis, Ecole supérieure ouvrière, Brussels, 1964), 29.

50 See notably, "Une centaine d'étudiants manifestent contre l'assassinat de Patrice Lumumba," *Le soir*, February 18, 1961, 3.

51 Nzuzi became involved in nationalist politics first as the president of the Union de la jeunesse du Kongo (UJEKO), a platform of the youth branches of Congo's political parties, and then as the leader of the youth section of Lumumba's MNC.

52 See Houart, *La pénétration communiste*, 95; Kamitatu, *La grande mystification*, 74; De Witte, *L'assassinat de Lumumba*, 324–30; and Kabamba and Kasulula, *Rapport sur les assassinats*, 75–80.

53 Interview with Paul-Henri Kabayidi, unrecorded, Kinshasa, February 12, 2011.

54 'Appel!,' Cercle d'études africaines Patrice Lumumba, bulletin intérieur 1 (March 1961): 2.

55 In an interview, the former Belgian communist youth leader Eddy Poncelet confirmed the importance of the Lumumba Club in the eyes of the party: Eddy Poncelet, personal interview, unrecorded, Ostend, September 7, 2011.

56 Cercle d'études africaines Patrice Lumumba, "Grande journée nationaliste africaine," April 1961, DP.

57 F. Brenner, letter to the rector of the Free University of Brussels, March 14, 1961, ULB.

58 Cercle d'étude africaine Patrice Lumumba, letter to the rector of the Free University of Brussels, September 27, 1961, ULB.

59 In a strange twist, the Belgian press blamed the Congolese students for the incidents, denouncing "the belligerent conduct of some Congolese students" as having caused a general deterioration in the relationship between Belgian students and their African peers. "La commémoration de le mort de Lumumba: Violents incidents à l'Université de Bruxelles," *Le soir* (January 1963).

60 *Séminaire de l'UGEC sur la réorganisation de l'UGEC, la lutte contre l'analphabétisme, les institutions politiques, la réforme et la démocratisation de l'enseignement, Bruxelles, February 22–24, 1963* (Brussels: COSEC,1963), 5.

61 See, for instance, Secrétaire General OSPAAL to Comité solidarité avec résistance congolaise, telegram, January 23, 1968, DP.

62 Young and Turner, *Rise and Decline*, 209.

63 Paget, *Patriotic Betrayal*.

64 Congolese students in Belgium, who had created their own organization, enjoyed a more direct access to pro-communist youth groups. In 1959, a dozen of these students participated in the World Festival of Youth and Students organized by the Soviet-front World Federation of Democratic Youth in Vienna (see Tshimanga, *Jeunesse, formation et société*, 258–59). The festival was an opportunity to socialize with left student activists from around the world, but a few students in the Congolese delegation spent most of their time at the CIA-sponsored "anti-festival" that was concurrently taking place in the Austrian capital (Jacques Bongoma, personal interview, recorded, Kinshasa, July 22, 2011; [James T. Harris], "Report on the Republic of the Congo," August 1960, p. 4, USNSA International Commission, Box 187, HIA).

65 Together with Angola and South Africa, the Belgian Congo was one of the three most important areas of concentration in sub-Saharan Africa for the NSA: Paget, *Patriotic Betrayal*, 262.

66 The trip was Young's first visit to the Congo. Three years later, he returned to the country to conduct doctoral research on Congolese politics. Crawford Young, personal interview, unrecorded, Madison, June 12, 2009.

67 James Scott interviewed by Alan Macfarlane, March 26, 2009, video, http://www.alanmacfarlane.com/DO/filmshow/scott1_fast.htm. The Paris office of the NSA served as an important point of connection between the CIA and the student union (see Paget, *Patriotic Betrayal*, 61–78). It was also a strategic position considering the NSA's strong involvement with Algerian student politics. One of Scott's predecessors in Paris had been Crawford Young, who was there before moving to COSEC in Leiden.

68 James Scott, "Report by NSA Representative on Louvanium [*sic*]," 7.

69 Bob Backhoff, "Conversation with Leonard Thako, President Swiss section of UGEC," February 25, 1963, p. 3, USNSA International Commission, Box 188, HIA.

70 Even a 1966 article that denounced the CIA's surveillance of Congolese students in Belgium did not mention NSA's or COSEC's possible role as a tool of American intelligence ("Qu'est-ce que la C.I.A.," *L'Eclair* 10 [May–June 1966]: 22–24). But after *Ramparts* magazine published a bombshell article that revealed the extent of CIA involvement with the NSA in March 1967, Congolese students forcefully denounced the fact that the Congo had become an American battlefield filled with CIA agents infiltrating labor unions, youth organizations, and the army ("Congrès annuel—UGEC Belgique," *L'avant-garde: Revue mensuelle de l'*UGEC [July 1967]: 6).

71 Duncan Kennedy, "Report on the Second Congress of UGEC-USA held at Detroit, June 13–16, 1964," p. 5, USNSA International Commission, Box 188. Kennedy by then still believed that the NSA's "deceptive activities were within the range of acceptable costs of containing the Soviets," but he changed his mind soon after that (Kennedy, "A Semiotics of Critique," 1167).

72 E. Wamba, "L'UGEC est-elle devenue lettre morte?," *La voix des étudiants congolais* 5, no. 6 (April 1966): 5.

73 Jean-Marie Mutamba has argued that Takizala refused to join the college for ideological reasons (Mutamba, *Autopsie du gouvernement*, 12). An interview of Takizala with *Jeune Afrique* in 1968 does suggest he may have found himself in an awkward position vis-à-vis the orientation of the college: Takizala said that Lumumba had "not made a great impression" on him in 1960 with his demand for immediate independence but that he was still convinced of Lumumba's "patriotism and sincerity" and that he "came to his aid" the moment "Patrice had difficulties," which resulted in accusations of being a communist ("H. D. Takizala: A Tough Man with a Tender Heart," *United States of America Department of Commerce: Translations on Africa* 727 [August 1968]: 102–3). However, in January 1961, Takizala had proudly shared the news with his American interlocutors that the college had chosen him as the new general secretary of the Ministry of Education and Fine Arts: see James Scott, letter to Henri Takizala, February 2, 1961, USNSA International Commission, Box 92, HIA.

74 On the centrality of the CIA in the US Congo policy under Dwight D. Eisenhower, John F. Kennedy, and Lyndon B. Johnson, see Namikas, *Battleground Africa*, 98–99, 131–32.

75 Alexander Korns, letter to James Scott, February 7, 1961, USNSA International Commission, Box 187, HIA.

76 Lovemore Mutambanengwe, letter to James Scott, January 4, 1961, p. 2, USNSA International Commission, Box 187, HIA.

77 Henri Takizala, "Address to the Congress by the UGEC President," in *The Resolutions of the First UGEC Congress, Leopoldville, Congo, 4–7 May, 1961* (Leiden: COSEC, 1961), 7–11.

78 Adoula cultivated his relationship with UGEC by using government funds to support the Belgian section of the group. See Hockins-Kadiebo, "Quelques recherches," 23; and Dikonda wa Lumanyisha and Daniel Mulomba, "L'arrestation du ministre des affaires étrangères du Congo M. Mabika Kalanda," *Remarques congolaises* 5, no. 29 (December 1963): 472.

79 "Xylophones et balafongs," *Présence universitaire* 8 (January 1962): 56.

80 Muhirwa, *Le syndicalisme et ses incidences*, 85–88

81 "Congo Students Sack Embassy," *Daily Reporter*, January 15, 1963, 3.

82 Ferdinand Kayukwa, speech at the International Union of Students' 7th Congress in Leningrad, August 1962, IUS archival collections, IISH. See also I. R. A., "Quitte ou double" and "Editorial," *Echos de Lovanium* (April 1962): 1, 5, 7.

83 Alexander Korns, report on UGEC, May 1963, pp. 3–4, USNSA International Commission, Box 188, HIA.

84 These positions had been particularly popular among UGEC activists in Belgium. Moderates closely aligned with COSEC dominated there until around 1964 and were careful to assert the "non-xenophobic" nature of their nationalist politics and to explicitly reject Soviet Marxism as an alternative to Western colonialism. See, for instance, Daniel Mulomba, "L'étudiant congolais face au nationalisme," *L'étudiant congolais: Revue bimestrielle de l'UGEC-belgique* (March 1962): 6.

85 "Le deuxième congrès des étudiants congolais tenu à Léopoldville du 4 au 11 août," *Remarques congolaises* 5, no. 22 (September 1963): 317.

86 Zénon Mibamba, personal interview, recorded, Kinshasa, June 15, 2010.

87 Shringarpure, *Cold War Assemblages*, 91.

88 Scott, *Seeing like a State*.

89 On his critical work with Algerian students as the NSA representative in Paris in 1956 and 1957, see Paget, *Patriotic Betrayal*, 197–206.

90 The acknowledgments in Young's book, which was based on his dissertation, only mentions the Ford Foundation support and leaves out the logistical help that he received from the US authorities in the Congo. Young, *Politics in Congo*, v–viii.

91 In 1963 and 1964, Young produced at least two reports for the Bureau of Intelligence and Research, one of the main intelligence agencies of the US Department of State: the first report surveyed general political dynamics

in the Congo, and the second focused on the Simba and Mulele rebellions. See R. Palmer, "Further Materials on Congo Rebels," United States government memorandum, September 2, 1964, Records of the Bureau of African Affairs, 1958–66, Box 24, NARA.

Six. Revolution in the (Counter)revolution

1   The school, which delivered a degree after four years of theory classes and training courses, opened with a first cohort of 176 students in 1961. In 1964, it counted a total of 488 students. See Golan, *Educating the Bureaucracy*, 37.

2   See Paget, *Patriotic Betrayal*, 115–65. Before joining ENDA, Harris had also served as the associate director of another CIA-front organization in the cultural cold war, the American Association of African Culture. See Gaines, *American Africans*, 48–49; and Tolliver, *Of Vagabonds*, 85–86. On the Ford Foundation's relation with ENDA, see Berman, *The Influence*, 85–88.

3   Golan, *Educating the Bureaucracy*, xi.

4   Golan, *Educating the Bureaucracy*, 44.

5   F. X. Sutton, "Memo on the National School of Law and Administration (ENDA)," Leopoldville, May 10, 1961, Ford Foundation Papers, RAC.

6   Golan returned to the Congo in 1969 as a journalist. She covered student protests in Kinshasa, until she was expelled from the country because of her proximity to some of the student activists (François Kandolo, personal interview, recorded, Kinshasa, October 12, 2007; François Cros, personal interview, unrecorded, Paris, February 12, 2011). In contrast with her indictment of the ENDA students' conservativism, she called the students of 1969 "real heroes who deserve to be remembered" (author's personal correspondence with Tamar Golan, 2010–11). Later in her life, Golan served as Israel's first ambassador to Angola and as the director of the African studies department at Ben-Gurion University. See Avi Cohen, "The Ambassador of All," in *Focus Review*, January 1, 2011, 35–37; and Gideon Levy, "Tamar Golan, Israel's Queen of Africa, Dies at 76," *Haaretz*, March 31, 2011.

7   Jean-Paul Kabeya, personal interview, recorded, Kinshasa, March 28, 2010; Isidore Ndaywel e Nziem, personal interview, unrecorded, Kinshasa, July 27, 2011. See also Dikonda wa Lumanyisha and Daniel Mulomba, "L'arrestation du ministre des affaires étrangères M. Mabika Kalanda," *Remarques congolaises* 5, no. 29 (December 1963): 471–73.

8   Mabika, *Tabalayi*.

9   "Chronique de l'ENDA: Les étudiants chez Monsieur Mabika-Kalanda," *Génération nouvelle* 1, no. 4 (June 1963): 38–40. Mabika further developed his ideas about mental decolonization in a later book (Mabika, *La remise en question*). His thinking on this topic may have started as a critical engagement with the work of the Belgian missionary August De

Clerq, an early promoter of Luba authenticity and "incultured Christianity" in Kasai in the 1930s. Jean-Paul Kabeya, personal interview, unrecorded, Kinshasa, March 28, 2010; on De Clerq, see Mwamba Mputu, *Le Congo-Kasaï*, 188–89.

10 Anatole Malu, "République du Congo, an III," *Génération nouvelle* 1, no. 4 (June 1963): 4–7.

11 "Les dirigeants de demain," *Génération nouvelle* 1, no. 4 (June 1963): 14–16.

12 Delphin Banza Hangakolwa, personal interview, recorded, Kinshasa, August 11, 2011. See also "Editorial," *Génération nouvelle* 2, no. 1 (November 1963): 2–4; and Delphin S. R. Banza, "Considérations sur la philosophie de l'éducation," *Génération nouvelle* 4, no. 1 (1965): 12–22. On Banza's friendship with Kabila, see Kennes and Munkana, *Essai biographique*, 72–82.

13 Herbert Weiss, introduction to Coquery-Vidrovitch, Forest, and Weiss, *Rébellions-révolution*, 13.

14 See, for instance, Kalixte Mukendi, "Das Erbe Lumumbas und die Tragödie der Freiheit im Kongo," *Blätter für deutsche und internationale Politik* 9 (1964): 728–34.

15 On the term *second independence* as an emic description of the rebellion in the Kwilu, see Fox, De Craemer, and Ribeaucourt, "The Second Independence."

16 See Kalema, "Scars, Marked Bodies."

17 Bourdieu, "Révolution dans la révolution."

18 In this way, even though Golan's work did not otherwise lack originality, it conformed well to the tendency in the American sociology of third-world higher education of the time to emphasize structural functionalism and pay little attention to political imagination. See, for instance, Hanna, *University Students*.

19 Jean-Baptiste Mulemba, personal interview, recorded, Kinshasa, August 2, 2011; Kisonga, *45 ans d'histoire*, 53. According to Verhaegen, Mitudidi studied at Sorbonne and then in Moscow. See Verhaegen, *Rébellions au Congo*, 1:176; and Verhaegen, *Mulele et la révolution*, 342. However, Abdoulaye Yerodia, who knew Mitudidi in France, confirmed Kisonga's point that Mitudidi studied in Nancy (Abdoulaye Yerodia, personal interview, recorded, Kinshasa, August 5, 2011). On Mitudidi's role in the first Popular Republic of the Congo in Stanleyville in 1960 and 1961, see Kennes and Munkana, *Essai biographique*, 90–91.

20 Martens, *Pierre Mulele*, 137–40.

21 See Verhaegen, "La rébellion muléliste."

22 See Verhaegen et al., *Mulele et la révolution*, 355–72; and Weiss and Fulco, "Les partisans au Kwilu."

23 On Nendaka's powers under Adoula, see Gérard-Libois and Verhaegen, *Congo 1962*, 82–92; and Lloyd Garrison, "Congo Politics: Position

of Adoula Becomes Shaky as Opposition to Regime Rises," *New York Times*, December 2, 1962, 3.

24 A. R. Kithima, personal interview, recorded, Kinshasa, November 2, 2009. See also Bo-Boliko et al., "Prise de position des syndicats congolais," October 2 and 9, 1963, ICFTU Papers, IISH; and De Witte, *L'ascension de Mobutu*, 41–43.

25 See Bazenguissa-Ganga, *Les voies du politique*, 91.

26 See, among many other articles, "Bas les mains devant le Congo-Leo," *Dipanda* 2, no. 2 (November 1963): 1, 6; N'Dalla Graille, "Editorial: Lumumba vécut, Lumumba vit, Lumumba vivra toujours," *Dipanda* 13 (January 18, 1964): 2; "Le peuple vaincra," *Dipanda* 26 (April 25, 1964), 3; N'Dalla Graille, "Sous le sigle de la revolution africaine," *Dipanda* 34 (June 27, 1964), 2–5; and "Le chien Tshombe aboie, mais le peuple veille," *Dipanda* 42 (August 22, 1964): 1, 4. Most of these pieces were written by Ernest N'Dalla, a figure of the new regime who had studied in France and the Soviet Union and later looked back at a speech he delivered at Moscow's Lomonov State University after Lumumba's death as the foundational moment in his political trajectory (Etienne N'Dalla, personal interview, recorded, Brazzaville, March 31, 2010).

27 Abdoulaye Yerodia, personal interview, recorded, Kinshasa, August 5, 2011.

28 They did not fare much better when they started a small maquis in the region of Lake Leopold II (Martens, *Pierre Mulele*, 305–14).

29 See Verhaegen, *Rebellions au Congo*, 2:405–60, 577–88, 599–645.

30 Gleijeses, *Conflicting Missions*, 70–75; Borel, "La politique belge"; Vandewalle, *L'Ommegang.*

31 Pressure to organize the conference mostly came from Nasser, but the Vietnamese, Algerian, Moroccan, and Angolan delegations in Egypt also played a role, with the Chinese embassies financing the event. See Kisonga, *45 ans d'histoire*, 98–100.

32 Paul Indongo, personal interview, recorded, Berlin, April 5, 2011. See also Paul Fernand [Indongo], letter to Jules Chomé, October 18, 1965; and UGEC-RAU, letter to UGEC-Belgique, September 10, 1965, Gérard-Libois Papers, MRAC; as well as Jules Chomé, "La mort du Colonel Pakassa," *Remarques africaines* 252 (November 1965): 16–19.

33 See Moore, *Castro, the Blacks and Africa*, 165–230; Kennes and Munkana, *Essai biographique*, 158–86; and Galvez, *Che in Africa*.

34 Guevara, *Congo Diary*, 88–90.

35 Joseph Sébastien Ramazani, letter to Camarade Secrétaire du Comité de Solidarité avec la Résistance Congolaise de Belgique, June 19, 1968, Jacques Grippa Papers, CARCOB. A former postal employee turned chief of protocol for Lumumba in July 1960, Ramazani occupied diverse ministerial positions in rebel governments. Unlike many other rebel cadres, he acquired a strong reputation of incorruptibility. See Verhaegen, *Rébellions au Congo*, 435–41.

36 Thomas R. Kanza, "Congo, pays de surprises," *Remarques africaines* 271 (August 25, 1966): 398–401. Algiers and Accra had been two leading

supporters of the Congolese rebels, while Malcolm X had been obsessed with the Congo in the last months of his life. See Moore, *Castro, the Blacks and Africa*, 204; Marable, *A Life of Reinvention*, 36–37, 386–87, 394–96, 401; and Byrne, *Mecca of Revolution*.

37 See Kalema, "Scars, Marked Bodies"; and De Witte, *L'ascension de Mobutu*, 187–264.

38 See Althabe, *Les fleurs du Congo*, 297–302; Gleijeses, *Conflicting Missions*, 70–75; and Slobodian, *Third World Politics*, 137–41.

39 See, for instance, Brown, *West Germany*, 21–78.

40 Willame, "The Congo," 46–47; *Congo 1964*, 176. The choice of Kayukwa surprised, as he had served time in prison during the secession because of his opposition to Tshombe. Interestingly, Gbenye made very similar promises to the UGEC students he also courted, writing to them that once in power, the CNL would place "all our national institutions' levers of control in the hands of Congolese technicians, notably the students who are now slogging over school benches" (Christophe Gbenye, letter to Grégoire Dikonda wa Lumanyisha, April 20, 1964, Gérard-Libois Papers, MRAC).

41 See Gérard-Libois, *Congo 1966*, 86–87.

42 Henri Takizala, the founder and former president of UGEC, was also arrested after publicly criticizing the Tshombe government in December 1964: *Congo 1964*, 438–41.

43 T. W. McElhiney, "Confidential Memorandum: Administration of Liberated Areas," October 8, 1964, pp. 1, 8, RBAA, 1958–1966, Congo Kinshasa 1965–1966, Box 25, NARA. On the CIA's close association with the counterinsurgency campaign, see, for example, Devlin, *Chief of Station*, 249–68. And on the weaponization by the counterinsurgency of the Congo Protestant Relief Agency's humanitarian work in the former Simba territories, see Rich, *Protestant Missionaries*, 108–31.

44 "Minutes of the Country Team Youth Committee Meeting," July 9, 1965, RBAA, Congo Kinshasa 1965–1966, Box 27, NARA.

45 See, for instance, André Nkanza-Dolomingu and Anatole Malu, "L'UGEC et les événements du Kwilu," March 2, 1964, Gérard-Libois Papers, MRAC, Tervuren; Anatole Malu, "Réponse à 'Amis de l'UGEC, ceci ne signifie pas la révolution,'" October 27, 1964, unpublished pamphlet, in the author's possession; and Dikonda wa Lumanyisha, "L'UGEC Belgique et les événenements du Kwilu," February 1964, UGEC documents, DP. In private, UGEC activists' criticisms of the CNL leaders were even harsher, and they called them "incompetent, stupid and unworthy of political support" (Robert Backhoff, "Report on the Union ÿ énéralegénérale des étudiants du Congo," April 1965, USNSA International Commission, Box 188).

46 Ndaywel è Nziem, "La vie quotidienne à Lovanium," 58.

47 See Albert Mpase, "Rapport aux membres du Conseil d'administration sur la situation des étudiants pendant l'année académique 1965–1966," July 7, 1966, p. 14, VSP, LUA. See also Mpase, "Vivre le devenir," 265–68.

48 Jean-Baptiste Murairi, personal interview, recorded, Brussels, December 30, 2019.

49 Isidore Ndaywel è Nziem, personal interview, unrecorded, Kinshasa, July 27, 2011.

50 See Raymaekers, *Nzala*; and Paul Raymaekers, personal interview, unrecorded, Rhode-St-Genèse, July 25, 2009.

51 Isidore Ndaywel, personal interview, unrecorded, August 5, 2011.

52 Theophile Nkasa, speech at Lovanium, July 2, 1960, USNSA International Commission, Box 187.

53 See, for instance, B. Kalonji, "Conscience nationale et développement," *Présence universitaire* 11 (1963): 17–22; and C. M., "Le rôle national de l'esprit universitaire africain," *Présence universitaire* 11 (January 1963): 11–16.

54 "Nouvelles de Kinshasa," *L'Eclair* 5 (October 1965): 21.

55 Albert Mpase, "Rapport sur les étudiants et leurs problèmes," July 1965, VSP, LUA.

56 On Kasa-Vubu's turn to the left in 1965, see Kamitatu, *La grande mystification*, 123–49; and De Witte, *L'ascension de Mobutu*, 411–13.

57 Etienne N'Dalla Graille, personal interview, recorded, Brazzaville, March 31, 2010.

58 Tharcisse Mwamba, "Discours prononcé par le président de l'association générale des étudiants de l'Université Lovanium," *Echos de Lovanium* 1 (March 1966): 24–25.

59 Gillon's own speech that day, which he gave before Mwamba, was a warm embrace of the new president. The two men were on friendly terms. They knew each other well from their shared interest for flying. See Gillon, *Allocution de bienvenue*; and Gillon, *Servir en actes*, 186–200.

60 See, for instance, "Pour une éducation congolaise," *La voix des étudiants congolais* 5, no. 5 (March 1966): 1–2; "Mobutu et la prospérité," *La voix des étudiants congolais* 5, no. 7 (May 1966): 3–4; and Georges Ntalaja-Nzongola, "La sixième année," *La voix des étudiants congolais* 6, no. 1 (October 1966): 1.

61 See Turner, "Clouds of Smoke," 78.

62 Maspero published the text together with a long commentary by the anthropologist Gérard Althabe in 1972, and it was republished by Bogumil Jewsiewicki in 1997 (Althabe, *Les fleurs du Congo*). On Maspero, see Hage, "Une brève histoire."

63 See Lal, *African Socialism*.

64 Althabe, *Les fleurs du Congo*, 54.

65 François Maspero, email to the author, May 9, 2011; Althabe, *Les fleurs du Congo*, 9–10.

66 Althabe, *Les fleurs du Congo*, 76.

67 The manifesto may itself have illustrated the blurred boundaries between revolution and counterrevolution. According to Bogumil Jewsiewicki, the manifesto's authors were former Catholic seminarians from eastern

Congo who studied at Lovanium and may have later joined the intellectuals who theorized the Afrocentrist return to authenticity that Mobutu promoted as a national ideology in the early 1970s (see Althabe, *Les fleurs du Congo*, 394–400).

Seven. A Student Front

1 Sumbu was one of the few people in Cuba informed of Che Guevara's mission to eastern Congo in April 1965. At the beginning of 1967, Sumbu traveled to Egypt and from there to Cyprus, where he represented the Congo together with the rebel leader Gaston Soumialot (to whom he was personally related) at a meeting of the Organization for Solidarity for the People of Africa and Asia. Sometime after the meeting, he returned to Cuba, staying on the island as a refugee until his return to the Congo-Zaire in the 1980s, when he entered Mobutu's secret police services. Constantin-Marie Kibwe, letter to Jacques Grippa, Cairo, February 22, 1967, DP; N'Gbanda, *Ainsi sonne le glas*, 32; Kennes and Munkana, *Essai biographique*, 119; Moore, *Castro, the Blacks*, 211. See also Sumbu, *El Congo*.

2 In May 1963, during a meeting with John F. Kennedy in Washington, DC, Mobutu had asked to attend a two-week training program at Fort Bragg. The US president agreed to the request, but it is not clear if Mobutu did attend the program. See Schwar, *Foreign Relations*, 858–62.

3 See Folti, "Feltrinelli," 375.

4 Fidel Castro's publisher and a frequent traveler to Cuba, Feltrinelli was present when Sumbu gave a speech at the Havana International Cultural Congress in January 1968. See Rey and Gracia, "Role of Left-Wing Editors," 94. According to Feltrinelli's son, *Il sangue dei leoni* was one of the most popular political texts published by his father (usually pressed at around four thousand copies each). See Feltrinelli, *Feltrinelli*, 232.

5 Sumbu, *Il sangue dei leoni*, 61–62.

6 See Zénon Mibamba, "Au comité exécutif de l'Union générale des étudiants congolais," March 15, 1966, p. 2, DP; and Thomas Mukwidi, letter to Antoine Gizenga, August 29, 1964, Gérard-Libois Papers, MRAC.

7 Holm, *The Craft We Chose*, 176. Not all US officials believed that ideological considerations were irrelevant to understanding events in the Congo. As a diplomat mentioned in a memo in September 1964, "If the rebels are little more than unrelated bandit gangs hopped up with hashish . . . , how have they been able to pre-empt the word 'nationalist' by which the rebels . . . are generally known in the Congo?" (Curtis C. Strong, "Report on trip to Congo," September 1964, p. 2, RBAA, Box 24, NARA).

8 *In Support of the People of the Congo (Leopoldville) against U.S. Aggression* (Peking: Foreign Languages Press, 1964).

9 See Ross, *Communal Luxury*, 77.

10 "Compte-rendu de la Ve séance de travail," April 20, 1964, pp. 3–6, FPC documents, DP.

11 See "Compte-rendu de la IIIe séance," March 23, 1964, pp. 4–6; and "Compte-rendu de la Ve séance de travail," April 20, 1964, p. 6, DP.

12 For a nuanced discussion of African socialisms in the 1960s as part of broader current of "peripheral socialisms," see Lal, "Tanzanian *Ujamaa*."

13 "Compte-rendu de la Ve séance de travail," April 20, 1964, pp. 3–4.

14 See "Bedarf des FPC zur Reorganisierung und Fürhung der Volksrevolution im Kongo" [1964], DP; and Kalixte Wa Nsanga Mukendi, personal interview, recorded, Nouakchott, May 20, 2016.

15 Imani Lukale (Antoine Robert), "Proposition concernant l'organisation de cellules" [August 1964], DP.

16 See Valentin Okitakula, "L'Union des nationalistes fait la force de l' UGEC progessiste!" [November 1964], DP.

17 Beltchika was the son of Liévin Kalubi, who had been accused of masterminding the so-called conspiracy of 1944 in Elisabethville (see chapter 2). After independence, Kalubi had become a top civil servant in the ministry for foreign affairs and sent all his children to Belgium (François Beltchika Kalubye, personal interview, recorded, Kinshasa, July 22, 2011).

18 "Communiqué à la presse de l'UGEC devant la dégradation de la situation au Congo," November 1964, DP. The text was then distributed on Belgian cities' streets as a pamphlet by the pro-Chinese Belgian Communist Party. "Un courageux communiqué de presse de l'Union des étudiants congolais," November 1964, Georges Pétré Papers, CARCOB.

19 See International Union of Students, "Draft Resolution on Congo Leopoldville," December 1964, IUS Papers, IISH.

20 Oswald Ndeshyo, personal interview, recorded, Kinshasa, June 7, 2010; and "UGEC Discusses the Congo," *World Student News* 19, no. 1–2 (1965): 10–12. In February, Tshilenge wrote to a friend that he and Ndeshyo sometimes attended classes in Algiers but that they otherwise spent their time reading and strolling along the beach (Pontien Tshilenge, letter to Jean-Marie, February 3, 1965, DP). The two young men stayed in Algeria for more than a year until Mobutu, who was newly in power and attempt to co-opt the student left to his regime, offered them a fellowship that allowed them to finish their education in France (Oswald Ndeshyo, personal interview, recorded, Kinshasa, June 7, 2010).

21 See "Communiqué à la presse des étudiants congolais devant l'aggravation de la situation au Congo," *Dipanda* 56 (December 12, 1964): 8; "L'U.G.E.C. continue," *Remarques congolaises et africaines* 241 (April 28, 1965): 11; François Beltchika Kalubye, "Allocution d'ouverture aux journées d'études de l'Union générale des étudiants congolais—section Belgique," March 27, 1965, Grippa Papers, CARCOB; "U.G.E.C.-R.D.A., à la bonne attention de tous étudiantes et étudiants congolais membres de l'Union générale des étudiants congolais," *Remarques congolaises et africaines* 241 (April 28, 1965): 21–22; and "Qui sommes-nous?," *La voix des étudiants congolais* (October 1965): 1.

22 Buakasa, "Nation congolaise."

23 Gérard Buakasa Tulu Kia Mpansu, "Plan pour l'organisation et l'éducation au sein de l'U.G.E.C.," *Remarques africaines* 254 (December 1965): 18–22.

24 Kalixte Mukendi Wa Nsanga, personal interview, recorded, Nouakchott, May 20, 2016.

25 J. D. R., "K. Z. Mukendi, géologue, géographe et penseur: Le souci des structures," *Mwana Shaba* 138 (December 1966): 5–7.

26 K. Mukendi Wa Nsanga, letter to Eddy Poncelet, February 25, 1962, TP, CARCOB.

27 K. Mukendi Wa Nsanga, "Un programme à base du travail et le travail à base de la coopération," April 19, 1962, pp. 14–15, TP, CARCOB.

28 Wa Nsanga, letter to Terfve and Poncelet, October 6, 1963, TP, CARCOB.

29 He lived in a house where all his housemates were Congolese. In August 1963, he had traveled to Leopoldville with some of them to attend the second Congress of UGEC and had met with Gaston Soumialot and other nationalist politicians (Luc-Daniel Dupire, personal interview, unrecorded, Brussels, August 17, 2012).

30 "Ve séance de travail," April 20, 1964, p. 1, DP.

31 Dupire ultimately joined the party's central committee. He also became involved with the Committee of Solidarity with the Congolese Resistance (CSRC), which was launched in 1965 on the model of Committee of Solidarity with Vietnam. Although Maoist-dominated, the CSRC was bankrolled by Antoine Allard, the private secretary of Queen Elisabeth of Belgium and rich scion of a recently ennobled grand bourgeois banking family that counted financial interests in the Belgian Congo (see Adant, "Un baron rouge?").

32 See Thomas Turner, "Preparatory Seminar for 3rd UGEC (Congo) Congress," Cologne, April 17–20, 1965, USNSA International Commission, HIA.

33 Mukendi Wa Nsanga, "L'U.G.E.C. porte-t-elle l'espoir du peuple congolais déçu? Nos principes et méthodes de travail," *Remarques africaines* 244 (June 9, 1965): 23–28.

34 Jean-Robert Benza and Symphorien N'Kita-Kabongo, leter to Walter Ulbricht, February 7, 1966, p. 4, DY30/IV2/9.02/36, BA.

35 Dhimiter Mandro, "Relacion takimi me Kalikst Mukendi," August 11, 1965, Foreign Affairs Collection 14/15/612, GDA. Later on, the Albanians encouraged the transformation of the UJRC into a (short-lived) Congolese Communist Party (see "En avant vers la creation d'un veritable parti d'avant-garde, marxiste-léniniste!," *L'Eclair* 12 [April 1967]: 3–5). Discussions for the creation of the party began in Tirana and Rome in February 1967 in the presence of Grippa, Dupire, Théo Tango, and three CNL activists (Thomas Mukwidi, Constantin-Marie Kibwe, and Emmanuel-Willem Kabasubabo). Mukwidi's death during a military operation in June 1967 and the renunciation by Dupire, Tango, and Wa Nsango of revolutionary activism around 1968 prevented the actual creation of the party. However, Kibwe and Kabasubabo remained active and

resuscitated their relationship with Albania in the early 1970s when they launched a Parti révolutionnaire marxiste du Congo.

36 Michel-Ange Mupapa, personal interview, recorded, Kinshasa, July 11, 2011; Elikia M'Bokolo, personal interviews, unrecorded, Kinshasa, July 12, 2010, and July 6, 2021; Jean-Marie Mutamba, personal interview, unrecorded, Kinshasa, November 8, 2009.

37 After one of the members, Elikia M'Bokolo, was admitted to the prestigious Ecole Normale Supérieure in Paris, the group's center of gravity moved to the French capital, just in time for the events of May 1968. In Paris, they entered in contact with Abdoulaye Yerodia, who was back in France after the failure of the CNL, and took them under his wing. Besides M'Bokolo, two other future Congolese scholars, Michel-Ange Mupapa and Jean-Marie Mutamba, also participated in the Lyon group. Their affiliation to the UJRC and their companionship with Yeriodia strongly anchored them all to the left, but they each explored the French political scene independently, and the group included social democrats, Trotskyists, Maoists, and members of the French Communist Party.

38 See N'Zevu Zebula, "Les positions de l'UJRC: La nature révolutionnaire de l'engagement dans la lutte armée," *L'Eclair* 8 (February 1966): 3; and "Les positions de l'UJRC: L'impérialisme américain, ennemi n. 1 de notre peuple," *L'Eclair* 10 (May–June 1966): 2.

39 Twelve issues of *L'Eclair* came out between June 1965 and April 1967, each between thirty and fifty pages long. Total circulation went from 450 copies for the first issue up to 3,250 copies for the final issue in April 1967, which was sent to correspondents in eighty countries throughout Europe, Africa, and beyond ("Répartition par pays des expéditions du numéro 11 de Janvier 1967 de 'L'Eclair,'" undated typescript, DP).

40 "Editorial," *L'Eclair* 3 (August 1965): 1.

41 "Aux lecteurs de *L'Eclair*," *L'Eclair* 5 (October 1965): 4.

42 I. Lukale, "Le développement de la lutte de liberation nationale au Congo," *L'Eclair* 1 (June 1965): 3; Imani Lukale, "Le peuple congolais lutte pour le socialisme et le progrès sous la conduite du conseil suprême de la révolution," *L'Eclair* 3 (August 1965): 5–13. Robert seemed to have left the struggle after a few months in eastern Congo. Demoralizing dissensions within the revolutionary camp probably played a role in his decision to withdraw from the front. See R. I. Lukale, "Les progrès du peuple congolais en armes," *La voix du peuple* 82 (July 3, 1965): 2–5.

43 R. Imani Lukale, "Plus que jamais, aujourd'hui le peuple congolais est déterminé à vaincre," *Remarques congolaises et africaines* 235 (February 3, 1965): 6–9.

44 Imani Mwana Lukale, "Le peuple congolais lutte pour le socialisme et le progrès sous la conduite du CNL," undated typescript, DP.

45 Similarly, when Dupire disagreed with parts of the arguments in an article written by Zénon Mibamba from Brazzaville, he did not hesitate to

heavily editorialize it. See Gongo-Musengere, letter to Zénon Mibamba, October 2, 1966, DP.

46 See Hans Jürgen Krüger, "Aus tausend Flüssen strömt der Kongo," *Frankfurter Allgemeine Zeitung*, October 8, 1960, 18.

47 "Editorial," *L'Eclair* 2 (July 1965): 1.

48 "Editorial," *L'Eclair* 3 (August 1965): 2.

49 N'Zevu Zebula, "De l'audace, encore de l'audace, toujours de l'audace!," *L'Eclair* 4 (September 1965): 3.

50 "Le courrier," *L'Eclair* 10 (May–June 1966): 3.

51 "Le courrier," *L'Eclair* 12 (April 1967): 39.

52 "7 juin 1965, mort de Léonard Mitudidi," *L'Eclair* 10 (May–June 1966): 5.

53 "Deux étudiants révolutionnaires visitant un territoire libéré," *L'Eclair* 5 (October 1965): 3.

54 Gongo Musengere, "La violence révolutionnaire, arme essentielle du peuple congolais," *L'Eclair* 10 (May–June 1966): 31.

55 One moment of tension within UGEC-Belgium happened at the end of 1966 when a new direction decided to expel a group of vocal radical members, including UJRC activist Théo Tango. See "A propos du Congrès de l' UGEC: Les tonneaux vides font beaucoup de bruit . . . ," *L'Eclair* 11 (January 1967): 12–13.

56 N'Zevu Zebula, "Les positions de l'UJRC. Faire la révolution ou souffrir de la folie des grandeurs," *L'Eclair* (April 1966): 3.

57 Imani Mwana Lukale, "Le peuple congolais lutte pour le socialisme et le progrès," 28–30. See also "Du Lumumbisme à la science du Marxisme-Léninisme," *L'Eclair* 8 (February 1966): 9.

58 An article in the last issue of *L'Eclair* mentioned that "at the risk of their own lives," people in Kinshasa were hiding photographs of President Mao in their houses. The article cited the case of Congolese exiles in Cairo and Cuba, for whom the shared ownership of Mao's collected works was the most meaningful binding experience ("Le rayonnement de la pensée de Mao Tse-Toung," *L'Eclair* 12 [April 1967]: 8–9).

59 A 1966 book about the Western military intervention in Stanleyville and that consisted mainly in photographs of dead and tortured bodies of Simba fighters seemed to have particularly unnerved Congolese censors (Union des jeunesses révolutionnaires congolaises, *Mémorandum*).

60 Mbelolo ya Mpiku, personal interview, unrecorded, Kinshasa, July 11, 2015.

61 See "Conditions du mouvement révolutionnaire congolais," in Debord, *Oeuvres*, 697. On Mbelolo and his friend Simon Lungela, who joined the Situationist group in Paris, see Monaville, "On the Passage."

62 Although the Congolese were often critical of countercultural tendencies among some sectors of European youth, Mukadi embraced recreational drugs, frequently went on hitch-hiking adventures, and became acquainted with young bohemian African American expatriates. Radicalized by the events of 1968, he experienced increased police harassment and

was ultimately forced to leave the former metropole and move to Algeria (where he overlapped with Paul Kagongo) and then to Burundi. Around the end of the 1980s, he was forcefully returned to the Congo, where he was tortured and imprisoned. After he was released, he found employment with the national radio in Katanga. See Matala, *Dans la tourmente*.

63 Several of his texts came out in student journals, but his major accomplishment was the publication of a collection of poems with a prestigious Parisian publishing house: Matala, *Réveil*. The volume was dedicated to Matala's parents, to Kalubye-Belchika (the leader of the "Elisabethville plot" in 1944), and to the "fighters of the tricontinental."

64 See Riva, *Nouvelle histoire*, 116.

65 Matala, *Réveil*.

66 Sumbu, *Il sangue dei leoni*, 51–52.

67 Sumbu, *Il sangue dei leoni*, 52.

68 Sumbu, *Il sangue dei leoni*, 62.

Interlude IV. The Dictator and the Students

1 Jacques Bongoma, personal interview, recorded, Kinshasa, July 22, 2011.

2 See John Bulloch, "Mobutu Tries to Drop the Pilots," *Daily Telegraph*, February 2, 1967, 16; Judith Listowell, "The Congo," *The Listener*, June 22, 1967, 809; Henry Tanner, "The Congo: Still the 'Tshombe Problem' Short Careers," *New York Times*, August 13, 1967, E5; Malcolm Rutherford, "Mobutu's Shaking Throne," *Financial Times*, August 14, 1967, 13; and Arthur H. House, "Congolese Struggle to Regain Balance," *Christian Science Monitor*, October 16, 1967, 22–24.

3 See Nimy, *Je ne renie rien*, 151–52.

4 See Central Intelligence Agency, "Intelligence Cable regarding Assassination Activities of Paracommandos in the Congolese Town of Leopoldville," August 22, 1964, *US Declassified Documents Online*, http://link .galegroup.com/apps/doc/CK2349466494/GDCS?u=new64731&sid =GDCS&xid=56befdco. Hubert Tshimpumpu, Anastase Nzeza, Léon Lobitsh, Jean Patrick Nimy, Emmanuel Lokili, and Barthélémy Bisengimana are some of the members who joined the secretariat later. On the first years of the office, see Willame, *Patrimonialism and Political Change*, 139.

5 Jacques Bongoma, personal interview, recorded, Kinshasa, July 12, 2011.

6 Arthur House, phone interview, unrecorded, April 30, 2019.

7 "United States Government Memorandum," July 5, 1966, and L. Dean Brown, "A Possible Leftward Drift in the Congo (Kinshasa)," July 21, 1966, RBAA, 1958–1966, Box 27, NARA.

8 See, for instance, John Bulloch, "Mobutu Tries to Drop the Pilots," *Daily Telegraph*, February 2, 1967, 16.

9 John W. Mowinckel, "Random Thoughts on Congo," December 21, 1966, RBAA, 1958–1966, Box 27, NARA; and Department of State, "Cable regarding the Stability of the Congolese Copper Industry," Janu-

ary 11, 1967, *U.S. Declassified Documents Online,* http://link.galegroup
.com/apps/doc/CK2349475043/GDCS?u=new64731&sid=GDCS&xid
=6babd528. In the Congo, opponents to Bongoma and Kamanda included powerful figures such as Justin-Marie Bomboko and Monsignor
Malula who believed these young advisers risked turning Mobutu into
a new Lumumba (Justin-Marie Bomboko, personal interview, recorded,
Kinshasa, November 6, 2009; Vaïsse, *Documents diplomatiques: 1966,*
2:198). For further descriptions of Bongoma and Kamanda as "dangerous Marxist-trained extremists," see British Embassy Kinshasa, "Russian
Activity in the Congo," September 3, 1969, p. 4, Foreign Office records
31/322, NA.

10 The book abundantly quoted Frantz Fanon, but it drew most of its inspiration from the US liberal economist Kenneth Galbraith. The preface was
a true game of mirrors. It was signed by Mobutu, but it had been ghost-
written by Bongoma himself. One sentence that the young adviser put in
the mouth of the president was particularly emblematic of how he was
seeking to position himself at the time. It praised the book by arguing that
Bongoma demonstrated that "one [could] be a revolutionary . . . without
necessarily lapsing into verbal excesses and violence" (J. D. Mobutu,
"Préface," in Bongoma, *Indépendance économique,* 16).

11 There was no trial, and Bongoma was let go after thirty-six days in
jail. He continued to occasionally advise Mobutu informally in the
years that followed (see, for instance, Bureau of Congressional Relations, "Staffdel Bryan and Kraft Arrive Kinshasa," WikiLeaks cable
1976STATE270583_b, dated November 3, 1976, wikileaks.org), but his
access to power was much reduced and he had great difficulties making ends meet. A job at the Association of African Universities in Accra
and the pursuit of a doctoral degree in demography at the National
University of Australia offered him opportunities to rebound away from
the homeland for most of the 1970s. He then returned to Kinshasa and
successfully launched his own newspaper. *L'Analyste* occasionally took
positions against the regime. Yet, Bongoma remained loyal to Mobutu
until the very end, differentiating between the man and the system. Talking to me in 2011, he still remembered Mobutu as the tactile, magnetic,
glamorous Pygmalion that he had first met in London and then served in
Kinshasa.

12 See Paul Bihin, "Incidents Université Lovanium, Lubumbashi et Kisangani (rapport à P. Harmel, Ministre Aff. Etr.)," February 8, 1968,
Ministry of Foreign Affairs, Brussels, AD; and "Après le remaniement
ministériel du 1er août 1969," August 1969, Archives du secrétariat
national pour les affaires africaines et malgaches, CARAN.

13 Jacques Bongoma, personal interview, recorded, Kinshasa, July 22, 2011.
Other versions exist of how the decision to proclaim Lumumba a national hero was taken. Paul-Henri Kabayidi remembered that the idea
had emerged within the political bureau of his Corps des Volontaires de la

République (Paul-Henri Kabayidi, personal interview, recorded, Brussels, February 12, 2011). Cléophas Kamitatu presented it as a suggestion made to Mobutu by US diplomats after they conducted a survey on political opinions around the country (Kamitatu, *La grande mystification*, 177). Gérard Kamanda claimed that he had made it a condition of his collaboration with the president (Kalema, "Les congrès de l'union," 158–59).

14 Incidentally, Truman Capote based the character played by Audrey Hepburn in *Breakfast at Tiffany's* on a young German woman he had known in New York and who had then disappeared in the Belgian Congo (see Inge, *Truman Capote*, 142). Hepburn, a native of Brussels, played the role of a Flemish Catholic nun in the Belgian Congo in Fred Zinnemann's *The Nun's Story* (see Hunt, *Colonial Lexicon*, 129). Although there are no picnic scenes in *Breakfast at Tiffany's*, there is a famous one in Billy Wilder's *Love in the Afternoon*, which starred Hepburn alongside Gary Cooper.

15 Don Shannon, "Mobutu Proclaims Lumumba a Congolese National Hero," *New York Herald Tribune*, July 1, 1962, 2.

Eight. (Un)natural Alliances

1 See Semonin, "Mobutu and the Congolese."

2 Vaïsse, *Documents diplomatiques français: 1966*, 2:195–97.

3 "A propos du Congrès de l'UGEC: Les tonneaux vides font beaucoup de bruit . . . ," *L'Eclair* 11 (January 1967): 12.

4 "Congo de janvier 1965 à mars 1966," *Chronique de politique étrangère* 20, no. 1 (January 1967): 29.

5 Paul-Henri Kabayidi, personal interview, recorded, Brussels, February 12, 2011. The CVR emphasized its role as a quasi-militia in charge of collecting information on the activities of "shady individuals" and of intervening (using "intimidation if necessary") anytime they witnessed anti-regime activities ("Programme d'action du CVR," January 27, 1968, Gérard-Libois Papers, MRAC, Tervuren). The CVR also foreshadowed the personality cult that developed in the mid-1970s when Mobutism imposed itself as a state religion ("Catéchisme du CVR," January 1966, Gérard-Libois Papers, MRAC, Tervuren). On Kabayidi's relationship with the Bills, see Gondola, *Tropical Cowboys*, 175–76.

6 Coincidentally, radicals within the Brazzaville regime who had loathed Mobutu as one of Lumumba's murderers now proclaimed their willingness to give him a chance to show his sincerity in his attempt to "rescue the Congo from the clutches of the exploiters." N'Dalla-Graille, "Lumumba a vécu, Lumumba vit, Lumumba vivra toujours," *Dipanda*, January 15, 1966, 1.

7 See "CVR, Notes biographiques," n.d., Gérard-Libois Papers, MRAC, Tervuren; "L'UGEC et le nouveau régime," *Courrier africain T. A.* 77 (March 1968): 2; and Delphin Banza, personal interview, recorded, Kinshasa, August 11, 2011.

8 This was a description provided by Duncan Kennedy when he visited Kinshasa for the National Student Association (NSA) in July 1966 (see chapter 5). His report also mentioned Bongoy as "the most intelligent Congolese I met"; and it was similarly positive about another UGEC officer Anatole Malu (even if he found him "extremely hostile to US Vietnam position," and "under strong Marxist influence, but not a communist); by contrast, N'Kanza was a lost cause ("totally unreliable, shifty, anti-American, and very intelligent"): see Duncan Kennedy, "Report on the Congolese Student Situation," September 18, 1966, USNSA International Commission, Box 188, HIA.

9 See Thomas Turner, "Preparatory Seminar for the 3rd UGEC Congress, Cologne, April 17–20, 1965," USNSA International Commission, Box 188, HIA. The plan was to have the congress scheduled in between the Afro-Asian heads of state summit and the World Festival of Youth that Ben Bella had planned to host in the summer of 1965. Yet, all these events were canceled after Boumédienne's coup in June 1965. See Byrne, *Mecca of Revolution*, 257.

10 See "A propos du Congrès de l'UGEC," 12; and Willame, "The Congo," 48. See also René Beeckmans, "Que faut-il penser du socialisme scientifique de l'UGEC?," *Afrique chrétienne* 6, no. 15 (1967): 24–25; 6, no. 16 (1967): 25; 6, no. 17 (1967): 24–25; 6, no. 20 (1967): 22; and Sampassa Kaweta Milombe, *Conscience et politique au Congo-Zaïre*, 40–41.

11 N'Kanza-Dolomingu, "L'UGEC au service de la nation," *La voix des étudiants congolais* 6, no. 2 (November–December 1966): 3–15.

12 Robert LaGamma, "Report on the Meeting of the Union générale des étudiants congolais," December 9, 1966, CFP, 1944–66, Box 375, NARA.

13 John W. Mowinckel, "Random Thoughts on Congo," December 21, 1966, RBAA, 1958–66, Box 27, NARA.

14 Banyaku Luape Epotu, *Chronologie, monographie et documentation*, 77. American interferences may have played in this episode. The US Labor attaché at the time remembered that "the United States had . . . become virtually a proconsul there. . . . We had people in virtually every ministry telling them what to do. We had a major CIA [Central Intelligence Agency] operation that was even running its own airline. It was a totally different thing from anything I had ever seen before. The labor union was an important element in our overall strategy" (Kennedy, *Ambassador Herman J. Cohen*, 24).

15 N'Kanza Dolomingu, "La production sociale et l'enseignement (supérieur) ou Les bases rationnelles de l'enseignement (supérieur)," unpublished pamphlet, PDM. In parallel with his presidency of UGEC, N'Kanza was the director of an adult education center that trained state employees in the science of development. Quite ironically, at the end of 1967, some of the students at the center wrote an anonymous letter to demand N'Kanza's removal. N'Kanza, they wrote, was "mean, quite mean, very mean." He was a single man without any family charge, and he could not

understand how they as married men "had sacrificed the pleasures of Kin-la-Belle" to resume their education. They complained that N'Kanza failed too many students. He constantly talked about socialism, they noted, but he had not heart and compassion: "Destitution de Nkanza Dolomingu de la direction de l'ESDE," November 27, 1967, in the author's possession.

16 Anonymous, letter to Luc Dupire, March 29, 1968, p. 2, DP.

17 See "Ninth Congress of the International Union of Students, Ulan Bator, Mongolia, Report on the 2nd Point of the Agenda," April 5, 1967, IUS Papers, IISH, Amsterdam; and *Resolutions of the 9th IUS Congress, Ulan-Bator, Mongolia, 26 March–8 April 1967* (Prague: IUS, 1967), 67–68.

18 It is possible that around this time N'Kanza decided not to wait for the regime on the organizational structure for the revolution and that he began planning clandestinely the creation of a Congolese Communist Party: Jean-Baptiste Mulemba, personal interview, recorded, Kinshasa, July 21, 2015; Wembo Ossako, personal interview, unrecorded, Kinshasa, September 1, 2010.

19 Paul-Henri Kabayidi described the forced dissolution of the CVR as the beginning of McCarthyism in the Congo. He initially joined the executive committee of the MPR, but "like everybody," as he told me, he was ultimately arrested and sent to the prison island of Bula Mbemba, where he overlapped with Zénon Mibamba and other leftist detainees in 1969. Paul-Henri Kabayidi, personal interview, recorded, Brussels, February 12, 2011.

20 The scholarship on the MPR usually focuses on this period of "high Mobutism" in the 1970s: see Schatzberg, *Politics and Class*; Callaghy, *State-Society Struggle*; and Young and Turner, *Rise and Decline*.

21 Growing tensions with Belgium over the nationalization of Union Minière and the rebellions of remaining groups of white mercenaries prolonged Mobutu's dependence on the student left in 1967. These tensions culminated in August when youth protesters plundered the Belgian embassy in Kinshasa. See Jacques Brassine, "La coopération belgo-zaïroise 1960–1985," *Courrier hebdomadaire du CRISP* 34–35 (1985): 64. On the "emotional diplomacy" between Mobutu's Congo-Zaire and Belgium, see also De Villers, *De Mobutu à Mobutu*; and Vanthemsche, *La Belgique et le Congo*, 234–58.

22 See Laclau, *On Populist Reason*, 216–17.

23 Mobutu, *Manifeste du Mouvement Populaire de la Révolution*. See also J. D. Mobutu, *Conférence du Président Fondateur du MPR prononcé le 19 mai 1967 à Kisangani* (Kinshasa: Secrétariat National à l'Information, 1967).

24 Yoka Lye Mudaba, quoted in White, *Rumba Rules*, 227.

25 The day Sampassa learned he was co-opted to the leadership of the JMPR, he was giving a conference at the University of Lubumbashi on Leninism. See Sampassa, *Conscience et politique*, 44–45.

26 Delphin Banza, personal interview, recorded, Kinshasa, August 11, 2011.

27 Critics notably accused the committee of reproducing the dominance of Kasai and Katanga over the Congolese intelligentsia and of not including any member from Mobutu's home province of Equateur. Mathieu Nzanda-Bwana, personal interview, recorded, Kinshasa, March 8, 2010.

28 The service was first announced in August 1966 when the Belgian government threatened to recall 1,126 teachers in Congolese schools as a retaliation against Mobutu's nationalist agenda. Student recruits complained about working conditions and irregularly paid salaries, which did not fit with their idea of the standing and dignity to which they were entitled as the country's intellectual elite. Bitoma and Ntil, *Enquête sur les professeurs miliciens.*

29 Albert Mpase, "Rapport aux membres du conseil d'administration sur la situation des étudiants pendant l'année académique 1965–1966," July 7, 1966, Fonds Vander Schueren, LUA.

30 The politicization of ethnicity had been relatively limited at Lovanium, but it began to increase after Mobutu's coup. The president allied a strong nationalist agenda with a Manichean manipulation of ethnic rivalries. He himself at different times accused Luba politicians of conspiring against him, which in turn encouraged suspicions against students from this ethnic group on campuses and, later on, the introduction of quotas that aimed at limiting their numbers and favor students from underrepresented groups. Although ethnicity became a more relevant category in student politics, it remained a negative reference, something to be denounced. Even if regionalist solidarity played a role in everyday life on campuses, nationalism continued to dominate student political expression.

31 Mathias Nzanda-Buana and Etienne Kachama, "Le contentieux AGEL-UGEC," December 27, 1966, UNIKIN.

32 See Université Lovanium de Kinshasa, "Mémorandum," April 7, 1967, PP.

33 The modus operandi intentionally recalled the blood sausage revolution, but the atmosphere on campus was much more tense among students, the faculty, and the administration. So much so that retrospectively, Canon Maurice Plevoets, one of Gillon's main associates in the leadership of the university, would later come to speak of the 1964 events in strikingly positive terms, with the idea of contrasting them with Nzanda-Buana's strike: Maurice Plevoets, personal interview, recorded, Kinshasa, November 5, 2009.

34 Joseph Ndundu Kivuila, personal interview, recorded, Kinshasa, June 10, 2010; Mathias Nzanda-Buana, personal interview, recorded, Kinshasa, March 8, 2010.

35 "Situation à Lovanium," February 22, 1967, Vander Schueren Papers, LUA.

36 Paul Bihin, letter to Pierre Harmel, February 25, 1967, AD.

37 Luc Gillon, "Note personelle à M. Malgengreau, Mgr. Descamps, M. Vander Schueren et M. Borghraef," March 8, 1967, Vander Schueren Papers, LUA.

38 "Troubles à Lovanium," *Dipanda*, February 26, 1967, 1.

39 Athanase Djadi, letter to Luc Gillon, April 5, 1967, VSP, LUA.

40 Luc Gillon, "Memorandum," April 7, 1967, VSP, LUA.

41 M. Colin, letter to Luc Gillon, April 28, 1967, VSP, LUA.

42 See Mudimbe, *Invention of Africa*, 164.

43 Tharcisse Tshibangu, personal interview, recorded, Kinshasa, December 18, 2019.

44 In February 1967, Mobutu had attended a talk by Tshibangu on "Africa and the Future of African Civilization" (moderated by Lovanium visiting professor of African history Jan Vansina). See "Les grandes conférences universitaires de Lovanium," *Afrique chrétienne*, February 12, 1967, 20. See also V. Y. Mudimbe, *The Invention of Africa*, 171–72.

45 Mpase, *Au service d'un Congo*, 298 and "Hommage à Patrice Lumumba," *Afrique chrétienne* 6, no. 35 (September 1967): 10.

46 UGEC-Lovanium, "Manifeste pour l'Université Lovanium," November 3, 1967, Tervuren.

47 See Benoit Verhaegen, "Eloge de l'université," February 1967, PDM.

48 Mukendi, *Enterrons les zombies*, 225.

49 "University Student Discontent in Kinshasa," January 19, 1968, p. 1, CFP, 1967–69, Box 356, NARA.

50 François Kandolo, personal interview, recorded, Kinshasa, October 12, 2007.

51 For a detailed chronology of the events of January and February 1968, see Centre de Recherche et d'Information Socio-Politique, "Contestation ou stagnation étudiante au Congo," *Travaux Africains* 79 (September 1968): 1–20.

52 UGEC, "Communiqué du comité exécutif national," January 18, 1968, Gérard-Libois Papers, MRAC.

53 Inspection de la police de la ville de Kinshasa, "Informations recueillies à la date du 13 mars 1968," March 14, 1968, DP. At the same time, Mulelist rebels in Brazzaville released a pamphlet that denounced Mobutu as "an agent of the CIA, well-known reactionary, and murderer of Lumumba" ("Message du commissaire politique du front de l'ouest et du détachement Lumumba de l'Armée Populaire de Libération du Congo-Kinshasa," January 1968, DP).

54 Agence Congolaise de Presse, "Subversion à l'Université Lovanium," January 16, 1968, DP.

55 See Marc Lagneau, letter to L. Dupire, DP; and "Notes sur la position de l'université vis-à-vis des associations ou groupements d'étudiants," January 30, 1968, Guy Malengreau Papers, UCL. During his meeting with Tshibangu, Mobutu reportedly told him that he "would not permit student demonstrations until at least the year 2000" (American embassy in Kinshasa, telegram to the secretary of state, January 20, 1968, CFP 1967–1969, Box 356, NARA). What seems to have particularly angered Mobutu was what he perceived as a lack of respect on the part of the students; and one of the several students arrested at Lovanium in January 1968

included Joseph Kalala, the editor of the student satirical newspaper *Le Furet* (Joseph Kalala, personal interview, recorded, Kinshasa, October 19, 2007).

56 Paul Demunter, "Les relations entre le mouvement étudiant et le régime politique congolais: Le colloque de Goma," *Travaux Africains du CRISP* 126 (April 1971): 7. On the torture that Kalonji was allegedly subjected to in front of Mobutu, see François-Médard Mayengo, personal interview, recorded, Kinshasa, August 3, 2011. In a memo about the event shared with the campus community, Lovanium's rector, Tharcisse Tshibangu, mentioned he was also present when Kalonji was interrogated in front of Mobutu, but he stopped short of describing the conditions of the interrogation. See Comité de direction, "Avis aux étudiants," February 22, 1968, Lovanium Papers, UNIKIN.

57 See UGEC, "Répression en milieu congolais (Kinshasa) en Belgique," 1972, DP. The Belgian Sûreté was very careful to document Congolese student activities, both in the Congo and in Belgium. See, for instance, Ludovic Caeymaex, letter to Jean d'Ursel, March 21, 1968, AD.

58 See Jean-Baptiste Mulemba, personal interview, recorded, Kinshasa, August 2, 2011; and Matala Mukadi, *Dans la tourmente de la dictature*.

59 UGEC-Bruxelles, "N'Kanza Dolomingu, Kalonji Tshibola: Libération," June 30, 1968, UGEC Papers, ULB; Henri Badibanga, personal interview, recorded, Kinshasa, April 15, 2010; Célestin Luanghy, personal interview, recorded, Kinshasa, October 6, 2010; Jean-Baptiste Mulemba, personal interview, recorded, Kinshasa, July 27, 2011; Emile Ilunga, personal interview, recorded, Kinshasa, July 18, 2011; Ambroise Kalabela Misombo, personal interview, unrecorded, Liège, August 27, 2009; Raphaël Ghenda, personal interview, unrecorded, Kinshasa, June 30, 2011. The most important student organization to emerge from the suppression of UGEC was the Etudiants Congolais Progressistes, whose leadership, in 1977, joined the Front de Libération National du Congo in the context of the Shaba wars that spectacularly relaunched the idea of a possible victorious armed insurrection, a decade after the Mulelist and Simba rebellions. On the FLNC and the Shaba wars, see Kennes and Larmer, *Katangese Gendarmes*, 119–44.

60 Jean Ilunga Kabese, letter to *L'Eclair*, January 18, 1968, DP.

61 J. Kalombo and R. C. Kalala, "Procès-verbal de la réunion du 29 Janvier 1968," January 29, 1968, UNIKIN.

62 AGEL, "Colloque du 26 mars au 6 avril," April 1968, UNIKIN.

63 See "Rapport des principales activités de l'association d'amitié entre les peuples en 1968," February 10, 1969, IUSY Papers, IISH.

64 Vaïsse, *Documents diplomatiques: 1968*, 2:383–84.

65 Mobutu, *Paroles du président*.

66 Schatzberg, *Political Legitimacy*.

67 This was not the end of the story. A few days later, some of the students who had met with Mobutu in July to ask for N'Kanza's release published the memorandum that they had presented to the president. Although Mobutu tolerated hearing their criticisms in private, he viewed the public

circulation of the text as an outright attack and banished N'Kanza to his village for ten years before making him a member of the political bureau of the MPR.

68 See, for instance, Aubert Mukendi's description of his experience physical and psychological torture, constant diarrhea, and near madness during his imprisonment in 1964 and 1965. Mukendi, *Enterrons les zombies*.

69 See Ferguson, "Invisible Humanism."

70 CRISP, "Contestation ou stagnation étudiante au Congo?," *Travaux Africains* 79 (September 1968): 13–16.

Nine. A Postcolonial Massacre and Caporalisation in Mobutu's Congo

1 "Student Flare-Up," telegram from the American consulate in Lubumbashi to the Department of State, May 28, 1968, General Records of the Department of State, CFP, 1967–69, Box 356, NARA. As in Lovanium in 1964, discontent over food triggered the Lubumbashi protests. Students were upset about the lack of diversity at the campus restaurant and felt angered when the rector said that they should be happy to be given the same food as students in Belgian universities. François Lufuluabo, personal interview, recorded, Kinshasa, October 14, 2007.

2 Caporalisation, derived from the military rank of caporal, was notably used in relation to the military coups in Africa and to the struggle to disalienate education in the aftermath of 1968. Caporalisation is literally a form of subalternization. It can be compared to the concept of commandement, which Achille Mbembe has used as paradigmatic of the post-colony (see Mbembe, *On the Postcolony*, 24–65).

3 Robert McBride, "Kisangani: New Rector Named for Université Officielle du Congo," airgram to the Department of State, July 25, 1968, and "Kisangani: University Students End 48-Hour Strike," airgram to the Department of State, December 27, 1968, General Records of the Department of State, CFP, 1967–69, Box 356, NARA.

4 Quoted in Dworkin, *Congo Love Song*, 274.

5 *Discours prononcé par le citoyen A. R. Kithima, Ministre de l'Education Nationale, lors de l'ouverture de l'année académique 1968–1969 à l'Université Lovanium* (Kinshasa: Université Lovanium de Kinshasa, 1968).

6 After learning of the students' heckling of Kithima, Mobutu shut Lovanium down and suspended the payment of student scholarships. The university was only authorized to reopen after the security services arrested eight students, identified as the "ringleaders" behind Kithima's heckling. Detained for a few weeks, these students were ultimately "pardoned" on the third anniversary of Mobutu's coup. See "Congo (K) Government Clamps Down on Lovanium Students," telegram to the Department of State, November 1, 1968, and "Release of Lovanium Students," telegram to the Secretary of State, November 22, 1968, General Records of the Department of State, CFP, 1967–69, Box 356, NARA.

7 US Consulate in Lubumbashi, "University Academic Year Opens," telegram to the US embassy in Kinshasa, November 4, 1968, General Records of the Department of State, CFP, 1967–69, Box 356, NARA.

8 State and academic authorities regularly blamed these left-wing faculty members (many of them junior) for radicalizing Congolese campuses. Yet, students still very much acted autonomously from these faculty members and rarely consulted with them when staging protests (Jean-Claude Willame, personal interview, recorded, Brussels, December 2, 2009; Laurent Monnier, personal interview, recorded, Brussels, December 8, 2009).

9 "La situation des étudiants à Lovanium (point de vue d'un chrétien)," unsigned memo to Lovanium's board, July 27, 1969, LUA.

10 René Deckers, "Université Officielle du Congo, discours de rentrée," October 21, 1968, UNILU. The reference to Bantu values suggests a familiarity with the colonial library. After all, it was in Katanga that the Catholic missionary Placide Tempels wrote his famous treatise on *Bantu Philosophy*. On the place of Tempels's work in the colonial library, see Mudimbe, *Parables and Fables*.

11 In his speech at Lovanium, Kithima had asked students to dedicate a few hours every day to teaching people in underprivileged neighborhoods how to read, write, and count. Rector Tshibangu shared the same views and considered that a focus on "human formation," which meant encouraging volunteering among students, was an appropriate response to student protests. See "University Melting Pot," *The Times*, November 24, 1969, 41.

12 Anastase Nzeza, personal interview, recorded, Kinshasa, June 1, 2010; Elisabeth Mudimbe-Boyi, personal interview, unrecorded, Abu Dhabi, April 7, 2019.

13 The name of Makeba's first grandchild, a boy born a few months before her visit to Kinshasa, was emblematic of the singer's political imagination and certainly resonated with the students at Lovanium: he was called Nelson Lumumba.

14 On Makeba as a fashion icon for Black women across the Atlantic, see Ford, *Liberated Threads*.

15 The proportion of foreigners remained rather high among female students, with notably a sizable contingent from Biafra. Congolese male students expressed frustration at the sexual politics around the foreign female students because male peers who originated from the same countries as these women often actively prevented them from developing romantic relationships with Congolese: Alexandre Luba, personal interview, recorded, Lubumbashi, November 14, 2010; Célestin Kabuya Lumuna Sando, personal interview, recorded, Kinshasa, November 3, 2009.

16 Pierre-Aimé Mobembo, "Dans le roc de mon chemin," unpublished manuscript, [1971], nonpaginated, private collection. On sexism at Lovanium, see also Nyunda ya Rubango, "De Lovanium à la Kasapa via caserne."

17 There was only one publicly identified romantic couple among students on campus in the late 1960s, which everybody referred to as les amours célèbres, after the title of a popular French comedy starring Brigitte Bardot and Alain Delon. Jean-Baptiste Sondji, personal interview, unrecorded, Kinshasa, July 28, 2011. On accusations of snobbery and arrogance waved at Congolese female students, see Comhaire-Sylvain, *Femmes de Kinshasa*, 249–51.

18 See, for instance, "Les dix commandements de l'AGECE," *Le Furet, Canard de Lovanium* 13 (April 1965): 5.

19 Antoinette Bwanga Zinga (formerly Da Silva), personal interview, unrecorded, Kinshasa, October 15, 2007. Mudimbe took inspiration of this gendered imaginary for his novel *Le bel immonde*, centered on a female student at Lovanium who becomes the lover of a minister. On Lovanium's sexual culture, see also Kalulambi, "Sex@mour et pouvoir." On the intersection of generational and social tensions with sexual competition in Dar es Salaam around the same period, see Ivaska, *Cultured States*.

20 Grégoire Muteba, personal interview, recorded, Lubumbashi, September 28, 2007; Tambwe ya Kasimba, personal interview, recorded, Kinshasa, October 4, 2007.

21 Alexandre Luba, personal interview, recorded, Lubumbashi, November 14, 2010. Stanley Mika had led a contingent of the Congolese national army that fought against the Katanga secession between 1960 and 1963. Afterward, he became the head of the secret services in Lubumbashi. At the time, an American journalist described him as the "most powerful man" in Katanga, a "smooth 33 year old" known for his ruthlessness and love of fine restaurants and dancing clubs (Anthony Lewis, "Gaiety in a Congo City," *New York Times*, August 20, 1966, 7). Mobutu then took him onboard alongside him in Kinshasa. On his surveillance work at Lovanium and his relationship with his student girlfriend, see Kabamba and Kasulula, *Rapport sur les assassinats*, 87. And on two well-known male students who served as Mobutu's ears on campus, see Monguya, *Histoire secrète*, 155–56.

22 Yvonne Nsansa, personal interview, recorded, Kinshasa, December 2, 2010; Marie-Thérèse Mulanga, personal interview, recorded, Kinshasa, November 30, 2010; Elisabeth Boyi, personal interview, unrecorded, Abu Dhabi, March 31, 2019.

23 On the contradictions in Mobutu's discourse about female emancipation, see Mianda, "Du Congo des évolués"; and Covington, *Gesture and Power*, 137–86.

24 Josette Shaje, who brought up the importance of Kanza in her own path toward higher education also mentioned her own mother—an active member of the female section of the Republic's Volunteer Corps (CVR) in Kinshasa—to illustrate how the Mobutu regime offered opportunities for women to participate (Josette Shaje, personal interview, recorded, Kinshasa, December 6, 2010).

25 "Nombre d'étudiants à l'Université Lovanium de Kinshasa de 1954 à 1968," n.d., PP.

26 In 1968, an anonymous pamphlet called on students at Lovanium to refuse to participate in a research project conducted by German social scientists who were visiting the campus to investigate the students' sociopolitical attitudes. The pamphlet denounced their research as a co-lonial attempt to turn the Congo's future elite into guinea pigs. See Dias et al., *Les étudiants universitaires congolais*, 19–20.

27 A. R. Kithima Bin Ramazani, personal interview, recorded, Kinshasa, November 2, 2009.

28 See Paul Demunter, "Les relations entre le mouvement étudiant et le régime politique congolais: Le colloque de Goma," *Etudes africaines du CRISP*, T. A. 126 (April 1971).

29 A. R. Kithima, "Colloque National de l'enseignement supérieur, discours d'ouverture," February 15, 1969, PDM.

30 Bernadette Lacroix, personal interview, recorded, Brussels, August 13, 2009. See also Lacroix, *Pouvoirs et structures*.

31 Demunter, "Les relations entre le mouvement étudiant et les régimes politiques congolais," 20.

32 See *Le MPR a deux ans* (Kinshasa, 1969).

33 A former seminarian whose path to priesthood had been stopped after he advocated for a radical Africanization of theology and liturgy, Milingo had come to Lovanium with a strong rebellious spirit. Valérien Milingo, personal interview, recorded, Kinshasa, November 5, 2009.

34 Alice Makanda-Kuseke, personal interview, recorded, Brussels, Janu-ary 28, 2011.

35 Mudimbe, *Carnets d'Amérique*, 54. Readings that present student protests as apolitical because they focused on living conditions are therefore prob-lematic. See, for instance, Bechtolsheimer, "Breakfast with Mobutu," 106–7.

36 G. Sambwa, letter to Rector Tshibangu, February 26, 1969, UNIKIN.

37 Pierre-Aimé, "Dans le roc de mon chemin," unpaginated manuscript.

38 See Lacroix, *Pouvoirs et structures*, 77.

39 Some former students believe that N'Singa reached out to Kandolo after becoming aware of the incoming march to explicit warn the AGEL leader of the consequences of such a public manifestation of defiance vis-à-vis Mobutu: Thomas Makamu, personal interview, recorded, Kinshasa, May 24, 2010; Miatudila Malonga, personal interview, recorded, Rock-ville, Maryland, April 3, 2012. One of the reasons for Mobutu's ner-vousness about street protests was the precedent of the trois glorieuses insurrection that had overthrew President Fulbert Youlou from power in Brazzaville in August 1963. See Kamitatu, *La grande mystification*, 257.

40 Alice Makanda-Kuseke, personal interview, recorded, Brussels, Janu-ary 28, 2011; Valérien Milingo, personal interview, recorded, Kinshasa, April 18, 2010. Milingo's jaws and dentition were badly damaged and he still suffered the stigmas at the time of our interview.

41 Célestin Kabuya Lumuna Sando, personal interview, November 3, 2009. See also Gambembo, "De Lovanium à l'Université de Kinshasa," 67–76; and "Les événements du 4 juin 1969 à Kinshasa et leurs répercussions: Chronologie, informations, témoignages," June 28, 1969, tapuscript, PDM.

42 See the description of these events in Majambu, *Concours et circonstances*, 157–58. Talking to the US ambassador, the vice-minister of interior, Denis Sakombi, suggested that soldiers' inexperience in dealing with urban protests caused the massacre (Sheldon B. Vance, "Lovanium Students," telegram to the Department of State, September 18, 1969, NARA, CFP 1967–69, Box 356). Yet, American diplomats believed that Mobutu had "ordered military units to clobber the students without mercy" (Herman Cohen, "Lovanium Students Take the Street," telegram to the Department of State, June 6, 1969, CFP 1967–69, Box 356, NARA).

43 Mika continued to work closely with Mobutu after the massacre, serving as the head of the president's personal security service. See, for instance, L. Cayemaex, "Visite royale en République Démocratique du Congo: 17 juin–1er juillet 1970," June 1970, 18659, AD. See also Willame, *Patrimonialism and Political Change*, 136.

44 Omer Marchal, "Les matinées kinoises," *Spécial*, June 11, 1969, 12–14. Belgian officials also echoed this rhetoric in various notes. See, for instance, Emile Indekeu, "Telegram n. 1585 vertrouwelijk mt 15/78: Incidenten Kinshasa," June 5, 1969; and André Raes, letter to J. d'Ursel, June 25, 1969, 18518/14, AD.

45 Students at Lovanium compiled a list of seventeen victims, while an anonymous report estimated that forty-two protesters had been killed across the city and fifty more had suffered gun wounds. See Herman Cohen, "Congolese Student Situation," telegram to the Department of State, June 10, 1969, CFP, 1967–69, Box 356, NARA and "De la manifestation estudiantine du 4 juin 1969," unsigned letter, n.d., Jules Gérard Libois Papers, MRAC. See also "Liste des victimes," manuscript note, n.d., PP. Testifying at the National Sovereign Conference in 1991, Léon Kengo-wa-Dondo, who in 1969 served as general prosecutor, established the death toll at forty. See Kabamba and Kasulula, *Rapport sur les assassinats*, 87. Besides students, soldiers also took the lives of several children and teenagers who joined the march. An anonymous source mentioned, for instance, that five of the protesters killed at the Victoire roundabout in Matonge were secondary school students (see Léopold Caeymaex, letter to the Pierre Harmel, June 17, 1969, 18518/14, AD; see also Jacques Mangalaboyi, "1969: Massacres des étudiants à Kinshasa," Congonet Radio, June 4, 2009, congonetradio.blogspot.com/2009/06 /1969-massacre-des-etudiants-kinshasa.html).

46 "Le tract 'maoiste' de Révolution," *Remarques africaines* 388 (June 1969): 276–77.

47 For details on Sapwe's role in the assassination of Lumumba, see De Witte, *The Assassination of Lumumba*, 93–152. On his participation to

counterinsurgency operations in the mid-1960s, see "Congo Insurgents Said to Withdraw," *New York Times*, August 14, 1964, 1, 4. On his earlier background in colonial Katanga, see Tilman, "L'implantation du scoutisme," 136.

48 On necropower and the "nocturnal body" of politics, see Mbembe, *Necropolitics*. On the connection made at the time of the events between Mobutu's repression of student protests and colonial violence, see Martin Klein, "Congo (K) Simmers," *Africa Report*, January 1, 1970, 10–12.

49 "Student Problems Congo," telegram to the Department of State, June 9, 1969, CFP, 1967–69, Box 356, NARA; P. Vercauteren, telegram to Belgian Ministry of Foreign Affairs, June 5, 1969, AD; Robert Strand, "ULC Vice Rector Comments on June Student Protests," airgram to the Department of State, June 18, 1969, CFP, 1967–69, Box 356, NARA.

50 See Comité de Solidarité avec le Peuple Congolais, "Les événements du 4 juin 1969 à Kinshasa et leurs répercussions: Chronologie, informations, témoignages," June 28, 1969, PDM.

51 J. M. Lubabu and Sambay Mukendi, "Qui est le cerveau de la manifestation du 4 juin à Kin?," *L'étoile*, June 25, 1964, 5.

52 The government seems to also have given some credit to groundless accusations from Nigerian students at Lovanium that their Biafran peers had masterminded the protest. See Herman Cohen, "Biafran Students in Congo (K) to Ivory Coast," airgram to the Department of State, June 26, 1969, CFP, 1967–69, Box 356, NARA.

53 See, for instance, Emile Indekeu à Pierre Harmel, "Professeur Verhaegen/ Lovanium," June 20, 1969, AD, 18518-14.

54 See Verhaegen, *L'enseignement universitaire*, 95–118. Echoes of Verhaegen's talk may be seen in some of the literature produced by the CEK in preparation for the June march. See Comité de Solidarité avec le Peuple Congolais, "Les événements du 4 juin 1969 à Kinshasa et leurs répercussions: Chronologie, informations, témoignages," June 28, 1969, pp. 20–21, PDM.

55 Daniel Gambembo, personal interview, recorded, Kinshasa, October 2, 2010.

56 The specter of tribalism, which was not mentioned at the trial, was brought up in an anonymous tract, most certainly produced by Mobutu's secret police, that circulated widely in Kinshasa at the end of June. It argued that Luba students from the Kasai had manipulated the student movement and that the June 4 march was part of a broader plot to impose a Luba domination over the country. "Aux étudiants des provinces [du] Katanga, Kasai Occidental, Kivu, Bandundu, Orientale, Equateur, Kongo-Central," anonymous tract, June 1969, PP; see also "Balubas Blamed for Student Disorders," telegram to the Department of State, June 19, 1969, CFP, 1967–69, Box 356, NARA.

57 Alice Makanda-Kuseke, personal interview, recorded, Brussels, January 28, 2011.

58 On the father chief figure, see Schatzberg, *Political Legitimacy.*

59 Tshungu Bamesa, personal interview, recorded, Kinshasa, September 22, 2007; Médard Kayamba, personal interview, recorded, Lubumbashi, September 27, 2007; Célestin Kabuya Lumuna Sando, personal interview, unrecorded, Kinshasa, April 3, 2010. While the cancres were relatively isolated, the group's revolutionary intentions mattered in themselves (especially given the volatile political climate of the time). It is impossible to know what the cancres would have done if they had been given more time, but some of their thinking brings to mind the types of discussions that happened in the student circles that were paving way for the Ethiopian revolution at the same time (see Zeleke, *Ethiopia in Theory,* 87–147).

60 Because the curriculum in medicine was longer than in other disciplines, students from that faculty greatly contributed to the continuity of the student movement and to processes of transmission from one generation of activists to another. Tshungu Bamesa Zakama, personal interview, recorded, Kinshasa, October 19, 2007.

61 Guy Yangu, personal interview, recorded, Kinshasa, June 1, 2010.

62 Pondja, together with Moreno Kinkela, another member of the committee, had been active in the Ligue des jeunes vigillants, an anti-imperialist group that had functioned in Kinshasa in 1965 and 1966. The league organized several violent protests in front the embassies of Belgium, Portugal, and the United Kingdom in November 1965. After Mobutu's coup, several animators of the league joined the CVR, while others attempted to create a clandestine Communist Party. Kinkela's older brother, the labor activist François Mayala (see preface), was one of the league's animators; he introduced the young men to key figures in Kinshasa's Marxist scene (including the UGEC president N'Kanza Dolomingu and the writer Aimé Diakanwa) and connected them to left-wingers in Congo-Brazzaville.

63 Kinkela-vi-Kan'Sy, *Contestation et prison: Mémoire de bagne d'un étudiant sous Mobutu,* unpublished manuscript (2003), 16.

64 Jean-Baptiste Sondji, personal interview, recorded, Kinshasa, October 4, 2007.

65 Kinkela-vi-Kan'Sy, *Contestation et prison,* 35–36 and Jean-Baptiste Sondji, personal interview, recorded, Kinshasa, July 28, 2011. Baudouin saw Lovanium as a major source of Belgian influence in postcolonial Congo and the request to visit the Inspired Hill had come from him directly. The Congolese authorities initially resisted this demand, which the Belgians interpreted as a sign of Mobutu's fear of the students, but they ultimately agreed to accommodate the king's desire after more insistence on the part of the Belgians. André Schöller, "Rapport annexe confidentiel," April 16, 1970, 18808/1, AD.

66 C. M. Sikitele and D. M. Nsabimana, "Lovanium 4 juin 1970, récit d'un anniversaire," *Présence universitaire* 33 (1970): 36–41.

67 Majambu, *Concours et circonstances,* 163.

68 Jean-Baptiste Sondji, personal interview, unrecorded, Kinshasa, July 19, 2011.

69 See Pain, *Kinshasa*, 87–100. See also Young and Turner, *Rise and Decline*, 276–325.

70 A. Cahen, "Renseignements émanant des services de la Sûreté belge: Relations République démocratique du Congo–République populaire du Congo," April 8, 1971, p. 6, AD.

71 Kinkela-vi-Kan'Sy, *Contestation et prison*, 80.

72 One of the organizers of the June 4 march managed to get elected as the president of the section of the JMPR at the University of Lubumbashi, where he had just transferred (Prosper Malangu Mposhi, personal interview, recorded, Lubumbashi, October 2, 2007).

73 See Devisch, "What Is an Anthropologist?," 92–102.

74 Jacques Paulus, "Rapport des rencontres du Home XX (mai–juin 71)," June 25, 1971, Vander Schueren Papers, LUA.

75 Pascal Ntsomo Payanzo et al., "Mémorandum du Mouvement populaire de la révolution, section de l'ULC aux membres du conseil d'administration de l'ULC," December 10, 1970, SWP.

76 Z. Lutumba-Buzangu, "Université libre du Congo, procès-verbal n°01-71 du Conseil rectoral du 22 mars 1971," March 22, 1971, SWP.

77 Weissman had participated in antiwar activism and in the civil rights movement in New York. The introductory course he was teaching that semester went from Augustine to Mao. The authorities presented his syllabus as a proof that he was an "anti-American American" who pushed students to rebel. See Stephen Weissman, "My Coming of Age in the Congo," unpublished manuscript, SWP.

78 Mathurin Dienayame, a Marxist activist well known on Brazzaville's left, participated in the event. He had been invited for his expertise and because the cancres wished to develop their connections with existing pockets of opposition to Mobutu outside the campus. See Kinkela vi-Kan'Sy, *Contestation et prison*, 25–26; and Yangu Sukama, *Les manifestations des étudiants*, 49–50.

79 The origin of the pamphlet is a highly disputed question among former student activists. Several have argued that two medical students, Jean-Baptiste Sondji and Célestin Kabuya, authored the text, something they vigorously denied. See Jean-Baptiste Sondji, personal interview, recorded, Kinshasa, October 4, 2007; and Célestin Kabuya Lumuna Sando, personal interview, recorded, Kinshasa, October 5, 2007.

80 Nkiko Munya Rugero, personal interview, recorded, Lubumbashi, October 3, 2007.

81 Mama Yemo had often been presented as someone who moderated Mobutu's authoritarian impulses and her death coincided with a clear acceleration in Mobutu's cult of personality. On this point, see Young and Turner, *Rise and Decline*, 174.

82 Médard Kayamba, personal interview, recorded, Lubumbashi, September 27, 2007. The CND agent had been seen on campus the day before to supervise a tour of Lovanium by Jacques Foccart, the late general De Gaulle's main adviser for African affairs. Although he was an extremely influential man (and the godfather of the so-called Françafrique), Foccart maintained a rather low public profile. His visit at Lovanium apparently went unnoticed by student activists. In his memoirs, Foccart even noted that he was well received by the students he talked to and to whom he shared his views that Congolese students had specific obligations of dedication to their studies because of their role as their country's future elite (Foccart in this way recycled a discourse quite common among Mobutu's ministers who claimed that African students could not have the luxury of vain protests like their peers in Europe and America because of their greater responsibilities toward their nation). Foccart noted how surprised he was that students reacted positively to this discourse: "It is rather extraordinary to be able, in 1971, to preach to students in such a way and be warmly applauded" (Foccart, *Dans les bottes*, 738).

83 Thysman later told Belgian officials that he had considered the students' request to have the tomb blessed ridiculous but that he had complied because of the importance of "symbolism among the Bantus" (A. Lebrun, "Résumé de la rencontre avec le Père Thysman," June 14, 1971, ID-135, AD).

84 See Nyunda, "Du 4 juin à la genèse."

85 Raymond Thysman, untitled statement, June 9, 1971, PP.

86 In a public statement, Mobutu called Thysman an anarchist who "was nostalgic for the trouble times in our nation's history" and was known for having taken part in many "obscure manifestations" in the past ("Le curé belge de Lovanium est expulsé du Congo," *Le Soir*, June 10, 1971, 2). Father Thysman, both at the time and years later, contested his having been at all involved in student politics besides his participation in the symbolic burial (Raymond Thysman, personal interview, unrecorded, Louvain-la-Neuve, September 5, 2009). Still, he was expelled from the Congo, while his Congolese assistant, Father Munzihirwa, joined the students in the army when they were conscripted by the regime by force a few days later (see De Dorlodot, "L'engagement politique").

87 On the impact of the draft on the wives of married students, see Vansina, "Mwasi's Trials." In Lubumbashi, students decided to enlist in the army, hoping that the state would not have the capacity to cope with the massive influx of new recruits and may reconsider the forced enrollment of the Lovaniards. After two days of protest by the students, the government agreed to open a recruiting office but announced that each student could choose in confidence to either proceed with the enrollment or to sign a pledge of obedience to the MPR that would allow them to continue their studies. Fewer than 300 students opted for the military service and more

than 2,800 decided to stay at the university. The activist core denounced trickeries, corruption, and betrayals. Some wanted to pull back from the enrollment, but this was not an option and they were immediately flown to the military base of Kitona on the Atlantic Ocean (Stanislas Maroyi, personal interview, recorded, Kisangani, October 12, 2010). See also Luabeya, *Une jeunesse congolaise*, 40–84.

88 See in particular Mwifi, "*Mésaventure d'une étudiante*"; Marie-Madeleine Mwifi, personal interview, recorded, Kinshasa, July 19, 2015; Noël Obotela, personal interview, recorded, Kinshasa, September 10, 2010; Jacob Sabakinu, personal interview, unrecorded, Kinshasa, July 11, 2011; Joseph Yaone, personal interview, recorded, Kinshasa, November 30, 2010; Josette Shaje, personal interview, recorded, Kinshasa, December 6, 2010; and Damase Ndembe, personal interview, unrecorded, Kinshasa, September 9, 2010.

89 André Yoka, personal interview, recorded, Kinshasa, September 20, 2007; Dieudonné Kadima Nzuji, personal interview, recorded, Brazzaville, September 22, 2010; Léopold Mbuyi Kapuya, personal interview, recorded, Kinshasa, November 1, 2010.

90 See Monaville, "June 4th 1969."

91 Young and Turner, *Rise and Decline*, 174. See also Mobutu, *Dignité pour l'Afrique*, 22–24; and Langellier, *Mobutu*, 7–16.

92 "Communiqué de l'AFP à partir des révélations de Mobutu faites à l'ACP," June 10, 1971, ID-135, AD.

93 The army invited the students to adopt a new identity. Ultimately, many of them sympathized with soldiers, and several stayed their whole career in the army. Yet, as one interviewee expressed sharply, the new recruits remained painfully aware that the stultifying discipline, the quotidian humiliations, and the "toilet drills," when corporals selected soldiers who had to defecate on command in front of the troop, were meant to "break" students and "crush their personalities" (Salamu Yamba Yamba, personal interview, recorded, Kinshasa, October 5, 2007). On scatology and the "aesthetic of vulgarity" as constitutive of political power and the "intimacy of tyranny" in postcolonial Africa, see Mbembe, *On the Postcolony*, 102–72.

94 Accusations of Maoist allegiances resurfaced as in 1969, but the prosecutors also focused on the students' commemoration of the Paris Commune to make their case about the "import of foreign subversive ideology." See Kinkela vi-Kan'Sy, *Contestation et prison*, 75–79.

95 They included members of the Ligue congolaise pour la paix et l'amitié avec les peuples (LICOPA), a philo-Soviet group created in 1962 and that had somehow escaped the ban on political organizations. Together with Nicolas Olenga, a general in the Simba rebel army that captured Stanleyville in 1964, LICOPA members were convicted for plotting against Mobutu's life during a highly publicized trial at the beginning of

August 1971, only days before the cancres' own trial (Tharcisse Kayembe, personal interview, unrecorded, Kinshasa, November 20, 2010). At the center of the prosecution's case were a series of cartographic coordinates: the supposed backing of the group by the Brazzaville embassy in Kinshasa, alleged connections to revolutionaries in Cameroon, written correspondence with Chinese, Cuban, and East German associations, and subversive contacts forged by LICOPA president Jean-Willy Tshimbila during his years of exile in Karthoum and Cairo. For more, see Albert Kisonga, *45 ans*, 131–32; "Ouverture du premier procès des réseaux subversifs," *Le monde*, August 17, 1971, 3; and J. R. Vanden Bloocks, "Samenzwering tegen republiek," telegram n. 1949, Kinshasa, July 8, 1971, AD. On the cancres' experience of imprisonment, see notably Kabuya Lumuna Sando, *Les prisonniers du président*.

96   J. R. Vanden Bloocks, telegram n. 2225, Kinshasa, August 3, 1971, AD; K. Philipps, untitled note, August 5, 1971, Foreign and Commonwealth Office Papers, FCO 31-804, NA.

97   On more recent associations between university science and the worlds of occultism and sorcery in Kinshasa's popular imagination, see Lambertz, *Seekers and Things*.

98   The later evolution of the Mobutu regime did not necessarily realize these totalitarian ambitions and some suggested that "while the party was to have, in theory, absorbed the state, in practice the reverse occurred" (Schatzberg, "*Fidélité au guide*").

99   The organization of daily singing and dancing sessions in praise of Mobutu, which became another iconic figure of caporalisation in Congo-Zaire, emerged in the aftermath of the 1971 crisis (see White, *Rumba Rules*, 65–96; and Covington, *Gesture and Power*, 137–64). Anicet Mobe has suggested that the creation of the General Commissioners Committee was the first act in Mobutu's caporalisation of intellectuals. See Mobe, "Intellectualités estudiantines," 117.

100   Tharcisse Tshibangu, "Rapport au Conseil d'administration," Kinshasa, July 21, 1971, Vander Schueren Papers, LUA.

101   Although the creation of UNACO was presented as a direct consequence of the events of June 1971, it had been decided several months beforehand, when Lovanium faced important financial problems that forced the Congolese government to raise its contribution to the Catholic university. See J. R. Vanden Bloockx, letter to Harmel, March 24, 1971, AD. Years earlier, Gillon had already envisioned the possibility of fusing certain disciplines across the different universities ("Procès-verbal de la 94e réunion du Conseil d'administration," November 4, 1967, PP).

102   Ndaywel, *Histoire générale*, 690–91.

103   The new rhetoric of the "search for authenticity" allowed the regime to retire its previous motto of "authentic nationalism," which evoked now-unwanted connections with the Congolese Lumumbist left but also to a

tricontinentalism explicitly rejected by Mobutu. See J. D. Mobutu, *Message du president de la république au parti frère du Sénégal, 14 février 1971* (Kinshasa: Ministère de l'information, 1971).

Epilogue

1 E. W. Lamy, "Mort de Lovanium," *Les Temps Modernes* 301–2 (1971): 374. Willame first arrived at Lovanium in 1962 at the age of twenty-four as a researcher at the Centres d'études politiques. In 1966, he moved to the University of California, Berkeley, where he immersed himself in student politics and obtained a doctorate in political science. He came back to Lovanium only weeks before the June 4, 1971, events (Jean-Claude Willame, personal interview, recorded, Brussels, December 2, 2009).

2 Vansina, *Living with Africa*, 163–66; Vansina, "Some Perceptions," 84. Vansina resigned from his visiting position at Lovanium because he believed that three of his students had been killed during the forced military draft (Jan Vansina, personal interviews, unrecorded, Madison, June 12, 2009).

3 Kangafu, *Demain la promotion*, 13–14. The anti-institutional ethos that transpired in Willame's call to destruction did feature in some speeches of Mobutu and members of his entourage at the time, who called for the abolition of schools and prisons, for instance. See Kengo, *Vers une société*.

4 Jacques Ali Risasi, the minister who oversaw the reform, had been a teaching assistant in psychology at Lovanium until February 1971. He wrote the first draft of the reform together with several politicians who were or had been active as university faculty or researchers, including Mario Cardoso, Paul Mushiete, Claude Mafema, Mabika Kalanda, Charles Bokonga, and Etienne Tshisekedi. The final version of the reform was adopted during a weeklong colloquium at the MPR's headquarters in Nsele to which all Congolese academics had been summoned.

5 *Discours prononcé par Mr. Mabika Klanda, recteur de l'Ecole Nationale d'Administration à l'occasion de l'ouverture de l'année académique 1967–1968* (Kinshasa: ENDA, 1967), 6.

6 For an important reappraisal of the politics of authenticity, see Van Beurden, *Authentically African*, 100–27.

7 Gambembo, Kazadi, and Mpinga, *Le nationalisme congolais*.

8 Daniel Gambembo, personal interview, recorded, Kinshasa, October 2, 2010. Both Gambembo and Mpinga served as directors of the MPR's party school in the 1970s; the latter was also prime minister (premier commissaire d'état) from 1977 to 1979.

9 Hull, "Education in Zaire," 151.

10 For instance, Kinyongo Jeki, "Le Zaïre en quête de son authenticité," March 22, 1974, Plevoets Papers. Some students also took part in the

Mobutist scholarship. Crawford Young remembered, for instance, that one of the brightest students he supervised during the two years he spent as faculty and dean at UNAZA in the early 1970s wrote his senior thesis on the charisma of Mobutu, "in which he firmly believed" (Crawford Young, personal communication, July 11, 2016).

11 See Bokonga, *La politique culturelle*; and Ndaywel, *Les années UNAZA* (particularly the following chapters: Ndaywel, "De Lovanium au campus de Lubumbashi"; Ngandu Nkashama, "La colonisation"; and Lufunda, "Eloge de l'UNAZA").

12 Kasereka, "L'authenticité comme cadre."

13 See Mudimbe, *L'autre face du royaume* and *L'odeur du père*. See also Kasereka, *L'Afrique, entre passé*, 139–63; Fraiture, *Mudimbe*, 50–79; and Robert Young, "Preface," in Sartre, *Colonialism and Neocolonialism*, viii–xix.

14 Bogumil Jewsiewicki, personal interview, unrecorded, Brussels, November 10, 2009. See also Bogumil Jewsiewicki, "Préface," in Ndwaywel, *Les années UNAZA*, 1:11–18.

15 See Ndaywel and Mudimbe-Boyi, *Images, mémoires et savoirs*, 757–812; and Fabian, *Ethnography as Commentary*, 1–3.

16 Jacob Sabakinu Kivulu, personal interview, unrecorded, Kinshasa, July 11, 2011. See also Nyunda, "Du 4 juin."

17 Mudimbe, *Les corps glorieux*, 79, 210–11. On Zairianization as the cause of a more general collapse of the infrastructure of the whole education system, see Lagae, De Raedt, and Sabakinu, "'Pour les écoles.'"

18 Erny, *Sur les sentiers de l'université*, 104.

19 Willame defined it "as a system of rule incorporating three fundamental and related elements: appropriation of public offices as the elite's primal source of status, prestige and reward; political and territorial fragmentation through the development of relationships based on primordial and personal loyalties, and the use of private armies, militias and mercenaries as instruments of rule." Willame, *Patrimonialism*, 2.

20 Willame, *Patrimonialism*, 163.

21 See, for instance, Nimer, "Congo Politics"; Willame, "Art of Misquotation"; Nimer, "Concerning Willame's Reply"; Janzen, "Review of *Patrimonialism*"; and Young, "Review of *Patrimonialism*."

22 See Jean Rymenam [pseud. of B. Verhaegen], "Le pouvoir absolu d'un militaire d'occasion," *Le Monde diplomatique*, December 1975, 10–11; Nzongola-Ntalaja, "The Continuing Struggle"; Schatzberg, *Politics and Class*; Elikia Mbokolo, "La triple stratification zaïroise," *Le Monde diplomatique*, November 1981, 21; Callaghy, *State-Society Struggle*; and Young and Turner, *Rise and Decline*. See also Bayart, *L'Etat en Afrique*, 114–17; Reno, "Congo"; Young, *The Postcolonial State*, 56–58; and De Villers, *Histoire du politique*, 208–36.

23 Mbembe, "Banality of Power," 30.

24 On dynamics of elite reproduction in today's Congo, see Trapido, "Masterless Men."

25 The two major literary texts about the massacre of June 4—André Yoka's *Le fossoyeur* and Pius Ngdandu Nkashama's *La mort faite homme*—are important contributions to a broader production on the imaginary and pedagogy of death and suffering in Congolese literature. Yoka's novella, dedicated to the memory of Symphorien Mwamba, approaches the massacre from the perspective of a gravedigger requisitioned by the army to bury the bodies of the victims of the march and who realizes that his own son is among the cadavers he has to make disappear; Ngandu's punctuation-less novel of confinement and mental alienation tells the existential travails of a jailed student leader. Sony Labou Tansi's *L'anté-peuple* is also emblematic of this literary genre. It does not directly engage with the massacre of June 4. Yet, its story begins in 1969 and focuses on a school director and Lovanium graduate in Kinshasa who finds himself plunged into an unstoppable cycle of suffering and death.

26 There were no student strikes at UNAZA until 1976. And even though the late 1970s were a more turbulent time, students' direct challenges to the regime only reappeared in 1989 and 1990 at the Universities of Kinshasa and Lubumbashi. On the latter campus, the state repression of dissent gave way to a new massacre on May 11, 1990 known as Lititi Mboka, which precipitated the chaotic period of the so-called democratic transition. See Abemba Bulaimu and Ntumba Lukunga, *Mouvements étudiants*; and Nzongola-Ntalaja, *The Congo*, 155–56.

27 Appadurai, *Modernity at Large*, 1–10.

28 See Gondola, "Dream and Drama"; and Trapido, *Breaking Rocks*.

29 See Lambertz, *Seekers and Things*.

30 See Yoon, "Figuring Africa and China."

31 See Pype, *Making Pentecostal Melodrama*, 29–32.

32 See Geenen, "Sleep Occupies No Space"; and De Boeck and Baloji, *Suturing the City*, 211–56.

33 See Rivers Ndaliko, *Necessary Noise*.

34 Biaya, "Société parallèle," 72–76, 79.

35 Fabian's theorization of coevalness, which emerges from a specific debate about writing in anthropology, is useful in this context. Fabian, *Time and the Other*.

36 See Yoka, "4 juin 1969."

37 André Yoka Mudiba Lye, personal interview, recorded, Kinshasa, September 20, 2007; Medard Kayamba, personal interview, recorded, Lubumbashi, September 27, 2007; Guy Yangu, personal interview, recorded, Kinshasa, June 1, 2010; Alexandre Luba, personal interview, recorded, Lubumbashi, November 14, 2010; Marie-Therese Mulanga, personal interview, recorded, Kinshasa, November 30, 2010; Polydor Muboyayi Mubanga, personal interview, recorded, Kinshasa, July 25,

2011; Jacques Mangalaboyi, personal interview, unrecorded, Lille, June 3, 2012. See also Yangu Sukama, *Les manifestations*, 7.

38 Roblès, *Montserrat*. World War II and the history of the anti-Nazi resistance in occupied France was an obvious subtext to the play (as was the case for Anouilh's *Antigone*), but so was the resistance to French colonialism in Indochina and Madagascar. See Freeman, *Theatres of War*, 88–102.

39 Elisabeth Mweya T'Olande, personal interview, recorded, Kinshasa, July 13, 2011.

40 See, for instance, Mweya, "Courrier des lecteurs," *Afrique chrétienne* 6, no. 2 (1967): 4.

41 Mweya, "Courrier d'Elisabeth," *Afrique chrétienne* 6, no. 9 (1967): 22.

42 Mweya, *Remous de feuilles*, 4. Ironically, Mweya's book was awarded the first Mobutu Sese Seko prize for poetry in 1972.

Archives

AA	Archives africaines, Service publique fédéral affaires étrangères, Brussels
ACIA	Archives du Centre-Interdiocésain, Kinshasa
AD	Archives diplomatiques, Service publique fédéral affaires étrangères, Brussels
AGR	Archives générales du royaume, Brussels
AN	Archives nationales, Paris
ARNACO-K	Archives nationales du Congo, Kikwit
BA	Bundesarchiv, Berlin
CARAN	Archives nationales de France, Paris
CARCOB	Centre des archives communistes en Belgique, Brussels
CEGES	Center for Historical Research and Documentation on War and Contemporary Society, Brussels
DP	Luc-Daniel Dupire papers, privately owned
GDA	General Directorate of Archives, Tirana
GMMA	George Meany Memorial Archives, AFL-CIO, Silver Spring, Maryland
HIA	Hoover Institute Archives, Stanford
IISH	International Institute of Social History, Amsterdam
KADOC	Documentation and Research Center on Religion, Culture and Society, Leuven
LOC	Library of Congress, Washington, DC
LUA	Leuven Universiteitsarchief, Leuven

MHSL	Minnesota Historical Society Library, Saint Paul
MRAC	Royal Museum for Central Africa, Contemporary History Section, Tervuren
NA	National Archives, London
NARA	United States National Archives and Records Administration, College Park, Maryland
PDM	Paul Demunter Papers, privately owned
PP	Maurice Plevoets Papers, UNIKIN
RAC	Rockefeller Archive Center, Sleepy Hollow, New York
SUL	Stanford University Libraries' Special Collections and University Archives, Stanford
SWP	Steven Weissman Papers, privately owned
UCL	Archives de l'Université catholique de Louvain, Louvain-la-Neuve
ULB	Archives de l'Université libre de Bruxelles, Brussels
UNA	United Nations Archives, New York
UNIKIN	Archives rectorales, Université de Kinshasa, Kinshasa
UNILU	Archives de l'Université de Lubumbashi, Lubumbashi

Interviews

Awaka, Augustin. Kinshasa, August 17, 2010.
Badibanga, Henri. Kinshasa, April 15, 2010.
Banza Hangakolwa, Delphin. Kinshasa, August 11, 2011.
Beltchika Kalubye, François. Kinshasa, July 22, 2011.
Bomboko, Justin-Marie. Kinshasa, November 6, 2009, and May 2, 2010.
Bongoma, Jacques. Kinshasa, July 5, 12, and 22, 2011.
Bongoy, Yvon. Kinshasa, December 12, 2010.
Bwanga Zinga (formerly Da Silva), Antoinette. Kinshasa, October 15, 2007.
Cros, François. Paris, February 12, 2011.
Dupire, Luc-Daniel. Brussels, August 17, 2012.
Ekwa, Martin. Kinshasa, December 7, 2010.
Elesse, Michel. Kinshasa, July 28, 2015.
Gambembo Fumu a Utadi, Daniel. Kinshasa, October 2, 2010.
Ghenda, Raphaël. Kinshasa, June 30, 2011.
Ilunga, Emile. Kinshasa, July 18, 2011, and September 5, 2011.
Indongo-Imbanda Isseewanga, Paul. Berlin, April 5, 2011.
Jewsiewicki, Bogumil. Brussels, November 10, 2009.
Kabayidi, Paul-Henri. Brussels, February 12, 2011.
Kabeya, Jean-Paul. Kinshasa, March 28, 2010.
Kabeya, Tshikuku. Kinshasa, August 3, 2010.
Kabongo, Isidore. Kinshasa, February 15, 2010.
Kabongo, Paul. Kinshasa, July 8, 2011.

Kabuya Lumuna Sando, Célestin. Kinshasa, October 5, 2007, November 3, 2009, and April 3, 2010.
Kadima Nzuji Mukala, Dieudonné. Brazzaville, September 22, 2010.
Kalabela Misombo, Ambroise. Liège, August 27, 2009.
Kalala, Joseph. Kinshasa, October 19, 2007.
Kandolo, François. Kinshasa, October 12, 2007.
Kayamba, Médard. Lubumbashi, September 27, 2007.
Kayembe, Tharcisse. Kinshasa, November 20, 2010.
Kimoni Ivay, Valentin. Kikwit, May 31, 2010.
Kithima Bin Ramazani, Alphonse-Roger. Kinshasa, November 2, 2009, April 6, 2010, April 22, 2010, and April 30, 2010.
Kitutu Oleontwa, Stéphane. Kinshasa, November 25, 2010.
Lacroix, Bernadette. Brussels, August 13, 2009.
Liétard, Edouard. Kinshasa, August 17, 2010.
Losembe Batwanyele (formerly Cardoso), Mario. Kinshasa, July 23, 2015.
Luanghy, Célestin., Kinshasa, October 6, 2010.
Luba, Alexandre. Lubumbashi, November 14, 2010.
Lubuele, Jules. Kinshasa, March 17, 2010.
Lufuluabo, François. Kinshasa, October 14, 2007.
Makamu, Thomas. Kinshasa, May 24, 2010.
Makanda Kuseke, Alice. Brussels, January 28, 2011.
Malangu Mposhi. Lubumbashi, October 2, 2007.
Mambo (formerly Santos), Thomas. Brussels, February 26, 2011.
Mangalaboyi, Jacques. Lille, June 3, 2012.
Maroyi, Stanislas. Kisangani, October 12, 2010.
Mayala, François. Kinshasa, August 10, 2010, and December 3, 2010.
Mayengo, François-Médard. Kinshasa, August 3, 2011.
Mbelolo Ya Mpiku. Kinshasa, unrecorded, July 11, 2015.
M'Bokolo, Elikia. Kinshasa, July 12 and September 3, 2010; Paris, July 6, 2021.
Mbuyi Kapuya Meleka, Léopold. Kinshasa, November 1, 2010.
Miatudila, Malonga. Rockville, April 3, 2012.
Mibamba, Zénon. Kinshasa, May 27, 2010, June 15, 2010, September 9, 2010, and July 13, 2011.
Milingo, Valérien. Kinshasa, October 6, 2007, November 5, 2009, April 18, 2010, April 30, 2010, and July 12, 2011.
Moke Motsüri, Eugène. Kinshasa, October 14, 2007.
Monnier, Laurent. Brussels, December 8, 2009.
Mpeye Nyango, Nestor. Kinshasa, April 6 and 10, 2010.
Mrazek, Rudolph. Ann Arbor, May 2, 2013.
Muboyayi Mubanga, Polydor. Kinshasa, July 25, 2011.
Mudimbe-Boyi, Elisabeth. Abu Dhabi, April 7, 2019.
Mugaruka, Richard. Kinshasa, November 3, 2009.
Mukendi, Germain. Liège, April 22, 2011.

Mukendi Ntite Kizito, Aubert. Paris, January 15, 2011.
Mukendi Wa Nsanga, Kalixte. Nouakchott, May 19–21, 2016.
Mukengechay, Grégoire. Berlin, April 6, 2011, and July 30, 2014.
Mulanga, Marie-Thérèse. Kinshasa, November 30, 2010.
Mulemba, Jean-Baptiste. Kinshasa, July 18, 2011, July 27, 2011, August 2, 2011, and July 21, 2015.
Mupapa Say, Michel-Ange. Kinshasa, September 6, 2010, and July 11, 2011.
Murairi, Jean-Baptsite. Brussels, December 30, 2019.
Mutamba Makombo, Jean-Marie. Kinshasa, November 8, 2009, and February 15, 2010.
Muteba, Grégoire. Lubumbashi, September 28, 2007.
Mweya T'olande, Elisabeth. Kinshasa, December 8, 2010, and July 13, 2011.
Mwifi, Mari-Madeleine. Kinshasa, July 19, 2015.
N'Dalla (Graille), Etienne. Brazzaville, March 31, 2010.
Ndaywel è Nziem, Isidore. Kinshasa, October 13, 2010, and July 27, 2011.
Ndembe Nsasi, Damase. Kinshasa, September 9, 2010.
Ndeshyo, Oswald. Recorded. Kinshasa, June 7, 2010.
Ndundu Kivuila, Joseph. Kinshasa, June 10, 2010.
Nkiko Munya Rugero. Kinshasa, October 3, 2007.
Nsansa Ndundu, Yvonne. Kinshasa, December 2, 2010.
N'Singa Udjuu, Joseph. Kinshasa, December 2, 2010.
Ntil, Julien. Kinshasa, August 17, 2010.
Nzanda-Bwana, Mathieu. Kinshasa, March 8, 2010.
Nzeza, Anastase. Kinshasa, June 1 and October 10, 2010.
Obotela Rashidi, Noël. Kinshasa, September 10, 2010.
Palambwa, Daniel. Kinshasa, August 10, 2010, August 17, 2010, September 5, 2010, and July 12, 2011.
Plevoets, Maurice. Kinshasa, November 5, 2009.
Poncelet, Eddy. Ostend, September 7, 2011.
Raymaekers, Paul. Rhode-St-Genèse, July 25 and September 17, 2009.
Sabakinu Kivulu, Jacob. Kinshasa, July 11, 2011, and December 19, 2019.
Salamu Yamba Yamba. Kinshasa, October 5, 2007.
Shaje a Tshiluila, Josette. Kinshasa, December 6, 2010.
Sondji, Jean-Baptiste. Kinshasa, October 4, 2007, April 22, 2010, July 19, 2011, and July 28, 2011.
Thysman, Raymond. Louvain-la-Neuve, September 5, 2009.
Tshibangu, Tharcisse. Kinshasa, December 18, 2019.
Tshungu Bamesa Zakama. Kinshasa, September 22, 2007, and October 19, 2007.
Vansina, Jan. Madison, June 12, 2009.
Wamba dia Wamba, Ernest. Kinshasa, November 7, 2010, and December 19, 2019; Dar Es Salaam, October 23, 2016, and June 10, 2017; and Abu Dhabi, April 9, 2019.
Wembo Ossako. Kinshasa, September 1, 2010.
Wenda Tshilumba, Patrick. Kisangani, October 11, 2010.
Willame, Jean-Claude. Brussels, December 2, 2009.

Yangu, Guy. Kinshasa, April 12, June 1, and July 28, 2010.
Yaone, Joseph. Kinshasa, November 30, 2010.
Yerodia, Abdoulaye. Kinshasa, December 3, 2010, and August 5, 2011.
Yoka Lye Mudaba, André. Kinshasa, September 20, 2007, and July 21, 2015.
Young, Crawford. Madison, June 12, 2009.

Books, Book Chapters, Journal Articles

Abemba Bulaimu, Jean, and Hubert Ntumba Lukunga M. *Mouvements étudiants et évolution politique en République démocratique du Congo.* Kinshasa: CEP, 2004.

Abiola, Irele. "In Praise of Alienation." In *The Surreptitious Speech: Présence africaine and the Politics of Otherness 1947–1987*, edited by V. Y. Mudimbe, 201–22. Chicago: University of Chicago Press, 1992.

Achebe, Chinua. *Home and Exile.* Oxford: Oxford University Press, 2000.

Adant, Jérôme. "Un baron rouge? Les activités pacifistes d'Antoine Allard de 1945 à 1965." *Brood en rozen* (2004): 7–27.

Ahlman, Jeffrey. *Living with Nkrumahism: Nation-State, and Pan-Africanism in Ghana.* Athens: Ohio University Press, 2017.

Allman, Jean. "Phantoms of the Archive: Kwame Nkrumah, a Nazi Pilot Named Hanna, and the Contingencies of Postcolonial History-Writing," *American Historical Review* 118, no. 1 (2013): 104–29.

Allman, Jean. "The Fate of All of Us: African Counterrevolutions at the Ends of 1968." *American Historical Review* 123, no. 3 (2018): 728–31.

Althabe, Gérard. *Les fleurs du Congo: Une utopie du Lumumbisme.* Paris: L'Harmattan, 1997.

Ambar, Saladin. *Malcolm X at Oxford Union.* Oxford: Oxford University Press, 2014.

Amin, Samir. *Le développement du capitalisme en Côte d'Ivoire.* Paris: Editions de Minuit, 1967.

Anderson, Benedict. *Imagined Communities: Reflections on the Origin and Spread of Nationalism.* London: Verso, 2006.

Appadurai, Arjun. *Modernity at Large: Cultural Dimensions of Globalization.* Minneapolis: University of Minnesota Press, 1996.

Apter, Emily. "On Oneworldedness: Or Paranoia as a World System." *American Literary History* 18, no. 2 (2006): 365–89.

Arrighi, Giovanni, and John S. Saul. *Essays on the Political Economy of Africa.* New York: Monthly Review Press, 1973.

Autesserre, Séverine. *The Trouble with the Congo: Local Violence and the Failure of International Peacebuilding.* Cambridge: Cambridge University Press, 2010.

Bandeira Jeronimo, Miguel. "Restoring Order, Inducing Change: Imagining a 'New (Wo)man' in the Belgian Colonial Empire in the 1950s." *Comparativ: Zeitschrift für Globalgeschichte und vergleichende Gesellschatsforschung* 28, no. 5 (2018): 77–96.

Banyaku Luape Epotu, Eugène. *Chronologie, monographie et documentation sur l'histoire politique du Congo des années 60 aux années 90.* Kinshasa: Editions Compodor, 1999.

Barber, Karin, ed. *Africa's Hidden Histories and Making the Self.* Bloomington: Indiana University Press, 2006.

Barrès, Maurice. *La colline inspirée.* Paris: Emile Paul, 1913.

Bayart, Jean-François. "Africa in the World: A History of Extraversion." *African Affairs* 99 (2000): 217–67.

Bayart, Jean-François. *L'Etat en Afrique: La politique du ventre.* Paris: Fayard, 1989.

Bazenguissa-Ganga, Remy. *Les voies du politique au Congo: Essai de sociologie historique.* Paris: Karthala, 1997.

Bechtolsheimer, Götz. "Breakfast with Mobutu: Congo, the United States and the Cold War, 1964–1981." PhD diss., London School of Economics, 2012.

Beeckmans, René, ed. *Voies africaines du socialisme.* Léopoldville: Bibliothèque de l'Etoile, 1963.

Bennington, Geoffrey. "Postal Politics and the Institution of the Nation." In *Nation and Narration,* edited by Homi K. Bhabha, 121–37. London: Routledge, 1990.

Berman, Edward. *The Influence of the Carnegie, Ford, and Rockefeller Foundations on American Foreign Policy.* Albany: State University of New York Press, 1983.

Bernard, Guy. *Ville africaine, famille urbaine: Les enseignants de Kinshasa.* Paris: Mouton, 1968.

Bernard, Marion. "Le monde comme problème philosophique." *Les études philosophiques* 98, no. 3 (2011): 351–73.

Bernault, Florence. *Colonial Transactions: Imaginaries, Bodies, and Histories in Gabon* Durham, NC: Duke University Press, 2019.

Bernault, Florence. "The Politics of Enclosure in Colonial and Post-Colonial Africa." In *A History of Prison and Confinement in Africa,* edited by Florence Bernault, 1–53. Portsmouth, NH: Heinemann, 2003.

Biaya, T. K. "Ethnopsychologie de quelques anthroponymes africains des missionnaires du Kasai occidental." *Annales aequatoria* 16 (1995): 183–227.

Biaya, T. K. "La culture urbaine dans les arts populaires d'Afrique: Analyse de l'ambiance zaïroise." *Canadian Journal of African Studies* 30, no. 3 (1996): 345–70.

Biaya, T. K. "Société parallèle, 'Mobutucratie' et nationalisme post-colonial en République démocratique du Congo." *African Journal of Political Science* 4, no. 1 (1999): 63–82.

Biebuyck, Daniel, and Kahombo C. Mateene, eds. *The Mwindo Epic: From the Banyanga (Congo Republic).* Berkeley: University of California Press, 1969.

Bitoma, Ghislain, and Julien Ntil, *Enquête sur les professeurs miliciens en République démocratique du Congo, année scolaire: 1968–1969.* Kinshasa: Office national de la recherche et du développement, 1970.

Blum, Françoise. "Années 68 postcoloniales? 'Mai' de France et d'Afrique." *French Historical Studies* 41, no. 2 (2018): 193–218.

Blum, Françoise. *Révolutions africaines: Congo, Sénégal, Madagascar, années 1960–1970*. Rennes: Presses universitaires de Rennes, 2014.

Blum, Françoise, Pierre Guidi, and Ophélie Rillon, eds. *Etudiants africains en mouvement: Contribution à une histoire des années 68*. Paris: Publications de la Sorbonne, 2016.

Bodart, Roger. "Entretien avec Lomami Tshibamba." In *Aspects de la culture à l'époque coloniale en Afrique Centrale: Littérature, théâtre (Congo-Meuse, 7)*, edited by Marc Quaghebeur, 101–8. Paris: L'Harmattan, 2008.

Bokonga Ekanga Botombole, ed. *La politique culturelle en République du Zaïre*. Paris: Les Presses de l'UNESCO, 1975.

Boltanski, Luc. *De la critique: Précis de sociologie de l'émancipation*. Paris: Gallimard, 2009.

Bongeli Yeikelo ya Ato, Emile. *L'Université contre le développement au Congo-Kinshasa*. Paris: L'Harmattan, 2009.

Bongoma, Jacques-Daniel. *Indépendance économique et révolution*. Kinshasa: Editions du Léopard, 1969.

Bontinck, François. "Le directeur d'école, alias Tata Raphaël." In *Figures et paradoxes de l'histoire au Burundi, au Congo et au Rwanda*, edited by Marc Quaghebeur, 58–66. Paris, L'Harmattan, 2002.

Bontinck, François. "Les missions catholiques à Léopoldville durant la seconde guerre mondiale." In *Le Congo belge durant la seconde guerre mondiale: Recueil d'études*, 399–418. Brussels: ARSOM, 1983.

Bontinck, François. "Mfumu Paul Panda Farnana 1888–1930: Premier (?) nationaliste congolais." In *La dépendance de l'Afrique et les moyens d'y re-médier: Actes de la 4e session du Congrès international des études africaines, Kinshasa*, edited by V. Y. Mudimbe, 591–610. Paris: Berger Levrault, 1980.

Borel, Philippe. "La politique belge à l'égard du Congo pendant la période des insurrections (1963–1964)." In *Rébellions-révolutions au Zaire 1963–1965*, edited by Catherine Coquery-Vidrovitch, Alain Forest, and Herbert Weiss, 2:7–35. Paris: L'Harmattan, 1987.

Bostoen, Koen, and Inge Brinkman, eds. *The Kongo Kingdom: The Origins, Dynamics and Cosmopolitan Culture of an African Polity*. Cambridge: Cambridge University Press, 2018.

Bourdieu, Pierre. "L'illusion biographique." *Actes de la Recherche en sciences sociales* 62, no. 63 (1986): 69–72.

Bourdieu, Pierre. "Révolution dans la révolution." *Esprit* 29, no. 1 (January 1961): 27–40.

Bouwer, Karen. *Gender and Decolonization in the Congo: The Legacy of Patrice Lumumba*. New York: Palgrave Macmillan, 2010.

Boyle, Patrick. *Class Formation and Civil Society: The Politics of Education in Africa*. Aldershot, UK: Ashgate, 1999.

Breckenridge, Keith. "Reasons for Writing: African Working Class Letter-Writing in Early-Twentieth-Century South Africa." In *Africa's Hidden*

Histories: Everyday Literacy and Making the Self, edited by Karin Barber, 143–54. Bloomington: Indiana University Press, 2006.

Brown, Timothy. *West Germany and the Global Sixties: The Antiauthoritarian Revolt, 1962–1978.* Cambridge: Cambridge University Press, 2013.

Buakasa, Gérard. "Nation congolaise et responsabilités de l'indépendance." In *Voies africaines du socialisme,* edited by René Beeckmans, 148–58. Léopold-ville: Bibliothèque de l'Etoile, 1963.

Buakasa, Gérard. *Réinventer l'Afrique: De la tradition à la modernité au Congo-Zaïre.* Paris: L'Harmattan, 1996.

Buakasa, T. K. M. *L'impensé du discours: "Kindoki" et "Nkisi" en pays Kongo du Zaïre.* Kinshasa: Presses universitaires du Zaïre, 1973.

Burbank, Jane, and Frederick Cooper. *Empires in World History: Power and the Politics of Difference.* Princeton, NJ: Princeton University Press, 2010.

Burton, Eric, ed. "Journeys of Education and Struggle: African Mobility in Times of Decolonization and the Cold War." Special issue of *Vienna Journal of African Studies* 34 (2018).

Byrne, Jeffrey. *Mecca of Revolution: Algeria, Decolonization and the Third World Order.* Oxford: Oxford University Press, 2016.

Cabrita, Joel. *The People's Zion: Southern Africa, the United States, and a Transatlantic Faith-Healing Movement.* Cambridge, MA: Harvard University Press, 2018.

Calhoun, Craig. "The Public Sphere in the Field of Power." *Social Science History* 34, no. 3 (2010): 301–35.

Callaci, Emily. *Street Archives and City Life: Popular Intellectuals in Postcolonial Tanzania.* Durham, NC: Duke University Press, 2017.

Callaghy, Thomas M. *The State-Society Struggle: Zaire in Comparative Perspective.* New York: Columbia University Press, 1984.

Casanova, Pascale. *The World Republic of Letters.* Cambridge, MA: Harvard University Press, 2004.

Casement, Roger. *Correspondence and Report from His Majesty's Consul at Boma Respecting the Administration of the Independent State of the Congo Presented to Both Houses of Parliament by Command of His Majesty.* London: Harrison, 1904.

Césaire, Aimé. *Une saison au Congo.* Paris: Seuil, 1973.

Chafer, Tony. "Students and Nationalism: The Role of Students in the Nationalist Movement in Afrique Occidentale Française." In AOF: *Réalités et héritages: Sociétés ouest-africaines et ordre colonial, 1895–1960,* edited by Charles Becker, Saliou Mbaye, and Ibrahima Thioub, 388–407. Dakar: Direction des Archives du Sénégal, 1997.

Challaye, Sylvie. "Jean-Marie Serreau, l'architecte d'un rêve théâtral aux couleurs d'Afrique." *Revue d'histoire du théâtre* 65, no. 4 (2013): 351–64.

Chalux. *Un an au Congo belge.* Brussels: Albert Dewit, 1925.

Cherki, Alice. *Fanon: A Portrait.* Ithaca, NY: Cornell University Press, 2006.

Chomé, Jules. *L'ascension de Mobutu: Du sergent Joseph Désiré au général Sese Seko.* Brussels: Complexe, 1975.

Christiansen, Samantha, and Zachary Scarlett, eds. *The Third World and the Global 1960s*. New York: Berghahn, 2012.

Clark, Katerina. *Moscow, the Fourth Rome: Stalinism, Cosmopolitanism, and the Evolution of Soviet Culture, 1931–1941*. Cambridge, MA: Harvard University Press, 2011.

Codding, George. *The Universal Postal Union: Coordinator of the International Mails*. New York: New York University Press, 1964.

Colard, Sandrine. "Photography in the Colonial Congo." PhD diss., Columbia University, 2016.

Coleman, James, ed. *Education and Political Development*. Princeton, NJ: Princeton University Press, 1965.

Collier, Delinda. *Repainting the Walls of Lunda: Information Colonialism and Angolan Art*. Minneapolis: University of Minnesota Press, 2016.

Comhaire, Jean. "Vie et oeuvre d'une folkloriste en Afrique." In *Folklore in Africa Today: Proceedings of the International Workshop, Budapest 1–4 XI, 1982*, edited by Szilard Biernaczky, 103–18. Budapest: Department of Folklore, 1984.

Comhaire-Sylvain, Suzanne. *Femmes de Kinshasa: Hier et aujourd'hui*. Paris: Mouton, 1968.

Comhaire-Sylvain, Suzanne. *Food and Leisure among the African Youth of Leopoldville (Belgian Congo)*. Cape Town: University of Cape Town, 1950.

Congo 1964: Political Documents of a Developing Nation, Compiled by C.R.I.S.P. Princeton, NJ: Princeton University Press, 1966.

Connery, Christopher Leigh. "The World Sixties." In *The Worlding Project: Doing Cultural Studies in the Era of Globalization*, edited by Rob Wilson and Christopher Leigh Connery, 77–107. Berkeley, CA: North Atlantic Books, 2007.

Conrad, Joseph. *Almayer's Folly: A Story of an Eastern River and Tales of Unrest*. London: Dent, 1961.

Cookey, S. J. R. "West African Immigrants in the Congo 1885–1896." *Journal of the Historical Society of Nigeria* 3, no. 2 (December 1965): 261–70.

Cooper, Frederick. *Africa in the World: Capitalism, Empire, Nation-State*. Cambridge, MA: Harvard University Press, 2014.

Cooper, Frederick. "Conflict and Connection: Rethinking Colonial African History." *American Historical Review* 99, no. 5 (December 1994): 1516–45.

Cooper, Frederick. *Decolonization and African Society: The Labor Question in French and British Africa*. Cambridge: Cambridge University Press, 1996.

Coquery-Vidrovitch, Catherine, Alain Forest, and Herbert Weiss, eds. *Rébellion-révolution au Zaïre, 1963–1965*. 2 vols. Paris: L'Harmattan, 1987.

Counet, Oscar. *Deux ans au service de la T. S. F. au Congo belge, 1920–1922, sous la direction de MM. R. Goldschmidt et le Lieutenant-Colonel Wibie*. Liège: Georges Thone, 1924.

Covington, Yolanda. *Gesture and Power: Religion, Nationalism, and Everyday Performance in Congo*. Durham, NC: Duke University Press, 2015.

Craven, Matthew. "Between Law and History: The Berlin Conference of 1884–1885 and the Logic of Free Trade." *London Review of International Law* 3, no. 1 (2005): 31–59.

Davis, Mike. *Planet of Slums*. London: Verso, 2006.

De Boeck, Filip. "Inhabiting Ocular Ground: Kinshasa's Future in the Light of Congo's Spectral Urban Politics." *Cultural Anthropology* 26, no. 2 (2011): 263–86.

De Boeck, Filip, and Sammy Baloji. *Suturing the City: Living Together in Congo's Urban Worlds*. London: Autograph APB, 2016.

De Boeck, Filip, and Marie-France Plissart. *Kinshasa: Tales of the Invisible City*. Ghent: Ludion, 2004.

Debord, Guy. *Oeuvres*. Paris: Gallimard, 2006.

Dedieu, Jean-Philippe, and Aïssatou Mbodj-Pouye. "The Fabric of Transnational Political Activism: 'Révolution Afrique' and West African Radical Militants in France in the 1970s." *Comparative Studies in Society and History* 60, no. 4 (2018): 1172–208.

De Dorlodot, Philippe. "L'engagement politique de Mgr Christophe Munzihirwa, 1922–1996." In *Mission et engagement politique après 1945*, edited by Caroline Sappia and Olivier Servais, 333–42. Paris: Karthala, 2010.

De Groof, Matthias, ed. *Lumumba in the Arts*. Leuven: Leuven University Press, 2020.

De Luna, Kathryn. "Affect and Society in Precolonial Africa." *International Journal of African Historical Studies* 46, no. 1 (2013): 123–50.

De Luna, Kathryn. "Hunting Reputations: Talent, Individuals, and Community in Precolonial South Central Africa." *Journal of African History* 53 (2012): 279–99.

Demunter, Paul. "Les relations entre le mouvement étudiant et le régime politique congolais: Le colloque de Goma." *Travaux Africains du CRISP* 126 (April 1971): 1–23.

Depaepe, Marc. *Between Educationalization and Appropriation: Selected Writings on Modern Educational Systems*. Leuven: Leuven University Press, 2012.

Depaepe, Marc. "Parallélisme belgo-congolais dans l'histoire de l'enseignement." In *La chanson scolaire au Congo belge: Anthologie*, edited by Pierre Kita Masandi and Marc Depaepe, 9–30. Paris: L'Harmattan, 2004.

Depaepe, Marc, and Lies Van Rompaey. *In het teken van de bevoogding: De educatieve actie in Belgisch-Kongo (1908–1960)*. Leuven: Garant, 1995.

De Quincey, Thomas. *The English Mail-Coach and Other Essays*. London: Dent, 1961.

De Rezende, Isabelle. "Visuality and Colonialism in the Congo: From the 'Arab War' to Patrice Lumumba, 1880s to 1961." PhD diss., University of Michigan, 2012.

Derrida, Jacques. *La carte postale: De Socrate à Freud et au-delà*. Paris: Flammarion, 1980.

De Saint Moulin, Léon. *Oeuvres complètes du Cardinal Malula*. Kinshasa: Facultés catholiques de Kinshasa, 1997.

De Sousa Santos, Boaventura. *Epistemologies of the South: Justice against Epistemicide*. New York: Routledge, 2016.

De Villers, Gauthier. *De Mobutu à Mobutu: Trente ans de relations Belgique-Zaïre*. Brussels: De Boeck, 1995.

De Villers, Gauthier. *Histoire du politique au Congo-Kinshasa: Les concepts à l'épreuve*. Louvain-la-Neuve: Academia-L'Harmattan, 2016.

Devisch, René, and Francis B. Nyamnjoh. *The Postcolonial Turn: Re-imagining Anthropology and Africa*. Leiden: African Studies Center, 2011.

Devlin, Larry. *Chief of Station, Congo: Fighting the Cold War in a Hot Zone*. New York: Public Affairs, 2009.

De Vos, Luc, Emmanuel Gerard, Jules Gérard-Libois, and Philippe Raxhon. *Les secrets de l'affaire Lumumba*. Brussels: Racine, 2005.

De Vos, Pierre. *Vie et mort de Lumumba*. Paris: Calman-Levy, 1961.

De Witte, Ludo. *L'ascension de Mobutu: Comment la Belgique et les USA ont installé une dictature*. Brussels: Investig'action, 2017.

De Witte, Ludo. *The Assassination of Lumumba*. London: Verso, 2001.

Diagne, Souleymane Bachir. *Bergson postcolonial: L'élan vital dans la pensée de Léopold Sédar Senghor et de Mohamed Iqbal*. Paris: CNRS éditions, 2011.

Dias, Patrick V., Theodor Han, Franz-Wilhelm Heimer, and William M. Rideout. *Les étudiants universitaires congolais: Une enquête sur leurs attitudes socio-politiques*. Dusseldorf: Bertelsmann, 1971.

Dibwe dia Mwembu. "Popular Memories of Patrice Lumumba." In *A Congo Chronicle: Patrice Lumumba in Urban Art*, edited by Bogumil Jewsiewicki, 59–72. New York: Museum for African Art, 1999.

Di-Capua, Yoav. *No Exit: Arab Existentialism, Jean-Paul Sartre and Decolonization*. Chicago: University of Chicago Press, 2018.

Dikonda Wa Lumanyisha. *Face à face*. Brussels: Editions remarques africaines, 1964.

Djungu-Simba Kamatenda. "Ce sorcier de Zamenga." In Zamenga Batukezanga, *Chérie Basso*. Kinshasa: Editions Saint Paul Afrique, 1983.

Du Four, Jean. *Cinquante ans d'histoire postale*. Brussels: Revue Postale, 1962.

Dunn, Kevin C. *Imagining the Congo: International Relations of Identity*. New York: Palgrave Macmillan, 2003.

Dworkin, Ira. *Congo Love Song: African American Culture and the Crisis of the Colonial State*. Chapel Hill: University of North Carolina Press, 2017.

Eggers, Nicole. "Kitawala in the Congo: Religion, Politics and Healing in 20th–21st Century Central African History." PhD diss., University of Wisconsin, 2013.

Ekwa bis Isal, Martin. *La RD Congo contée autrement: Jalons pour l'avenir, entretiens avec Clémentine Faïk-Nzuji*. Kinshasa: Editions Loyola, 2012.

Ekwa bis Isal, Martin. *L'école trahie*. Kinshasa: CADICEC, 2004.

Erny, Pierre. *Sur les sentiers de l'université: Autobiographies d'étudiants zaïrois*. Paris: La pensée universelle, 1977.

Ewing, Adam. *The Age of Garvey: How a Jamaican Activist Created a Mass Movement and Changed Global Black Politics*. Princeton, NJ: Princeton University Press, 2014.

Fabian, Johannes. *Ethnography as Commentary: Writing from the Virtual Archive*. Durham, NC: Duke University Press, 2008.

Fabian, Johannes. *Remembering the Present: Painting and Popular History in Zaire*. Berkeley: University of California Press, 1996.

Fabian, Johannes. "Text as Terror: Second Thoughts about Charisma." *Social Research* 46, no. 1 (1979): 166–203.

Fabian, Johannes. *Time and the Other: How Anthropology Makes Its Object*. New York: Columbia University Press, 1983.

Fanon, Frantz. *Alienation and Freedom*. Edited by Jean Khalfa and Robert J. C. Young. Translated by Steven Corcoran. London: Bloomsbury, 2018.

Fanon, Frantz. *Ecrits sur l'aliénation et la liberté: Oeuvres II, Textes réunions, introduits et présentés par Jean Khalfa et Robert Young*. Paris: La découverte, 2015.

Fanon, Frantz. *Peau noire, masque blanc*. Paris: Seuil, 1971.

Fanon, Frantz. *Toward the African Revolution: Political Essays*. New York: Grove, 1967.

Featherstone, David. *Solidarity: Hidden Histories and Geographies of Internationalism*. London: Zed Books, 2012.

Fejzula, Merve. "The Cosmopolitan Historiography of Twentieth-Century Federalism." *Historical Journal* 64, no. 2 (2021): 477–500.

Feltrinelli, Carlo. *Feltrinelli*. New York: Harcourt, 2001.

Ferguson, James. *Global Shadows: Africa in the Neoliberal World Order*. Durham, NC: Duke University Press, 2006.

Ferguson, James. "Invisible Humanism: An African 1968 and Its Aftermaths." In *The Long 1968: Revisions and New Perspectives*, edited by Daniel Sherman, Ruud van Dikj, Jasmine Alinder, and A. Aneesh, 120–38. Bloomington: Indiana University Press, 2013.

Fierens, Marie. "Reporting on the Independence of the Belgian Congo: Mwissa Camus, the Dean of the Congolese Journalists." *African Journalism Studies* 37, no. 1 (2016): 81–99.

Findlay, Edward. *Caring for the Soul in a Postmodern Age: Politics and Phenomenology in the Thought of Jan Patočka*. Albany: State University of New York Press, 2002.

Foccart, Jacques. *Dans les bottes du général: Journal de l'Elysée: Volume III: 1969–1971*. Paris: Fayard, 1999.

Folti, Omero. "Feltrinelli." In *La piste rouge (Italia, 69–72)*, edited by Ornella Volta, 347–403. Paris: Union Générale d'Editions, 1973.

Ford, Tanisha. *Liberated Threads: Black Women, Soul, and the Politics of Soul*. Chapel Hill: University of North Carolina Press, 2015.

Foucault, Michel. *Dits et écrits*. Paris: Gallimard, 1994.

Foucault, Michel. *Technologies of the Self: A Seminar with Michel Foucault*. Amherst: University of Massachusetts Press, 1988.

Fox, Renée, Willy de Craemer, and Jean-Marie Ribeaucourt. "'The Second Independence': A Case Study of the Kwilu Rebellion in the Congo." *Comparative Studies in Society and History* 8, no. 1 (October 1965): 78–109.

Fraiture, Pierre-Philippe. *V. Y. Mudimbe: Undisciplined Africanism.* Liverpool:
Liverpool University Press, 2013.

Fraiture, Pierre-Philippe, and Daniel Orrells. *The Mudimbe Reader.* Charlot-
tesville: University of Virginia Press, 2016.

Freeman, Ted. *Theatres of War: French Committed Theatre from the Second
World War to the Cold War.* Exeter, UK: University of Exeter Press, 1998.

Gaines, Kevin. *American Africans in Ghana: Black Expatriates and the Civil
Rights Era.* Chapel Hill: University of North Carolina Press, 2006.

Galvez, William. *Che in Africa: Che Guevara's Congo Diary.* New York:
Ocean Press, 1999.

Gambembo, Daniel, Ferdinand Kazadi, and Honoré Mpinga. *Le nationalisme
congolais, idéologie de l'authenticité.* Kinshasa: Imprimerie de l'université,
1971.

Gambembo Fumu wa Utadi, Daniel. "De Lovanium à l'Université de Kinshasa."
In *L'Université dans le devenir de l'Afrique: Un demi-siècle de présence
au Congo-Zaïre,* edited by Isidore Ndaywel è Nziem, 67–76. Paris:
L'Harmattan, 2007.

Geenen, Kristien. "'Sleep Occupies No Space': The Use of Public Space by
Street Gangs in Kinshasa." *Africa* 79, no. 3 (2009): 347–68.

Gerard, Emmanuel, and Bruce Kuklick. *Death in the Congo: Murdering Patrice Lumumba.* Cambridge, MA: Harvard University Press, 2015.

Gérard-Libois, Jules. *Congo 1966.* Brussels: CRISP, 1967.

Gérard-Libois, Jules, and Jean Van Lierde. *Congo 1965.* Brussels: CRISP, 1966.

Gérard-Libois, Jules, and Benoît Verhaegen. *Congo 1962.* Brussels: CRISP,
1963.

Gérard-Libois, Jules, and Benoît Verhaegen. *Congo 1960.* 2 vols. Brussels:
CRISP, 1961.

Getachew, Adom. *Worldmaking after Empire: The Rise and Fall of Self-
Determination.* Princeton, NJ: Princeton University Press, 2019.

Gibbs, David N. *The Political Economy of Third World Intervention: Mines,
Money and US Economy in the Congo Crisis.* Chicago: University of Chicago Press, 1991.

Gijs, Anne-Sophie. *Le pouvoir de l'absent: Les avatars de l'anticommunisme
au Congo (1920–1961).* 2 vols. Brussels: Peter Lang, 2016.

Gikandi, Simon. "*Arrow of God*: The Novel and the Problem of Modern
Time." *Research in African Literatures* 49, no. 4 (2018): 1–13.

Gillon, Luc. *Allocution de bienvenue prononcée par Mgr L. Gillon, recteur
de l'Université Lovanium a l'occasion de la première visite officielle du
Lieutenant-General Joseph-Desiré Mobutu, président de la République
démocratique du Congo, le 14 décembre 1965.* Leopoldville: Université de
Lovanium, 1965.

Gillon, Luc. *Servir en actes et vérité.* Gembloux: Duculot, 1988.

Glassman, Jonathon. "Creole Nationalists and the Search for Nativist Authenticity in Twentieth-Century Zanzibar: The Limits of Cosmopolitanism." *Journal of African History* 55 (2014): 229–47.

Gleijeses, Piero. *Conflicting Missions: Havana, Washington and Africa, 1959–1976*. Chapel Hill: University of North Carolina Press, 2002.

Goebel, Michael. *Anti-imperial Metropolis: Interwar Paris and the Seeds of Third World Nationalism*. Cambridge: Cambridge University Press, 2015.

Golan, Tamar. *Educating the Bureaucracy in a New Polity*. New York: Teachers College Press, 1968.

Goldschmidt, Robert, and Raymond Braillard, *La télégraphie sans fil au Congo belge: Une oeuvre du roi*. Brussels: Hayez, 1920.

Gondola, Ch. Didier. "Ata Ndele . . . et l'indépendance vint: Musique, jeunes et contestation politique dans les capitales congolaises." In *Les jeunes en Afrique: La politique et la ville*, edited by Hélène d'Almeida-Toper, Catherine Coquery-Vidrovitch, and Odile Goerg, 463–83. Paris: L'Harmattan, 1992.

Gondola, Ch. Didier. "'Bisengo ya la joie': Fête, sociabilité et politique dans les capitales congolaises." In *Fêtes urbaines en Afrique: Espaces, identités et pouvoirs*, edited by Odile Goerg, 87–111. Paris: Karthala, 1999.

Gondola, Ch. Didier. "Dream and Drama: The Search for Elegance among Congolese Youth." *African Studies Review* 42, no. 1 (1999): 23–48.

Gondola, Ch. Didier. *Tropical Cowboys: Westerns, Violence, and Masculinity in Kinshasa*. Bloomington: Indiana University Press, 2016.

Gondola, Ch. Didier. *Villes miroirs: Migrations et identités à Brazzaville et Kinshasa, 1930–1970*. Paris: L'Harmattan, 1997.

Goswami, Manu. "Colonial Internationalisms and Imaginary Futures." *American Historical Review* 117, no. 15 (2012): 1461–85.

Grabli, Charlotte. "La ville des auditeurs: Radio, rumba congolaise et droit à la ville dans la cité indigène de Léopoldville (1949–1960)." *Cahiers d'études africaines* 233 (2019): 9–45.

Grant, Kevin. *A Civilised Savagery: Britain and the New Slaveries in Africa, 1884–1926*. New York: Routledge, 2005.

Grant, Kevin. "The Limits of Exposure: Atrocity Photographs in the Congo Reform Campaign." In *Humanitarian Photography: A History*, edited by Heide Fehrenbach and Davide Rodogno, 64–88. New York: Cambridge University Press, 2015.

Gray, Christopher. "Territoriality and Colonial 'Enclosure' in Southern Gabon." In *Enfermement, prison et châtiments en Afrique*, edited by Florence Bernault, 99–132. Paris: Karthala, 1999.

Griferro, Tonino. *Atmospheres: Aesthetics of Emotional Spaces*. London: Routledge, 2010.

Guevara, Ernesto. *Congo Diary: The Story of Che Guevara's Lost Year in Africa*. New York: Ocean Press, 2011.

Gueye, Omar. *Mai 1968 au Sénégal: Senghor face aux étudiants et au mouvement syndical*. Paris: Karthala, 2017.

Guyer, Jane I., and Samuel M. Eno Belinga. "Wealth in People as Wealth in Knowledge: Accumulation and Composition in Equatorial Africa." *Journal of Africa History* 36 (1995): 91–120.

Hage, Julien. "Une brève histoire des libraires et des éditions Maspero 1955–1982." In *François Maspero et les paysages humains*, edited by Bruno Guichard, Julien Hage, and Alain Léger, 93–160. Paris: A plus d'un titre, 2009.

Halen, Pierre. *"Le petit Belge avait vu grand": Une littérature coloniale.* Brussels: Labor, 1993.

Hanna, William John, ed. *University Students and African Politics.* New York: Africana, 1975.

Hédo, Gaston. *Mosselmans, ombre blanche: Impressions et souvenirs du Congo.* Brussels: Editions de la Gaule, 1930.

Hendrickson, Burleigh. "Imperial Fragments and Transnational Activism: 1968(s) in Tunisia, France, and Senegal." PhD diss., Northeastern University, 2013.

Hendrickson, Burleigh. "March 1968: Practicing Transnational Activism from Tunis to Paris." *International Journal of Middle East Studies* 44 (2012): 755–74.

Henkin, David. *The Postal Age: The Emergence of Modern Communications in 19th Century America.* Chicago: University of Chicago Press, 2009.

Henriet, Benoit. "Elusive Natives: Escaping Colonial Control in the Leverville Oil Palm Concession, Belgian Congo, 1923–1941." *Canadian Journal of African Studies/Revue canadienne des études africaines* 49, no. 2 (2015): 339–61.

Henriet, Benoit. "The Concession Experience: Power, Ecology and Labour in the Leverville Circle (Belgian Congo 1911–1914)." PhD diss., Université Saint-Louis, 2016.

Higginson, John. *A Working Class in the Making: Belgian Colonial Labor Policy, Private Enterprise, and the African Mineworker, 1907–1951.* Madison: University of Wisconsin Press, 1990.

Hill, Robert A. *The Marcus Garvey and Universal Negro Improvement Association Papers: Volume IX: Africa for the Africans, 1921–1922.* Berkeley: University of California Press, 1995.

Hill, Robert A., and Edmond J. Keller, eds. *Trustee for the Human Community: Ralph J. Bunche, the United States and the Decolonization of Africa.* Athens: Ohio University Press, 2010.

Hodgkin, Thomas. *Nationalism in Colonial Africa.* London: Frederick Muller, 1956.

Hodgkinson, Dan, and Luke Melchiorre, eds. "Student Activism in an Era of Decolonization." Special issue of *Africa: Journal of the International African Institute* 89 (2019).

Hodgkinson, Dan, and Luke Melchiorre. "The Vietnam War in Africa." In *Protest in the Vietnam War Era*, edited by Alexander Sedlmaier. New York: Palgrave Macmillan, forthcoming.

Hofmeyr, Isabel. *Gandhi's Printing Press: Experiments in Slow Reading.* Cambridge, MA: Harvard University Press, 2013.

Hofmeyr, Isabel. *The Portable Bunyan: A Transnational History of "The Pilgrim's Progress."* Princeton, NJ: Princeton University Press, 2003.

Holm, Richard. *The Craft We Chose: My Life in the CIA.* Mountain Lake Park, MD: Mountain Lake Press, 2011.

Holt, Elizabeth. "'Bread or Freedom': The Congress for Cultural Freedom, the CIA, and the Arabic Literary Journal *Hiwār* (1962–1967)." *Journal of Arabic Literature* 44 (2013): 83–102.

Houart, Pierre. *La pénétration communiste au Congo.* Brussels: Centre de documentation international, 1960.

Hountondji, Paulin. *The Struggle for Meaning: Reflections on Philosophy, Culture, and Democracy in Africa.* Athens: Ohio University Press, 2002.

Howland, Nina, David Humphrey, and Harriet Schwar, eds. *Foreign Relations of the United States, 1964–1968: Volume XXIII, Congo, 1960–1968.* Washington, DC: United States Government Printing Office, 2013.

Hull, Galen. "Education in Zaire: Instrument of Underdevelopment." In *Zaire: The Political Economy of Underdevelopment*, edited by Guy Cran, 149–54. New York: Praeger, 1979.

Hunt, Nancy Rose. *A Colonial Lexicon of Birth Rituals, Medicalization and Mobility in the Congo.* Durham, NC: Duke University Press, 1999.

Hunt, Nancy Rose. *A Nervous State: Violence, Remedies, and Reverie in Colonial Congo.* Durham, NC: Duke University Press, 2016.

Hunt, Nancy Rose. "An Acoustic Register, Tenacious Images, and Congolese Scenes of Rape and Repetition." *Cultural Anthropology* 23, no. 2 (2008): 220–53.

Hunt, Nancy Rose. "Domesticity and Colonialism in Belgian Africa: Usumbura's Foyer Social, 1946–1960." *Signs* 15, no. 3 (1990): 447–74.

Hunt, Nancy Rose. "Espace, temporalité et rêverie: Ecrire l'histoire des futurs au Congo belge." *Politique africaine* 135 (2014): 115–36.

Hunt, Nancy Rose. "Letter-Writing, Nursing Men and Bicycles in the Belgian Congo: Notes towards the Social Identity of a Colonial Category." In *The Paths towards the Past: Essays in Honor of Jan Vansina*, edited by Robert Harms, Joseph Miller, David Newbury, and Michele Wagner, 187–210. Atlanta: African Studies Press, 1994.

Hunt, Nancy Rose. "Noise over Camouflaged Polygamy, Colonial Morality Taxation, and a Woman-Naming Crisis in Belgian Africa." *Journal of African History* 32, no. 3 (1991): 471–94.

Hunt, Nancy Rose. "Rewriting the Soul in a Flemish Congo." *Past and Present* 198 (2008): 185–215.

Hunt, Nancy Rose. "Tintin and the Interruptions of Congolese Comics." In *Images and Empires: Visuality in Colonial and Postcolonial Africa*, edited by Paul S. Landau and Deborah Kaspin, 90–123. Berkeley: University of California Press, 2002.

Hunter, Emma. *Political Thought and the Public Sphere in Tanzania: Freedom, Democracy and Citizenship in the Era of Decolonization.* New York: Cambridge University Press, 2015.

Inge, Thomas. *Truman Capote: Conversations.* Jackson: University Press of Mississippi, 1987.

Ivaska, Andrew. *Cultured States: Youth, Gender, and Modern Style in 1960s Dar es Salaam.* Durham, NC: Duke University Press, 2011.

Ivaska, Andrew. "Movement Youth in a Global Sixties Hub: The Everyday Lives of Transnational Activists in Postcolonial Dar es Salaam." In *A Global Age: Transnational Histories of Youth in the Twentieth Century*, edited by Richard Ivan Jobs and David Pomfret, 188–201. New York: Palgrave Macmillan, 2015.

Jackson, Michael. *Lifeworlds: Essays in Existential Anthropology.* Chicago: University of Chicago Press, 2013.

Janzen, John. "Review of *Patrimonialism and Political Change in the Congo* by J.-C. Willame." *Journal of Asian and African Studies* 8 (1973): 134–35.

Jewsiewicki, Bogumil. "African Peasants in the Totalitarian Colonial Society of the Belgian Congo." In *Peasants in Africa: Historical and Contemporary Perspectives*, edited by Martin Klein, 45–75. London: Sage, 1980.

Jewsiewicki, Bogumil. *Mami wata: La peinture urbaine au Congo.* Paris: Gallimard, 2003.

Jewsiewicki, Bogumil. "Political Consciousness among African Peasants in the Belgian Congo." *Review of African Political Economy* 19 (1980): 23–32.

Jewsiewicki, Bogumil. "Reading in Kinshasa: Between Colonial Modernization and Globalization." *Research in African Literatures* 39, no. 4 (2008): 105–19.

Jewsiewicki, Bogumil, ed. *A Congo Chronicle: Patrice Lumumba in Urban Art.* New York: Museum for African Art, 1999.

Jesse Jones, Thomas. *Education in Africa.* New York: Phelps-Stokes Fund, 1922.

Jian, Chen, Martin Klimke, Masha Kirasirova, Mary Nolan, Marilyn Young, and Joanna Waley-Cohen, eds. *The Routledge Handbook of the Global Sixties: Between Protest and Nation-Building.* London: Routledge, 2018.

Joyce, Patrick. "Filling the Raj: Political Technologies of the Imperial British State." In *Material Powers: Cultural Studies, History and the Material Turn*, edited by Tony Bennett and Patrick Joyce, 102–23. London: Routledge, 2010.

Kabamba Mbwebwe K. and Kasulula Djuma Lokali. *Rapport sur les assassinats et violations des droits de l'homme.* 2 vols. Kinshasa: Yerodia Abdoulaye Ndombasi, 2004.

Kabemba Biabululu wa Mayombo, Joseph. *Le destin de Biabululu, l'enfant de la patience.* Kinshasa: Editions universitaires africaines, 1998.

Kabongo, Ilunga. *Crise à Lovanium (1964).* Brussels: CRISP, 1964.

Kabongo, Ilunga. "The Catastrophe of Belgian Decolonization." In *Decolonization and African Independence*, edited by W. Roger Louis and Prosser Gifford, 381–400. New Haven, CT: Yale University Press, 1988.

Kabuya Lumuna Sando, Célestin. *Les prisonniers du président*. Paris: Société des écrivains, 2012.

Kabuya Lumuna Sando, Célestin. *Lovanium: La Kasala du 4 juin*. Brussels: A.F.R.I.C.A., 1982.

Kadima Nzuji Mukala, *La littérature zaïroise de langue française: 1945–1965*. Paris: Karthala, 1984.

Kalb, Madeleine G. *The Congo Cables: The Cold War in Africa, from Eisenhower to Kennedy*. New York: Macmillan, 1982.

Kalema, Emery. "Les congrès de l'union générale des etudiants congolais (1961–1969)." Undergraduate thesis, Université de Kinshasa, 2011.

Kalema, Emery. "Scars, Marked Bodies, and Suffering: The Mulele 'Rebellion' in Postcolonial Congo." *Journal of African History* 59, no. 2 (2018): 263–82.

Kalulambi Pongo, Martin. "Le manifeste *Conscience africaine*: Genèse, influences et réactions." In Nathalie Toussignant, *Le manifeste* Conscience africaine: *Elites congolaises et société coloniale, regards croisés*, 59–81. Brussels: Facultés Universitaires Saint-Louis, 2009.

Kalulambi Pongo, Martin. "Sex@mour et pouvoir en milieu universitaire congolais." In *Les années UNAZA (Université nationale du Zaïre): Contribution à l'histoire de l'université africaine*, edited by Isidore Ndaywel è Nziem, 2:101–37. Paris: L'Harmattan, 2018.

Kamitatu, Cléophas. *La grande mystification du Congo-Kinshasa: Les crimes de Mobutu*. Paris: Maspero, 1971.

Kangafu Gudumbagana. *Demain la promotion*. Kinshasa: Presses africaines, 1975.

Kanza, Thomas. *Eloge de la révolution*. Brussels: Remarques congolaises, 1965.

Kanza, Thomas. *The Rise and Fall of Patrice Lumumba: Conflict in the Congo*. London: Rex Collings, 1978.

Karagiannis, Nathalie, and Peter Wagner. "Introduction: Globalization or World-Making?" In *Varieties of World-Making: Beyond Globalization*, edited by Nathalie Karagiannis and Peter Wagner, 1–14. Liverpool: Liverpool University Press, 2007.

Kasa-Vubu, Justine M'Poyo. *Douze mois chez Kabila (1997–1998)*. Brussels: Le Cri, 1998.

Kasereka Kavwahirehi. *L'Afrique, entre passé et futur: L'urgence d'un choix public de l'intelligence*. Brussels: Peter Lang, 2009.

Kasereka Kavwahirehi. "L'authenticité comme cadre de pensée et d'écriture au Congo-Kinshasa entre 1970 et 1982." In *Images, mémoires et savoirs: Une histoire en partage avec Bogumil Koss Jewsiewicki*, edited by Isidore Ndaywel è Nziem and Elisabeth Mudimbe-Boyi, 624–48. Paris: Karthala, 2009.

Kasereka Kavwahirehi. "Mudimbe Senghorien? La négritude, la critique des évidences et la modernité dans l'oeuvre de V. Y. Mudimbe." *Les lettres romanes* 54, no. 1–2 (2000): 115–35.

Kashamura, Anicet. *De Lumumba aux colonels*. Paris: Buchet-Chastel, 1966.

Kasongo-Ngoy Makita-Makita. *Capital scolaire et pouvoir social en Afrique: À quoi sert le diplôme universitaire*. Paris: L'Harmattan, 1989.

Katsakioris, Constantin. "Students from Portuguese Africa in the Soviet Union 1960–1974: Anticolonialism, Education, and the Socialist Alliance." *Journal of Contemporary History* 56, no. 1 (2020): 142–56.

Katsakioris, Constantin. "The Lumumba University in Moscow: Higher Education for a Soviet-Third World Alliance, 1960–91." *Journal of Global History* 14, no. 2 (2019): 281–300.

Kengo-wa-Dongo. *Vers une société sans prison*. Kinshasa: Cour surpême de justice de la République du Zaïre, 1975.

Kennedy, Charles Stuart. *Ambassador Herman J. Cohen*. Washington, DC: Foreign Affairs Oral History Collection of the Association for Diplomatic Studies and Training, 1996.

Kennedy, Duncan. "A Semiotics of Critique." *Cardozo Law Review* 22, no. 5 (2001): 1147–89.

Kennes, Erik, and Miles Larmer, *The Katangese Gendarmes and War in Central Africa: Fighting Their Way Home*. Bloomington: Indiana University Press, 2016.

Kennes, Erik, and Munkana N'Gee. *Essai biographique sur Laurent-Désiré Kabila*. Paris: L'Harmattan, 2003.

Kent, John. *America, the UN and Decolonization: Cold War Conflict in the Congo*. New York: Routledge, 2010.

Kiangu, Sindani. *Le Kwilu à l'épreuve du pluralisme identitaire 1948–1968*. Paris: L'Harmattan, 2009.

Kiangu, Sindani. *Préparer un peuple parfait: Mgr Joseph Guffens, 1895–1973*. Kinshasa: Editions Saint-Paul, 1992.

King, Michael. *The Penguin History of New Zealand*. New York: Penguin, 2003.

Kisonga Mazakala, Albert. *45 ans d'histoire congolaise: L'expérience d'un lumumbiste*. Paris: L'Harmattan, 2005.

Kita Kyankenge Masandi. *Colonisation et enseignement: Cas du Zaire avant 1960*. Kinshasa: Editions du CERUKI, 1982.

Kita Masandi, Pierre, and Marc Depaepe. *La chanson scolaire au Congo belge: Anthologie*. Paris: L'Harmattan, 2004.

Klimke, Martin. *The Other Alliance: Student Protest in West Germany and the United States in the Global Sixties*. Princeton, NJ: Princeton University Press, 2010.

Krings, Matthias. *African Appropriations: Cultural Difference, Mimesis, and Media*. Bloomington: Indiana University Press, 2015.

Laborie, Léonard. "Global Commerce in Small Boxes: Parcel Post, 1878–1913." *Journal of Global History* 10 (2015): 235–58.

Labou Tansi, Sony. *L'anté-peuple*. Paris: Le Seuil, 1983.

Labrique, Jean. *Congo politique*. Leopoldville: Editions de l'avenir, 1957.

Lacalau, Ernesto. *On Populist Reason*. London: Verso, 2005.

Lacroix, Bernadette. "Pouvoirs et structures de l'Université Lovanium." *Cahiers du CEDAF* 2, no. 3 (1972): 1–207.

La Fontaine, Jean Sybil. *City Politics: A Study of Leopoldville, 1962–1963*. Cambridge: Cambridge University Press, 1970.

Lagae, Johan, Kim De Raedt, and Jacob Sabakinu Kivulu. "'Pour les écoles: Tant mieux qu'elles sont là': Patrimoine scolaire, pratiques mémorielles et politiques de sauvegarde en République démocratique du Congo." *Politique africaine* 135 (2014): 47–70.

Lal, Priya. *African Socialism in Postcolonial Tanzania*. New York: Cambridge University Press, 2015.

Lal, Priya. "Tanzanian *Ujamaa* in a World of Peripheral Socialisms." In *The Routledge Handbook of the Global Sixties: Between Protest and Nation-Building*, edited by Chen Jian, Martin Klimke, Masha Kirasirova, Mary Nolan, Marilyn Young, and Joanna Waley-Cohen, chap. 27. London: Routledge, 2018.

Lambertz, Peter. *Seekers and Things: Spiritual Movements and Aesthetic Difference in Kinshasa*. New York: Berghahn, 2018.

L'an 3 de la révolution congolaise: Analyse des expériences et perspectives de la révolution Congolaise. Brussels: Livre International, 1966.

Langellier, Jean-Pierre. *Mobutu*. Paris: Perrin, 2017.

Langland, Victoria. *Speaking of Flowers: Student Movements and the Making and Remembering of 1968 in Military Brazil*. Durham, NC: Duke University Press, 2013.

Laqua, Daniel. *The Age of Internationalism and Belgium, 1880–1930: Peace, Progress and Prestige*. Manchester: Manchester University Press, 2013.

Larkin, Brian. *Signal and Noise: Media, Infrastructure and Urban Culture in Nigeria*. Durham, NC: Duke University Press, 2008.

Lauro, Amandine. "'J'ai l'honneur de porter plainte contre ma femme': Litiges conjugaux et administration coloniale au Congo belge (1930–1960)." *Clio: Histoire des femmes et sociétés* 33 (2011): 65–84.

Lauro, Amandine. "Suspect Cities and the (Re)making of Colonial Order: Urbanization, Security Anxieties and Police Reforms in Postwar Congo (1945–1960)." In *Policing New Risks in Modern European History*, edited by Jonas Campion and Xavier Rousseaux, 57–85. London: Palgrave, 2016.

Lauro, Amandine. "Violence, Anxieties, and the Making of Interracial Dangers: Colonial Surveillance and Interracial Sexuality in the Belgian Congo." In *The Routledge Companion to Sexuality and Colonialism*, edited by Chelsea Schields and Dagmar Herzog, 327–38. London: Routledge, 2021.

Lauro, Amandine. "Women in the Democratic Republic of Congo." *Oxford Research Encyclopedia of African History* (May 2020 ed.). https://oxfordre.com/africanhistory/view/10.1093/acrefore/9780190277734.001.0001/acrefore-9780190277734-e-544.

Lee, Christopher J. "Between a Moment and an Era: The Origins and Afterlives of Bandung." In *Making a World after Empire: The Bandung Moment and Its Political Afterlives*, edited by Christopher J. Lee, 1–44. Athens: Ohio University Press, 2010.

Lemarchand, René. *Political Awakening in the Belgian Congo*. Berkeley: University of California Press, 1964.

Le martyr des Congolais: Rien de changé au Congo: Principaux témoignages publiés à l'étranger depuis le rapport de la Commission d'enquête. Gand: Volksdrukkerij, 1907.

Lengelo Guyisa, *Mukanda, l'école traditionnelle pende.* Bandundu: CEEBA, 1980.

Lerner, Mitch. "Climbing off the Back Burner: Lyndon Johnson's Soft Power Approach to Africa." *Diplomacy & Statecraft* 22, no. 4 (2011): 578–607.

Les cahiers de Gamboma: Instructions politiques et militaires des partisans congolais (1964–1965). Brussels: CRISP, 1965.

Likaka, Osumaka. *Rural Society and Cotton in Colonial Zaire.* Madison: University of Wisconsin Press, 1997.

Loffman, Reuben. *Church, State and Colonialism in Southeastern Congo, 1890–1962.* Cham: Springer Nature, 2019.

Lopez Alvarez, Luis. *Lumumba ou l'Afrique frustrée.* Paris: Cujas, 1964.

Losso Gazi. *Culture, littérature et enseignement au Zaïre: Essai de bilan.* Brussels: CEDAF, 1984.

Louis, William Roger. *Ends of British Imperialism: The Scramble for Empire, Suez and Decolonization.* London: Tauris, 2006.

Luabeya Mesu'a Kabwa. *Une jeunesse congolaise: De Luluabourg à Kinshasa; confidences d'un enfant de l'indépendance.* Paris: L'Harmattan, 2014.

Lufunda Samajiku Kaumba. "Eloge de l'UNAZA: De l'édification d'une université congolaise." In *Les années UNAZA (Université Nationale du Zaïre): Contribution à l'histoire de l'université africaine,* edited by Isidore Ndaywel è Nziem, 2:187–220. Paris: L'Harmattan, 2018.

Lugard, Frederick. *Education in Tropical Africa.* London: Colonial Office, 1930.

Lumumba, Patrice. *Le Congo, terre d'avenir, est-il menacé?* Brussels: Office de publicité, 1961.

Mabika Kalenda, [Auguste]. *La remise en question: Base de la décolonisation mentale.* Brussels: Remarques africaines, 1967.

Mabika Kalenda, [Auguste]. *Tabalayi: Bana betu.* Leopoldville: Concordia, 1963.

MacGaffey, Wyatt. *Kongo Political Culture: The Conceptual Challenge of the Particular.* Bloomington: Indiana University Press, 2000.

MacGaffey, Wyatt. "Zamenga of Zaire: Novelist, Historian, Sociologist, Philosopher and Moralist." *Research in African Literatures* 13, no. 2 (1982): 208–15.

Magaziner, Daniel. *The Art of Life in South Africa.* Athens: Ohio University Press, 2016.

Magaziner, Daniel. "Two Stories about Art, Education, and Beauty in Twentieth-Century South Africa." *American Historical Review* 118, no. 5 (2013): 1403–29.

Majambu Mbikay. *Concours et circonstances: Tome 1.* L'Ile-Perrot: Akulà, 2015.

Malengreau, Guy. *L'Université Lovanium des origines lointaines à 1960.* Kinshasa: Editions universitaires africaines, 2008.

Malkki, Liisa. "Citizens of Humanity: Internationalism and the Imagined Community of Nations." *Diaspora* 3, no. 1 (1994): 41–68.

Malkki, Liisa. *The Need to Help: The Domestic Arts of International Humanitarianism.* Durham, NC: Duke University Press, 2015.

Mamdani, Mahmood. "The African University." *London Review of Books* 40, no. 14 (July 2018): 29–32.

Manjpara, Kris. "Third World Humanities from South Asian Perspectives: An Oral History Approach." *South Asia: Journal of South Asian Studies* 41, no. 4 (2018): 1–18.

Mann, Gregory. *From Empires to NGOs in the West African Sahel: The Road to Nongovernmentality.* New York: Cambridge University Press, 2015.

Mantels, Ruben. *Geleerd in de tropen: Leuven, Congo, en de wetenschap, 1885–1960.* Leuven: Universitaire Pers, 2007.

Marable, Manning. *A Life of Reinvention.* New York: Viking, 2011.

Markowitz, Marvin D. *Cross and Sword: The Political Role of Christian Missions in the Belgian Congo, 1908–1960.* Stanford, CA: Hoover Institution Press, 1973.

Martens, Ludo. *Abo: Une femme du Congo.* Antwerp: EPO, 1992.

Martens, Ludo. *Pierre Mulele ou la seconde vie de Patrice Lumumba.* Antwerp: EPO, 1985.

Matala Mukadi, Tshiakatumba. *Dans la tourmente de la dictature (autobiographie d'un poète).* Paris: L'Harmattan, 2000.

Matala Mukadi, Tshiakatumba. *Réveil dans un nid de flammes (la foudre et le feu).* Paris: Seghers, 1969.

Matera, Marc. *Black London: The Imperial Metropolis and Decolonization in the Twentieth Century.* Oakland: University of California Press, 2015.

Mazov, Sergey. *A Distant Front in the Cold War: The USSR in West Africa and the Congo, 1956–1964.* Stanford, CA: Stanford University Press, 2010.

Mazrui, Ali A. *Political Values and the Educated Class in Africa.* Berkeley: University of California Press, 1978.

Mbembe, Achille. "Decolonizing the University: New Directions." *Arts and Humanities in Higher Education* 15, no. 1 (2016): 29–45.

Mbembe, Achille. *Necropolitics.* Durham, NC: Duke University Press, 2019.

Mbembe, Achille. *On the Postcolony.* Berkeley: University of California Press, 2001.

Mbembe, Achille. *Sortir de la grande nuit: Essai sur l'Afrique décolonisée.* Paris: La Découverte, 2010.

Mbembe, Achille. "The Banality of Power and the Aesthetics of Vulgarity in the Postcolony." *Public Culture* 4, no. 2 (1992): 1–30.

Meier, Prita. *Swahili Port Cities: The Architecture of Elsewhere.* Bloomington: University Indiana Press, 2016.

Merriam, Alan. *Congo: Background of a Conflict.* Evanston, IL: Northwestern University Press, 1961.

Mianda, Gertrude. "Colonialism, Education, and Gender Relations in the Belgian Congo: The Evolué Case." In *Women in African Colonial Histo-*

ries, edited by Jean Allman, Susan Geiger, and Nakanyike Musisi, 144–61. Bloomington: Indiana University Press, 2002.

Mianda, Gertrude. "Du Congo des évolués au Congo des universitaires: La représentation du genre." In *L'Université dans le devenir de l'Afrique: Un demi-siècle de présence au Congo-Zaïre*, edited by Isidore Ndaywel è Nziem, 221–36. Paris: L'Harmattan, 2007.

Millford, Ismay. "More than a Cold War Scholarship: East-Central African Anticolonial Activists, the International Union of Socialist Youth, and the Evasion of the Colonial State (1955–65)." *Stichproben Wiener Zeitschrift für kritische Afrikastudien* 18, no. 34 (2018): 19–43.

Mobe Fansiama, Anicet. "Les intellectualités estudiantines congolaises revisitées: 1954–1965." In *Aspects de la culture à l'époque coloniale en Afrique: Presse-archives*, 115–44. Paris: L'Harmattan, 2007.

Mobutu, Joseph-Désiré. *Dignité pour l'Afrique: Entretiens avec Jean-Louis Remilleux*. Paris: Albin Michel, 1988.

Mobutu, Joseph-Désiré. *Manifeste du mouvement populaire de la révolution*. Kinshasa: MPR, 1967.

Mobutu, Joseph-Désiré. *Paroles du président*. Kinshasa: Editions du Léopard, 1968.

Moke, Eugène. *Itinéraire et mémoires: Souvenirs personnels*. Kinshasa: Saint-Paul, 1989.

Monaville, Pedro. "Histoires politiques congolaises: Esquisse d'une réflexion sur la chronologie." In *L'Afrique belge au XIXe et XXe siècles: Nouvelles recherches et perspectives en histoire coloniale*, edited by Patricia Van Schuylenbergh, Catherine Lanneau, and Pierre-Luc Plasman, 73–88. Brussels: Peter Lang, 2014.

Monaville, Pedro. "June 4th 1969: Violence, Political Imagination, and the Student Movement in Kinshasa." In *The Third World in the Global Sixties*, edited by Samanta Christiansen and Zachary Scarlett, 159–70. New York: Berghahn, 2012.

Monaville, Pedro. "La crise congolaise de juillet 1960 et le sexe de la décolonisation." *Sextant* 25 (2008): 87–102.

Monaville, Pedro. "On the Passage of a Few Congolese through the Situationist International." In *The Other Country/L'Autre Pays*, edited by Vincent Meesen, 57–66. Berlin: Sternberg Press, 2018.

Monaville, Pedro. "The Political Life of the Dead Lumumba: Cold War Histories and the Congolese Student Left." *Africa* 89, no. 1 (2019): 15–39.

Monguya Mbenge, Daniel. *Histoire secrète du Zaïre*. Brussels: Editions de l'Espérance, 1977.

Moore, Carlos. *Castro, the Blacks and Africa*. Los Angeles: University of California Press, 1988.

Moorman, Marissa. *Powerful Frequencies: Radio, State Power, and the Cold War in Angola, 1931–2002*. Athens: Ohio University Press, 2019.

Mpase Nselenge Mpeti, Albert. *Au service d'un Congo aux milles visages, mémoires*. Kinshasa: Academic Express Press, 2010.

Mpase Nselenge Mpeti, Albert. "Vivre le devenir de l'université comme étudi-ant, responsable universitaire et ministre." In *Les années Lovanium: La première université francophone d'Afrique subsaharienne*, edited by Isidore Ndaywel è Nziem, 1:247–319. Paris: L'Harmattan, 2010.

Mrazek, Rudolf. *A Certain Age: Colonial Jakarta through the Memories of Its Intellectuals*. Durham, NC: Duke University Press, 2010.

Mudimbe, V. Y. *Carnets d'Amérique, septembre–novembre 1974*. Paris: Edi-tions Saint-Germain-des-Prés, 1976.

Mudimbe, V. Y. *L'autre face du royaume: Une introduction à la critique des languages en folie*. Lausanne: L'age d'homme, 1973.

Mudimbe, V. Y. *Le bel immonde*. Paris: Présence africaine, 1976.

Mudimbe, V.Y. *Le corps glorieux des mots et des êtres: Esquisse d'un jardin africain à la bénédictine*. Paris: Présence africaine, 1994.

Mudimbe, V. Y. *L'odeur du père: Essai sur les limites de la science et de la vie en Afrique noire*. Paris: Présence africaine, 1982.

Mudimbe, V. Y. *Parables and Fables: Exegesis, Textuality, and Politics in Cen-tral Africa*. Madison: University of Wisconsin Press, 1991.

Mudimbe, V.Y. *Tales of Faith: Religion as Political Performance in Central Africa*. London: Athlone, 1997.

Mudimbe, V. Y. *The Invention of Africa: Gnosis, Philosophy, and the Order of Knowledge*. Bloomington: Indiana University Press, 1988.

Mudimbe-Boyi, Elisabeth. "Le français, langue paternelle." In *La culture fran-çaise vue d'ici et d'ailleurs: Treize auteurs témoignent*, edited by Thomas Spear, 73–96. Paris: Karthala, 2002.

Mudimbe-Boyi, Elisabeth. "Vivre (à) la mission: Mémoires individuelles, his-toire collective." In *Religion, Colonization and Decolonization in Congo, 1885–1960*, edited by Vincent Viaene, Bram Cleys, and Jan De Mayer, 209–37. Leuven: Leuven University Press, 2020.

Muhirwa, Gassana. *Le syndicalisme et ses incidences socio-politiques en Af-rique: Le cas de l'UNTZA*. Kinshasa: Presses universitaires du Zaïre, 1982.

Mukendi, Aubert. *Enterrons les zombies: Essai de remise en question de la politique nationale*. Paris: France-Ouest, 1969.

Mukendi, Germain, and Bruno Kasonga. *Kabila: Le retour du Congo*. Ottigi-nies: Editions quorum, 1997.

Murairi Mitima, Jean-Baptiste. *Le festin des vautours: Mémoires d'un ambas-sadeur congolais*. Lille: Editions sources du Nil, 2012.

Mutamba Makombo, Jean-Marie. *Autopsie du gouvernement au Congo-Kinshasa: Le Collège des commissaires généraux (1960–1961) contre Patrice Lumumba*. Paris: L'Harmattan, 2015.

Mutamba Makombo, Jean-Marie. *Du Congo belge au Congo indépendant, 1940–1960: Emergences des "évolués" et genèse du nationalisme*. Kin-shasa: IFEP, 1998.

Mutamba Makombo, Jean-Marie. "La destinée de Patrice Lumumba (1925–1961)." In *A la redécouverte de Patrice Emery Lumumba*, edited by Mabiala Mantumba-Ngoma, 11–52. Kinshasa: Institut de formation et d'études politiques, 1996.

Mutamba Makombo, Jean-Marie. "Les auteurs du manifeste de conscience africaine: Blancs ou noirs?" In *Images, mémoires et savoirs: Une histoire en partage avec Bogumil Koss Jewsiewicki*, edited by Isidore Ndaywel è Nziem and Elisabeth Mudimbe-Boyi, 611–24. Paris: Karthala, 2009.

Mutongi, Kenda. "'Dear Dolly's' Advice: Representations of Youth, Courtship, and Sexualities in Africa, 1960–1980." *International Journal of African Historical Studies* 33, no. 1 (2000): 1–23.

Mwamba Mputu, Baudouin. *Le Congo-Kasaï (1865–1950): De l'exploration allemande à la consécration de Luluabourg*. Paris: L'Harmattan, 2011.

Mweya, Elisabeth Françoise. *Remous de feuilles*. Kinshasa: Edition du mont noir, 1972.

Mwifi Bodibatu, Marie-Madeleine. "*Mésaventure d'une étudiante religieuse et soldat.*" In *Les années Lovanium: La première université francophone d'Afrique subsaharienne*, edited by Isidore Ndaywel è Nziem, 2:121–33. Paris: L'Harmattan, 2010.

Namikas, Lise. *Battleground Africa: Cold War in the Congo, 1960–1965*. Stanford, CA: Stanford University Press, 2013.

Ndaywel è Nziem, Isidore. "De Lovanium au campus de Lubumbashi: Production d'une modernité culturelle congolaise." In *Les année UNAZA (Université Nationale du Zaïre): Contribution à l'histoire de l'Université Africaine*, edited by Isidore Ndawel è Nziem, 1:107–25. Paris: L'Harmattan, 2010.

Ndaywel è Nziem, Isidore. *Histoire générale du Congo: De l'héritage ancien à la république démocratique*. Paris: Duculot, 1998.

Ndaywel è Nziem, Isidore. "La première écriture de l'élite universitaire du Zaïre: Présence universitaire, 1959–1971." In *Papier blanc encore noire*, edited by Marc Quaghebeur et al., 401–31. Brussels: Labor, 1992.

Ndaywel è Nziem, Isidore. "La vie quotidienne à Lovanium." In *Les années Lovanium: La première université francophone d'Afrique subsaharienne*, edited by Isidore Ndaywel è Nziem, 2:43–75. Paris: L'Harmattan, 2010.

Ndaywel è Nziem, Isidore, ed. *Les années Lovanium: La première université francophone d'Afrique subsaharienne*. 2 vols. Paris: L'Harmattan, 2010.

Ndaywel è Nziem, Isidore, ed. *Les années UNAZA (Université Nationale du Zaïre): Contribution à l'histoire de l'Université Africaine*. 2 vols. Paris: L'Harmattan, 2018.

Ndaywel è Nziem, Isidore, ed. *L'université dans le devenir de l'Afrique: Un demi-siècle de présence au Congo-Zaïre*. Paris: L'Harmattan, 2007.

Ndaywel è Nziem, Isidore, and Elisabeth Mudimbe-Boyi, eds. *Images, mémoires et savoirs: Une histoire en partage avec Bogumil Koss Jewsiewicki*. Paris: Karthala, 2009.

Newell, Stephanie. *The Power to Name: A History of Anonymity in Colonial West Africa*. Athens: Ohio University Press, 2013.

Ngandu Nkashama, Pius. "La colonisation, tombeau de l'authenticité." In *Les années* UNAZA *(Université Nationale du Zaïre): Contribution à l'histoire de l'université africaine,* edited by Isidore Ndaywel è Nziem, 2:29–46. Paris: L'Harmattan, 2018.

Ngandu Nkashama, Pius. *La mort faite homme.* Paris: L'Harmattan, 1986.

N'Gbanda, Honoré. *Ainsi sonne le glas: Les derniers jours du maréchal Mobutu.* Paris: Groupe international d'édition et de publication de presse économique, 1998.

Ngoma-Binda, P. *Zamenga Batukezanga: Vie et oeuvre.* Kinshasa: Editions Saint-Paul afrique, 1990.

Nimer, Benjamin. "Concerning Willame's Reply." *International Journal of African Historical Studies* 7, no. 2 (1974): 312–17.

Nimer, Benjamin. "Congo Politics and the Pitfalls of Ideal Type Analysis." *International Journal of African Historical Studies* 6, no. 2 (1973): 315–34.

Nimy Mayidika Ngimbi, José. *Je ne renie rien, je raconte: L'histoire d'un parcours d'histoires.* Paris: L'Harmattan, 2006.

Nkay Malu, Flavien. *La mission chrétienne à l'épreuve de la tradition ancestrale (Congo belge, 1891–1933).* Paris: L'Harmattan, 2007.

Nkrumah, Kwame. *Challenge of the Congo.* London: Nelson, 1967.

Nkrumah, Kwame. *Neocolonialism: The Last Stage of Imperialism.* London: Nelson, 1965.

Nyunda ya Rubango. "De Lovanium à la Kasapa via caserne: Mémoires d'un pélerin metis." In *L'université dans le devenir de l'Afrique: Un demi-siècle de présence au Congo-Zaire,* edited by Isidore Ndaywel è Nziem, 97–124. Paris: L'Harmattan, 2007.

Nyunda ya Rubango. "Du 4 juin à la genèse de l'UNAZA: Fragments de mémoires d'un Lovaniard-milicien-Kasapard." In *Les années* UNAZA *(Université Nationale du Zaïre): Contribution à l'histoire de l'université africaine,* edited by Isidore Ndaywel è Nziem, 1:31–61. Paris: L'Harmattan, 2018.

Nyunda ya Rubango. "Mémoires de la colonie en vrac." In *Aspects de la culture à l'époque colonial en Afrique centrale (Congo-Meuse, 6),* edited by Marc Quaghebeur and Bibiane Tshibola Kalengayi, 145–90. Paris: L'Harmattan, 2007.

Nyunda ya Rubango. "Tango ya Ba-Papa Bol: Ou une page de chronique lovaniarde." In *Littérature francophone, université et société au Congo-Zaïre: Hommage à Victor Bol,* edited by Nyunda ya Rubango and Bogumil Jewsiewicki, 151–83. Paris: L'Harmattan, 1999.

Nzongola-Ntalaja, Georges. *Patrice Lumumba.* Athens: Ohio University Press, 2014.

Nzongola-Ntalaja, Georges. *The Congo from Leopold to Kabila: A People's History.* New York: Zed Books, 2002.

Nzongola-Ntalaja, Georges. "The Continuing Struggle for National Liberation in Zaire." *Journal of Modern African Studies* 17, no. 4 (1979): 595–614.

O'Malley, Allana. *The Diplomacy of Decolonisation: America, Britain and the United Nations during the Congo Crisis 1960–1964.* Manchester: Manchester University Press, 2018.

Omasombo Tshonda. "Lumumba, drame sans fin et deuil inachevé de la commission." *Cahiers d'études africaines* 173, no. 174 (2004): 221–61.

Omasombo Tshonda, Jean, and Benoît Verhaegen. *Patrice Lumumba acteur politique: De la prison aux portes du pouvoir, juillet 1956–février 1960.* Paris: L'Harmattan, 2005.

Omasombo Tshonda, Jean, and Benoît Verhaegen. *Patrice Lumumba: Jeunesse et apprentissage politique.* Paris: L'Harmattan, 1998.

Osseo-Osare, Abena Dove. *Atomic Junction: Nuclear Power in Africa after Independence.* Cambridge: Cambridge University Press, 2019.

Paget, Karen. *Patriotic Betrayal: The Inside Story of the CIA's Secret Campaign to Enroll American Students in the Crusade against Communism.* New Haven, CT: Yale University Press, 2015.

Pain, Marc. *Kinshasa: La ville et la cité.* Paris: Editions de l'ORSTOM, 1984.

Pavlakis, Dean. *British Humanitarianism and the Congo Reform Movement, 1896–1913.* London: Routledge, 2015.

Peck, Raoul. "It's about the Image." In *Lumumba in the Arts*, edited by Matthias De Groof, 173–79. Leuven: Leuven University Press, 2020.

Pedersen, Susan. *The Guardians: The League of Nations and the Crisis of Empire.* Oxford: Oxford University Press, 2015.

Peterson, Derek. *Ethnic Patriotism and the East African Revival: A History of Dissent, c. 1935–1972.* Cambridge: Cambridge University Press, 2012.

Petit, Pierre. *Patrice Lumumba: La fabrication d'un héros national et panafricain.* Brussels: Académie Royale de Belgique, 2016.

Prestholdt, Jeremy. *Icons of Dissent: The Global Resonance of Che, Marley, Tupac, and Bin Laden.* Oxford: Oxford University Press, 2019.

Prichard, Andreana. "'Let Us Swim in the Pool of Love': Love Letters and Discourses of Community Composition in Twentieth-Century Tanzania." *Journal of African History* 54 (2013): 103–22.

Pursley, Sara. "The Stage of Adolescence: Anticolonial Time, Youth Insurgency, and the Marriage Crisis in Hashemite Iraq." *History of the Present* 3, no. 2 (2013): 160–97.

Pype, Katrien. "Bolingo ya face: Digital Marriages, Playfulness and the Search for Change in Kinshasa." In *New Media Practices in a Changing Africa*, edited by Jo Helle-Valle and Ardis Storm-Mathisen, 93–122. Oxford: Berghahn, 2020.

Pype, Katrien. "Dancing to the Rhythm of Léopoldville: Nostalgia, Urban Critique and Generational Difference in Kinshasa's TV Music Shows." *Journal of African Cultural Studies* 29, no. 2 (2017): 158–76.

Pype, Katrien. "Political Billboards as Contact Zones: Reflections on Urban Space, the Visual and Political Affect in Kabila's Kinshasa." In *Photography in Africa: Ethnographic Perspectives*, edited by Richard Vokes, 187–204. Woodbridge, UK: James Currey, 2012.

Pype, Katrien. *The Making of the Pentecostal Melodrama: Religion, Media, and Gender in Kinshasa.* New York: Berghahn, 2012.

Quaghebeur, Marc, and Bibiane Tshibola Kalengayi, eds. *Aspects de la culture à l'époque coloniale en Afrique centrale: Formation, réinvention (Congo-Meuse, 6)*. Paris: L'Harmattan, 2007.

Quaghebeur, Marc, and Bibiane Tshibola Kalengayi, eds. *Aspects de la culture à l'époque coloniale en Afrique centrale: Littérature, théâtre (Congo-Meuse, 7)*. Paris: L'Harmattan, 2008.

Quaghebeur, Marc, and Bibiane Tshibola Kalengayi, eds. *Aspects de la culture à l'époque coloniale en Afrique centrale: Presse, archives (Congo-Meuse, 8)*. Paris: L'Harmattan, 2008.

Ranger, Terence. "The Invention of Tradition in Colonial Africa." In *The Invention of Tradition*, edited by Eric Hobsbawm and Terence Ranger, 211–62. Cambridge: Cambridge University Press, 1983.

Ray, Carina. *Crossing the Color Line: Race, Sex, and the Contested Politics of Colonialism in Ghana*. Athens: Ohio University Press, 2015.

Raymaekers, Paul. *L'organisation des zônes de squatting: Elément de résorption du chômage structurel dans les milieux urbains des pays en voie de développement: Application au milieu urbain de Léopoldville (République du Congo)*. Paris: Editions universitaires, 1964.

Raymaekers, Paul. *Nzala: Autobiographie d'un coopérant en Afrique centrale*. Braine-l'Alleud: J. M. Collet, 1993.

Raymaekers, Paul. *Prédélinquance et délinquance juvénile à Léopoldville (1960–1961): Cliché sociologique*. Brussels: Paul Raymaekers Foundation, 2010.

Reno, William. "Congo: From State Collapse to 'Absolutism,' to State Failure." *Third World Quarterly* 27, no. 1 (2006): 43–56.

Revel, Jacques. *Un parcours critique: Douze exercices d'histoire sociale*. Paris: Galaade, 2006.

Rey Tristan, Eduardo, and Guillermo Gracia Santos. "The Role of the Left-Wing Editors on the Diffusion on the New Left Wave." In *Revolutionary Violence and the New Left: Transnational Perspectives*, edited by Alberto Martin Alvarez and Eduardo Rey Tristan, 89–109. New York: Routledge, 2016.

Rich, Jeremy. "Manufacturing Sovereignty and Manipulating Humanitarianism: The Diplomatic Resolution of the Mercenary Revolt in the Democratic Republic of Congo, 1967–68." *Journal of African History* 60, no. 2 (2019): 277–96.

Rich, Jeremy. *Protestant Missionaries and Humanitarianism in the DRC: The Politics of Aid in Cold War Africa*. Woodbridge, UK: James Currey, 2020.

Richards, Yevette. *A Personal History of Race, Labor and International Relations, Conversations with Maida Springer*. Pittsburgh, PA: University of Pittsburgh Press, 2004.

Richards, Yevette. *Maida Springer: Pan-Africanist and International Labor Leader*. Pittsburgh, PA: University of Pittsburgh Press, 2000.

Rikir, Milou, ed. *Le P.C.B. et la scission "Grippiste" de 1963*. Brussels: Carcob, 2002.

Riva, Silvia. *Nouvelle histoire de la littérature du Congo-Kinshasa*. Paris: L'Harmattan, 2006.

Rivers Ndaliko, Chérie. *Necessary Noise: Music, Film, and Charitable Imperialism in the East of Congo*. New York: Oxford University Press, 2016.

Robbins, Hollis. "Fugitive Mail: The Deliverance of Henry 'Box' Brown and Antebellum Postal Politics." *American Studies* 50, no. 1–2 (Spring/Summer 2009): 5–25.

Roberts, Jennifer. *Transporting Visions: The Movement of Images in Early America*. Berkeley: University of California Press, 2014.

Roblès, Emmanuel. *Montserrat*. Paris: Le Seuil, 1962.

Roessler, Philip, and Harry Verhoeven. *When Comrades Go to War: Liberation Politics and the Outbreak of Africa's Deadliest Conflict*. Oxford: Oxford University Press, 2016.

Ross, Kristin. *Communal Luxury: The Political Imaginary of the Paris Commune*. New York: Verso, 2015.

Ross, Kristin. *May '68 and Its Afterlives*. Chicago: University of Chicago Press, 2002.

Rubin, Andrew, *Archives of Authority: Empire, Culture, and the Cold War*. Princeton, NJ: Princeton University Press, 2012.

Sabakinu Kivulu, ed. *Elites et démocratie en République Démocratique du Congo*. Kinshasa: Presses Universitaires de Kinshasa, 2000.

Salkin, Paul. *Etudes africaines*. Brussels: Larcier, 1920.

Salkin, Paul. *Le problème de l'évolution noire: L'Afrique centrale dans cent ans*. Paris: Payot, 1926.

Sampassa Kaweta Milombe, G. M. *Conscience et politique au Congo-Zaïre: De l'engagement aux responsabilités*. Paris: L'Harmattan, 2003.

Sartre, Jean-Paul. *Being and Nothingness: A Phenomenological Essay on Ontology*. New York: Washington Square Press, 1984.

Sartre, Jean-Paul. *Colonialism and Neocolonialism*. London: Routledge, 2001.

Schatzberg, Michael G. "*Fidélité au guide*: The JMPR in Zairian Schools." *Journal of Modern African Studies* 16, no. 3 (1978): 417–31.

Schatzberg, Michael G. *Political Legitimacy in Middle Africa: Father, Family, Food*. Bloomington: Indiana University Press, 2001.

Schatzberg, Michael G. *Politics and Class in Zaire: Bureaucracy, Business and Beer in Lisala*. New York: Africana Publishing, 1980.

Schatzberg, Michael G. *The Dialectics of Oppression in Zaire*. Indianapolis: Indiana University Press, 1988.

Schmidt, Elizabeth. *Foreign Intervention in Africa: From the Cold War to the War on Terror*. Cambridge: Cambridge University Press, 2013.

Schmitt, Carl. *The* Nomos *of the Earth in the International Law of the* Jus Publicum Europaeum. New York: Telos, 2003.

Schramme, Jean. *Le bataillon Lépoard: Souvenirs d'un Africain blanc*. Paris: Robert Laffont, 1969.

Schwar, Harriett Daschiell. *Foreign Relations of the United States, 1961–1963, Volume XX: Congo Crisis.* Washington, DC: United States Government Printing Service, 1994.

Scott, David. *Omens of Adversity: Tragedy, Time, Memory, Justice.* Durham, NC: Duke University Press, 2014.

Scott, James. *Domination and the Arts of Resistance: Hidden Transcripts.* New Haven, CT: Yale University Press, 1990.

Scott, James, ed. *Seeing like a State: How Certain Schemes to Improve the Human Condition Have Failed.* New Haven, CT: Yale University Press, 1998.

Segaert, Henri. *Un terme au Congo belge: Notes sur la vie coloniale, 1916–1918.* Brussels: A. Van Assche, 1919.

Seibert, Julia. "More Continuity than Change? New Forms of Unfree Labor in Colonial Congo, 1908–1930." In *Humanitarian Intervention and Changing Labor Relations: The Long-Term Consequences of the Abolition of the Slave Trade*, edited by Marcel Van der Linden, 369–86. Leiden: Brill, 2011.

Semonin, Paul. "Mobutu and the Congolese." *World Today* 24, no. 1 (January 1968): 20–29.

Senghor, Léopold Sédar. *De la négritude/Marxisme et humanisme.* Dakar: Grande imprimerie africaine, [1970].

Serufuri Hakiza, Paul. "Les Etats-Unis d'Amérique et l'enseignement en Afrique noire (1910–1945)." In *La nouvelle histoire du Congo: Mélanges offerts à Frans Bontinck, c.i.c.m.*, edited by Pamphile Mabiala Mantuba-Ngoma, 229–49. Paris: L'Harmattan, 2004.

Shinn, David H., and Joshua Eisenman. *China and Africa: A Century of Engagement.* Philadelphia: University of Pennsylvania Press, 2012.

Shringarpure, Bhakti. *Cold War Assemblages: Decolonization to Digital.* New York: Routledge, 2019.

Siegert, Bernard. *Relays: Literature as an Epoch of the Postal System.* Stanford, CA: Stanford University Press, 1999.

Signaté, Ibrahima. *L'Afrique entre ombre et lumière: Carnet de route d'un journaliste.* Paris: L'Harmattan, 2004.

Slobodian, Quinn. *Foreign Front: Third World Politics in Sixties West Germany.* Durham, NC: Duke University Press, 2012.

Solberg, Carl. *Hubert Humphrey: A Biography.* New York: Norton, 1984.

Sorensen, Diana, ed. *Territories and Trajectories: Cultures in Circulation.* Durham, NC: Duke University Press, 2018.

Stanard, Matthew. "Revisiting Bula Matari and the Congo Crisis: Successes and Anxieties in Belgium's Late Colonial State." *Journal of Imperial and Commonwealth History* 46, no. 1 (2018): 144–68.

Stearns, Jason. *Dancing in the Glory of Monsters: The Collapse of the Congo and the Great War of Africa.* New York: Public Affairs, 2011.

Stewart, Gary. *Rumba on the River: A History of the Popular Music of the Two Congos.* London: Verso, 2000.

Straker, Jay. *Youth, Nationalism, and the Guinean Revolution.* Bloomington: Indiana University Press, 2009.

Stoler, Ann Laura. "'In Cold Blood': Hierarchies of Credibility and the Politics of Colonial Narratives." *Representations* 37 (Winter 1992): 151–89.

Sumbu, Edouard-Marcel. *El Congo: Revolucion armada*. Havana: CTCR, n.d.

Sumbu, Edouard-Marcel. *Il sangue dei Leoni*. Milan: Liberia Feltrinelli, 1969.

Suri, Jeremi. *The Global Revolutions of 1968*. New York: Norton, 2007.

Tagore, Rabindranath. *Selected Stories from Rabindranath Tagore*. New Delhi: Ocean Books, 2011.

Tead, Diana. *What Is a Race? Evidence from Scientists*. Paris: UNESCO, 1952.

Telepneva, Natalia. "'Code Name Sekretar': Amilcar Cabral, Czechoslovakia and the Role of Human Intelligence during the Cold War." *International History Review* 42, no. 6 (2019): 1257–73.

Temkin, Moshik. "American Internationalists in France and the Politics of Travel Control in the Era of Vietnam." In *Outside In: The Transnational Circuit of US History*, edited by Andrew Preston and Doug Rossinow, 247–68. Oxford: Oxford University Press, 2017.

Terretta, Meredith. *Nation of Outlaws, State of Violence: Nationalism, Grassfields Tradition, and State Building in Cameroon*. Athens: Ohio University Press, 2014.

Thomas, Kate. *Postal Pleasures: Sex, Scandal, and Victorian Letters*. New York: Oxford University Press, 2012.

Tilman, Samuel. "L'implantation du scoutisme au Congo belge." In *Itinéraires croisés de la modernité, Congo belge (1920–1950)*, edited by Jean-Luc Vellut, 103–40. Paris: L'Harmattan, 2001.

Tödt, Daniel. *The Lumumba Generation: African Bourgeoisie and Colonial Distinction in the Belgian Congo*. Oldenbourg: De Gruyter, 2021.

Tolliver, Cedric. *Of Vagabonds and Fellow Travelers: African Diaspora Literary Culture and the Cultural Cold War*. Ann Arbor: University of Michigan Press, 2019.

Toulier, Bernard, Johan Lagage, and Marc Gemoets. *Kinshasa: Architecture et paysage urbains*. Paris: Somogy, 2010.

Trapido, Joe. *Breaking Rocks: Music, Ideology and Economic Collapse from Paris to Kinshasa*. Oxford: Berghahn, 2017.

Trapido, Joe. "'Masterless Men': Riots, Patronage, and the Politics of Surplus Population in Kinshasa." *Cultural Anthropology* 62, no. 2 (2021). https://doi.org/10.1086/713765.

Trefon, Théodore, ed. *Reinventing Order in the Congo: How People Respond to State Failure in Kinshasa*. London: Zed Books, 2004.

Tshimanga, Charles. *Jeunesse, formation et société au Congo-Kinshasa, 1890–1960*. Paris: L'Harmattan, 2001.

Tshimanga, Charles. "La jeunesse étudiante dans l'évolution socio-politique du Congo-Kinshasa, 1954–1973." In *Histoire et devenir de l'Afrique noire au vingtième siècle: Travaux en cours*, edited by Catherine Coquery-Vidrovitch et al., 55–65. Paris: L'Harmattan, 2001.

Tsing, Anna. *Friction: An Ethnography of Global Connection*. Princeton, NJ: Princeton University Press, 2005.

Turner, Thomas. "Clouds of Smoke: Cultural and Psychological Modernization in Zaire." In *Zaire: The Political Economy of Underdevelopment*,
edited by Guy Cran, 69–84. New York: Praeger, 1979.

Twain, Mark. *King Leopold's Soliloquy*. Boston: Warren, 1906.

Union des jeunesses révolutionnaires congolaises. *Mémorandum: L'agression
armée de l'impérialisme américano-belge à Stanleyville et Paulis*. Brussels:
Livre International, 1966.

Vaïsse, Maurice, ed. *Documents diplomatiques français: 1966*. 2 vols. Brussels:
Peter Lang, 2006.

Vaïsse, Maurice, ed. *Documents diplomatiques français: 1968*. 2 vols. Brussels:
Peter Lang, 2009.

Van Beurden, Sarah. *Authentically African: Arts and the Transnational Politics
of Congolese Culture*. Athens: Ohio University Press, 2015.

Van Beurden, Sarah. "The Art of (Re)possession: Heritage and the Cultural
Politics of Congo's Decolonization." *Journal of African History* 56 (2015):
143–64.

Vanderlinden, Jacques. *Main d'oeuvre, église, capital, et administration dans le
Congo des années trente: Journal de Pierre Ryckmans*. Brussels: Académie
royale des sciences d'outre-mer, 2007.

Vanderlinden, Jacques. *Pierre Ryckmans, 1891–1959: Coloniser dans
l'honneur*. Brussels: De Boeck, 1994.

Vandewalle, Frédéric. *L'Ommegang: Odysée et reconquête de Stanleyville,
1964*. Brussels: Témoignage africains, 1969.

Vandewoude, E. *Le voyage du Prince Albert au Congo en 1909*. Brussels: Académie royale des sciences d'outre-mer, 1990.

Van Keerberghen, Joseph. *Histoire de l'enseignement catholique au Kasayi,
1891–1947*. Kananga: Editions de l'archidiocèse, 1985.

Van Lierde, Jean, ed. *La pensée politique de Patrice Lumumba*. Paris: Présence
universitaire, 1963.

Van Lierde, Jean, and Guy de Bosschère. *La guerre sans armes: Douze années
de luttes non-violentes en Europe, 1952–1964*. Brussels: Editions Luc Pire,
2002.

Vansina, Jan. *Being Colonized: The Kuba Experience in Rural Congo, 1880–
1960*. Madison: University of Wisconsin Press, 2010.

Vansina, Jan. *Living with Africa*. Madison: University of Wisconsin Press, 1995.

Vansina, Jan. "Mwasi's Trials." *Daedalus* 111, no. 2 (1982): 49–70.

Vansina, Jan. *Paths in the Rainforests: Toward a History of Political Tradition
in Equatorial Africa*. Madison: University of Wisconsin Press, 1990.

Vansina, Jan. "Some Perceptions on the Writing of African History: 1948–
1992." *Itinerario* 16, no. 1 (1992): 77–91.

Vanthemsche, Guy. *La Belgique et le Congo: Empreintes d'une colonie
1885–1980*. Brussels: Complexe, 2007.

Valtat, Jean-Christophe. "Vitesse, réseau, vision: La malle-poste anglaise de
Thomas de Quincey." *Conserveries mémorielles* 17 (2015). http://journals
.openedition.org/cm/2084.

Vellut, Jean-Luc. *Congo: Ambitions et désenchantements 1880–1960.* Paris: Karthala, 2017.

Vellut, Jean-Luc. "Le Katanga industriel en 1944: Malaises et anxiétés dans la société coloniale." In *Le Congo belge dans la seconde guerre mondiale: Recueil d'études,* 495–523. Brussels: Académie royale des sciences d'outre-mer, 1983.

Vellut, Jean-Luc. *Simon Kimbangu, 1921: De la prediction à la déportation; Les Sources.* 2 vols. Brussels: Académie royale des sciences d'outre-mer, 2005–15.

Verbeek, Léon. "D'une thèse de doctorat à la constitution d'une banque de données: Naissance d'un projet de recherché et d'une équipe." In *Les arts plastiques de l'Afrique contemporaine: 60 ans d'histoire à Lubumbashi,* edited by Léon Verbeek, 11–23. Paris: L'Harmattan, 2008.

Verdery, Katherine. *The Political Lives of Dead Bodies: Reburial and Postsocialist Change.* New York: Columbia University Press, 1999.

Vergès, Françoise. "Vertigo and Emancipation, Creole Cosmopolitanism and Cultural Politics." *Theory, Culture and Society* 18, no. 2–3 (2001): 169–83.

Verhaegen, Benoît. "Communisme et anticommunisme au Congo." *Brood and rozen* 4, no. 2 (1999): 113–28.

Verhaegen, Benoît. *Congo 1961.* Brussels: CRISP, 1962.

Verhaegen, Benoît. "La rébellion muléliste au Kwilu: Chronologie des événements et essai d'interprétation (janvier 1962–juillet 1964)." In *Rébellions-révolutions au Zaire 1963–1965,* edited by Catherine Coquery-Vidrovitch, Alain Forest, and Herbert Weiss, 1:120–46. Paris: L'Harmattan, 1987.

Verhaegen, Benoît. *L'enseignement universitaire au Zaire: De Lovanium à l'UNAZA 1958–1978.* Paris: L'Harmattan, 1978.

Verhaegen, Benoît. "Les trois héros tragiques de l'histoire du Congo: Lumumba, Mulele, Guevara." In *Figures et paradoxes de l'histoire au Burundi, au Congo et au Rwanda,* edited by Marc Quaghebeur, 299–331. Paris: L'Harmattan, 2002.

Verhaegen, Benoît. *Rébellions au Congo: Tome 1.* Brussels: CRISP, 1966.

Verhaegen, Benoît. *Rébellions au Congo: Tome 2.* Brussels: CRISP, 1969.

Verhaegen, Benoît, et al. *Mulele et la révolution populaire au Kwilu (République démocratique du Congo).* Paris: L'Harmattan, 2006.

Volta, Ornella, ed. *La piste rouge (Italia 69–72).* Paris: Union Générale générale d'éEditions, 1973.

Wack, Henry Wellington. *The Story of the Congo Free State: Social, Political, and Economic Aspects.* New York: Putnam, 1905.

Wallerstein, Immanuel. "1968, Revolution in the World-System: Theses and Queries." *Theory and Society* 18, no. 4 (1989): 431–49.

Wallerstein, Immanuel. *Africa: The Politics of Independence.* New York: Vintage, 1961.

Weiner, Tim. *Legacy of Ashes: The History of the CIA.* New York: Anchor, 2007.

Weiss, Herbert F. *Radicalisme rural et lutte pour l'indépendance au Congo-Zaïre: Le Parti solidaire africaine, 1959–1960.* Paris: L'Harmattan, 1994.

Weiss, Herbert, and Adrienne Fulco. "Les partisans au Kwilu: Analyse des origines sociales des membres et cadres des équipes de base." In *Rébellions-révolutions au Zaire 1963–1965*, edited by Catherine Coquery-Vidrovitch, Alain Forest, and Herbert Weiss, 1:168–81. Paris: L'Harmattan, 1987.

Weissman, Steven R. *American Foreign Policy in the Congo, 1960–1964.* Ithaca, NY: Cornell University Press, 1974.

White, Bob W. *Rumba Rules: The Politics of Dance Music in Mobutu's Zaire.* Durham, NC: Duke University Press, 2008.

White, Bob W. "The Political Undead: Is It Possible to Mourn for Mobutu's Zaire?" *African Studies Review* 48, no. 2 (2005): 62–85.

White, Luise. "Hodgepodge Historiography: Documents, Itineraries, and the Absence of Archives." *History in Africa* 42 (2015): 309–18.

Wilder, Gary. *Freedom Time: Negritude, Decolonization and the Future of the World.* Durham, NC: Duke University Press, 2015.

Willame, Jean-Claude. *Patrice Lumumba: La crise congolaise revisitée.* Paris: Karthala, 1990.

Willame, Jean-Claude. *Patrimonialism and Political Change in the Congo.* Stanford, CA: Stanford University Press, 1972.

Willame, Jean-Claude. "The Art of Misquotation: A Reply to Benjamin Nimer." *International Journal of African Historical Studies* 7, no. 1 (1974): 120–23.

Willame, Jean-Claude. "The Congo." In *Students and Politics in Developing Nations*, edited by Donald K. Emerson, 37–63. New York: Praeger, 1968.

Williams, Suzanne. *Spies in the Congo: America's Atomic Mission in World War II.* New York: Public Affairs, 2016.

Williams, Suzanne. *Who Killed Hammarskjöld? The UN, the Cold War and White Supremacy in Africa.* London: Hurst, 2011.

Williamson, F. H. "The International Postal Service and the Universal Postal Union." *Journal of the Royal Institute of International Affairs* 9, no. 1 (January 1930): 68–78.

Yakemtchouk, Romain. *L'Université Lovanium et sa faculté de théologie: L'action éducative de l'Université catholique de Louvain en Afrique centrale.* Chastre: Bureau d'études en relations internationales, 1983.

Yambuya Lotika Kibesi, Pierre. *Le néocolonialisme au Congo: La révolution, le parcours, les hommes.* Paris: Jouve, 2006.

Yangu Sukama, Guy. *Les manifestations des étudiants du Congo-Kinshasa du 4 juin 1969 et 4 juin 1971.* Kinshasa: Imprimerie Sakalemady, 2014.

Yates, Barbara. "The Missions and Educational Development 1876–1908." PhD diss., Columbia University, 1967.

Yoka Lye Mudaba, [André], "4 juin 1969: Témoignage d'un survivant." In *Les années Lovanium: La première université francophone d'Afrique subsaharienne*, edited by Isidore Ndaywel è Nziem, 107–12. Paris: L'Harmattan, 2010.

Yoka Lye Mudaba, [André]. *Kinshasa, signes de vie.* Paris: L'Harmattan, 2000.

Yoka Lye Mudaba, [André]. *Le fossoyeur, et sept autres nouvelles primées dans le cadre du concours radiophonique de la meilleure nouvelle de langue française.* Paris: Hatier, 1986.

Yoon, Duncan. "Figuring Africa and China: Congolese Literary Imaginaries of the PRC." *Journal of World Literature* 6, no. 2 (2021): 167–96.

Young, Crawford. *Politics in Congo: Decolonization and Independence.* Princeton, NJ: Princeton University Press, 1965.

Young, Crawford. "Review of *Patrimonialism and Political Change in the Congo* by J.-C. Willame." *Journal of Politics* 35, no. 2 (1973): 506–8.

Young, Crawford. *The Postcolonial State in Africa: Fifty Years of Independence, 1960–2010.* Madison: University of Wisconsin Press, 2012.

Young, Crawford, and Thomas Turner. *The Rise and Decline of the Zairian State.* Madison: University of Wisconsin Press, 1985.

Young, Robert. "Sartre: The African Philosopher." In Jean-Paul Sartre, *Colonialism and Postcolonialism*, ix–xxvii. London: Routledge, 2006.

Zamenga Batukezanga. *La carte postale.* Kinshasa: Editions Saint-Paul afrique, 1976.

Zana Aziza Etambala. *In het land van de Banoko: De geschiedenis van de Kongolese/Zaïrese aanwezigheid in België van 1885 to heden.* Leuven: Hoger Instituut voor de Arbeid, 1993.

Zana Aziza Etambala. "L'armée du salut et la naissance de la 'mission des noirs' au Congo belge, 1934–1940." *Annales aequatoria* 26 (2005): 67–164.

Zana Aziza Etambala. "Lumumba en Belgique, du 25 avril au 23 mai 1956: Son récit de voyage et ses impressions, document inédit." In *Figures et paradoxes de l'histoire au Burundi, au Congo et au Rwanda*, edited by Marc Quaghebeur, 191–229. Paris: L'Harmattan, 2002.

Zana Aziza Etambala. "Stefano Kaoze, sa formation, son ordination et son voyage en Europe (1899–1921)." In *Aspects de la culture à l'époque coloniale en Afrique centrale (Congo-Meuse, 6)*, edited by Marc Quaghebeur and Bibiane Tshibola Kalengayi, 17–61. Paris: L'Harmattan, 2008.

Zimmerman, Andrew. *Alabama in Africa: Booker T. Washington, the German Empire, and the Globalization of the New South.* Princeton, NJ: Princeton University Press, 2010.

Zeleke, Elleni Centime. *Ethiopia in Theory: Revolution and Knowledge Production, 1964–2016.* Leiden: Brill, 2019.

Zewde, Barhu, ed. *Documenting the Ethiopian Student Movement: An Exercise in Oral History.* Addis Ababa: Forum for Social Studies, 2010.

Zewde, Barhu. *The Quest for Socialist Utopia: The Ethiopian Student Movement, c. 1960–1974.* Woodbridge, UK: James Currey, 2014.

…

The letter *f* following a page number denotes a figure.

Ben Bella, Ahmed, 62, 98, 136, 148, 232n28, 267n9
Benot, Yves, 142
Benza, Jean-Robert, 151–52
Berlin Conference, 26, 27
Biafra: students from, 273n15, 277n52
Biaya, T. K., 208
Bills (Kinshasa's youth gangs), 95, 168, 244n37, 266n5
Bisengimana, Barthélémy, 264n4
blackness, 46, 69, 92, 113, 141, 142, 148
Bokata, Hubert, 50
Bol, Victor, 193
Bomboko, Justin-Marie, 57, 87, 112, 115, 116, 171, 193, 242n14, 248n10, 265n9
Bongoma, Jacques, 161–65
Bongoy, Yvon, 99, 100, 101, 169, 246n63, 267n8
Bosango, Séraphin, 195–96
Botamba, Joseph, 57–58
Botike, Michel, 135
Bourdieu, Pierre, 132
Brazzaville. See Congo-Brazzaville
Breakfast at Tiffany's, 164
Brown, Irving, 55–56, 234n53
Brussels: Amis de Présence Africaine, 113; Lumumba protest, 117–18; round-table conferences, 45, 113–14; Sartre in, 8; La Voix de l'Amitié (radio program), 6; World Fair of 1958, 228n76. See also student expatriates, Congolese; Université Libre de Bruxelles
Buakasa, Gérard, 13, 149, 154
Buisseret, Auguste, 33, 76–77

CADULAC (Centre agricole de l'Université de Louvain au Congo), 87
Caesarism, 206
Cairo, 117, 118; Congolese rebels in, 104, 135, 150, 152, 263n58, 282n95; Radio Cairo, 6
caporalisation, 180, 198, 272n2
Cardoso, Mario, 185, 283n4
La carte postale (Zamenga), 21–22, 222n3
Castro, Fidel, 62, 172, 179, 259n4
Catholic Church: communism and, 231n27; expansion of school system by, 12, 76; relations between state

and, 81; social Catholicism, 8, 181; Vatican, 114. See also Lovanium; missionaries; schools, Catholic; seminary education
CEK (Cercles de Etudiants de Kinshasa), 185–86
censorship: banned publications, 31; banned publications and, 226n54; of communist pamphlets, 230n17; escaping, 39, 49, 60; postal system and, 36, 50; students and self-censorship, 176
Central Intelligence Agency (CIA): Brown and, 55, 234n53; the College of General Commissioners and, 116; central role in the Congo, 253n74, 267n14; counterinsurgency operations by, 135, 136, 146, 219n56; covert support by, 10, 119–22, 252n70; Harris and, 129; and Lumumba's assassination, 2, 215n7; Mibamba and, 125; Mobutu as agent of, 270n53; on post in Leopoldville, 44; report on youth radicalization, 9; student politics and, 127, 215n10, 219n50, 251n64. See also USNSA
Centre National de Documentation (CND), 194, 198, 280n82
Césaire, Aimé, 104, 107, 113, 118, 170, 181
Ch'en Chia-k'ang, 235n64
China (PRC), People's Republic of: diplomats from, 6; Mobutu and, 126, 202; PCB and, 49; support from, 62. See also Maoism; Mao Zedong
CIA. See Central Intelligence Agency
cinq chantiers, xiii
citizenship: colonial, 34; and decolonization, 4, 78; in the world, x
CNL. See Comité National de Libération
co-gestion, 100–101, 184–86
Colard, Sandrine, 223n15
Cold War: in Congo, xiv, 10; insurrection and, 146; letter writing during, 54, 58; nationalist camp and, 111; neocolonial violence and, 43; political alignment during, 54–55; student activists and, xiv, 9; student politics and, 119; UGEC and, 127; US Cold War liberals, 1, 119–25, 219n50. See also Congo crisis; imperialism

as horizon for students, 19; interracial sexuality and, 51; of knowledge, 129–30, 193; of Lovanium, 139; Palambwa on, 73–74; as pedagogy of the world, 209; student activists and, 101–2, 197; student politics and, 16; as unfinished, 8, 180, 216n19; of universities, xi, 129; US response to, 43

decolonization era: characteristics of, 12; domestic front, 22; foreign front of, 21–22; postal correspondences and, 21; postcolonial humanities in, 13. *See also* mobility; postal communications

De Coninck, Albert, 235n64

De Quincey, Thomas, 23–24, 222n1 (chap. 1)

Diagne, Blaise, 31

Dibwe, Donatien, 226n62

Dienayame, Mathurin, 279n78

Diop, Alioune, 113, 174

Diop, Cheikh Anta, 46, 113, 203

Dipanda (newspaper), 133–34

distance learning, 34–37; APIPO and, 33, 35–37; Institute for Human Culture, 34–35; Kingansi and, 34–35; Liwatwa and, 34; Lumumba's, 33–34, 35; Nyssens and, 34–35; PCB and, 49–51

distinction: in Central African traditions, 108; class, 140; generational, 4–5; of Josephite education, 72; missionaries and, 69; postal correspondence and search for, 52; of students, 13, 92, 120, 197, 201, 207. *See also* cosmopolitanism; elitism

Dominican Republic, 153

Du Bois, W. E. B., 31

Dupire, Luc-Daniel, 151, 153, 155–56, 261n31, 262n45

Dutschke, Rudi, 6

East Germany, 150, 151, 152, 233n49

Ebony article, 42–43, 44

L'Echo Postal (periodical), 36–37, 40

L'Eclair (periodical), 153–60, 176, 262n39, 263n58

Ecole Nationale de Droit et d'Administration (ENDA), 129–30, 142, 175, 185

education system: about, 17; in Belgian colonial period, 60, 67, 81, 82; Belgian teachers in Congo, 83; Catholic Church and, 11, 12; development of, xiii; expansion of in Congo, 11–12; foreign study, 82–83; importance of, 63–64; overeducation, 68–70; paths of, 76–78; in post-independence era, 67, 78–80, 81–83; progressive pedagogy, 72–75, 81; state-controlled secondary school, 76–77, 82–83; UN and, 54; universalism and, 7. *See also* education system; schools, Catholic; schools, Pamba; schools, Protestant; schools, state; seminary education; university education

Egyptology, 7

Ekwa, Martin, 65–66, 72, 73, 78, 79, 82, 83

Elanga, Adou, 94

Elisabethville. *See* Lubumbashi

elitism: as alienation, 132, 197; critiques of, 170, 189; in education xi, 75, 88, 90, 93, 238n32; students and, 94, 109, 184, 204, 216n20; UGEC and, 158, 167. *See also* distinction

ENDA (Ecole Nationale de Droit et d'Administration), 129–32, 142, 175, 185

Engels, Friedrich, x

Equateur, 269n27

Erny, Pierre, 82, 205

Ethiopia, 9, 163, 218n44, 227n64, 278n59

Etudiants Congolais Progressistes, 271n59

évolués: assimilationist relation to Europe, 140; cellular incarceration of, 38; colonial libraries for, 23; distance learning, 34–36; Kingansi as, 34–35, 228n76; as "Europeanized Blacks," 69, 71; Lomami as, 238n30; Lumumba and, 33, 36; in politics and, 44, 77, 95, 110, 137, 220n66; postal system and, 25, 26; and print media, 227n68, 238n30; respectable masculinity of, 37, 228n88; salaries for, 38; school reforms and, 76–77; university students as children of, 11, 239n47

existentialism, 7, 210. *See also* Sartre, Jean-Paul

extraversion, 13–15, 62, 112–15

global movement of refusal, 7
Golan, Tamar, 129, 130–32
Gold Coast: Lumumba in, 45; self-government in, 11, 95
Goldschmidt, Robert, 29, 30, 225n43
Goma Charter, 184–85, 186
Grand Kalle (Joseph Kabasele), 191
Grippa, Jacques, 151, 261n35
Gudumbangana, Kangafu, 201
Guevara, Ernesto "Che," 140; in Congo, 135–36; Guevarism, 155; influence on students, 6, 182, 191, 219n56, 259n1
Guinea, 49, 59

Harriman, Averell, 219n57
Harris, James T., 129
Harvard, 121
hazing rituals, 85–86, 97
Heart of Darkness (Conrad), 66
Hepburn, Audrey, 266n14
Herskovits, Melville, 64
higher education. *See* university education
Ho Chi Minh, 2, 179
Hodgkin, Thomas, 11
Hogbood, Ben, 193–94
Hountondji, Paulin, 14–15
human rights, 28, 44, 57, 113, 113, 178, 234n60
Humphrey, Hubert, 121; African tour, 1–2, 3f; anti-Humphrey rally, 2, 5–8, 175, 180, 185; Lumumba and, 215n7; Mobutu and, 2, 18; one-worldedness of, 10; student/state antagonism and, 4, 218n44
Humphrey, Muriel, 1, 2, 215n12
Hunt, Nancy, 11

identity politics, 182–84
Iléo, Joseph, 102
Il sangue dei leoni (Sumbu), 144–45, 160
Ilunga, Jean-Claude, 52–53
Ilunga Kabese, Jean, 176
Ilunga Kabongo, André, 246n63
imagination: political imagination, x, 16–17, 40, 44, 62, 153, 180, 209, 216n15, 219n51, 255n18, 273n13; popular imagination and sorcery, 282n97; spatial imagination, xiv, 4,

10, 14, 95, 181, 202; temporal imagination, xiv, 7, 217n36
imperialism: anti-colonial nationalism and Western, 15; Belgian, 116; British, 224n25; French cultural, 217n33; Marxist-Leninist, 116; Mobutu and, 169, 175, 181; mutations in structures of, 19; postal system and, 27; radical critiques of, xi; Soviet, 62, 119, 121, 252n71; US, 2, 8, 10, 120–21, 134, 136, 141, 146, 175, 180
independence: about, 19; Bomboko and, 112; Cold War and, 5; granting of, 45; Lumumba as advocate for, 39, 110; mutiny after, 43, 44; optimism after, 47; Palambwa on, 73–74; postal correspondences and, 15, 17; postal system and, 61; radical anti-imperialism and, xiv; student activists and, 12; unfinished business of, xiv
India, 5–6, 70, 119, 227n64, 237, 19
Inspired Hill. *See* Lovanium
Institut d'Etudes Politiques (Brazzaville), 103
Institut Politique Congolais, 46, 114
international correspondence: about, 17; anti-imperialist rhetoric of, 15; boundaries and, 21
internationalism: and anti-colonialism, 31; postal system and, 26–27; liberal internationalism, 6; rhetoric of, 2, 44, 216n20; of student activists, xii, 4, 113, 122, 175, 180, 182
internationalization: about, 17; importance of, 61; self-rule transition and, 6
international solidarity: Afro-Asian, 6–7, 49, 126, 267n9; student movement's cultivation of, x; with Vietnam, 2, 4, 7–8, 174–75, 267n8. *See also* internationalism; Tricontinental Conference; tricontinentalism; Vietnam
International Union of Socialist Youth (IUSY), 53, 60f, 233n44
International Union of Students (IUS), 119, 120, 121, 170, 219n56, 250n48
IUS. *See* International Union of Students
IUSY (International Union of Socialist Youth), 53, 60f, 233n44

Lovanium (continued)
Mobutu at, 171–72; Mount Amba, 88–89; Mwamba and, 171–72; nationalization of, 114; nicknamed as *la colline inspirée* (the inspired hill), 89; N'Singa at, 109–10; Nzanda-Buana and, 172–74; Nzuji at, 6–7; occupation of, 171–75; nuclear reactor, 242n11; protest movement, 194–96; restoration work of, 116; Senghor at, 7; strikes at, 99–101, 102, 173; student governance, 96–98, 184–86; student politics at, x, 13, 95–96, 101; student protests in Kinshasa, 2; tenth anniversary celebration, 98–99; UNECRU and, 119; USNSA and, 109, 111; Wa Nsanga at, 13, 104; Zamenga at, 20. *See also* Gillon, Luc

Lower Congo, xx, 20, 24, 79, 94, 225n45, 240n53

Lubumbashi: clerks' letter of 1944, 32, 37, 260n17; COSEC and, 119; events in, 6, 98; Kabasela in, 57; Katanga State in, 43, 188; N'Kanza Dolomingu in, 170; Saint Boniface Institute in, 90, 243n25; students in, 24, 50, 107, 119, 171, 175, 179, 181, 189, 231n27, 248n18. *See also* Université Officielle du Congo

Lubumbashi, University of. *See* Université Officielle du Congo

Lukusa, André, 55

Luluabourg, 83, 103

Lumumba, Patrice, 281n95; about, 2, 17, 18, 25; as advocate for independence, 39; APIPO and, 33, 35–37; assassination of, 2, 7, 17–18, 43, 54, 58, 101, 116–18, 123; Bomboko and, 115; breaking of diplomatic ties, 5; commemoration of death, 2, 118, 175, 177, 193; and communism, 215n7; during Congo crisis, 66; *L'Echo Postal* (periodical), 36–37; forensic investigations of death, 230n10; Gizenga and, 73; in Gold Coast, 45; images of, 59, 235n68; Kabongo and, 103; Kashamura and, 78; labor unions and, 55; Leroy and, 83; long-distance teaching program, 33–34, 35; Lova-

nium against, 114–16; Lovanium students and, 109, 110; as man of letters, 46; Marxism and, 156; memory of, 4, 118, 124, 147; Mibamba and, 126; in missionary school, 65; MNC and, 39, 41, 45; Mobutu on, 164–65; Mulele and, 73; as national hero, 164–65; N'Singa and, 110; postal correspondences and, 39, 41, 42; postal system and, 33, 40–41, 229n90; as prime minister, 43; prison letters, 37–39, 41, 58; professional correspondence, 46–48; Soviet Union and, 43; student movement and, 62, 110; student protests, 116–18; *Une saison au Congo* (theater play) (Césaire), 104; United States and, 43, 55, 109; Verhaegen and, 116; Wa Nsanga and, 105

Lumumba Club, 118

Lumumba monument protest, 2, 6, 8, 10, 175, 215n7, 215n10

Lumumbism, 40–41, 118, 156

Mabika Kalanda, Auguste, 129, 130, 202

Madrandele, Prospère, 199

Mafwa, Victor, 60f

Makanda, Hubert, 99–101

Makeba, Miriam, 182, 191, 273n13

Makwambala, Alphonse, 95

Malaya, François, 5–6

Malcolm X, 6, 154f, 158, 180, 186

Malengreau, Fernand, 87

Malengreau, Guy, 87–88, 100

Malimba, Paul, 112, 248n13

Malinowski, Bronislaw, 64

Malkki, Liisa, 213n7

Malu, Anatole, 267n8

Malula, Joseph, 71, 77, 95–96, 101, 115, 182, 210, 238n29, 265n9

Mama Yemo, 193, 194, 196

Mambo, Thomas, 93

Mandala, Louis, 45–46

Mandel, Ernest, 163

Manjpara, Kris, 13

Maoism, 179; *L'Eclair* (journal), 153–59, 176, 262n39, 263n58; in France, 104, 262n37; Mobutu and, 202; and the Proletarian Brotherhood, 141; revolutionary correspondence on, 118, 152;

Mitudidi, Léonard, 133, 135, 155, 255n19

MNC. *See* Mouvement National Congolais

Mobe, Anicet, 282n99

mobility: letter of Congo crisis and, 56–58; letter writing and, 14, 25; of students, 4, 13; Zamenga and, 21. *See also* student expatriates, Congolese

Mobutu, Joseph-Désiré, 2; Bongoma and, 161–65; during Congo crisis, 66; coup of, 167; electoral win, 192–93; Humphrey and, 2; journalists and, 168; Kabila and, 106; Kamanda and, 163–64; Kasa-Vubu and, 115; Kennedy and, 259n2; left politics and, 171; Lovanium and, 173–74; in Luluabourg, 103; on Lumumba, 164–65; Lumumba and, 47, 115; Mibamba and, 126; Mpase and, 101; Mulele and, 126; N'Singa and, 109–11; opposition to, xii; postage iconography and, 44; school administrators and, 185; student activists and, xiii, 18, 164, 175–78; Sumbu and, 259n1; university graduates and, 162; on university training, 115

Mobutu administration: Congolese student movement and, 3; co-opting of student ideas and energies, 3; female emancipation claims, 183; Kabila's rout of, xii; Kithima in, 55; plans to overthrow, xi; radical rhetoric of student movement and, 3, 18; removal of Lumumba, 110; renaming by, xvii; student activists as threat to, 8; student activists in, 18; US and, 8; violence against student activists, 3–4; women under, 274n24

modernization theory, 9

Moke, Eugène, 71

Montesquieu, 23–24, 222n2 (chap. 1)

Montserrat (play) (Roblès), 209–10

Morel, Edmund, 28–29, 31, 153

La mort faite homme (Ngandu Kashama), 285n25

Moumié, Félix, 78

Moumouni, Abdou, 142

Mouvement National Congolais (MNC), 39, 41, 45, 49, 103, 112, 114, 116, 126, 233n52, 235n68, 250n51

Mouvement Populaire de la République (MPR), ix, 199, 268n20, 283n8; cooptation of activists by, 202, 206, 268n19, 272n67; manifesto, 170–71; and state repression, 176, 196, 280n87; and reform of universities, 198–99, 283n4. *See also* Jeunesse du Mouvement Populaire de République (JMPR)

Mpase, Albert, 101

Mpeye, Nestor, 92, 96

Mpinga, Honoré, 202–3

Mpolo, Maurice, 116

MPR. *See* Mouvement Populaire de la République

Mrazek, Rudolph, 65, 67

Mudimbe, V.Y., 13, 72–73, 186, 193, 203, 211, 217n38, 218n40, 239n41, 274n19

Mugaruka, Richard, xiii

mukanda (paperwork), 31–32, 61, 226n58, 226n60

Mukeba, Cléophas, 49, 231n24

Mukendi, Aubert, 90, 243n26

Mukengechay, Grégoire, 231n23

Mukwidi, Thomas, 145, 159, 261n35

Mulago, Vincent, 77, 97

Mulele, Pierre: in Cairo, 150; and distance learning, 48–49; Kinzambi and, 73, 74–75; launching of rebellion, 126, 133; as Lumumba's minister of education, 114–15; murder of, 177, 208

Mulelist rebellion, xvi, 105, 126, 131, 133–36, 140–42, 151, 157, 158, 159–60, 254n91, 270n53, 271n59

Mulemba, Jean-Baptiste, 93–94

Mungul-Diaka, Bernardin, 175

Munzihirwa, Christophe, 195–96

Mupapa, Michel-Ange, 262n37

music: Afro-Club, 93; Congolese rumba, 20, 52, 93, 94, 102; dancing bars, 15, 68, 92, 93, 204, 274n21. *See also* ambiance; Makeba, Miriam

Mutamba, Jean-Marie, 252n73, 262n37

Mwamba, Symphorien, 209–11

Mwamba, Tharcisse, 139, 171–72

Mweya, Elisabeth, 210–11

Nasser, Gamal Abdel, 135, 256n31

nationalism: Getachew on, 15; Congolese, 18, 46; Lumumba and, 54, 118; Kabila and, 214n10; Mobutu and, 5, 140, 178, 179, 203; student activists and, 4, 6, 119, 123, 167, 171, 185, 208; Zamenga and, 20

nation building: in the 1960s, 208; academics' demands about, 202; Catholic church and, 67; students' views on, 3, 112–13; United States and, 127

N'Dalla, Ernest, 256n26

Ndaywel, Isidore, 137–38

Ndele, Albert, 98–99

Ndeshyo, Oswald, 89–90, 148–49, 158

Ndundu, José, 100

Negritude, 6–8, 181, 202, 217n33, 217n38

Nendaka, Victor, 133, 193, 255n23

neocolonialism: mobilization against, xi, 53, 98, 117–18, 119, 139, 159, 174, 208; Nkrumah on, 5; and stamps in Congo, 43, 44; Tshombe and, 136; US embassy and, 124; violence of, 43

newspapers: in Belgian Congo, 30, 31, 39, 60, 71; in CFS, 26; cultural sovereignty and, 39; insurrection fears and, 30–31; Lumumba and, 33, 47, 59; Mobutu and, 176, 197; political, 50, 133–34, 226n54; and postal communications, 24, 222n2 (int. I); read by students, 105, 147, 149; student, 96, 271n55

Ngandu Kashama, Pius, 285n25

Ngoie, Venant, 120

Ngô Manh Lân, 147

N'Kanza Dolomingu, André: adult education and, 267n15; on communism, 170, 268n18; and Mobutu, 168–69, 175–77, 271n67; on racism at Princeton, 124; as UGEC leader, 137, 267n8, 278n62

N'Kita Kabongo, Symphorien, 151–52, 155

Nkrumah, Kwame, 11, 136; influence on students, 98, 181–82, 192; Lumumba and, 45, 230n13; on necolonialism, 5; as pan-African icon, xiii

Nouakchott, 106–7

Nsengi-Biembe, Gaston, 168–69

N'Singa Udjuu, Joseph, 171, 247n2; at Lovanium, 109–10; Lumumba and, 110; Mobutu and, 109–11

Ntil, Julien, 74–75

Nyerere, Julius, 141, 167

Nyssens, Paul, 34–35, 227n71, 228n76

Nzanda-Buana, Mathieu, 172–74

Nzeza, Anastase, 7–8, 264n4

Nzongola, George, 13

Nzuji, Dieudonné Kadima, 6–7, 8

Nzuzi, Emmanuel, 117–18, 250n51

occultism: and distance learning, 34; Mobutu's repression of, 198

Okito, Joseph, 116

Olenga, Nicolas, 281n95

Omolo, Isaac, 119

Operation Ommegang, 135

Oppenheimer, Robert, 84

oral history. See memory work

Organization for Solidarity for the People of Africa and Asia, 259n1

Organization of African Unity, 174

Oriental Province, 33, 36, 37, 83

Pakassa, Victor, 135

Palambwa, Daniel, 65, 73–75

pamba schools (écoles pamba), 80

Pan-Africanism: conversations on, 113; Makeba as icon of, 182; pamphlets, 26; Pan-African conference, 63; Lumumba and, 45; Panda and, 31; student activists and, 21, 113, 149

Panda Farnana, Paul, 31, 220n64

Paris: Belgian embassy protest, 18; Commune, 194, 281n94; Kabongo in, 104; Negritude literary movement and, 6–7; West African expatriates in, 9

Park, Daphne, 79

Parti Communiste Belge (PCB): anticolonialism of, 231n19; Drapeau Rouge, 226n54; gatekeeping in Congo, 235n64; Lumumba club and, 118, 251n55; postal correspondence with, 13, 48–52, 57–58, 150, 232n42; pro-Chinese split, 151; support to Lumumba, 233; Wa Nsanga and, 150–51; youth branch, 231n18

Union de la Jeunesse Révolutionnaire du Congo (UJRC), 151–57, 159, 160

Union Minière du Haut Katanga, 98, 104, 163, 172, 268n21

Union Nationale des Etudiants du Congo et Ruanda-Urundi (UNECRU), 119, 120

Union Nationale des Travailleurs Congolais (UNTC), 77; power decline of, ix. *See also* Mayala, François

United Arab Republic, 6

United Nations: Congolese postal service and, 54; criticisms of Belgium in, 87–88; education and, 54, 115; mission in Congo, 54, 61–62, 230n3, 230n5; vote on civilian and military mission, 5–6

United States: on 1969 student massacre, 276n42; Congolese dreams about, 63; overt support by, 119, 215n11; influence in Congo, 62, 124, 136, 267n14; funding of Lovanium, 86; Lumumba and, 43, 54, 115–16; Mibamba and, 125; Mobtubu and, 8, 163, 266n13; Pax Romana, 137; policies in Africa, 120; and Simba uprising, 146, 148, 259n7; support of Latin American dictatorships, 10; UGEC and, 127, 169–70; US scholars in Congo, xii, 47, 119, 129–30, 193–94. *See also* African Americans; American Federation of Labor (AFL-CIO); CIA; Cold War; Ford Foundation; Humphrey, Hubert; imperialism; usnsa; Vietnam

United States National Student Association (USNSA), 109, 111–12, 117, 119, 120–21, 122, 127, 129

universalism: creole, 64; educational system and, 7; in *La carte postale* (Zamenga), 21–22; of postal system, 27; and theology at Lovanium, 174

Universal Postal Union (UPU), 223n18; banned publications and, 31; Berlin Act and, 27; creation of, 26; participation in, 224n21

Université Catholique de Louvain, 11, 13, 84, 87, 88, 149, 201, 249n34

Université de Lubumbashi, 285n26

Université Libre de Bruxelles, 117, 118, 151, 232n28, 248n10

Université Libre du Congo (Kisangani), 180, 181, 193–94

Université Nationale du Zaïre, 82, 107, 198–99, 201, 203–7, 284n10, 285n26

Université Officielle du Congo (Lubumbashi), 119, 170, 171, 175, 179–80, 181, 268n25, 279n72

university education: colonial essence of, 7; curriculums, 11; decolonization movement and, 7; as gendered, 4–5; political establishment opposition and, 4; social stratification and, 216n15; symbolic and financial rewards of, xiii

University of Lovanium. *See* Lovanium

University of Massachusetts, 107

UNTC (Union Nationale des Travailleurs Congolais), 77; power decline of, ix. *See also* Mayala, François

UPU. *See* Universal Postal Union

urbanization: letter writing and, 33; missionary education and, 75–76; urban spaces, xiv

USNSA (United States National Student Association), 109, 111–12, 117, 119, 120–21, 122, 127, 129

Van Beurden, Sarah, 216n19

Vaneigem, Raoul, 157

Van Lierde, Jean, 230n13

Vansina, Jan, 12, 201, 220n72, 270n44, 283n2

Vatican, 114

Vergès, Jaques, 147

Verhaegen, Benoît, 99, 114, 116, 174, 189, 248n23

Vietnam: articles on, 152–53; Congo stabilization and, 219n57; solidarity with, 2, 4, 7, 174, 261n31; Tonkin Bay incident, 123; US imperialism and, 8, 175; Vietnamization of Congo, 152

violence: colonial violence, 9, 26, 28, 45, 220n72; of Congo crisis, 43, 55, 116; Congolese experiences of, xv; of counterinsurgency, 136; education and, 81;

guerilla warfare, 133, 134, 138, 159; June 4, 1969 massacre, 186–88, 206; Lumumba's assassination and persistence of colonial, 54, 117; Mobutu and, 177, 180, 190, 197, 207–8; in rhetoric of students, 99, 151, 186; of Simba and Mulelist rebellions, 75, 132, 134–35, 137; against student activists, 3, 19, 188, 209; in South Africa, 133

Wamba, Ernest, 24, 121
Wangata, Pierre, 45–46
Wa Nsanga, Kalixte Mukendi, 12–13, 103–7, 149–56, 246n9, 247n15
Washington, Booker T., 225n48
Weber, Max, 206
Weissman, Stephen, 194
The West African Mail (periodical), 29
West Germany, 57, 105, 106, 217n31
Willame, Jean-Claude, 201, 206
Williams, George Washington, 28
Williams College, 117, 119
wireless telegraphic network, 29–30
women: after independence, 48; Ekwa's promotion of, 241n59; femmes libres, 93; limited access to university education, 4–5; Mobutu's promotion of, 183; in national university era, 204–5; participation in student protests, 185; restrictions on, 95–96; students at

Lovanium, 85, 182–84; white Belgian brides, 51–52
world: being in the, 207; curiosity for the, 20, 34, 44, 64, 105; in the eyes of the, 122, 145; Lumumba as student of the, 33; men of the, 5, 100; as mokili, 207–8; pedagogy of the, 24, 209; question of the, 15, 10; separation from the, 75, 89; third world, 4, 19, 43, 104, 113, 119, 125, 135, 255n18; world politics, 10, 17, 58, 87, 113, 174, 216n20, 218n46
World Congress for Lay Apostolate (Rome), 8
worldedness, xiv, 8, 10, 208, 218n41
World Festival of Youth and Students (Vienna, 1959), 162, 232n35, 251n64
world-making and student politics, 16
Wright, Richard, 113

Yerodia, Abdoulaye, 134–34, 255n19, 262n37
Yoka Lye Mudaba, André, 285n25
Youlou, Fulbert, 103, 133, 275n39
Young, Crawford, 119, 127–28, 252n67, 284n10

Zaire: renaming of Congo as, xii, 199–200
Zairian academia, 201, 202–3
Zamenga Batukezanga, 20–22, 222n3